Terry Breverton was born in Barry in 1946, educated at Barry Grammar School and studied at the universities of Manchester, Birmingham and Lancaster. After a career in management consultancy, strategic planning and international marketing during which he found himself in the Paris of the student revolts, in Lisbon during the Portuguese Revolution and trapped in Iran when the Shah fled the country, he returned to the comparative peace of Wales in 1993 to lecture in marketing at the UWIC Business School, Cardiff.

He has in the past had published works in his specialist field as well as books for children and of poetry. This is his first book on aspects of Welsh life and its history.

AN A–Z
OF WALES
AND THE WELSH

Terry Breverton

SWANSEA
CHRISTOPHER DAVIES
– 2000 –

To Mam and Dad

Published in 2000 by
Christopher Davies (Publishers) Ltd.
P.O. Box 403, Swansea, SA1 4YF

A CIP catalogue record for this book is
available from the British Library.

ISBN 0 7154 0734 1

Printed and bound in Wales by
Dinefwr Press Ltd.
Rawlings Road, Llandybie
Carmarthenshire, SA18 3YD

CONTENTS

ACKNOWLEDGEMENTS

For permission to reprint extracts from works in copyright the author and the publishers thank the following for items from titles listed here:

The estate of Dylan Thomas and David Higham Associates for the extracts from *A Child's Christmas in Wales, Under Milk Wood, Poem in October* and *And death shall have no dominion.*

For the extract from *Reservoirs*, R. S. Thomas, *Selected Poems 1946-1968* (Bloodaxe Books 1986).

Gomer Press for the extract from Rachel Bromwich's translation of *Morfydd fel yr haul* by Dafydd ap Gwilym.

The estate of Idris Davies and Gomer Press for the poems *Capel Calvin* and *Psalm* and the extract from *Gwalia Deserta, Do you remember 1926?*

The publishers, Weidenfeld and Nicolson for the extract of the translation of *Cylch Atgof* by Owen M. Edwards

from *The Book of Wales* edited by Meic Stephens.

The author and publishers would also like to thank and acknowledge the following for the illustrations on the book cover:

Front cover: Welsh girl in Gwent costume, The National Library of Wales; The Red Kite, Nigel Sheppeard; Cromlech, The Wales Tourist Board; Catherine Zeta-Jones, Capital Pictures; Dylan Thomas, Llew Thomas. The background illustration is based on the statue of Owain Glyndŵr at City Hall, Cardiff. Tal-y-llyn Railway, source unknown.

Back cover: Coracle man, Wil y Dŵr, National Museums and Galleries of Wales; Coetan Arthur burial Chamber, St David's, Paul R. Davis; Gareth Edwards, Colorsport; Tintern Abbey, CADW Welsh Historic Monuments; National Eisteddfod and Millennium Stadium, sources unknown.

INTRODUCTION

What is Wales? 140 miles long, varying between 40 and 100 miles wide, 8000 square miles, most of it high plateau, hills and mountains. Europe's cleanest rivers dissect the mountain ranges and lead into a 750 mile coastline. A small country, two-thirds the size of Belgium, on the periphery of the continent, with the oldest living language in Europe. Over 20% of the land is designated as a National Park, and Forestry Commission woodland covers another 6%. Around 60% of Wales is over 500 feet high, 25% is over 1,000 feet and 6% over 1,500 feet. Mountainous, it has fifteen mountain summits over 3,000 feet, and another 153 that are over 2,000 feet. The Welsh population is around 2,900,000, about 5% of that of the United Kingdom, in 8% of the area of the UK. So how has this little mountainous region retained its identity, heritage, language and pride, when so close to a mighty neighbour, with an international language, that once controlled the world?

Upon my travels all over the world, no-one seems to know where Wales is, nor anything about it, unless they have some interest in rugby. The Bretons know us, and the rugby-playing areas of South-West France, South Africa, New Zealand and Australia. In Italy, some of the older people remember the great John Charles who played football for Juventus and Wales. In the rest of the world, nothing. Those that have heard of us usually have family connections or know people who have come to Wales for a holiday. Only one in thirty of overseas visitors to Britain visit Wales, and many of them are just passing through on their way to Ireland. Foreign tourists spend less than a fiftieth of what they purchase elsewhere in Britain. Some Japanese and Koreans know us because of inward investment marketing. Other foreigners think of us as part of England, but for the vast majority, it has never heard of Wales. Unless Wales can get a football team into the semi-finals of the FIFA World Cup, we will stay in this backwater of knowledge, unlike England, Scotland and Ireland that are known worldwide.

The problem is compounded by the lack of information available to native Welsh people. Many in the Anglicised South-East and the Border-Marches are quite happy to be considered part of England. But Wales has contributed to the development of the modern world. And Welshness has a nature of gentleness, respect for women, resilience in the face of oppression, togetherness and a Socialist-Christian character, that derives from its history and can serve as an exemplar for civilised society in the new millennium. It is this that gives us our *Cymreictod*, our sense of belonging to Wales, our sense of a place in history that has never needed to be shouted from the rooftops.

Wales is a fascinating country with a rich history and a marvellous countryside. There is an attractive 'softness' about the character of its people that explains the concept of *hiraeth* – that pure longing for home that all expatriate Welshmen feel. The purpose of this book is to try and explain what makes Wales different, how Wales has survived because of the bending nature of the population, and why it is important for fellow Welshmen as well as tourists to have a 'feel' for a country.

Nothing defines Wales so much as the remains, humps and stones that scatter its countryside. The Industrial Revolution started here and ended years ago, leaving overgrown lead, copper and silver workings half-hidden in famous beauty spots. Coal has gone and with it the heartache of the decision as to whether to work in the pit or leave Wales to find employment. A few collieries have been converted into heritage centres, but the employment that this 'black gold' gave Wales can never be replaced.

From previous centuries, Wales seems to have more historical remains per square metre than just about anywhere else in the world. Constant invasion by Celts, Romans, Irish, Vikings, Mercians, Saxons, Normans and Plantagenets have left us not only the legacy of a 'World Heritage Site' of North Wales Castles, but defensive fortifications and burial mounds going back 4000 years. If we just scan an Ordnance Survey Map from the centre and north of Cardiff across the Vale of Glamorgan to Llanilltud Fawr (Llantwit Major), an area of perhaps 40 square miles, we can list the following noted sites that can still be seen:

> Eighteen *Norman Castles*, a *Castellated Manor House* at Old Beaupre, two *Castle Ditches*, two *Civil War Battlefields*, a *Monastic Grange*, two *Mediaeval Dovecotes*, a *Roman Fort and walls*, a *Moat*, five *Norman Mottes*, a *Norman Motte and Bailey*, a *Cathedral* dating from the 6th century at Llandaff, the *Mediaeval Bishop's Palace* at Llandaff, also *Mediaeval Town Walls and Gates*, *Enclosures*, an *Elizabethan*

> *Mansion*, *Roman Villas*, *Stone Crosses*, five *Monastic Settlements*, *Settlements*, The *Beacons*, a *Homestead*, *Earthworks*, a *Fort* at Caerau, five *Ancient Wells*, four *Long Cairns*, seven *Tumuli*, a *Deserted Village* at Marcross, a *Castellated Priory* at Ewenny, and four *Iron Age Forts*.

This quick scan does not mention scores of ancient chapels and churches like the hidden Saxon church at Cogan, nor other historic monastic sites at Llancarfan and Llantwit Major. My own small village of Sain Tathan has a Norman church, and nearby two ruined castles (West Orchard and East Orchard), two castle-farmhouses (Flemingstone and Castleton), a manor-castle (Fonmon) and several mediaeval wells. Nearby Llancarfan has the sites of monasteries, and Llanilltud Fawr can claim to be Europe's first university. Wherever you are in Wales, you are walking across and over history, a history that is based upon the Christian tradition layered onto a Celtic feel for nature and a refusal to be changed by military dominance.

So few people seem to know of this historical background, because of the reticence born out of hundreds of years of stubborn resistance to a more powerful neighbour. The Llywelyns and Owain Glyndŵr should be as famous as Robert the Bruce or William Wallace – incidentally, Wallace was known as William Wallensis, 'the Welshman' and had a noble Welsh mother. We have no-one writing books with titles like 'How the Irish saved Christianity and Civilisation' although the Irish patron saint was Welsh, and the early Welsh church also carried the embers of Christianity back into Ireland and Europe. There is none of the arrogance with which more recent countries like Germany, England and America seem sometimes to face the rest of the world. Wales has kept itself to itself more than any other country in Europe – it is a secret nation which will outlast many others for this reason. Even the newcomers eventually become absorbed into its way of life – slow, quiet, socialist and respectful of tradition. Over the last few hundred years, leading Welshmen have shown the country that it dies without its language, so the language has survived and with it, all the culture that was not destroyed by the religious fundamentalism of the eighteenth and nineteenth centuries.

The book takes the form of a dip-in, dip-out A to Z, rather than a linear history or travelogue. It is intended as a supplement for conventional tourist books or histories. As such, there may be elements of repetition when areas cross over, for example in the entries upon 'Christianity' and 'The Rewriting of History'. It is meant to be interesting, to be a guide to Welsh achievement and pride, and to make both fellow-Welshmen and visitors alike want to learn more about this wonderful country. So what this book attempts to do is to show you the secret of 'hwyl', that natural pride, passion and feeling that lies close to the surface but never breaks out into violence.

There is a socialist, anti-authority, egalitarian motif running through Welsh heritage from Celtic times. This is a personal book and it is unashamedly pro-Welsh. Every nation's reference to its history omits the correct weightings of facts – most British history does not fairly relate its treatment of native 'colonials' or great military losses, just as many French people have never heard of Agincourt, Crécy, Poitiers or

Ramillies. Japanese education upon the treatment of Allied prisoners of war, and the Rape of Nanking is equally lacking. Americans are inculcated with the doctrine that they can trust a President, to effectively rule the world, when even his family cannot trust him. However, the Welsh have not been major players on the world scene – the days of 'glory' were when the Celts ruled Europe before the controlled power of Rome took over. Wales has a relic population and an ancient language, with a history of stubborn resistance for two thousand years against massive forces that possessed superior resources. Its story deserves to be told, not only to Welshmen so we can hang on for another millennium, but so that other nations can see that a pride in the past does not have to be justified by aggression.

If anyone can add or correct anything, I would be most grateful and attribute them in future editions. This is a sort of 'Hitch-Hiker's Guide to the Galaxy' of Wales, and will need constant amending and updating until we can all 'sing from the same hymnsheet' about why we are so proud of Wales and what it can offer to the visitor. As Castaneda said, *'without a knowledge of history, we are condemned to repeat the mistakes of the past'*. With a knowledge of history of countries comes a respect for their peoples, both of the past and present. I hope both Welsh nationals and other nationals learn from reading this book, what made Wales and why it is so important to keep our sense of historical duty. The major problem with 'true' British history was that it was rewritten by successive waves of conquerors to justify their dominance – starting with the Saxons and Normans, Welsh achievement and history was deliberately destroyed and obliterated. Ireland never suffered in the same way. However, the Hanoverians are responsible for a massive change in the way the British were taught about history. An alien monarchy changed perceptions of Britain's heritage and culture for its own ends and denigrated anything that did not fit with their Germanic model of justification of power. If anyone is offended by any strong sentiments expressed in this book, they are not directed against the British of England, but against their lords and masters over the centuries. Political, economic and military power has been directed against the Welsh over the centuries, and the people of England and Wales have never possessed any such power. This book tries to be an antidote to the power that starts wars, wastes scarce resources, corrupts historical fact, and has transformed itself into the arrogance of denial of Welsh achievement and culture.

There is, at last, a revival in Wales. Over the next decade people all over the world will realise the global con-tribution of this beautiful country and its gentle people. The survival of Cymru and its language has been a miracle, and its people's inward pride is best summed up in the stirring chorus of the Catatonia song: *'Every day, when I wake up, I thank the Lord I'm Welsh.'*

I must thank Professor Sir Glanmor Williams, the doyen of Welsh historians, for checking the many discrepancies in this publication. My background is more pragmatic than academic, and thus this book is unashamedly populist. The choice of headings is somewhat eclectic and stems from my own interests.

I only hope that some of the *hwyl* and *hiraeth* that make up the Welsh character is transmitted through the following pages.

Please contribute to future editions by sending any extra information or corrections to T. D. Breverton at UWIC, Colchester Avenue, Cardiff CF3 7XR, fax: 01222-506932; e-mail t.breverton @uwic.ac.uk. or breverton @lineone.net. All contributions will be gratefully acknowledged in future editions.

A

ACTORS

Notable Welsh actors include Gwen Frangcon Davies, Hugh Griffith, Ray Milland, Stanley Baker, Sian Phillips, Jonathan Pryce, Catherine Zeta Jones, Richard Burton and Anthony Hopkins, the latter three being noted international film actors. **Ray Milland**, born Reginald Truscott-Jones, won a best actor 'Oscar' in 1945 for his portrait as an alcoholic writer in 'The Lost Weekend'. The statuette has vanished since his death in 1986. He also starred in 'Dial M for Murder' and 'Love Story'. Hugh Griffith, a noted stage actor, won a best supporting actor 'Oscar' for his role in 'Ben Hur'. **Myrna Loy**, star of the 1930s 'Thin Man' films, was born Myrna Williams, of Welsh parents. The actress-singer **Deanna Durbin** had parents from Tredegar, and for over a decade from 1936 she was one of Universal Studio's biggest stars.

Jonathan Pryce starred with Madonna in the film, 'Evita', and also had the lead role in the musical 'Miss Saigon'. He has won 'Tonys' for 'Comedians' in 1976 and 'Miss Saigon' in 1990, two Olivier awards, 'Best Actor' at Cannes for 'Carrington', and has also played in all the major works of Shakespeare and Chekhov.

Catherine Zeta Jones co-starred with Antonio Banderas in the hit movie 'The Mask of Zorro', in which she rode, tangoed and fenced without any 'doubles' carrying out her stunts. Reviews include *'The most spectacular ingredient of all is newcomer Catherine Zeta Jones, whose dark eyes, porcelain skin and meltingly radiant smile remind me of the late, great, Natalie Wood'* (New York Observer); *'A Celtic riposte to Sophia Loren'* (Premier); and she was described as *'ravishingly beautiful and wonderfully spirited'* (Time). Jones also stars in Sean Connery's $100 million production 'Entrapment.'

Well-known for his best actor 'Oscar' for his portrayal of Hannibal Lecter in 'Silence of the Lambs', **Anthony Hopkins** is now concentrating upon films after a distinguished stage career. He has also won two 'Emmys'. Theatre appearances include 'Macbeth', 'Equus' and 'King Lear', while his films include 'Lion in Winter', 'A Bridge Too Far', 'The Elephant Man', 'Howards' End', 'Shadowlands' and 'The Remains of the Day'. In the 1998 Steven Spielberg film 'Amistad', Hopkins was nominated for an 'Oscar' for his portrayal of the American President, John Quincy Adams, who was himself of Welsh stock. He has also been contracted at a record fee of £15,000,000 to reprise his role as Hannibal Lecter. This notable Welshman has donated a million pounds to the fund to purchase a large part of Mount Snowdon for the National Trust.

Mention should also be given to the film director Richard Marquand, who made the highest grossing of the first three Star Wars films, 'Return of the Jedi', and also the psychological thriller 'Jagged Edge', before his early death. Jack Howells won a best short documentary Oscar for 'Dylan' in 1962.

Richard Burton, born Jenkins, came from the same neighbourhood as Anthony Hopkins and after Oxford University trained at RADA. A superb stage actor, he also received seven Academy Award nominations and twice married Elizabeth Taylor prior to his death in 1984. His villa where he was buried, on Lake Geneva, was called 'Pays de Galles' (French for 'Wales'), and 'Sospan Fach' was played at the funeral of this hard-drinking Celtic genius.

Sir Stanley Baker was a devoted Socialist who helped produce party political broadcasts for Harold Wilson and campaigned for Michael Foot in Ebbw Vale in 1972. Before his early death in 1978, aged forty-eight, he had made many films and is regarded as 'by far Wales's most important movie star' (Peter Stead, *Western Mail*, June 13, 1998). He had played Captain Horatio Hornblower aged just twenty-four, and starred in 'The Cruel Sea' a couple of years later. At the age of only thirty-three he made and starred in the award-winning film 'Zulu', giving Michael Caine his big break into films (see Zulu). There was a lovely story recounted about Stanley Baker by the director Michael Winner in 1998. In his Sunday Times food column, 'Winner's Dinner's', he wrote about *'the wonderfully vibrant actor Stanley Baker, belatedly knighted as he lay dying of cancer. Stanley was a macho movie actor of immense wit and charm. At the premiere of my film The Games, in which he starred, Stanley appeared, immaculate as ever in a dinner suit, and said: "Well, what do you think?" "About what?" I asked. "Me", he said. "Look at me!" I did notice something, but it couldn't possibly be what he was referring to. "My toupee," he finally said. "How do you like my new toupee?"*

The great tragedienne, possibly Britain's greatest actress, **Sarah Siddons**, was born in Brecon on 5th July 1775, in the 'Shoulder of Mutton' pub. Her parents belonged to the Brecon Company of strolling players, and after her discovery by David Garrick was the biggest draw in Drury Lane. He offered her the huge salary for the time of £5 a week. Sarah Siddons was said to have been the greatest Lady Mac-Beth of all time, and both Byron and Dr. Samuel Johnson sang her praises. Before she died in 1831, both Sir Joshua Reynolds and Thomas Gainsborough had painted her. She has a memorial in Westminster Abbey, and the Brecon High Street inn has been renamed The Sarah Siddons, with a reproduction of her painting by Gainsborough acting as a pub sign.

AMERICA

Wales has many connections with the USA, and has to a major extent shaped both its history *and* its independence.

PRINCE MADOC (see Madoc)
In 1170, thirteen ships and three-hundred men left the islands of Ynys Fadog in the mouth of the Glaslyn. A memorial plaque marks the point of departure in Llandrillo-yn-Rhos, near Llandudno. Legend says that America was discovered by the expedition's leader, Prince Madoc, son of the heroic Prince Owain Gwynedd (see Owain Gwynedd) and that there was a tribe of Welsh-speaking Indians, the Madogwys or Mandans. Sources describe Prince Madoc's Welshmen moving up from Alabama, fighting the Iroquois in Ohio, and the remnants heading west where they were discovered in the Revolution (as the Mandan Indians) in North Dakota.

In Welsh mythology, Madoc's ship, the 'Gwennan Gorn' still haunts the coast off Abergele. The 'Gwennan Gorn' was made with stag-horn nails so that Madoc could use a lodestone to navigate safely. He picked up his brother at Lundy Island on the way to America, and returned several years later with a small crew. The others had been left to start a colony in this fabulous new land. Prince Madoc then went again to America with ten ships filled with men and women. The fact that there are traditions associated with Alabama and Georgia, as well as North Dakota, may mean that the two parties never met up.

Charles Morgan, a Welsh West Indian known as Jacques Clamorgan, operated from St Louis, and led The Missouri Company for Spain, trying to open up the unexplored American interior, win control of the fur trade, and reach the Pacific before the British and Americans. A French trader from St Louis in 1792 had come across a tribe of Indians in the Upper Missouri, the Mandans, and had described them as 'white, like Europeans'. Jacques Clamorgan organised a Spanish expedition to find them.

The artist George Catlin painted some of these 'Welsh-speaking' Mandans before the tribe was decimated by the new white man's illness of small-pox in 1838. Scholars claimed that many of their customs and their use of coracles for catching fish 'proved' their Welsh ancestry. Professor Gwyn Williams also recounts that *'Mandan girls were celebrated for their good looks and amiability and were said to be more adept than moSt They chattered endlessly even when making love – a fact which one later observer cited as further proof of their Welsh descent!'*

Madoc's story is recounted in Hakluyt's 'Voyages' (1582) and Lloyd and Powell's 'Cambria' 1584. John Dee, the Welsh *'magus of his age'* claimed America for Queen Elizabeth I on the basis of this tale, which was developed by Southey in his long poem 'Madoc' in 1805. At Mobile, Alabama is a plaque erected by The Daughters of the American Revolution *'In Memory of Prince Madoc who landed on the shores of Mobile Bay in 1170 and left behind, with the Indians, the Welsh language'*. There are also references to Prince Madoc in relation to an ancient stone wall in Fort Mountain State Park, near Chatsworth, Georgia. Robert Southey's long poem 'Madoc' is based on Montezuma's statement to Cortez, that a white leader *'from the east'* brought an American tribe south into Mexico.

EXPLORATION

Some say that America was named after Richard ap Meurig, othewise known as Richard Amerik, a merchant from Glamorgan who sponsored John Cabot's second voyage from Bristol. A successor in American exploration, like Cabot looking for the passage to India and China, was Robert Mansel of Margam, who named Mansel Island. New Wales in Hudson's Bay was named by Welshmen under Thomas Button of St Lythan's also seeking the North-West Passage.

John Lloyd, also known as John Scolvus ('the skilful') was a Welsh sailor who carried on an illegal trade with Greenland and is claimed to have reached North America, sailing as far south as Maryland, in 1477. This was 15 years before the voyage of Columbus.

COLONIZATION

In 1617, the Welsh poet William Vaughan set up a colony in Newfoundland, and Roger Williams (c.1604-1684) founded Rhode Island colony in 1636, upon the basis of democracy and complete religious freedom. Williamsburg was founded in 1632, and this historic tourist venue was capital of the colony of Virginia from 1699 to 1779.

A colony of Welshmen and their fellow Cornishmen dating from 1607 is still crab-fishing in the islands around Chesapeake Bay in Maryland. The community has survived almost unscathed since Captain John Smith landed there in Queen Elizabeth's reign. However, the population of Ewell, Tylerton and Rhodes Point has fallen from 805 in 1910 to around 300 now, some of whom are from other parts of Maryland. The locals call themselves 'the watermen', and Glenn Evans made the point, in a cross between a Welsh accent and a Maryland drawl, that a group of ecologists are legislating them out of business. Crabs are plentiful, but quota restrictions have been imposed, and the local health department is stopping the watermen skinning and preparing crabs in their homes. The school opened at Tylerton on Smith Island in 1790, and its only teacher, April Tyler, was forced to close it in 1996 because there were only two pupils.

'*The heart of this community is the school and the (Methodist) church*' said Ms Tyler tearfully, '*With its closure, part of the heart has stopped pumping. I'm sure they are just jealous of our conditions and want things to change*'. It seems that bureaucracies everywhere hate anomalies – the state has spent £200,000 on a gleaming new visitors' centre and museum to document the island's history for the thousands of tourists who make brief excursions there every year. The Maryland state is destroying living history, because it makes more money from tourism than from its oldest community.

Jennings Evans, an ex-waterman who has chronicled the history of the settlement, says '*Soon we may have no more history to document. The restrictions on crabbing and the closure of the school represent the death of our community. In the next few years, we will lose even more islanders and others will come in from outside to buy homes here. They're real friendly but they don't understand our society. They don't understand our ways*'. The same feelings were expressed in Trefeglwys near Newtown in my maternal grandmother's time, as Birmingham and Liverpool people started moving in. She spoke no English – now it is difficult to find anyone there who speaks Welsh.

Welsh Quakers were the founding fathers of Pennsylvania in the late seventeenth century. William Penn had promised them a Welsh-speaking colony, '*New Wales*', 40,000 acres forming the so-called '*Welsh Barony*'. A letter of Penn's in 1690 confirms this fact. However, also in 1690 the Welsh Tract (Charter) took authority from the Welsh Quaker meetings, placing it in the hands of the colonial government.

Dr Thomas Wynne of Caerwys planned the layout of Pennsylvania itself, and his house, Wynnewood, still stands, the first stone-built house in the state. A trial at Bala in North Wales in 1679 for non-payment of tithes to the church had convinced many Welsh Quakers to emigrate and they set up the settlements of Bangor, Narberth, Radnor, Berwyn, St Davids, Haverford, Bala-Cynwyd and Bryn Mawr in Pennsylvania. Large tracts of Pennsylvania today are still called Gwynedd, Uwchlyn, Llanerch, Merion, St Davids, North Wales, Treddyfryn and so on. The Welsh Society of Philadelphia, dating from 1729, is the oldest ethnic language society in the USA. Baptists from Swansea flocked to Swanzey, Connecticut, and an attempt was made to establish a *'Utopia'* called New Cambria in Pennsylvania. Ohio also had very strong Welsh immigration.

At Towamencin near Lansford in Pennsylvania is the Morgan Log House, over 300 years old. This is the oldest, unchanged colonial dwelling in America, built by Edward and Elizabeth Morgan, the grandparents of Daniel Boone. Boone (1735-1820) was one of many American Welshmen who moved to Kentucky via the Carolinas. From 1769 he lived in the forests as a frontiersman with his brother and was twice captured by Indians. From 1775-1778 he repelled Indian attacks on his stockade fort, which Boonesboro has grown up around.

THE AMERICAN REVOLUTION
Robert Morris, of a Montgomery family, was known as *'the financier of the American Revolution'*. A member of the Continental Congress, he organised the finances for Washington's military supplies and signed the Declaration of Independence. In 1782 he founded The Bank of North America, but died bankrupt in 1806.

Fourteen of the generals of the Revolutionary Army were Welshmen and The Declaration of Independence was written by a Welshman, Thomas Jefferson. A third (eighteen of fifty-six) of its signatories were of Welsh descent. Jefferson's original draft was severely pruned by Congress, and North Carolina and Georgia were responsible for the removal of anti-slavery promises. Jefferson said that his father came from the Snowdon foothills, and a US State Department official unveiled a plaque at Llanfair Ceiriog in 1933, *'To the*

Memory of a Great Welshman, Thomas Jefferson'.

Jefferson, imbued with the Welsh traditions of social equality, used them to great effect when he drafted the Declaration of Independence. His original draft declares, *'We hold these truths to be sacred and undeniable; that all men are created equal and independent, that from that equal creation they derive rights inherent and inalienable, among which are the preservation of life, and liberty, and the pursuit of happiness.'*

Another Welshman, the one-legged lawyer Gouverneur Morris (1755-1835), wrote the final draft of the Constitution and as such is commemorated on a plaque on Philadelphia Town Hall, along with William Penn, Jefferson, Robert Morris and John Marshall. Gouverneur Morris was later Minister to France and a senator:

'Perpetuating the Welsh heritage, and commemorating the vision and virtue of the following Welsh patriots in the founding of the City, Commonwealth and Nation:

William Penn, *1644-1718, proclaimed freedom and religion and planned New Wales, later named Pennsylvania;*
Thomas Jefferson, *1743-1826, third President of the United States, composed the Declaration of Independence;*
Robert Morris, *1734-1806, foremost financier of the American Revolution and signer of the Declaration of Independence;*
Gouverneur Morris, *1752-1816, wrote the final draft of the Constitution of the United States;*
John Marshall, *1755-1835, Chief*

Justice of the United States and father
of American constitutional law.'

John Marshall (1755-1835), 'the father of
American Constitutional law', was of
Welsh stock. After serving in the army
in the War of Independence he was a
congressman and then Chief Justice
from 1801-1835. He established the
doctrine of judicial review, placed the
Supreme Court in a position of independence and power and his decisions
are the standard authority of constitutional law.

THOMAS JEFFERSON

As third President after George Washington, Jefferson negotiated and signed
the Louisiana Purchase of French territories from Napoleon. For $15 million,
the USA doubled in size at a cost of
just 4 cents an acre.

*'He was also an architect, builder and
carpenter. Into his stately Virginia home,
Monticello, went gadgets that were
designed to save time and energy for its
occupants. He built a circular staircase
to save space. He also installed a dumb-
waiter to save the servants many need-
less trips up and down the stairs. There
were folding tables, and chairs than
folded back into the walls when not in
use. Sliding panels were built into some
of the walls so that dishes and other
small objects could be passed from one
room to another with ease. He designed
a trick bed. From one side he emerged
to his study, from the other, to his
breakfast. During the day the bed was
raised out of the way.'*

J. F. Kennedy at a dinner honouring
Nobel Prize winners said, *'I think this is
the most extraordinary collection of talent,
of human knowledge, that has ever gathered*

*together at The White House – with the
possible exception of when Thomas Jefferson dined alone.'*

This greatest and most unassuming
American president composed his own
epitaph . . . *'Here was buried Thomas
Jefferson, Author of the Declaration of
American Independence, of the Statute of
Virginia for Religious Freedom, and Father
of the University of Virginia.'*

Jefferson was very proud of his
Virginian statute. He enshrined the
separation of the church and state as
he believed in religious liberty. A poli-
tically-aligned religion would mean
minority persecution. He believed that
*'the care of human life and happiness . . . is
the first and only legitimate object of good
government.'* This belief in the welfare
of citizens is alien to present Western
governments, which seem to kow-tow
to the multinational business interests
which control them.

The American Republic's first budget
was drawn up by the radical reformer
Dr Richard Price, who also influenced
the French Revolution (see literature).
Jefferson based The Declaration of
Independence upon Price's 'Observations on the Nature of Civil Liberty'.

LEWIS AND CLARK

Jefferson's friend and protege, a fellow-
Welshman called Meriwether Lewis,
opened up the American West, with
fellow explorer William Clark. Lewis
commanded and completed the first
overland expedition to the Pacific
Coast and back (1803-1806). They had
used the maps of John Thomas Evans
of Waunfawr, who had explored the
Missouri Valley in 1792 for the first
time looking for Prince Madoc's Welsh
Indians. Evans had entered the service
of Spain and Jacques Clamorgan and
reached the Mandans, enduring a ter-

rible winter with them, and held the Mandans for Spain against the Canadians, thus helping to fix the current American-Canadian border. He died of drink in New Orleans, aged only 29.

At least two of the Lewis and Clark party, Sergeant Ordway and Private Whitehouse, believed that they would find Prince Madoc's fair-skinned Indian descendants still in possession of Welsh treasure. They met light-skinned Indians in The Flatlands of Montana, speaking a strange *'gurgling kind of language spoken much through the throat'*, and Whitehouse was *'sure of it'* that they were the lost Welsh tribe.

The President had told Congress that he expected Lewis and Clark to discover a 'mountain of salt', 180 miles long and 45 miles wide (nearly the size of Wales!) They made contact with new Indian tribes, and found 'new species' such as prairie dogs, horned lizards, coyotes, bighorns, sage grouse, porcupines, jack rabbits, trumpeter swans, steelhead salmon trout, mule deer and pronghorn antelopes. One hundred and twenty two animals new to science were discovered, along with one hundred and seventy new types of plant.

Over the two years, four months and ten days they took to reach the Pacific Coast and return, the expedition encountered over forty Indian tribes, including the Oto, Missouri Osage, Yankton Sioux, Omaha, Teton Sioux, Arikaras, Mandans, Hidatsas, Flatheads, Nez Pierce, Shoshoni, Warapams, Chinooks, Clatsops, Walla Walla, Crow and the tribe feared most by all the other Indians, the Blackfeet.

Lewis followed the Missouri to its source, crossed the unknown Rockies (aided by an Indian woman, Sacajawea) and followed the Columbia River to Pacific Ocean, returning overland to St Louis from 1804-1806. He had designed a collapsible canoe, 'The Experiment', to transport equipment around rapids. According to his biographer, S. E. Ambrose, in 'Undaunted Courage', Meriwether Lewis was *'the first great American celebrity after the Revolutionary War – a superstar in today's terms.'*

Jefferson rewarded Lewis with the governorship of the huge new territories acquired by the Louisiana Purchase, but it looks like he acquired syphilis, drank to obsession, drifted into debt and committed suicide in Tennessee in 1809 aged just 35. Controversy now rages as to whether he was murdered and experts from George Washington University wish to dig up his bones. The main account of his death comes from an innkeeper, Mrs Grinder, who recounts hearing two shots, then finding Lewis with bullet wounds in his head and chest, using a razor, *'busily engaged in cutting himself from head to foot'*. Robbery by the innkeeper may be a motive, and pathologists wish to look at the angle of bullet entry into his bones to assess whether it was murder.

At Lemhi Pass in Idaho, Lewis had become the first white man to cross the Continental Divide and he named the Missouri River canyon in Montana, *'The Gates of the Mountains'*. Americans can now follow his trail, stopping at isolated campsites.

MORE WELSH PRESIDENTS
Penbanc farm, near Llanboidy, is the ancestral home of the second and sixth Presidents of the United States, John Adams and his son, giving Wales three of the USA's first six Presidents. (America has had eleven Presidents of

Welsh origin). John Adams (second President 1797-1801) had been a member of the Continental Congress and signed the Declaration of Independence, during which he was 'the colossus of the debate'. He proposed Washington as commander-in-chief of the armed forces. In 1779 he went to France and negotiated the treaty with England which ended the American War of Independence.

His son, John Quincy Adams, was sixth President from 1825-1829 and had negotiated the famous Treaty of Ghent to end the War of 1812 between England and America. This treaty warned off any further European colonisation in the Western Hemisphere in return for US non-interference in Europe. He was the real author of this 'Monroe Doctrine' which has been a recurring strategic theme in American policy ever since. Adams also negotiated the treaty to take Florida from Spain and was a noted anti-slaver. Thus Welshmen were responsible for peaceably taking both Spanish and French territories for the new country.

Incidentally, their grandson and great-grandson was Henry Brooks Adams (1838-1918), the famous American man of letters and noveliSt In 1807 he described the complexity of the 'multiverse' of modern society, and the predicament of modern man in an increasingly technological world. Henry Adams was posthumously awarded the Pulitzer Prize for his autobiography that had been published in 1907. His brother Brooks Adams (1848-1927) was a noted geopolitical historian. Their father Charles Francis Adams (1807-1886) was a diplomat and author and minister to Britain in The Civil War.

Samuel Adams (1722-1803) was a second cousin of John Adams, and the chief instigator of The Boston Tea Party in 1773. He had organised opposition to The Stamp Act in 1765 and organised the Non-Importation Association in 1798 and the Boston Committee of Correspondence in 1722. After the Tea Party he was delegate to the International Congresses of 1774 and 1775, before being one of the signatories to The Declaration of Independence in 1776. Samuel Adams called the English *'a nation of shopkeepers'* long before Napoleon and Boston's famous beer is named after him.

EDUCATION
The name Yale derives from Ial, the village of Llanarmon yn Ial, near Wrexham in Clwyd. The Yales had a house here and David Yale was one of the Pilgrim Fathers who sailed to America. Yale University was founded by Elihu Yale (1648-1721), David Yale's grandson. He had made a fortune with The East India Company, and had been Governor of Madras. 'Hiraeth' pulled him home to Wrexham, and he is buried in a tomb in The Church of St Giles, Wrexham where is carved *'Born in America, in Europe bred'*. Bryn Mawr (Great Hill), the leading female college in the USA, is of Welsh origins and Brown University, Rhode Island, was founded by a Welshman, Morgan Edwards of Pontypool who died in Delaware in 1795. Another Welshman instrumental in founding an American university (and a hospital) was John Hopkins (1795-1873). Both Johns Hopkins University and Morgan State University in Baltimore have strong Welsh connections.

Jonathan Edwards helped inspire the religious movement known as *'The Great Awakening'*, and was famous for his preaching. Dismissed as a minister, he became a missionary to Indians in Massachusetts, then became President of the College of New Jersey – now Princeton Univerity – in 1757. He was the greatest theologian of American Puritanism and a close friend of Samuel Hopkins. His *'System of Doctrines'* (1797) became known as 'Hopkinsianism', telling us that all sin is selfishness and that all virtue is disinterested benevolence.

In 1851, George Jones, whose parents emigrated from Llanwyddelan, co-founded the New York Times.

THE AMERICAN CIVIL WAR
John Davies emigrated from Wales to Philadelphia in 1701. His son Evan married a Welsh widow named Jane Williams, and the couple had a son, Samuel. The family moved to Augusta, Georgia when Samuel was a boy and her two Welsh sons by her earlier marriage enlisted in the Revolutionary army. Young Samuel Davies followed as a mounted gunman, later forming his own infantry company, fighting the British in Georgia and the Carolinas. At the end of the war, he was granted land in Georgia, then moved to Kentucky to breed racing horses on 600 acres of land, later known as Christian County. Here, in 1808, the last of his ten children was born, and named Jefferson, after the great Welshman just finishing his second term as President of the United States.

The cradle in which his mother Jane rocked the Jefferson Davis is in The Confederate Museum in New Orleans. (At some stage the spelling of Davies changed to Davis).When the child was three years old the family moved to Louisiana and in 1812 to Mississippi. While Thomas Jefferson had created the new country of the United States,

Jefferson Davis grew up to almost break it in two. A graduate of West Point, Jefferson Davis served in the Indian Wars, and was wounded becoming a hero in the Battle of Buena Vista against the Mexicans. In 1838 he was elected to the House of Representatives and sat in the US Senate from 1847 to 1851. Davis was Secretary of War from 1853 until 1857 when he returned to the Senate becoming leader of the Southern Democrats.

In 1860 South Carolina issued a declaration of secession from the USA. By January 1861, Georgia, Florida, Alabama, Mississippi, Louisiana, Texas and Arkansas had also seceded from the union. Virginia and North Carolina soon followed. Jefferson Davis was elected in February 1861 as President of the Confederate States of America. The ensuing bitter Civil War lasted from 1861 to 1865 with the vast military capability of the Union North eventually overcoming the Confederate Southern states.

The great and brutal battles of Manassas (where Davis took the field), Appomatox, Shiloh, Gettysburg, and the two battles at Bull Run echo through history and the South has still not forgotten Sherman's devastation. 359,528 Union and 258,000 Confederate troops had died in the young republic. The turning point in the war, more than any other, was the mass-production of the Springfield rifle in Connecticut. It had greater accuracy and three times the range of the old smooth-bore rifle. On the fateful third day of Gettysburg, 12,000 Confederate soldiers had mounted one last, great, Napoleonic assault on the Union lines. All but 300 were mown down before they reached the Northerners. After his capture, Jefferson Davis was put in shackles and imprisoned. His Welsh wife, Varina Howell, fought for his early release after two years in poor conditions.

The 'New York World', not a Southern sympathiser, called Jefferson Davis *'the best equipped man, intellectually, of his age, perhaps, in the country'*. Joseph McElroy, in his biography of Davis, says that *'Lincoln sought to save the Union; Davis did not wish to destroy the Union; he sought to preserve states' rights, under his interpretation of the Constitution.'* Like Jefferson before him, the right to liberty justified revolution for Davis. For him the Civil War was not about slavery but about freedom for the states and their individuals. He *'was convinced that Lincoln's aim was to convert a Federal republic of sovereign states into a consolidated nation with the right to dominate the states, the old idea which had precipitated the American Revolution.'* In the South, the Civil War is still referred to as 'The War of the States'.

The *'demon of centralisation, absolutism and despotism'* which is *'well-known by the friends of constitutional liberty'* has modern parallels with former German Chancellor Kohl's ideas for a united Europe with national sovereignty being subverted to central committees. A central over-riding bureaucracy could not work for Russia, so the European Union seems to be struggling against the natural flow of history. Welsh people from Glyndŵr to Thomas Jefferson to Jefferson Davis have always been rightly suspicious of both central-isation of power and rule by procedure and committees. Interestingly Lincoln had said that if he could win the Civil War without freeing the slaves he would. Lincoln's main reason for pursuing this course of action *'was not to free the slaves, but to cause discomfiture to the South in the Civil War'* (Brian Walden,

BBC TV, 13th January 1998). The distinction of Jefferson Davis being pro-slavery and Lincoln being anti-slavery has been a useful myth to help centralise power in Washington.

MORGAN'S RAIDERS

Jefferson Davis' biographer calls the Welsh *'militant nightingales'* possibly because of the activities of Morgan's Raiders during the Civil War. These guerrilla Confederates, officially called the Second Kentucky Cavalry Regiment, roamed behind the Union lines under John Morgan, capturing generals, fighting battles and cutting supply lines. They nicknamed themselves 'The Alligator Horses' and carried out a breath-taking 1,000 mile raid behind Union lines in 1862, destroying Federal supplies, capturing seventeen towns and taking twelve hundred prisoners. Morgan's Raiders lost ninety men, missing, killed or wounded. The next raid behind enemy lines brought about two-thousand enemy losses, against two killed, twenty-four wounded and sixty-four missing of the Kentuckians.

This flying column of expert horse-men fought battles in ten states, tied down enemy troop movements, and forced them to use valuable manpower to guard strategic targets behind their lines. In July 1863, Morgan's Raiders reached the furthest North of any Confederate troops. 'The Great Raid' reached Ohio before running out of horses and ammunition. Morgan was captured but tunnelled to freedom and managed to get back to the South. Nearly all of his imprisoned troops were systematically tortured by a special invention known as *'Morgan's Mule'* and some were simply shot at random by their vicious guards. Morgan's five raids into Union territory and his escape had terrorised the North and the prison authorities ignored these atrocities.

Gathering the remnants of his forces, Morgan still fought on as Confederate resistance crumbled. His brothers John, Richard, Calvin, Charlton, Tom and Key, and many Morgan cousins and nephews had fought with him in the Second Kentucky Regiment, along with other Welshmen like William Jones, Bowlin Roberts, William Davis, David Llewelyn and Greenberry Roberts. He was shot dead in 1864, refusing to return to a certain death in the appalling Union prison camps. His 'Alligator Horsemen' were the most hated and feared of all the Confederate soldiers. Courageous guerrillas, led by a Welshman, no atrocities can be held against their name in this dirty war. By 1865, the Second Kentucky was a scattered regiment of foot soldiers as the Union rampaged through the Southern States. Even now they were so highly rated that they were the chosen elite troops to assist the Welsh Confederate President Jefferson Davis in his flight from Richmond, before his capture.

A Union major-general who served in the Mexican War and the Civil War was Lewis Wallace. He saved Washington DC from capture by Confederate forces. He later became governor of New Mexico and minister to Turkey, but is better known as the author of Ben Hur (1880) which was twice made into a spectacular film (1936 and 1959).

JESSE WOODSON JAMES
The Reverend Robert James, a Baptist Minister, helped found William Jewell College in Liberty, Missouri. His son Jesse (1847-1882) had an entirely different life, first coming to our notice when riding with Quantrell's Raiders in the Civil War. After the war, he was wounded while surrendering to Union troops, and his treatment by them turned him against authority for the rest of his notorious life. His Welsh mother, the formidable Zerelda James Samuels ('Zee') lost her hand when Pinkerton's detectives threw a grenade into her house. It also killed Archie Samuels, Jesse's half-brother, further embittering him against the forces of law.

JOHN PIERPOINT MORGAN
After the Civil War, another man of Welsh descent, John Pierpoint Morgan (1837- 1913) built his father's firm into most influential private banking house in the USA. After the 1893 financial panic, Morgan formed a syndicate to float a dollar bond issue for President Grover Cleveland to finance an increased gold reserve. This stabilised the American economy. His bank financed the development of the railroad system to open up America, and by 1900 Morgan controlled one of the six major railway lines. He set up US Steel Corporation in 1901, then the largest corporation in the world, and International Harvester in 1902. Morgan controlled large chunks of the economy, including Equitable Life Assurance Society. He put together one of the greatest art collections in history which he bequeathed to the Metropolitan Museum of Fine Art in New York and his private library became the public Pierpoint Morgan library. Morgan's control of American public and private financing is without parallel. The 1998 'Forbes' survey put Bill Gates' worth, from his Microsoft shares, at $51 billion. However, Morgan controlled a percentage of American Gross Domestic Product many times that of Gates.

'Peter Drucker calculated recently that Morgan was rich enough to finance all of America's capital investments, whether private or public sector (except housing), for a period of four months – but that to do so today would take the fortunes of the top 60 American billionaires combined.' (Daily Telegraph, 28th June 1998).

AMERICAN WHISKY

Swingeing English taxation and the Nonconformist religious movement made Welsh whisky production increasingly fraught with financial problems. As a result of emigration, the first whisky distillery in America was started by the Evan Williams family, from West Wales, in Bardstown, Kentucky in the early 1700s. They left the family distillery in Dale, Pembrokeshire to set it up and Bardstown was named after Bardsey Island, the birthplace of Whisky (see Whisky entry). It is still one of the largest distilleries in the USA, selling 2,000,000 cases a year. Kentucky Bourbon dates from this time.

Eighty years later, in the early 1800s, the Daniels family from Cardigan, with another Welsh family, the Molows, started up production of the Jack Daniels brand in Lynchburg Tennessee. In 1866, Jack Daniels became the first registered distillery in the USA. Jack Daniels was born in New York of Cardiganshire parents. The current president of the company is Lem Molow. Jack Daniels Old No.7 Sour Mash is known world-wide. Southern Comfort is also a drink of Welsh origin, first distilled by settlers from a traditional Welsh recipe.

IMMIGRATION

In the nineteenth century, Welsh emigrants, driven to move by tolls, tithes for an Anglican Church they did not believe in, infant mortality, appalling working conditions and wage reductions looked to America. Between 1815 and 1850, around 75% of Welsh emigrants left the rural West and Mid-Wales to go to New York, Pennsylvania, Ohio, Wisconsin and Illinois, mainly carrying out agricultural work. They were then joined by workers from the South Wales and Clwyd coal and steel areas some of whom joined the California Gold Rush. But two towns in particular were the magnets, Scranton and Wilkes-Barre in Pennsylvania. More than 40,000 Welsh went to Scranton alone, and at the start of the nineteenth century, there were 19,000 Welsh speakers in the town of Scranton. The fledgling American ironworks industry drew on equipment and skilled workers from Pontypool, in order to get started. Benjamin Franklin had visited Pontypool to see how iron could be rolled instead of being hammered flat and the first American rolling mill was built by David Morgan from Pontypool in South Wales, in the Pennsylvanian town of Sharon in 1871.

By 1872 there were 384 Welsh Language chapels in the USA, and 24 Welsh periodicals. The oldest ethnic language newspaper in America, 'Y Drych', was established in Utica. It took over 'Banner America' of Scranton in 1868 and still survives, although the Welsh communities dispersed.

The Mormon Tabernacle Choir was formed by two-hundred and forty-nine Welsh Mormon immigrants in 1848 in Salt Lake City.

THE TWENTIETH CENTURY

The father of the epic movie, David Lewelyn Wark Griffith – DW – used to boast of his Welsh ancestry from

Gruffydd ap Llewelyn, King of Wales. Born in Kentucky, a favourite domicile of expatriate Welshmen, he made hundreds of short films before his masterpieces 'The Birth of a Nation' (1915) and 'Intolerance' (1916). Other major films made between 1918 and 1922 were 'Hearts of the World', 'Broken Blossoms' and 'Orphans of the Storm'. 'Hearts of the World' broke new ground by showing war scenes actually filmed at the front in World War I. Griffith revolutionised cinema techniques, innovating the fade-in, fade-out, close-up and flashback.

Another great American film-maker was also a businessman and aviator. Howard Robard Hughes had Welsh ancestry. From an oil industry background, he moved into movies in the 1920s, making 'Scarface' and 'Hells' Angels'. He then turned entirely to designing, building and flying aircraft in the 1930s and broke most of the world's air speed records. Returning to film-making in 1943 he made the controversial 'The Outlaw', starring Jane Russell. Moving back again into plane-manufacture he designed and built Hercules, a huge wooden seaplane that flew only once but yielded valuable technical information to the industry. After a severe plane crash in 1946, he became increasingly reclusive, controlling his business empire from sealed-off hotel suites and died in 1976 aged 71.

On the other end of the work-scale, John Llewelyn Lewis (1880-1969) was president of the United Mine Workers' Union from 1920-1960, making it one of the most powerful unions in the USA.

In 1916, Charles Evans Hughes, the Welsh-speaking son of a Tredegar immigrant, was only just beaten by Woodrow Wilson for the Presidency (277 to 254 electoral college votes, 9,129,606 to 8,538,221 popular votes).

William Randoph Hearst ('Citizen Kane') bought the Norman St Donats Castle on the Vale of Glamorgan coast, and spent millions of pounds on it, including demolishing Bradenstoke Priory in Wiltshire and part-reassembling it in the castle. As Atlantic College it became the first international college for talented children to study with their peers from other countries, helping promote pre-University understanding across nations.

In politics, Charles Evans Hughes was Secretary of State and Chief Justice between 1921 and 1925, and 1931-1940 respectively. Joseph Davies helped shape American foreign relations, and Harry Lloyd Hopkins headed the New Deal projects under F. D. Roosevelt. As Roosevelt's closest confidante, Hopkins undertook special missions to Russia and Britain in World War II.

Frank Lloyd Wright, the leading 20th century architect, along with Le Corbusier, was so proud of his Welsh heritage that he called the Wisconsin home he built for himself, 'Taliesin', after the legendary Welsh bard. Another home and school, Taliesin West, was built near Phoenix, Arizona in 1938. A controversial and daring architect, his weekend home of Falling Water (near Pittsburgh) is famous worldwide, as are the earthquake-proof Imperial Hotel in Tokyo, and the brilliantly designed Guggenheim Museum of Modern Art in New York. His mother had been born in Llandysul and his Welsh upbringing is described lovingly in his sister's book *'The Valley of the God Almighty Joneses'* (by Maginel Wright Barney).

Perhaps the greatest golfer in history, Bobby (Robert Tyre) Jones had Welsh roots. A qualified lawyer from Atlanta, he won the US Open four times and the British Open three times. After winning the 'Grand Slam' of the US Open, the British Open and both Amateur Championships in his golden year of 1930, he retired from the game as there were no challenges left. He was just 28 years old and he went on to build the Augusta National Golf Course and found the Masters Tournament. Welsh Americans since 1978 have been running the Bobby Jones Golf Tournament at Ann Arbor (twinned with Brecon), open to all those citizens named Robert or Roberta Jones. Entrants are given nicknames such as 'Computer', 'Too-Tall' and 'Hubcap' to distinguish them.

In American military history, the spiritual successors to Morgan's Marauders were 'Carlson's Raiders', led by the marine colonel Carlson Evans. In World War II, the 2nd Raider battalion became known as Carlson's Raiders because of its lightning attacks behind the Japanese lines at Guadalcanal.

It is thought that Elvis Aron Presley was of Welsh descent (from the Preseli Hills), not Scottish, and his father had the typical Welsh Christian name of Vernon. South of the Preseli Mountains, there is an ancient chapel devoted the Saint Elvis, the only one known in Britain. His dead twin, Jesse Garon Presley, had a Welsh second name, and his mother Gladys had a Welsh name. His grandmother Doll Mansell may have come from the famous family of Mansel from Oxwich on the Gower Peninsula. The first Presley recorded in the USA was David 'Pressley' in 1700, David being the most popular Welsh name and a direct Presley ancestor in the USA was called Dunnan. Most

'Elvisologists' believe that Elvis came from Scottish and Cherokee blood, but further research would probably solidify the Welsh connection at the expense of the Scottish.

Jerry Lee Lewis is also of Welsh stock, as is the man who discovered Elvis and founded the great Sun Records, Sam Phillips of Memphis. Jerry Lee ('Killer') stated *'I never said I was the King of Rock 'n' Roll. I said I'm simply the best.'* 'The Killer' is still the only man to top all three US pop, country music and R&B charts with one record, 'Great Balls of Fire' in 1958. Unfortunately his popularity waned when he married his thirteen-year old cousin, Myra. Sam Phillips was responsible for popularising Ike Turner, BB King, Carl Perkins, Roy Orbison, Jerry Lee Lewis, Charley Rich and Johnny Cash, amongst others, turning minority blues into the rock and roll we know today.

The modern American crooner Jack Jones had an equally famous singing father, Alan Jones from Wales who starred in musicals and had a worldwide hit with The Donkey Serenade. Hiram (Hank) Williams (1923-1953) from Alabama revolutionised country music in his short life. George Jones is another country singer of Welsh stock. Looking at Elvis, 'The Killer', Hank Williams and George Jones, we can safely say that Americans of Welsh ancestry have transformed popular music across the world. Also, the Hall of Fame country star, Conway Twitty, was born Harold Lloyd Jenkins.

ANIMALS

dafad – sheep; ceffyl – horse; gwartheg – cattle; mochyn – pig; ci – dog; gafr -goat.

SHEEP

Wales has the highest density of sheep in the world, which has given rise to countless jokes. It has 15% of the EU's sheep, but only 1% of the population. Welshpool's Monday fair is the largest sheep auction in Europe. To fit with our Welsh Black Cattle, cobs (horses) and pigs there is obviously a 'Welsh Black Mountain Sheep', and the Llanwaenog Sheep from West Wales has a strange tuft like that of a unicorn. Both can be seen at The Museum of Welsh Life at Saint Fagans, near Cardiff. The oldest sheep in the world last lambed at the age of 24 and died just before her 29th birthday, near Aberystwyth in 1988. The UK sheep-shearing record of 625 ewes was set by N. Beynon of Gower at Carno, Powys in 1993.

Other Welsh sheep breeds include the rare Dafad Rhiw on the Llŷn Peninsula, the Dafad Torddu, the Beulah Speck-Faced, the black-faced Clun Forest, the Welsh Mule, and the Badge-Faced (Black-Bellied) sheep. The rare Hill Radnor sheep were favoured in the eighteenth century to make fine woollens and women travelled from village to village knitting stockings to sell as they walked. There is a flock at The Museum of Welsh Life. Our newly-shorn Welsh Mountain Sheep are not the prettiest sheep in the world, especially compared to another native breed, the speckle-faced Kerry Hill, but they are definitely the cleverest. If you watch them rolling over cattle grids, or wandering up back alleys in valley towns trying gates to get to a rubbish bin or molesting you for food if you stop on the Brecon Beacons you will realise why grocers in the Valleys do not display their wares outside their shops. I have been lucky enough to watch Welsh sheep teach their lambs how to roll over the cattle grids. This appears to be a habit that no other sheep in the world has mastered.

HORSES

Horses were revered in Celtic literature and the finest horse-trappings found in Britain were the Bronze Age hoard from Parc-y-Meirch (the ancient Horse Park) in Clwyd. Hywel Dda's laws recognised five types of horse: the charger, hunter, hack, pack-horse and draft-horse. Wales is now famous world-wide for two types of horse, the lively Welsh mountain pony and the stocky Welsh Cob. Welsh mountain ponies are sold all over the world, with a record pony price of £22,050 being paid for a stallion, Coed Coch Bari, by an Australian in 1978. Possibly the largest horse-fair in Europe is held every month at Llanybydder in Carmarthenshire.

CATTLE

The native (pre-Roman) breed of Wales, Welsh Black Cattle, were the ancient Britons' most prized possessions as they retreated westwards under successive waves of Saxon invasion.

For centuries Welsh Black Cattle were herded in huge numbers along the old drove roads to England, giving them the nickname of *'black gold'*. John Williams, the Welsh Archbishop of York, called the droves *'the Spanish fleet of Wales, which brings hither the little gold and silver we have'*. The returning Welshmen were prey to highwaymen, providing the stimulus for Britain's first commercial bank, the Welsh Bank of the Black Ox, now Lloyds Bank. Until this century, Welsh Blacks were also used for ploughing and pulling wagons.

Smaller and far hardier than the Friesian and Charolais interlopers, they are making a comeback as a breed for both meat and milk. Their climatic adaptability makes them a suitable breed for North Canadian winters or Saudi Arabian summers, and because herd records go back to the last century, each animal can be traced over many generations – Welsh Black Beef is free of BSE.

Of the ancient Celtic White (or Park) Cattle, with their long horns, there is a relic wild population at Dinefwr Castle, and at Glynllifon and Vaynol in Gwynedd. These former are the descendants of the *white kine of Denefawr* mentioned in Hywel Dda's Law a thousand years ago. Yr Ychen Bannog, long-horned oxen, often appear in Welsh mythology and one of Culhwch's tasks in 'The Mabinogion' was to reunite the remaining pair on either side of Mynydd Banawg. Llanddewi Brefi church preserved a horn-core of one of these beasts, known as 'Mabcorn yr Ych Bannog' and it is now in The Museum of Welsh Life. It belonged to the 'great urus', Bos Primogenius, the pre-Roman wild long-horned cattle which are thought to be the ancestors of the Celtic White Cattle.

There is also a herd of the rare Glamorgan Cattle at Margam Country Park, a pretty, light brown breed with a white stripe along the backbone. These *red cattle* were bred in the Southern lowlands, along with oxen.

Water Buffalo are being bred at Rhydlewis in Cardiganshire, to supply the milk for a mozzarella-type cheese.

PIGS
The Welsh Pig was claimed to be the oldest breed in history, and like other animals is featured strongly in Celtic legend and place-names. One of the most popular terms for a child who gets a mucky face eating is still 'mochyn du' (black pig), even in Anglicised areas of Wales.

DOGS
The ancient, crinkle-haired White Welsh Hound which is still used by some Welsh hunts may be descended from the hounds at the courts of the Welsh princes. Welsh dog breeds include the Corgi beloved by the English Royal Family since George VI had one in 1936. This 'dwarf-dog' was bred to be close to the ground, and nip the ankles of the cattle it was herding rather than leap up and bite their flanks. It is an extremely old breed – some claim it to be Neolithic, and others that it came to Wales with the Vikings. The popular Pembrokeshire variety has hardly any tail. The much rarer Cardiganshire Corgi has a long tail and legs so short that its stomach almost touches the ground.

Other breeds include the Welsh Setter, the Sealyham, the red and white Welsh Springer Spaniel (a sporting dog with its own world-wide web site), the Welsh Terrier (used for fox-hunting in North Wales) and the Welsh Collie. The Welsh Terrier Club of America was founded in 1900, with an annual show competition for these black and tan dogs. A Welsh Terrier won the Champion of Champions accolade at Crufts in 1998. The Sealyham Terrier, a particularly snappy little dog, was bred to hunt otters near Haverfordwest in 1890 by Captain John Owen. A Welsh Collie called Taffy lived for almost 28 years, dying in 1980, so Wales in 1996 held the record for both Europe's oldest living man, dog and sheep.

Corgis (Dwarf-Dogs) were bred short to nip the ankles of cattle and avoid their kicks, and were used by the old drovers to take cattle across Wales to market. The typical Welsh sheepdog is probably a type of Border Collie. It wins sheep trials everywhere, is faithful, hardworking and to the Welsh the best dog in the world. The annual sheepdog trials at Bala are the oldest established anywhere, first staged in 1873. I have seen photographs of a beautiful Welsh sheepdog called the Blue Cambrian, but am unsure if the breed still exists. The eighty-six year-old farmer across the road from my barn, Arthur Hammett, has a scraggy blue-pale grey sheepdog he calls a 'Welsh Blue'. I am also informed that most 'seeing-eye dogs' (guide-dogs for the blind) in Japan are Welsh labradors.

One of the best known of Welsh dogs was a retriever called Swansea Jack who was famous for saving the lives of people and other dogs in the waters of Swansea Docks in the 1930s. A simple carved stone on the Swansea waterfront commemorates the dog.

GOATS

A Welsh song about coloured goats has made generations of children (and adults) collapse with laughter as it becomes quicker and quicker, and more and more difficult, to call out the colours of the goats. There are still a few feral herds in the wilds of Snowdonia, and a colony of seventy wild Kashmiri goats has lived on the Great Orme since Victorian times. The mascot of the Royal Welch Fusiliers is a Kashmiri billy-goat, usually called Taffy.

The regimental mascot of the Royal Regiment of Wales is also a goat. During the Crimean War, Private Gwilym Jenkins was on night-watch, guarding a herd of cattle destined as food for the troops. He had for company a small goat kid and fell asleep. The kid's bleating woke him up and alerted him to a sneak attack by the Russians. Jenkins sounded the alarm and the regiment was alerted to fight off the attack. The goat and its successors have led regimental processions ever since with the official rank and title of Lance-Corporal Gwilym Jenkins familiarly nicknamed Shenkin.

OTHER ANIMALS

Carrying on the Welsh Black tradition, the British Black Adder is only found in Tregaron Bog, and Dyfed's Black Bog Ant is only found elsewhere in parts of Dorset and Hampshire in England.

Hares, along with cockerels and geese, were regarded as sacred by the Celts. They are often represented in Celtic arts, and Caesar tells us that it was unlawful to eat them. Queen Buddig (Boadicea) of the Iceni released a hare while praying to her goddess before beginning her anti-Roman campaign and hare legends run through Celtic folklore. Saint Melangell is the patron saint of hares.

Pine Martens and polecats roam the great swathes of Forestry Commission land, both increasing in numbers, and a unique type of vole lives on Skomer Island. Martens' fur is almost as beautiful as sable and the old Welsh laws dictated that marten fur could only be worn by kings. Iits value was only beaten by the fur of a beaver.

Beavers lingered on in Wales long after the rest of Britain. According to Giraldus Cambrensis, on his 1188 Journey Through Wales, the last beavers in England and Wales lived in the River Teifi in Cardiganshire. The Laws of Hywel Dda mention beavers and wolves and the last wild wolves of Britain were said to be those of seventeenth-century Powys, the last of which kept watch in Chirk Castle in the 1680s. However, another report states that the last wolf was killed on Cader Idris in 1768. The last Welsh wild cat is thought to have lived in the eighteenth century near Usk (Brynbuga), but other reports say they lasted in the hills until the nineteenth century. Brown bears may have lasted until medieval times.

Probably the biggest freshwater fish in Britain was a 388 pound sturgeon caught in the River Towi at Nantgaredig, Carmarthenshire on 25th July 1933. Alec Allen was the lucky angler. The fish was so heavy that it had to be transported from the riverbank by horse and cart. (Many recent records feature 'imported' fish). Salmon (eog) are common in Welsh rivers and estuaries as are sea trout or sewin.

The rare Gwyniad, a type of whiting, lives in Snowdon's lakes (see Lakes). Also Saint Ffraid (Bride) was said to have thrown rushes into the River Conwy which turned miraculously into fish and averted a famine. These small 'brwyniad' (which means 'rush-like') or sparlings are related to the trout and are very uncommon (Osmerus Eperlanus).

A third of the world's population of grey seals are found around the Pembrokeshire islands and coasts.

Wales has the oldest rocks in Britain, and off the coast of Harlech in 1964, the oldest surviving life form in the world was found, the organism Kakabekia Barghoorniana, which has been in existence for 2000 million years.

AP

Map, or Mab (the p is mutated to b in front of vowels) is the equivalent of mac in Scottish lineage, meaning son of. Mab is the Welsh word for youth. This is one of the reasons that Welsh is the branch of Celtic languages known as Brythonic, or p-Celtic, while Erse and Gaelic are c-Celtic or q-Celtic (map compared to mac). The reason the custom died out in Wales (but is being revived) was that the Act of Union in 1536 stated that Welsh could no longer be used for legal or official purposes, so surnames had to be Anglicised.

Thus Llywelyn ap Robert became Llywelyn Probert; ap Hywel became Powell; ap Siencyn, Jenkins; ap Rhys became Price, Prees, Preece; ap Harri became Parry; ap Huw changed to Puw or Pugh; ap Henri to Penri, etc. Equally, ap Evan became Bevan, ap Owen became Bowen and so on, with the mutation to 'b' being caused by the vowel starting a name. For females, merch means daughter or girl, so Eira ferch Gwenllian served the same purpose as ap.

The nickname for someone who pretended to have forgotten his language and identity was Dic Sion Dafydd. From the sixteenth century it became necessary for Welshmen to petition Parliament to be 'made English' so they could enjoy privileges restricted to Englishmen such as the right to buy or hold land. It was at this time that the custom of using ap or ferch began to die out, and that Ioan became Jones, ap Hywel became Powell, etc. (see Names). Other noble families Anglicised their names under English pressure. For instance the House of Gwenwynwyn became 'de la Pole'.

Bishop Rowland Lee, President of the Council of Wales from 1534, had ordered the deletion of ap and the introduction of English surnames, so in many cases English Christian names were chosen. This is why there are so many Hughes, Davies, Johns, Williams etc. in Wales. Jones (from Ioan) is the most common Welsh surname but there is no 'j' in the Welsh alphabet. Gwyn Alf Williams in *'When Was Wales'* records the bankrupt Welshman who signed himself as *'Sion ap William ap Sion ap William ap Sion ap Dafydd ap Ithel Fychan ap Cynrig ap Robert ap Iorwerth ap Rhyrid ap Iorwerth ap Madoc ap Edwain Bendew, called after the English fashion John Jones.'*

Thomas Pennant (1726-1798) noted the lineage of Evan Llwyd whose family had lived at Cwm Bychan since at least 1100. *'Evan ap Edward ap Richard ap Edward ap Humphrey ap Edward ap Dafydd ap Robert ap Howel ap Dafydd ap Meurig Llwyd o Nannau ap Meirig Vychan ap Ynyr Vychan ap Ynyr ap Meuric ap Madog ap Cadwgan ap Bleddyn ap Cynfyn, prince of North Wales and Powys'* ... Thomas ap Rhisiart ap Hywel ap Ieuan Fychan (lord of Mostyn) and his brother Piers (founder of the family of Trelacre) were the first who abridged their names. Bishop Rowland Lee, sitting at one of the courts on a Welsh cause, wearied with the number of aps on the jury, directed that the panel should assume their last name or that of their residence and that Thomas ap Richard ap Hywel ap Ieuan Fychan should for the future be reduced to the poor dissyllable Mostyn, no doubt to the great mortification of many an ancient line.

ARCHERS

The longbow was developed by the Welsh in Gwent from the shorter bow in popular use, and gained popularity under Edward I for use against the Scots in the Highlands. In the Scottish wars, the English soon discovered that foot soldiers, armed with longbows and trained to keep a disciplined line, could repulse a charge of armoured knights by aiming at their horses. Thus, in 1337, in preparation for his French wars, Edward III prohibited on pain of death all sport except archery, and cancelled the debts of all workmen who manufactured the bows of yew and their arrows. The longbow rapidly became the critical success factor in battles before the development of reliable cannons and guns. Measuring about six feet and with arrows measuring around three feet the bow was easily portable. A skilled archer could fire ten to twelve arrows a minute, with an accurate killing range of over two-hundred yards. A hail of arrows demoralised any army and its rapid rate of fire made the crossbow obsolete. A crossbow could fire one to two bolts per minute, but in the rain was useless. The longbow was lighter, and strings were kept dry in the archers' hats.

With the salvage of Henry VIII's 'Mary Rose' in 1982, it was found that the draw-weight of these bows was twice what had been previously thought – up to one hundred and eighty pounds – which some experts said could not be drawn. To shoot arrows using this power needed practice from youth and from then on a regular daily basis.

With Edward III in command, for the sea battle at Sluys, he placed only one ship of men-at-arms between each two ships of longbowmen, with extra ships full of archers in reserve. From their 'castles' or fighting platforms Welsh archers in Edward's pay decimated the French. It was said afterwards that the *'fish drank so much French blood that they could have spoken French if God had given them tongues'.*

CRÉCY

The French belief in the power of the armoured nobility should have been shattered at Crécy in Picardy in 1346. Of Edward III's invasion army of twelve thousand men almost eight thousand were recruited from landowners in Wales and the Marches. Four thousand were Welsh archers, with around three thousand five hundred Welsh spearmen. King Edward's army almost reached Paris, but it was decided not to besiege it as Edward had no idea where Philip VI's French army was. By forced marches, the French army of 40,000 caught up with the Anglo-Welsh army at Crécy at 4pm. King Philip wished to rest for the night, but his army saw the smaller force and advanced expecting an easy and glorious victory.

Seeing the momentum could not be halted, Philip VI ordered his six thousand Genoese crossbowmen to shatter the foreign army. The battle was an unholy mess from the French point of view and all the luck came Edward III's way. A sudden downpour made the Genoese crossbow strings slack, but the Welsh archers kept their strings dry, coiled under their helmets. When the sun reappeared, the Genoese were trying to replace their bow strings, while the Welsh slaughtered them at a range of almost three hundred yards, aiming six arrows a minute – a contemporary report said that the arrows *'fell like snow'*. The French cavalry charged through the dead, dying and retreating Genoese and some reached the British line where they were held on the right flank by Edward's fifteen year-old son, the Prince of Wales –

later called 'the Black Prince'. Some fifteen hundred French knights were killed in his sector of the field.

Welsh archers relentlessly poured arrows into fourteen or fifteen French cavalry charges until midnight, when the carnage stopped. The French king had been led away, wounded by an arrow, and the Welsh followed up with long knives skewering around four thousand fallen knights as they lay helpless on the ground. The Prince of Wales had been in charge of one of the English battle groups, and took the crest of three ostrich feathers and the motto *'Ich Dien'* from the dead King John 'the Blind' of Bohemia, ever after to serve as the crest of Wales. French losses were eleven thousand compared to just a thousand suffered by the invading force. This battle with the consequent capture of Calais effectively started the 'Hundred Years War' between England and France and made the longbow an integral part of European battle plans for the next two hundred years.

The English knights railed at the Welsh "knifemen" for killing nobles who could be ransomed. However, the Welsh saw the fallen French as armoured enemies on armoured horses who had just scared them to death and tried to kill them. They received no reward for capturing the enemy, with all the attendant problems, and took the simple option – a dead enemy is no danger. The Welsh bowmen wore the national colours of green and white, the same colours later worn by Henry Tudor at his coronation in 1485. This was probably the first national uniform in European warfare.

The Welsh also knew that if the French caught them, the two fingers of their draw hand were cut off to stop them ever firing an arrow again. This is the origin of the infamous *'V' sign*, where the Welsh gesticulated to distant troops that they had the full use of their right hands.

POITIERS

A decade later, in 1356, the Prince of Wales (now called 'The Black Prince'), found himself at Poitiers, near Tours, with an Anglo-Gascon army of eight thousand men. He faced King Jean's army of at least twice as many soldiers. The Prince played for time by negotiating while his troops frantically set up defensive positions and palisades for his archers. Marshal Clermont advised blockading the English and starving them out but the proposal was rejected. However, the only access to the English enemy was a narrow passage allowing only four men to ride through.

The French flank was crushed by Welsh archers before they could approach the centre of the field. Their frontal attack was beaten back by arrows that fell so thick that they *'darkened the air'*. Shooting from positions protected by dismounted knights and foot soldiers, archers aimed at the unarmoured rumps of the retreating horses. Their riders were then knifed and piked to death. After repulsing three assaults in seven hours, the Black Prince and the Captal de Buch charged out and captured the French King. Several thousand of the French nobility had died, and the King, Constable, Marshalls, thirteen counts, five viscounts, twenty-one barons and two thousand knights and men-at-arms were captured. On the Black Prince's side was Hywel ap Gruffydd, known as Hywel y Fwyall, or 'Hywel the Axe'. His battle-axe was so feared that

for many years after his death a feast was served before it then given to the poor in honour of Hywel. Against the English was Owain Lawgoch (see Assassination), Owain 'Red Hand', the heir to the Princes of Gwynedd, who somehow survived the slaughter.

Even today, the descendants of the bowmen of Crécy and Poitiers, The Society of the Black Hundred, has an annual celebration in Llantrisant. (The rights to Llantrisant Common were granted in perpetuity, for the service of the archers who were with the Black Prince at Crécy in 1346). The longbow, a Welsh invention, changed the face of European warfare causing the end of the armoured cavalry charge and preceding reliable artillery. It changed combat from hand-to-hand to killing from distance.

AGINCOURT

Harry of Monmouth, Henry V, became king at the age of twenty-five, in 1413. With France divided between the Houses of Burgundy and Orleans, he prepared to invade and landed unopposed near Harfleur, which he besieged for six weeks until it fell. His army was struck down by dysentery and his Council of War recommended that he return to England in the face of the oncoming main French army. Instead he sent home the sick and wounded, about two thousand archers and fifteen hundred knights and men-at-arms. The remaining army set out to march the hundred miles to his fortress at Calais.

Almost sixty years after Poitiers, Harry of Monmouth met the French around thirty miles from Crécy, at Agincourt. He was outnumbered. Against twenty thousand French troops he had just four thousand archers and a thousand knights, squires and foot soldiers remaining of his invasion force.

On the morning of St Crispin's Day, 25th October 1415, Henry made the speech made famous by Shakespeare to his small army, who had spent the night listening to the French carousing and celebrating their assumed victory-to-be. Tired from their long march, hungry, and dysentery-ridden, the troops had no choice but to fight against these overwhelming odds. Following the king's example, the whole army dismounted and sent their horses to the rear. There was to be no retreat.

Realising that morale would sink if he stayed still, and with the French remaining in place, Henry ordered the English banner forward, to meet the attacking French. With cries of 'St George for England', the army advanced to within three hundred yards of the French. The Welsh archers drove forward-pointing stakes into the ground as some protection against a French cavalry charge. Henry's army had advanced to a point where both ends of their line touched the woods on either side.

As the larger French force assembled near the English line, they became compressed, and this restricted the field of fire of their cannons and cross-bowmen. At this point the Welsh archers unleashed the first onslaught of arrows from their longbows. Henry had deployed solid wedges of Welsh archers between his men-at-arms and two blocks on either wing to shoot through the compressed three lines of French cavalry.

The first line of 18,000 Frenchmen, dismounted knights and men-at-arms about 30 deep, churned the heavy ground into a real quagmire. As heavily armoured knights died, pierced by

arrows, those following could not get through the rider-less horses, the dead, wounded and dying. Hundreds of thousands of arrows had poured into the French. Many nobles were captured by the lightly-armoured archers for later ransom.

The second line was led forward by the Duke of Alençon and fierce hand-to-hand fighting only stopped when the Duke fell and the French line broke and retreated. At this moment, with the third French line intact, and his own men tired, weakened and losing shape, news came to Henry that the English camp in his rear was under attack. He took the terrible decision to slaughter all the prisoners, not realising that it was not a serious attack and had been beaten off easily. The third French line retired from the field.

From just a hundred yards, Welsh archers had been able to pinpoint the joints in the armour that allowed the limbs to move. They had used armour-penetrating arrow heads with four cutting edges, waisted to part the metal and for the arrow to slide through into the muscle. The arrows weighed seventy grammes and moved at two hundred feet per second, about two hundred km.p.h., shattering muscle and bone. One shot in the shoulder would spin a knight around and leave him incapacitated on the ground.

Thousands of Frenchmen had been killed (including three dukes, five counts and ninety barons) and thousands captured in this most one-sided battle of The Hundred Years War. Among the French dead was Henry Gwyn, Lord of Llansteffan, and many of Owain Glyndŵr's old soldiers lay among the slaughtered French. English losses were only five hundred, including the Welsh Davy Gam, who was knighted as he lay dying on the battlefield. He appears to have been the model for Shakespeare's Fluellen. It seems that he had tried to assassinate Owain Glyndŵr in 1404, so his loss was not felt deeply in Wales. The Welsh archers had been led by William ap Thomas, the builder of Raglan Castle. In 1420, Henry V was recognised by Charles VI as heir to the throne of France by the Treaty of Troyes. However, he died of dysentery at Vincennes in 1422 before this man born in Wales could claim the crown of France.

The Welsh longbow at Crécy (1346), then Poitiers (1356) and finally at Agincourt (1415) extended the 'killing zone' from an arm's length to hundreds of yards, altering the nature of war. French nobles in armour plate and chain mail were cut to shreds by starving soldiers from the lowest ranks of society. Some were pinned to their dead horses. The concept of chivalry was dead. Interestingly enough, as with language and religion, history has been consistently rewritten against the Welsh to the greater glory of its neighbour. This military innovation is now the 'English' longbow, used by 'English' archers. A 1997 BBC TV documentary on 26th February 1998, extolled it as such, ignoring that four thousand seven hundred Welsh archers went to Normandy with Henry and that it has as much to do with an English invention as a Cruise missile. All archery books and history books do the same. From Crécy, Poitiers and Pilleth, where Glyndŵr's archers decimated Mortimer's forces in 1402, the longbow was regarded as a Welsh weapon, invented in Gwent. With Agincourt, the Welsh archers suddenly transmogrify into English ones using English weapons. The experts also claimed that the rele-

vant archers were the English middle classes, 'yeomen', whereas in fact they were poor Welsh mercenaries, many from the Welsh-speaking border areas.

After the defeat of Llywelyn the Last, Edward I had used Welsh troops to win the battle of Falkirk against the Scots in 1298. Ten thousand five hundred of his twelve thousand five hundred infantrymen were Welsh, and the battle was the first that proved the superiority of the longbow, the speciality of the men of Glamorgan. Five thousand Welshmen were in Edward II's army at Bannockburn in 1314, and six thousand two hundred served in his 1322 Scottish campaign. We see unbroken battles from 1298 to 1415 with Welsh bowmen with Welsh bows, but modern history books record only 'English' archers with the 'English' invention of 'English' longbows. If any historian wishes to state that the inventors were the 'men of Gwent', Gwent was almost completely Welsh-speaking only as far back as 1850, with more Welsh monoglots than any other Welsh county (see Chartists, Language).

ARCHITECTURE

For anyone wanting a taste of traditional Welsh buildings over the last five-hundred years, a visit to The Museum of Welsh Life at Saint Fagans, Cardiff is thoroughly recommended. In the castle grounds, over thirty buildings from all over Wales have been re-erected.

Wales is about castles and churches, not great mansions and palaces. However, the great **Inigo Jones** (of Welsh parentage) has many houses and bridges attributed to him in Wales. He founded classical English architecture, designing the Queen's House at Greenwich, rebuilding the Banqueting Hall at Whitehall and laying out Covent Garden and Lincoln's Inn Fields. He also designed two Danish royal palaces and worked with Ben Jonson, introducing the proscenium arch and movable scenery to the English stage.

John Nash of Haverfordwest, lived in Carmarthen from 1784-1796, designing several local houses before his *Bath terraces* and crescents and the wonderfully oriental Prince Regent's Pavilion at Brighton. He laid out Regent's Park, Trafalgar Square, St James Park, Carlton House Terrace and Regent Street. One of the greatest town planners, his 1779 patent for improvements to the piers and arches of bridges led the way for the introduction of steel girders in building. The beautiful house he designed in Llanerchaeron, near Aberaeron, is now a National Trust property.

In 1787, Margam Orangery was built, still the biggest in the world at three hundred and thirty feet long. Margam Park, 1830, was designed by Thomas Hopper, the architect of Penrhyn Castle. In the nearby church attached to a ruined abbey, are some of the most important Celtic crosses in Europe, including the celebrated Wheel Cross of Cynfelin c.900AD. One of the owners of this Margam estate, Christopher Rice Mansel Talbot, sailed his luxury yacht 'Lynx' as the first ship through the Suez Canal in 1869. In fifty-nine years as the Member of Parliament representing Glamorgan, he was known to speak only once in the House of Commons to ask another MP to close his window because he was 'sitting in a draught'.

Owen Jones (1809-1874), son of the antiquary of the same name, was an architect and designer, being superintendent of works for The Great Exhibition of 1851 and director of decoration for the Crystal Palace. He designed St James Hall and wrote the superb 'Grammar of Ornament'. **Frank Lloyd Wright**, the American architect of Welsh descent, used the motto 'Y Gwir yn Erbyn y Byd', Truth Against the World (see America).

Clough Williams-Ellis (1883-1978) built the surreal Italianate village, Portmeirion, between 1922 and 1975. The cult 1960s series, The Prisoner, starring Patrick McGoohan, was set here and it defies description as one of the world's strangest villages. It was inspired by the architect's many visits to Portofino and its colourful exterior disguises some important pieces of salvage such as the ballroom from Emral Hall now installed in the 'Town Hall'. In the 175 acres of subtropical gardens overlooking the sea, you pass through a gatehouse into a world of grottoes, colonnades, a campanile, a watchtower and a variety of buildings ranging from Baroque to traditional Welsh, from Classical to Gothic. Williams-Ellis wrote *'Some day, somewhere, I would even assuredly erect a whole group of buildings on my own chosen site for my own satisfaction; an ensemble that would body forth my chafing ideas of fitness and gaiety and indeed be me.'*

The National Trust's Plas Newydd, on the banks of the Menai Strait, is an elegant eighteenth century country house designed by James Wyatt, with Whistler's largest wall painting and a military museum devoted to the battle of Waterloo.

Penrhyn Castle is another National Trust property, a neo-Norman fantasy designed by Thomas Hopper near Bangor. With an important collection of old masters, it was financed by the workers operating in slave conditions in slate mines, so has echoes of the massive inequalities of recent centuries.

William Burges rebuilt medieval fantasy castles at Cardiff and Castell Coch. Cardiff's City Hall, the jewel in the crown of one of the finest civic centres in the world, was built in only five years and opened in 1906. The Hall cost £129,708 and the adjoining Law Courts £96,583, massive costs at the time. With the adjoining National Museum, Temple of Peace, Welsh Office and University buildings, these glittering white Portland stone edifices represent a time when Britannia really did rule the waves. Spread across 60 acres, next to the splendid castle, Bute Park, near the River Taff, and a couple of minutes from one of the best shopping centres in Europe, other European (perhaps world) capitals find it difficult to rival this merging of history, nature, civic centre and city centre.

One can follow the adjoining park alongside the River Taff, walking through the country for a couple of miles to Llandaff Cathedral and its ruined Bishop's Palace (sacked by Glyndŵr). Huge 12 ton and 15 ton blocks of Portland stone were carried by teams of six shire horses to the Town Hall site, where eight 5-ton cranes lifted and placed them. The cranes, operated by a local firm, Turner and Sons, made the Civic Centre the first all-electric building site in the world. There were double celebrations for the 1906 opening ceremony as Cardiff had been designated a City in 1905. Cardiff is also the only capital city with its rugby stadium in the heart of the city, specifically rebuilt for the 1999 Rugby World Cup.

At the other end of the scale, a typical Welsh house was the *ty-hir*, 'long-house', thousands of which can still be seen, converted into family homes. On either side of a central corridor was a room, one for humans and one for animals. The heat from the animals served as a rudimentary central heating system, not quite as elegant a solution as the Roman villa but quite effective. Similar houses can be seen in Brittany.

A notable example of community co-operation was the *ty unnos*, 'one-night house' where twenty to forty men built a house overnight, usually on moorland, in the erroneous belief that such a building became the legal property of the builder if smoke issued from the chimney the following morning. This turf dwelling would then be superseded by a second, more permanent house by the autumn, and be converted into a cowshed. The unenclosed lands upon which these squatters' cottages were built were later enclosed by acts of Parliament in the late 18th century. Squatters who had occupied their houses for at least 20 years before the acts were allowed to keep them. Fields in the Llŷn Peninsula show the effects of this haphazard settlement, compared to the neatly geometric holdings where land was legally parcelled out.

Because of the religious revivalism, seven thousand chapels were built in Wales of which five thousand are left, but only four hundred listed. Merioneth (Meirionydd) had a chapel for every 159 people, and they dominated Welsh culture and education. Nowhere in Europe, probably in the world, had so many places of worship per person as Wales at the end of the 19th century. The rights to the great hymn 'Guide Me O Thy Great Jehovah' were sold to build a chapel in Cwm Rhondda (the Rhondda Valley) after which the tune was named. The Church is planning to dispose of 2,000 chapels in Wales *'with a view to establishing church unity in the next millennium'*.

The smallest house in Britain is a fisherman's cottage on the quay in Conwy with just two small rooms and a staircase. It is only 10 foot 2 inches high (3.09m), 6 foot wide (1.82m) and 8 foot 6 inches (2.58m) in depth.

The longest breakwater in Britain is at Holyhead. Built in 1873, it is almost 1.5 miles long (2.4 km). Wales has the most powerful lighthouse in Britain, at Strumble Head off Fishguard, with a visible range of 25 miles (39km).

Britain's longest railway tunnel connects Wales with England under the River Severn, and is 4 miles long (7km). Built over a period of 13 years, and completed in 1886, it used over 76 million bricks.

ARCHITECTURE – BRIDGES
Being a nation of hills and rivers, Wales is obviously notable for its number of bridges. The arched bridge in Pontypridd, built in 1775, was once the largest single-span bridge in the world, a single high arch of 160 feet, successfully erected after three collapsed attempts by its self-taught stonemason, the Methodist Reverend William Edwards. His three sons also became bridge-builders.

Thomas Telford's Menai Suspension Bridge, completed in 1825, was the world's first iron suspension bridge, carrying the London to Holyhead (A5) road across the Menai Straits. A masterpiece of nineteenth century engineering, it is 1265 feet long (386m) with a central span of 579 feet (176m), the longest single span of its time. It had to be 100 feet above the Strait to allow sailing ships to pass. All the wrought iron work was heated and soaked in linseed oil before being put in place, not quite as the White Knight told Alice:

'I heard him then, for I had just
Completed my design
To keep the Menai Bridge from rust
By boiling it in wine.'

The great Robert Stephenson's Britannia rail bridge, finished in 1850, also stands near the Menai Bridge.

The second Severn Bridge, completed in 1996, is the UK's longest-span cable-stayed bridge, with a main span of almost 1500 feet (456m). The overall length of the structure, around 17000 feet (5168m) makes it the longest bridge in Britain.

The tallest multispan bridge in Britain was the Crumlin Viaduct at 200 feet (61m), which was demolished in 1966. The tallest bridge is now the Mewbridge Bypass in Clwyd at 188 feet (57.3m).

The longest bridged aqueduct in Britain is the fantastic Pont Cystyllte, built to carry the Shropshire Union Canal over the River Dee. Designed by Thomas Telford, it was opened in 1805 and is still in use today. One thousand and six feet long (307m), it has nineteen arches up to one hundred and twenty-one feet (39m) higher than low water on the River Dee below it. Sir Walter Scott called this Pontcystyllte Aqueduct *'the greatest work of art the world has ever seen.'* Telford also built the beautiful Llangollen Canal aqueduct in 1801, in the Ceiriog Valley, seventy feet above the river.

Newport's Transporter Bridge is one of the three left in existence (Middlesborough and Australia have others). Built between 1902 and 1906 by a

Frenchman, Ferdinand Arnodin, it can carry cars across the river Usk on a cradle platform hung from cables. It was built to accommodate tall ships and some of the highest tides in the world. 250 feet high, four iron pillars support an iron grill, under which runs an electrically-powered platform holding the cars.

Barmouth Bridge is built on 113 wooded trestles to take the Cambrian coast railway across the wonderful Mawddach estuary. Opened in 1866, there is also a walkway which serves as a promenade to admire the river-mouth and mountains.

One of Wales' most beautiful villages is the thatched Merthyr Mawr, near Bridgend. The 'Dipping Bridge' over the Ogmore River has been used for centuries. A flock of sheep is driven onto the bridge, and improvised gates erected at both ends. Sheep are then pushed through special holes in the parapet to drop six feet into the cold waters below. They swim to the bank, where watchful sheepdogs guide them back into a flock.

ARGENTINA

In South America the existence of the Welsh-speaking colony, in Patagonia, stopped Chile claiming vast expanses of land from Argentina in 1865. One hundred and fifty-three Welsh emi-grants had boarded the sailing ship Mimosa and landed at Port Madryn there in the same year, trekking forty miles to found a settlement near the Chubut River. In 1885, some families crossed four hundred miles of desert to establish another settlement in Cwm Hyfryd at the foot of the Andes. *Y Wladfa* ('The Colony'), founded by the reformist preacher Michael D. Jones, was to be a radical colony where Non-conformism and the Welsh language were to dominate. Jones was deeply concerned about the Anglicisation of Wales – to preserve the heritage his people would have to move. He is regarded as the founder of the modern Welsh nationalist movement. The Argen-tine government was anxious to control this vast unpopulated territory, in which it was still in dispute with Chile, so granted one-hundred square miles for the establishment of a Welsh state, protected by the military.

For ten years after 1865, this Welsh state was completely self-governing, with its own constitution written in Welsh. The immigrants owned their own land and farmed their own farms – there was to be no capitalist state with its hated landlord system. Fe-males were given the vote – the first democracy in the world to show egali-tarianism, and this fifty years before British suffragettes started to try to change the British system. Boys and girls aged eighteen could vote, over a century before they could in Britain. Voting was by secret ballot and all were eligible – two more democratic innovations. The language of Parlia-ment and the law was Welsh, and only Welsh school books were used.

Back home in Wales, the use of Welsh was forbidden in schools. 'Y Wladfa' was 'the first example of a practical democracy in South America', and the first example of a practical, egalitarian, non-discriminatory democ-racy in the world.

There were massive problems in the settlement at first, until the native Teheulche Indians and their chief taught the Welsh to catch guanaco and rhea from the prairies. Also the Indians would exchange meat for bread, going from house to house saying *'poco bara'* – Spanish for 'a little' and Welsh for 'bread'. This was a 'green colony' whereby both sides gained. The Welsh taught them to break in horses, and they showed the Welsh how to use bolas to catch animals. By controlling the waters in the Camwy Valley, the settlers began to prosper. Unlike unsuccessful Spanish settlers before them, they had very few problems with the native Indians, who still empathise with the Welsh. When two were killed in the Chubut River uplands in 1883, Lewis Jones, the leader of the colony, refused to believe it. He told the messenger *'But John, the Indians are our friends. They'd never kill a Welshman.'* It transpired that an Argentine patrol had trespassed on Indian land, and the Welsh were tragically mistaken for the Indians' Argentine enemies. The bodies had their sexual organs stuffed into their mouths.

Butch Cassidy and the Sundance Kid were alleged to have formed a gang comprised of Welshmen in Patagonia , and Cassidy's old farm is still ranched. Their best friend was a Welshman called Daniel Gibbons, who helped them purchase horses. A son of Michael D. Jones, a grocer called Llwyd ap Iwan, was supposed to have been killed by the gang in 1909 in Arroyo Pescado in Northern Patagonia. It appears that a couple of renegade drifters from the USA carried out this act. It was this pair, named William Wilson and Robert Evans, who were also killed in the shoot-out with the Argentine military at Rio Pico and not the famous American outlaws. The Bolivian deaths were the fiction of a screen-writer. Butch, Sundance and Etta appear to have spent their time peaceably – they had no

need of money at first – and were assisted by the Welsh to settle in.

Butch Cassidy bought 12,000 acres near Cholila in 1901, and the following year Sundance and his 'wife', Etta Place arrived. However, in 1907 one of their gauchos saw Butch's picture in a Buenos Aires paper, although he could not read, and told everyone around him that this was his 'boss'. A couple of days later, Sheriff Perry (of Pinkerton's Detective Agency) heard the story and made his way down to Patagonia from the capital. The gaucho showed the outlaws the picture in the newspaper but the two escaped with Etta Place over the Andes into Chile just two days before Pinkerton's detectives arrived on the scene. According to his sister, Butch died in the 1930s in Washington State and Etta Place, it is believed, died in Denver some time after 1924.

The colony grew to three thousand people by the time Welsh immigration halted in 1912. Interestingly, the Welsh code of law established by the settlers was the first legal structure in Argentina and its *'influence in modern-day Argentinian law can still be seen'*. Three hundred and fifty people are currently learning Welsh in Patagonia, helping the language to survive there, and plans are underway with teacher exchanges to double this figure. However, only five thousand still speak the language regularly, most of them in their later years. The success of the colony attracted immigrants from Spain and Italy in the first decades of the twentieth century and the Welsh influence is declining steadily.

The Eisteddfod Fawr is still held in Chubut financially supported by the Argentinian government. It gives around a quarter of a million pounds a year to

support eisteddfodau in Gaiman, Tre-
felin and Trelew in recognition of the
service performed by the early settlers.
Gaiman is the 'most' Welsh town in
Patagonia, with signs on the road approaching *'Visit Tŷ Llwyd, the Welsh Tea
House'*, *'Stop at Tŷ Gwyn'* and *'Come to
Tŷ Te Caerdydd'*. In Tŷ Te Caerdydd, a
costumed group from the local school
sometimes dances and the traditional
Welsh tea is served by Welsh-speaking,
Welsh-costumed staff. Bruce Chatwin's
curious travelogue, *'In Patagonia'*, gives
a flavour of the place with characters
like Alun Powell, Caradog Williams,
Hubert Lloyd-Jones, Mrs Cledwyn
Hughes and Gwynneth Morgan.

In the 1920s, President Fontana was
the first President of Argentina to visit
the region. On horseback – there were
no roads or trains – the official party
could not cross the river into Trelew.
A tall, strong, red-haired youngster
called Gough offered to help and lifted
him up and carried him across the
raging river, to the town reception. A
couple of years later the boy was in the
ranks of conscripts in the main square
in Buenos Aires waiting for the president to address all those required to
carry out their National Service in the
military. The president stepped out onto
the square, surrounded by his generals
and bodyguard, when a Welsh voice
rang out loud and clear *'Hey, I know
you!'* Gough broke ranks and started
striding towards the president waving
his arms. A hundred guns trained on
him before President Fontana broke
into a smile and shouted to his guard
that this big red-haired youth was indeed not dangerous and known to him.

I am indebted to a friend, Rene
Griffiths, for the above story. He has a
ranch near Butch Cassidy's old farm in
Cholila and is fairly certain that the

gang carried out a maximum of two
robberies in South America, simply
because of the distances involved (at
Rio Gallegos, and Villa Mercedes de
San Luis in 1905). Butch and Sundance,
under their aliases were accepted into
the community and Welshmen helped
them get started in horse-breeding.

By an ironic twist of history, the
Argentinian pilot who fired the Exocet
missile, that killed twenty three Welsh
Guards and maimed Simon Weston in
The Falklands War, was a Welsh Pata-
gonian.

ART

The most famous 'Welsh' picture is
probably that by the Edwardian artist
Sydney Curnow Vosper, of the congre-
gation of Llanbedr's Salem Chapel.
The stove-pipe hatted old lady who
dominates the picture has a Paisley
shawl, allegedly with the face of the
Devil in it. Its massive popularity shows
the essential duality of Welshness – a
God-fearing up-front facade with an
acknowledged pagan past.

Wales has inspired many notable
English painters like J. M. W. Turner
and David Cox. There are good repre-
sentations of Welsh painters in the
National Museum at Cardiff and Swansea's Glynn Vivian Gallery.

Mold-born **Richard Wilson**, the 18th
century landscape artist, was influenced by Claude and Poussin and
studied in Italy and is best known for
his scenes of Snowdon and Cader Idris.
Wilson co-founded The Royal Academy
in 1768, and was championed by Ruskin,
but died in poverty in 1782, aged
around 69. The largest collection of his
pictures is in Cardiff but he is represented in art galleries and museums

from Adelaide to Berlin, and from Harvard to Hanover. As John Constable said, *'He was one of those appointed to show the world what exists in nature but which was not known till this time,'* and Wilson is considered to be the *'father'* of English landscape painting.

James Dickson Innes (1887-1914) was a superb landscape artist, much influenced by Richard Wilson and then Augustus John. He seemed to be developing towards the Fauve (Matisse, Vlaminck, Derain, Rouault) movement before his tragic early death. With Augustus John he rented a cottage in Snowdonia and they contributed to the post-Impressionist movement.

Augustus John (1878-1961), and his sister **Gwen John** (1876-1939), from Pembrokeshire, have many paintings in Welsh art galleries. Augustus John shocked even the Bohemian art world with his behaviour and promiscuity. A student at the Slade in the 1890s, he was invited to paint the Queen (now the Queen Mother) in 1937. He suggested that he stayed at a pub near Windsor Castle, where she would visit secretly for sittings, an offer she refused. In the 1940s he was offered a knighthood. His wife had died and he was told that he must marry his long-time mistress Dorelia. He had lived and procreated with her for 40 years, so he proposed and she demurred, thus depriving him of his recognition. His portraits and paintings can be found in Stockholm, Washington, Sydney, Detroit and Dublin. For 30 years he had been *the* portrait painter of British society, hailed as *'the last of the Old Masters'*, but was a wild child until the end. Dylan Thomas' wife, Caitlin, was one of the many artist's models who found herself compromised in a relationship with him. His sister Gwen-

doline's intensely expressive paintings can also be found in major galleries.

Sir Frank Brangwyn (1867-1956) painted huge murals for The Royal Exchange, Lloyds, the New York Rockefeller Centre etc. His murals for The House of Lords are now in Swansea Guildhall and there are museums dedicated to his life and work in Orange (France) and Bruges, his birthplace.

Goscombe John RA (1860-1952) was one of the most prominent Welsh sculptors and is well-represented in Welsh galleries. **Ivor Roberts-Jones** died in 1996, aged 83. In 1973 he *'had created one of the grandest works of public sculpture in Britain. It was also probably the last commemoration of its kind'*. The Times obituary of December 14th was referring to his brooding, indomitable, intense statue of Winston Churchill, commissioned to stand outside the Houses of Parliament. One of his best works is *'Two Kings'* at Harlech Castle and he was publicly commissioned for statues of Viscount Slim, Viscount Alanbrooke and Augustus John.

David Jones's (1895-1974) (see Literature) delicate water colour washes and elegant calligraphy took him away from the mainstream of British art and a reassessment of this most multi-talented man is overdue. Kathleen Raine describes the *'Turneresque evanescence'* of his *'Manawyddan's Glass Door'* in her wonderful appreciation of his writings, poetry and art in *'David Jones and the Actually Loved and Known'*. His luminous, visionary watercolours, redolent of Arthurian mysticism and the legends of The Mabinogion, can be seen in the Tate Gallery and many other museums.

Merlyn Evans (1910-1973) was a surrealist painter who won the Gold Medal for Fine Art at the 1966 National

Eisteddfod. **Will Roberts** was born in the same year and uses slabs of paint to evoke the hardship of crouching miners. A recent show at Cardiff's Albany Gallery celebrated Roberts' seventy years of dedicated work.

Ceri Richards (1903-1971) celebrated life in his abstract paintings, especially in his Dylan Thomas Suite of prints, with bold colours and a reaffirmation of the springs of life. His semi-surrealist, Celtic-inspired works are timeless and have many similarities to Graham Sutherland's Welsh-inspired works.

Like Turner, Graham Sutherland was inspired by Wales, in particular Pembrokeshire. He first visited in 1934 and the gnarled tree roots around Picton Beach, Porth Clais, the Daugleddau and Sandy Haven combined with the unique quality of light, inspired him. From 1967 he returned every year from his home in Menton, France, to paint. His friend John Ormond made a television documentary about him and Picton Castle near Haverfordwest holds a collection of his paintings.

George Chapman, born 1908, was equally moved by Wales, but in a diametrically different way, with his visit to Rhondda in 1953. His Rhondda Suite and all his later work reflect the importance of the industrialised valleys to his vision (see *'George Chapman at the Goldmark Gallery'*, published by Mike Goldmark, March 1992).

From the Llŷn Peninsula, **Kyffin Williams** RA uses wedges of oil paint to give the strength of the rocky landscapes and sheep farmers of Snowdonia. His work, like Josef Herman's, is instantly recognisable. He seeks to find *'the mood that touches the seam of melancholy that is within most Welshmen, a melancholy that derives from the dark hills, the heavy clouds and the enveloping sea mists.'* Aged eighty in 1998, Kyffin is still actively painting. His two-volume autobiography and his books *'Portraits'* and *'The Land and the Sea'* reveal a great painter, who states, *'I was lucky that I was born into a landscape so beautiful I had no need to go elsewhere. There was never any question of what I should paint.'*

Josef Herman, a Polish refugee from the dark years of 1938 influenced a generation of Welsh painters from his then base at Ystradgynlais. *'Jo Fach'*, now based in London, specialised in pictures of people, especially miners, struggling in gloomy surroundings. Using sombre colours he often depicted miners bent double but always portrayed the dignity of the working man. Awarded an OBE by Thatcher in 1984, he is still active, aged 85.

Andrew Vacari of Port Talbot was educated at Neath Grammar School, and is now a millionaire tax exile in Monaco. He studied art with Lucien Freud and Francis Bacon and is the only artist to have painted the whole royal family of Saudi Arabia. He was also invited by General Norman Schwarzkopf to paint scenes from the 1991 Gulf War. He calls himself *'a Celt and a Latin with an Anglo-Saxon education – a true European'*. The Welsh Rugby Union has commissioned him to be the official artist for the 1999 Rugby World Cup.

ARTHUR

Welsh military history falls into distinct phases.

1. The arrival of the new wave of Celts around 600BC.

2. The Roman Occupation from 78AD to around 390AD.

3. The Dark Ages until 600AD which saw the rise of Christianity (The Age of the Saints in Wales, and The Dark Ages in England). This was the time of the Celts fighting against the Picts and Irish invaders and the time of the fabled Arthur.

4. The Welsh Kingdoms fighting and uniting against the Vikings, Irish and Anglo-Saxons under Rhodri Mawr, Hywel Dda, and Gruffydd ap Llywelyn until 1066.

5. The fight against the Normans by the Welsh Princes including Owain Gwynedd and the two Llywelyns until the 1282 Statute of Rhuddlan.

6. Plantagenet oppression, with the Glyndŵr Rebellion, until 1485.

7. The taking of the English throne by the Welsh Tudor (Tudur, Tewdwr) dynasty at the Battle of Bosworth Field in 1485.

8. The English Civil War period.

The third phase, the time of Arthur is the most debated area of British history. This Arthur was a Celtic warlord around whom the mythology of Guinevere, Merlin, Lancelot, The Holy Grail and the Round Table revolve. He fought back the Saxon threat from the east and the Pictish threat from the north and west. It appears, after studying around twenty books on the legends surrounding Arthur, that he was Prince Athrwys, or Arthmael, the Bear Prince (Athruis ap Meurig ap Tewdrig), His son Morgan became King of Glamorgan.

'Journey to Avalon – the Final Discovery of King Arthur' (by C. Barber and D. Pykitt) makes a persuasive claim that Arthur's court of Gelli-weg was Llanmelin Hillfort, the ancient capital of the Silures, that overlooks Caerwent Roman town. In the Welsh Triads, Gelliwig in Cernyw was one of Arthur's three principal courts. Cernyw was once part of the coastal area of South-East Wales. Cornwall was not known as Cernyw until the 10th century, hundreds of years post-dating the Triads. At Coed Kernew, just west of Newport, the church was founded in the sixth century by Glywys Cernyw, a son of Gwynlliw Filwr (the Warrior).

Gelliwig means small grove and Llanmelin's previous name was Llan y Gelli (church of the grove). Llanmelin is situated in Gwent-is-Coed, Gwent below the Wood and now called Wentwood), where Arthur's uncle and chief elder Caradoc Freichfras (Sir Craddock) ruled when Arthur was campaigning. Barber and Pykitt believe that Caer Melin, as Llanmelin was known to the Romans, and where Scapula was defeated by the Silures in 53AD, was the site of the fabled Camelot.

Nennius, from South-East Wales, wrote around the end of the eighth century about Arthur and his famous twelve battles. He is also referred to in The Gododdin, written around the end of the sixth century, early Welsh poetry, some of the Lives of the Saints, and in the sixth-century Welsh Triads of the Islands of Britain.

Many of the characters in Arthurian legend previously appear in Welsh legend and literature. Merlin was identified with Myrddin in Welsh history, both St Illtud and Gwalchaved with Sir Galahad, both Gwalchmai and St Govan with Sir Gawain, Cei with Sir Kay, and Peredur and Bedwyr in 'The Mabinogion' with Sir Percival and Sir Bedivere. Peredur, who glimpses the Holy Lance and Grail in 'Peredur, Son of Erawc', has an uncle Bran the Blessed, who is the model for 'The Fisher King'. Eigyr passed into legend as Igraine, the mother of Arthur, and both Gwenhwyfar and Gwendoloena the flower maiden as

Guinevere. The Welsh prince Medraut ap Cawrdaf became Mordred, and the Druidic goddess Morgen has been associated with Morgen le Fay. Morgen was the patroness of priestesses, who lived on Avalon, Bardsey Island, with nine sisters. Peredur, or Pryderi, brought about the devastation of South Wales by sitting on a Perilous Mound, but as Percival, in *'Didot Perceval'* causes enchantments to fall on Britain by sitting on the Seat Perilous at King Arthur's Court.

Sir Lancelot may be based on Maelgwn Gwynedd or Llwch Llawinawg, Lord of the Lakes, and Sir Tristram with Drustanus the son of Marcus Conomorus, a prince of Glamorgan. Sir Howel is identified with Howel (Riwal) Mawr of Ergyng, who fought Lancelot, became Dux Britannorum after Arthur's death and was buried at Llanilltud Fawr. The fabulous Castell Dinas Bran, perched high on the rocks overlooking Llangollen, is identified with Grail Castle. Both Bran (from the Mabinogion) and the Fisher King had wounds which would not heal and King Bran is associated with the castle. Bran also had a magical 'cauldron of plenty' (see Thirteen Treasures), which is identified with the Holy Grail (see Holy Grail). Another of the Thirteen Treasures seems to be linked with Excalibur.

Lloegr was the Welsh name for England, and Logres is the name of England in Arthurian legend. Pendragon, the title first taken by Arthur's father Uther and then by Arthur, is a combination of the Old Welsh *dragwn*, dragon/leader, and the Brythonic *pen*, or head.

At the top of Snowdon, there was a tumulus commemorating one of Arthur's victims. Arthur sailed across Snowdonia's Llyn Llydaw on his way to Avalon, after fighting Mordred at Bwlch y Saethau ('Pass of the Arrows'). Bedevere threw Excalibur into Llyn Llydau, which seems to be a continuation of the Celtic throwing away of a dead warlord's weapons into water, which was sacred to them. Avalon seems to be Afallach, the sacred and holy isle of Bardsey off the Llŷn Peninsula. Barber and Pykitt believe that Arthur recovered from his wounds at the monastery of Bardsey, and went to Brittany, where he was known as St Armel.

Barber and Pykit also state that Arthur was born in 482 at Boverton (Trebeferad), a Roman camp site in the Vale of Glamorgan, fought his final British battle at 'Cadlan' on the Llŷn Peninsula where Mordred (Medraut) had territories, recovered from his wounds at Bardsey Island, and died in 562 at St Armel des Boschaux in Brittany.

A persuasive case for the final Battle of Camlan being at Maes-y-Camlan (Camlan Field) just south of Dinas Mawddwy has been made in a little booklet by Laurence Main. This local tradition was recorded in Welsh by a local bard in 1893. In the area are three Camlans: Bron-Camlan, Camlan-uchaf and Camlan Isaf. Across the valley from Maes Camlan are Bryn Cleifion and Dol-y-Cleifion (Hill of the Wounded and Meadow of the Wounded). The nearby ridge overlooking the Dyfi river is Cefn-Byriaeth (Mourning Ridge) where graves were discovered. Five miles east is the site where Mordred's Saxon allies are said to have camped the previous night and the stream there is still called Nant-y-Saeson (Saxon Stream). The date was 537 in the Welsh Annals, but the Celtic Church may have dated this from the crucifixion of Christ, making it 574. This Arthur ap Meurig ap Tewdrig was married to

Gwenhwyfar and his son Gwydre was killed by the Twrch Trwyth (in the Tale of Culhwch and Olwen in 'The Mabinogion') at Cwm Cerwyn, near Nevern. Nearby are the Stones of the Sons of Arthur (Cerrig Meibion Arthur). Arthur had returned from Brittany to defeat Mordred. Again tradition states that he survived the battle, but was grievously wounded while resting after he had won (by Eda Elyn Mawr, according to Harleian mss 4181 entry 42). Arthur was soon succeeded as Pendragon by Maelgwn Gwynedd, sometimes identified with Lancelot.

At Ogmore Castle was found a sixth century memorial stone recording a land grant by Arthur. It is now in the National Museum, and the Latin inscription reads *'Be it known to all that Arthmail has given this field to God to Glywys and to Netart and to Bishop Fili'*. In St Roque chapel ruins at nearby Merthyr Mawr, another stone reads *'Conbelan placed this cross for his (own) soul (and for) the soul of St Glywys, of Nertain, and of his brother and father prepared by me, Sciloc'*. And in the holy church of St Illtud at Llanilltud Fawr, just a few miles away, the famous Pillar of Abbot Samson reads:

'In the name of the MOST HIGH GOD
was begun the cross of the Saviour
which Samson the Abbot prepared for
  his soul
And for the soul of king Iuthahel
And for Artmal the dead'.

A recent book by Adrian Gilbert, Alan Wilson and Baram Blackett ('The Holy Kingdom', Bantam Press, 1998) agrees with much of the Barber and Pykit research but strangely makes no reference to their work. The author is researching the area from St Donat's

Castle (the seat of Caractacus) through Llanilltud Fawr (the centre of monastic learning) and Boverton (the possible birthplace of Arthur) to Caerleon and Llanmelin Hill Fort. This strip of the Vale of Glamorgan, the Roman forts of Cardiff and Caerleon and the inland Church of St Peter super Montem seem to hold the key to all the Arthurian legends. 'The Holy Kingdom' makes the case for 'Caer Melyn' just north of Cardiff being Camelot. The sulphur springs nearby colour the water yellow, so Caer Melyn means Yellow Fortress. As 'mellitus' means honeycoloured in Latin, perhaps it was corrupted to Caer Mellitus and hence to Camelot. The author's preference is for Arthur to have been based at Dinas Powys, but far more research will be undertaken on this topic. This same book seems to drift off into the hiding of the 'True Cross' in Wales but also reveals the finding in Glamorgan of a stone inscribed 'Rex Artorius Fili Mauricivs', 'King Arthur son of Maurice' (Meurig). If this stone is not a forgery then it is essential that public and university resources are directed towards enlightening these 'Dark Ages' (see the Rewriting of History).

Arthur's links with the West Country are extremely tenuous and based upon romances from the Middle Ages. The placing of Arthur, Merlin and the knights of the Round Table firmly in Wales can be a tremendous boost to the tourist industry. All it needs is someone in power with the vision and courage to challenge and change things. Unfortunately this is not the type of person who clambers to the top in politics or tourist boards. English Heritage has recently been trumpeting the find of a piece of slate from Tintagel in Cornwall as proof of Arthur in the sixth century being an English reality. Cornwall was Welsh at this time. The rough inscription *'Pater Coliavificit Artnogov'* means 'Artnogov, father of a descendant of Coll, has had (this building) constructed'. According to English Heritage it is *'the first evidence of a link between the Arthurian legend and historical fact'* (*Daily Telegraph*, August 7, 1990). Yet again publicity tries to overwhelm historical truth. Arthmael ap Meurig ap Tewdrig is known and recorded in history but does not 'fit' with the English tourist industry and its promotional power.

ASSASSINATION

Owain ap Thomas ap Rhodri was known in Wales as Owain Lawgoch (Llaw Goch means Red Hand) and on the continent as Yvain de Galles. He was nick-named 'red hand' because of his presence on battlefields across Europe. Owain was the grandson of Llywelyn II's brother, and the sole heir of the Princes of Gwynedd. Born about 1330 on his father's estate at Tatsfield in Surrey, in 1350 he bound himself to the service of the King of France and became his protégé. He constantly proclaimed himself the true heir of Aberffraw, the court on Anglesey of the Princes of Gwynedd, and only de Guesclin features more highly in French literature as an enemy of the English at this time. Described by Edward Owen as *'possibly the greatest military genius that Wales has produced'*, he crossed to England in 1365 to claim his inheritance but was forced to return to France.

Many Welshmen followed him, including Ieuan Wyn, who took over Owain's company of soldiers after his death. Owain still features in the folk literature of Britanny, France, Switzerland, Lombardy and the Channel Islands. His father having been executed by the King of England, 'Owen of Wales' had been brought up at the court of King Philip VI of France and was one of the most noted warriors of the fourteenth century. Described as *'high-spirited, haughty, bold and bellicose'* (Barbara Tuchman, *'A Distant Mirror'*), he had fought heroically against the English at Poitiers in 1356, somehow surviving against all the odds. Owain campaigned in the Lombard Wars of the 1360s, for and against the Dukes of Bar in Lorraine and with Bertrand du Guesclin in the campaigns of the 1370s. In 1366, he led the Compagnons de Galles (Company of Welshmen) to fight Pedro the Cruel in Spain.

An Anglesey man, Gruffydd Sais, was executed and his lands confiscated by the crown in 1369 for contacting *'Owain Lawgoch, enemy and traitor'* and in the same year Charles V gave Owain a fleet to sail to Wales from Harfleur. It was, sadly, repulsed by storms. The French King Charles now gave Owain 300,000 francs, another fleet and 4,000 men to win back his land. Owain proclaimed that he owned Wales *'through the power of my succession, through my lineage, and through my rights as the descendant of my forefathers, the kings of that country'*.

Taking Guernsey from the English, Owain captured the legendary Captal de Buch, the Black Prince's comrade, hero of Poitiers and one of England's greatest soldiers. Owain had taken a Franco-Castilian landing party to The Channel Islands and overpowered him at night. Such was the Captal's reputation that King Charles V kept him in prison in the Temple in Paris without the privilege of ransom. Both King Edward of England and delegations of French nobles repeatedly asked Charles to ransom him if he promised not to take up arms against France, but the King refused and the noble Captal sank into depression He refused food and drink and died in 1376.

Owain prepared to invade Wales after his seizure of Guernsey, but a message came from the French king to help the Spanish attack the English-occupied La Rochelle in 1372. Owain responded and fought again against the English, who had killed both his uncles. Owain never had another chance to return to Wales. In 1375, he took part in the successful siege of Saveur-le-Comte in Normandy, where for the first time cannon had been used successfully to break the English defences. He then took a contract from the great Baron de Coucy to lead four hundred men at a fee of four hundred francs per month, with one hundred francs per month going to his assistant, Owain ap Rhys. Any town or fortress taken was to be yielded to De Coucy.

The capture of Duke Leopold of Austria was to be worth 10,000 francs to Owain, who attracted 100 Teutonic knights from Prussia to his banner. With The Treaty of Bruges, English knights also came to offer their services under the leadership of Owain who was the King of England's son-in-law. Probably around 10,000 soldiers eventually formed an army for De Coucy and Owain. The knights wore pointed helmets and cowl-like hoods on heavy cloaks and their hoods called 'gugler', from the Swiss-German for cowl or point, gave their names to the 'The Gugler War'.

The companies making up the army plundered Alsace and took ransom of 3000 florins not to attack Strasbourg as Leopold retreated, ordering the destruction of all resources in his wake. He withdrew across the Rhine, relying on the Swiss to stave off the attack, although the Swiss hated the Hapsburgs almost as much as they hated the Guglers. The invaders were allowed entrance to Basel, but their forces became increasingly scattered as they sought loot in the wake of Leopold's depredations. Near Lucerne, a company of Guglers was surrounded by the Swiss and routed. On Christmas night a company of Bretons was ambushed by citizens of Berne, city of the emblem of the bear. On the next night the Swiss attacked the Abbey of Fraubrunnen, where Owain was quartered, setting fire to the Abbey and slaughtering the sleeping 'English'. Owain swung his sword 'with savage rage' but was forced to flee, leaving 800 Guglers dead at the Abbey.

Ballads tell of how the Bernese fought '40,000 lances with their pointed hats', how 'Duke Yfo (Owain) of Wales came with his golden helm' and how when Duke Yfo came to Fraubrunnen, "The Bear roared 'You shall not escape me! I will slay, stab and burn you!' In England and France the widows all cried 'Alas and woe!' Against Berne no-one shall march evermore!"

The following details are fully recounted in 'Froissart's Chronicles'. In 1378, Owain was conducting the siege of Mortagne in the Gironde on the Atlantic coast. As usual, early in the morning, he sat on a tree stump, having his hair combed by a new squire while he surveyed the scene of siege. His new Scots manservant, James Lambe, had been taken into service as he had brought news of 'how all the country of Wales would gladly have him to *be their lord'*. But with no-one around, Lambe stabbed Owain in the back, and escaped to Mortagne – the English king had paid £20 for the assassination of the person with the greatest claim to the Principality of Wales, the last of the line of Rhodri Fawr. Norman and Angevin policy had always been to kill Welsh male heirs and put females of the lineage into remote English monasteries, as we can see in the case of Llywelyn the Last (Llywelyn Olaf).

Owain Lawgoch was only second in valour to Bertrand du Guesclin in Europe through these years, a mercenary operating away from home compared to a national hero. His is an amazing story, yet he is unknown to ninety-nine per cent of Welshmen, only mentioned as an aside in specialist text-books. His importance to King Edward III of England is shown in a payment of 100 francs and in the Issue Roll of the Exchequer dated December 4, 1378: *'To John Lamb, an esquire from Scotland, because he lately killed Owynn de Gales, a rebel and enemy of the King in France . . . By writ of privy seal, &c., £20.'*

However, with Owain Lawgoch's death, the prior claim to the heritage of Llywelyn the Great and Llewelyn the Last passed on eventually to another Owain, Glyndŵr, another *'Mab Darogan'* ('Son of Prophecy') of the Welsh bards. When Owain Glyndŵr, in 1404, requested French help against England he reinforced his case by referring to Owain Lawgoch's great service to the French crown.

ATLANTIS

For every century in the last few thousand years, the sea has risen a quarter of a metre. Thus since the time of Christ, the sea around Britain has risen five metres, and from the time of Arthur around four metres.

Stories of drowned lands are prominent in old Welsh literature, perhaps based on folk memories of when Wales was only separated from Ireland by a narrow, shallow strip of water around 10,000 years ago. The Mabinogion story of Bran the Blessed describes him, a giant of a man, helping his soldiers to cross the sea to fight in Ireland. As early as the 17th century, expeditions were being made to see the sunken ruins of Llys Helig, an estate two miles off the mouth of the river Conwy. Traditionally this palace ('*llys*') had been flooded in the Dark Ages. Llys Helig, the lost realm of Helig ap Glannowg, joins Cantre'r Gwaelod and Caer Arianrhod to form a triad of lost kingdoms off the Welsh coast. In 1816 Edward Pugh identified the site and its causeway and in 1864 the site of the palace ruins was measured at five and a half acres. A nearby hill at Trwyn yr Wylfa, at Penmaenbach, is said to be where Helig's subjects fled from the sixth century inundation.

In this century straight lines of boulders have been found, some at right angles to each other, but modern scientific thought is that these are 'boulder trains' left behind by the retreating ice at the end of the Ice Age. The fabled Caer Ariánhod, off the southern entrance to the Menai Strait, also seems like a sunken castle. This is three quarters of a mile offshore from Dinas Dinlle on the Llŷn Peninsula. Nearby the great stone 'Maen Dylan' commemorates Arianrhod's lost son, Dylan eil Don (see Castles – Conwy).

Welsh folklore mentions a vast land from Bardsey Island in the North to the mouth of the River Teifi in the

South, extending over Cardigan Bay, around eight hundred square miles with sixteen cities, ruled by the Lord Garanhir of Gwyddno. This lowland was controlled by sluice-gates and embankments. However, Seithennin the gate-keeper drank too much at a banquet, forgot to close the sluices and the sea rushed in. An ancient Welsh triad tells of the flooding of Cantre'r Gwaelod (The Hundred Homesteads of the Bottom) – *'by this calamity sixteen fortified cities, the largest and finest that were in Wales, excepting only Caerleon upon Usk, were entirely destroyed, and Cardigan Bay occupies the spot where the fertile plains of the cantref had been the habitation and support of a flourishing population.'*

However, a new translation of 'The Black Book of Carmarthen' by Rachel Bromwich reads:

'Stand forth, Seithenhin,
and look upon the fury of the sea;
it has covered Maes Gwyddneu.
Accursed be the maiden
who released it after the feast;
the fountain cup-bearer of the barren
sea'.

The maiden has parallels in Breton folk-lore as the scourge of God, punishing the land because of the wickedness of its people. There are submerged petrified forests off Borth on the Cardigan coast and auroch bones have been found in the sands. There seem to be racial folk memories of a greater Wales, narrowly separated by the shallow sea (that Bran walked across) from Ireland. The original name of Borth was Porth Wyddno – 'The Gate of the City Under Wave', and spring tides still regularly flood the town.

The haunting old song, The Bells of Aberdyfi, was composed by Charles Dibdin for the 1785 operatic entertainment, 'Liberty Hall'. It tells the legend of old church bells still tolling in the waters of West Wales. Leland refers to the lost Cantref y Gwaelod (Lowland Hundred), eaten away by the Irish Sea. Legends of the times when Ireland was united by a land-bridge with Wales are linked with its ownership by Cynfelin (Shakespeare's Cymbeline, Cunobelinus) and one of the three strange ridges of rock reaching out from Cardigan Bay to Ireland is called *Sarn Gynfelin* ('Cymbeline's Causeway').

These ridges are exposed at very low tides. The most northerly is *Sarn Badrig* ('St Patrick's Way'), near Shell Island, traditionally thought to be the road to the flooded land known as Cantref Gwaelod where church bells still ring. It runs for fifteen miles (24 km) out into Cardigan Bay, and a giant boulder thirteen feet (4m) across can be seen. It is possible to land a boat on Sarn Badrig at certain low tides and is also known as Shipwreck Reef. The flattened glacial boulders that can be seen look very much like sea-battered embankments. King Bran Bendigeidfran in legend waded to Ireland across here, starting from Harddlech in Ardudwy (Harlech). Sarn Badrig is between Harlech and Barmouth. Intriguingly, an ancient stone was found in the sands off Barmouth about one hundred yards below the high water mark. The inscription read, *'here lies the boatman to King Gwynddo'* (sic), as reported in *'Journey to Avalon'* by C. Barber and D. Pykitt. Was this Gwyddno Garanhir's boatman?

Between Barmouth and Towyn is Sarn-y-Bwch, lying directly offshore from Tonfanau Iron Age fort. Sarn Cynfelin lies between Towyn and Aberystwyth, and can be walked for about half a mile when there is a falling spring tide. This twelve thousand year-old Ice Age remnant runs about six and a half miles towards Ireland and acted as a natural breakwater for small coasters landing limestone for local shore-based kilns.

Further south, Aberaeron has lost Castell Cadwgan to the sea and off the Glamorgan coast, Porthkerry (Porthceri) Castle has gone under the waves. Even recently the sea has hit coastal settlements. Three hundred years ago the village of Hawton near Ferryside in Dyfed was wiped out by a high sea and the twelfth century church at Cwm-yr-Eglwys ('Church Valley') was hit by the massive 1859 storm leaving only the belfry standing.

However, Wales has regained some land from the sea in the Gwent (Caldecot) Levels and Wentloog Levels which make up the most extensive ancient fenland in Wales. The Wentloog Levels are protected from the massive tidal differences in the Bristol Channel by Peterstone Great Wharf, a huge bank of earth. Reens (straightened drainage ditches) cover this marshland between the mouths of the Taff and Usk rivers. When a high spring tide allies with a strong south-westerly wind, the sea can still come over the bank. The 1606-7 floods claimed thousands of lives here, and the depth of the flood is marked by a plaque on the side of St Bride's Church at Wentloog. These marshes were reclaimed by the Romans' Second Legion, probably using slave labour. They also have strong Arthurian connections but seem to be doomed by urban planners over the next twenty years.

East of the Usk, the Caldecot Levels are marshland silt lying on top of peat, and changes in water levels have led to tilting buildings, for example Whitson church. Nash and Goldcliffe churches also have plaques recording the 1607 flood levels. Much of the drainage here dates from mediaeval, and probably Roman times. This unique ecological system of reeds, bulrushes and marsh birds is threatened by new housing and industry. The new Legend Park will also destroy some heritage areas, for the sake of those people wanting to be excited by ever more frightening fairground 'rides'.

Gwyddneu Garanhir, ruler of the lost country flooded under Cardigan Bay, asked for protection from Gwyn, the God of War and Death, in 'The Black Book of Carmarthen'. Gwyn's response includes:

> *I have been in the place where was killed Gwendolau,*
> *The son of Ceidaw, the pillar of songs,*
> *When the ravens screamed over blood.*

> *I have been in the place where Bran was killed,*
> *The son of Iweridd, of far extending fame,*
> *When the ravens of the battlefield screamed.*

> *I have been where Llacheu was killed,*
> *The son of Arthur, extolled in songs,*
> *When the ravens screamed over blood.*

> *I have been where Meurig was killed,*
> *The son of Carreian, of honourable fame,*
> *When the ravens screamed over flesh.*
> *I have been where Gwallawg was killed,*
> *The son of Goholeth, the accomplished,*
> *The resister of Lloegyr (England), the son of Lleynawg.*

> *I have been where the soldiers of Britain were slain,*

From the east to the north:
I am the escort of the grave.

I have been where the soldiers of
Britain were slain,
From the east to the south:
I am alive, they in death!

AUSTRALASIA

New South Wales was so named by **Captain Thomas Jones** of Llandewi Skirrid.

Samuel Walker Griffith (1845-1920) was born in Merthyr Tydfil and studied at Sydney University. He served as Prime Minister and Chief Justice of Queensland and had the major input into drafting Australia's Commonwealth Constitution in 1900. As the first chief justice of the following High Court of Australia from 1900 to 1919 he had a major and lasting influence on the interpretation of law in the 'new' country. His place in Australian legal history parallels that of John Marshall in the United States of America.

A Welsh migrant, **William Morris Hughes**, landed in Brisbane in 1884, aged 22. 'Billy Hughes' became an organiser for the Australian Workers' Union and after setting up a bookshop in 1894 was elected for the Labour Party to the New South Wales Parliament. Over seven years he campaigned for improved workers' conditions and old age pensions and he persuaded the Labour party to adopt the full adult franchise in its electoral programme. He then stood for the First Federal Parliament, winning West Sidney in 1901.

By 1903 he had qualified as a barrister, and after posts of Minister for External Affairs and Attorney-General became Prime Minister of Australia in 1915. He was given the Freedom of the City of Cardiff and shared a platform with Lloyd-George to encourage conscription for the First World War. He lost the Premiership in 1923 at the age of 61 but was Attorney-General and Minister for the Navy at the start of the Second World War. In 1952, still an MP, he died aged 90. His parliamentary career spanned 58 years, the Federation of Australia, two world wars, the great depression, and eight years as Prime Minister. (For further information, see the article by Peter Huw Davies, in *The Welsh Review*, January 1997).

From 1870, many Welsh artisans had taken up the offer of a free passage to Australia. As Merthyr Tydfil was probably the largest industrial exporting town in Europe at the time and Welsh industrial expertise was about a generation in front of the rest of Europe, this was equivalent to modern technology transfer as Australia wished to develop its massive mineral resources. (Similarly, although Welsh settlers had moved to farm in Natal from 1824, the discovery of gold in South Africa 30 years later led to an influx of Welsh miners and engineers to exploit the mineral).

New Zealand, to counter the move of emigrants to Australia, offered massive sheep farms to Welsh flockmasters and farmers. To some extent this lasting link with Wales has led to the development its national sport. New Zealand and Wales are the only two countries in the world where rugby has always been the sport of passion for the majority.

B

BARDS

'*Bardd*' means 'poet' in Welsh and '*barddoniaeth*' means 'poetry' (literally 'the work of bards'). A poem is a 'cerdd', so the head bard in each lord's household was known as the 'pencerdd' or 'head of poems'.

Like the druids, the bards were a class of learned men in early Celtic societies, principally concerned with music and poetry. Merlin was supposed to have retired to Bardsey (the Isle of the Bards) with nine bardic attendants, to guard the Thirteen Treasures of Britain. Bards survived after the Celtic era, attached to the courts of Welsh princes, and when the Lord Rhys established the first Eisteddfod in 1176, their existence gained a new life. Music and poetry contests carried on through the Middle Ages and were revived on a national basis in 1789, thanks to Iolo Morganwg. Their influence on the spoken word has affected the course of Welsh literature and its leaning towards poetry. The Celts prized bards more than warriors and the tradition has continued.

The four main periods in the history of Welsh literature begin with the age of the *Cynfeirdd*, or primitive bards, from around 460-500 to the middle of the eleventh century and their work was inspired by the struggles of the Britons against the invading Saxons. The Triads record that the original bards of Ynys Prydain ('the Isle of Britain') were Alawn, Gwron and Plenydd. The books of Aneirin, Carmarthen, Taliesin and Hergest commemorate some of these ancient poems. As well as Aneirin and Taliesin, Myrddin (Merlin) and Llywarch Hen were notable bards recorded in these manuscripts. The poems used rhyming and alliterative devices to assist the bards in repeating them and handing them down to future generations. Their work was called *cerdd dafod*, the craft of the tongue. Hywel Dda gave the bards legal status and high honour in his 'Laws' in the tenth century.

The next period was that of the *Gogynfeirdd*, from the eleventh century, when the bards began to travel from court to court, like troubadours. Over thirty poets from the twelfth and thirteenth centuries are known from existing works. Gwalchmai ap Meilyr, the pencerdd (chief bard) at the court of Owain Gwynedd was best known and Cynddelw is also famous. Some bards were also soldiers and nobles, such as Dafydd Benfras, who died fighting for Llewelyn Fawr in 1257 and Bleddyn Fardd, who died fighting the Normans. Owain Cyfeiliog and Hywel ab Owain Gwynedd were bardic poet-princes of this time, learned men with their own courts.

After the death of Llywelyn the Last in 1282, it was the age of *Beirdd yr Uchelwyr*, the Bards of the Nobles, who entertained the higher classes. They introduced a revolutionary new metre, the *cywydd*, to blend with traditional *cynghanedd*, (rhyming internal consonance) and Wales' greatest poet, Dafydd ap Gwilym, flourished. Between 1300 and 1420, the other leading bards were the remarkable Sion Cent, Rhys Goch Eryri and Iolo Goch, who composed the famous panegyric to Owain Glyndŵr. They were followed by Lewis Glyn Cothi, Llawdden, Guto'r Glyn and the great Dafydd ab Edmwnd of Hanmer. Edmwnd Prys and Gruffydd Hiraethog thrived under the Tudors, but apart from Huw Morus the bardic tradition began to be replaced by prose. In 1694, the last known household bard, Sion Dafydd Las, died. He was the family poet of the Nannau family in north-west Wales.

The renaissance and the fourth period of bardic activity was sparked by the Machynlleth Eisteddfod of 1702. Grinding poverty forced Goronwy Owen to emigrate to America. Lewis Morris, Alun (John Blackwell), Ceiriog (John Ceiriog Hughes), the wonderful Islwyn (William Thomas) and many others pushed out the frontiers of Welsh poetry with little reward. However, they set the background for our twentieth century poets (see Poetry).

Bards have directly been responsible for the survival of the Welsh language. Gaelic has all but died out in Ireland and Scotland, despite the former being an island and the latter a large mountainous region far from the English seat of power in London. Wales as a country was the first to be invaded and dominated by England, is within easy reach of it and had its language proscribed by the 1536 Act of Union. However, from Celtic times through to mediaeval times the bard was one of the most important members of a noble's household.

Bards remembered and retold in verse the battles and deeds of famous Welshmen against the Romans, Irish, Vikings, Saxons, Mercians, Normans, Angevins and Plantagenets. As scholars, they studied the language and wrote handbooks and dictionaries to maintain its purity. As the old Welsh aristocracy

and their attendant court bards died out in the sixteenth century, to be replaced by absentee English landowners, the 1588 translation of the Bible into Welsh saved the language. Bishop William Morgan's masterpiece has been a model for all future generations (see Language)

BEER

The *cyfarfod cymorth*, assistance meeting, was held for hundreds of years for the benefit of poor people or people having problems with their rent or to help a grieving widow meet her bills. It was a meeting with *cwrw bach*, small beer, brewed by the householder. The beer was free, to comply with legislation, but the *pice*, small cakes, were highly priced, to ensure the householder made a fair profit. There was dancing, singing and sometimes love tokens were exchanged, as this was one of the few free-wheeling occasions in Welsh society. *Meth*, mead, was also sometimes made. Even up until the late nineteenth century, mead was traditionally mixed with spiced beer in some villages to celebrate Easter Monday.

Brewing has been carried out from the same well at the Old Brewery, in Central Cardiff since 1713. Brains brewery has been synonymous with Cardiff since the other local brewers Rhymney and Hancocks were taken over by the big English brewers in the 1960s. Bass is closing the old Hancock's brewery in Cardiff, and Whitbread do not make Rhymney beers. Brains has won many awards for its beers. Back in the 1970s, it was the only brewery left in Britain that sold more dark than light beer and its Brains Dark is still a best-seller, a creamy rich mild with about the same strength as its estimable Bitter. Its flagship beer is SA, Strong Ale, variously known as Samuel Arthur (after the brewery's founder, S. A. Brain) or more often as Skull Attack.

Brains is a flagship for real ales, and often brews specials like Dylan's, Summer Ale or Winter Ale. In the 1998 Brewing Industry International Awards, bottled S.A. came first out of one hundred and nineteen entries, chosen by thirty-six international judges. Brain's Dark won in the dark mild category, and Brain's Bitter won a silver medal.

Until recently the only other major independent breweries left in Wales were Felinfoel and Crown Buckley's, both based in Llanelli. Felinfoel Double Dragon is a lovely pint, but like Brains, does not 'travel' well in its natural form. Felinfoel has just eighty-seven pubs in South-West Wales. Felinfoel used the local tin expertise to become the first brewery in Europe to market beer in cans, back in 1935. This development helped the depressed local tin industry. Unfortunately, with the swing to light beers and lager, Felinfoel has stopped brewing Dark beer because of falling sales. Its light bitter, Dragon, has 3.4% strength, and Double Dragon has 4.2%. CAMRA describes the latter as having '*a sulphurous aroma which fades to leave apple and malt. A taste of apple weaves around the malt and hops to give a distinctive finish. Very drinkable.*' Buckley's, which had taken over Crown Brewery, has been bought by Brains in 1998, and the Llanelli brewery closed in 1998 after two hundred and thirty-one years of brewing.

A small Welsh brewery is producing a special ale, Cwrw Caio, to commemorate Caio Evans, the self-styled leader of the Free Wales Army, who served a prison sentence in the 1960s. There are a few other small independent breweries in Wales, Bullmastiff in Penarth, Tomos Watkins in Llandeilo (run by a Buckley's descendant, Simon Buckley), Swansea Brewing Company in Bishopston, the Tynllidiart Arms in Capel Bangor, The Nag's Head in Boncath and the Red Lion, Llanidloes.

Unfortunately, most of Wales is covered by the big English brewers. Bass has 35% of the UK market, via all their regional brews; Scottish Courage has 31% and Whitbread 14% – three monolithic empires control four in every five pints of beer sold in Britain.

The first Act of Parliament that passed legislation specifically for Wales, was the 1881 Act that closed the pubs on Sundays. So for many years, all Welsh pubs were shut upon Sundays. The last remaining place where the Sabbath was 'dry' was Dwyfor, the Welsh-speaking heartland of North-West Wales, but the ban ended after a 1996 local referendum.

Courtesy of the back of a Brain's beer mat, the following phrases can be useful:

un peint o gwrw da – a pint of best beer
os gwelwch yn dda – please
iechyd da – cheers
eich rownd chi yw e – it's your round
yr un peth eto – same again.

BIRDS

Milvus Milvus, 'Barcud' in Welsh, the Red Kite, used to be common as a scavenger in London's streets in Shakespeare's time. By 1905, only five birds remained after centuries of persecution, in the Welsh Hills – a symbol of Welsh survival to many people. Now there are over a hundred pairs and this majestic predator draws tourists to Wales. Perhaps it should feature as the national bird, like America's Bald Eagle. By 1984 there were thirty three breeding pairs and by 1995 there were one hundred and eleven, rearing 90 young successfully. At Gigrin Farm just south of Rhayader one can watch up to forty at a feeding station (plus buzzards and ravens) at 2pm between October and April.

The word cuckoo seems to have originate from the Welsh *'cw-cw, cw-cw'- 'whither? whither?'*. The mention of a cuckoo in old Welsh poetry signifies a change to a sad tone, signifying something that is sadly lost, for example in one of the 9th century poems attributed to Llywarch Hen:

> *'At Aber Cuawg cuckoos are singing,*
> *Sad it is to my mind*
> *That he who once heard them will hear*
>   *them no more.'*

Thousands of Puffins and the rare Chough inhabit Welsh islands and cliffs. At Craig Aderyn (Birds' Rock), six miles inland on the Gwynedd coast, forty pairs of cormorants nest, their only British inland nesting site. Peregrine falcons and fulmars also inhabit the cliffs.

Grassholm Island has the world's second largest breeding colony of 30,000 pairs of gannets and nearby Skomer and Skokholm Islands support 6000 pairs of storm petrels and the internationally significant population of 140,000 pairs of the burrow-nesting Manx Shearwaters.

All members of the crow family (except the Hooded Crow) inhabit Wales, from the massive raven to the cocky jackdaw. Fairly rare in many parts of England, jackdaws raid bus-stop waste-paper bins in places like Tonypandy, jumping in and out and throwing litter onto the pavement, oblivious of nearby people. *Brân* is Welsh for crow but can also mean raven. In Welsh legend, Bran the Blessed's decapitated head was taken to be buried beneath the white hill beside the Thames, the site of the Tower of London. The myth that there must always be ravens at the Tower, or England will fall, could be the continuation of the story of Brân from the 'Mabinogion' (see Mabinogion).

The only domesticated bird of Welsh origin it seems is the Brecon Buff Goose, but there must be others – any information would be welcome. With hares and cockerels, geese were sacred to the Celts. As recently as 1880 in North Wales it was thought an evil omen to see geese on a lake at night. Such a sighting was said to signify that witches were about and the very worst time to see them was on the first Thursday of the lunar month.

BOGS

Wales possesses seven RAMSAR Sites, 'wetlands of international importance', at Burry Inlet, the Dee Estuary, Llyn Tegid (Lake Bala), Cors Caron, Cors Fochno and the Dyfi and Crymlyn Bog. The Dyfi Estuary is a Biosphere Reserve of 2100 hectares, designated in 1977 to conserve a major type of ecosystem.

Cors Llyn Farch and Llyn Fanod, near Tregaron, are acid bogs cared for by the West Wales Trust for Nature Conservation, home to many birds, invertebrates, dragonflies and plants like water lobelia and bogbean. (Tregaron has a statue to Henry Richards, 1812-88, the founder of the Peace Union, which in turn begat the League of Nations which begat The United Nations).

Cors Caranod, not far from Aberystwyth, is a fen-bog area with crowberry, white sedge, bottle sedge, cottongrasses and bog mosses.

Ynys Eidiol and Ynys Hir, near Machynlleth have areas of peat bogs and salt marshes, sustaining 31 species of butterfly, the rare nightjar, hen harrier, peregrine falcon, merlin, red-breasted merganser and many endangered plants such as the heath spotted orchid and bog asphodel.

Cors Geirch is a mire and fen area not far from Pwllheli on the Llŷn Peninsula with different types of bladderwort great fen-sedge and brook lamprey in its river.

The Afon Dwyfach flows through Cors Gyfelog, fenlands and willow woodlands outside Nasareth, near Porthmadog. This is one of the best areas to see dragonflies in Britain.

At Cors Caron, outside Lampeter, there is one of the finest examples of raised mire in Britain, formed by the action of glaciation during the last Ice Age. There are spectacular lichens and sphagnum mosses to be seen on the two walks that can be made around this Nature Conservancy Council reserve. Pied flycatchers, red kites, merlins, peregrines and harriers can also be seen and there is a superb display of dragonflies in the area. It is notable for its deer grass, bog mosses and other wetland vegetation, sundews, hen harriers, merlins and animals such as otters, polecats and the unique black adder. The River Teifi runs through the site.

'Rhos' is Welsh for marshy land, so many place-names are prefixed with it. Rhos Goch Common, near Painscastle, is a raised mire and fen swamp, with bogbean, bog asphodel, cottongrass, sedges, heather, bilberry, marsh fern, petty whin, lesser skullcap and marsh speedwell.

Cors y Llyn, near Newbridge-on-Wye, is a basin mire, with a very rare lichen, plus sundew, the insectivorous plant, bog asphodel, cranberry, crowberry, white-beaked sedge, heath spotted orchid and dyer's greenweed. Nearby Aberithon is a peat bog and fen, with abundant birdlife and similar plants to Cors y Llyn, including marsh cinquefoil, floating club-rush, meadow thistle, lesser bladderwort, and ivy-leafed bellflower.

While not really bogs, the saltmarshes, reed beds, fenland, mudflats and reclaimed grassland to the east and west of Newport, Gwent, are fascinating for the variety of wildlife so close to a built-up area. Peterstone Wentloog has avocet, wood sandpiper, little stint, ruff, long-tailed duck, common scoter, little ringed plover, grey plover, dunlin and shoveler ducks as well as plants such as spiny restharrow and bristly ox-tongue. Goldcliff and Magor Pill marshes have peregrine falcons, merlin, short-eared owl and redshank. Magor Marsh is important for birds, and supports grasshopper warblers, water rail, garganey, shoveler ducks and reed warblers. There are marsh marigolds, bulrushes, flowering rush, spearwort and arrowhead growing here. All these four sites are managed by the Gwent Trust for Nature Conservation.

Also nearby are wild orchids, around Penhow Castle, Cadicot Castle and nearby woodlands There are bird's-nest orchids, lesser-butterfly orchids, green-winged orchids, early purple orchids, wild daffodils, Tintern spurge and helleborines. These sites are also managed by the Gwent Trust.

Henllys Bog, near Cwmbran, has over eighty five plant species, including sundew and marsh helleborine. Llwyn-y-Celyn Bog, outside Shirenewton, is a one acre lowland bog with monks-hood, marsh-mallow, marshwort, lesser skullcap, water avens and bogbean. Near this south-east corner of Wales is the wonderful Forest of Dean. A former royal deer forest, it has many small bogs around its stream valleys and ancient oaks around the Speech House area. There are crossbills and pied flycatchers in the woodland and bog asphodel, bog pimpernel, helleborines and few-flowered spike-rush can be found.

BOTANY

Wales has several tracts of ancient woodland, including the Pengelli Forest in Pembrokeshire, with sessile oaks and midland hawthorn. The wild service tree appears to have its last foothold in Britain, in Wales, near Aberthaw.

Rare arctic-alpine plants, remants of the Ice Ages, are found in Cwm Idwal in the Ogwen Valley, the Brecon Beacons and Snowdonia, for example the Snowdon Lily (Lloydia Serotina) is only found around Snowdon, probably discovered in the 17th century by Edward Lhuyd. Other rare alpine species are the purple saxifrage, moss campion, tormentil and mountain avens.

The coastline supports Sea Holly, Sea Lavender, Devil's Bit Scabious, Sea Campion, Sea Vetch and Sea Aster, with glorious banks of pink sea thrift.

The Welsh Poppy, bright yellow, can sometimes be seen in mountain areas and the Tenby Daffodil and the Pembrokeshire Primrose, a pink variety, are fairly common in the South-West.

Wales used to be covered with oak trees and the famous oak at Bassaleg Village near Newport was converted into 2,426 cubic feet of timber for Nelson's warships in 1802, then the most ever recorded from a single tree. Unfortunately, the Forestry Commission has now covered vast swathes of Welsh hillsides with Sitka Spruce as a cash crop.

Lottery money has been granted to turn the Middleton gardens and estate in Carmarthenshire into a National Botanic Centre for Wales.

BRITTANY

Ancient Armorica, the North-West part of France, was the centre of a confederation of Celtic tribes. In the fifth and sixth centuries many British Celts fled there, across the old trading routes, to escape the growing pressure from Germanic Angles and Saxons invading Britain from the East. They called their new home Brittany or Britain, to distinguish it from Great Britain, Grande Bretagne. These Britons, later called Bretons, converted the Armorican Celts to the Celtic Christianity they had practised in their old land. The legend of Cynan (Conan) Meriadoc persists that he led an army of Britons from Wales to support Maxen Wledig, the emperor Maximus, to defeat the Roman emperor Gratian. Upon the death of Maximus, this army settled in Armorica, where they spoke the same language. Other legends link Bretons with founding America, or that Prince Madoc called the New World Armorica.

Brocielande, in Brittany, has strong connections with Arthur and Merlin. In its centre, the Abbey at Paimpont, I came across an exhibition of a dozen banners of the holiest Breton saints – three were of Welsh missionaries, St Brieuc (Briog), St Malo and St Samson of Dol. St Brieuc is on the Breton coastline near St Malo (see the entry on Saints for the Welsh influence on Breton Christianity). Saint Guenole was also important in Finistere and Landevennec, and Saint Alawn became bishop of Quimper. Brittany was settled in the fifth century by Welsh and Cornish Celts and their language is very similar to Welsh and Cornish. The Breton 'k' disappeared from Welsh a few hundred years ago, but the 'z' of Breton is in the Cornish alphabet though not the Welsh. The region the Bretons call Armor, the ports and nearby coastal villages, is made up of the Welsh words *ar* (at or on) and *môr* (the sea). Their internal, formerly heavily wooded areas, Argoat, has the same derivation – *ar* and *coed* (at the woods), with the 'c' being mutated to 'g' in Welsh making Argoed.

In 1488, Brittany lost its independence to France, just three years after their Welsh cousins took over the English throne. Duchess Anne of Brittany married Charles VIII of France. The Union was ratified in 1532, just four years before the Act of Union joined England and Wales under the Tudor dynasty. Since then the attempts to stamp out the Breton language have been even fiercer than those by the English government against the Welsh. The Bretons, however, kept their culture better by not going through the fervent religious revival that Wales underwent in the eighteenth and nineteenth centuries. As a result their dance,

song and costume have survived more or less intact. Each village still has processions 'pardons' devoted to its local saint on a special annual saint's feast day.

In 1996 Rita Williams of Fishguard was awarded the Silver Collar of Brittany, a cultural award dating back to the Middle Ages. Only the first Briton, and second non-Breton to receive the award, Rita Williams has translated Breton short stories and plays into Welsh and compiled a Welsh-Breton and Breton-Welsh dictionary.

The French word *'baragouiner'* means 'to speak nonsense'. Years ago, Breton farmers travelling with their herds and flocks to sell them in Paris used to ask on the way for 'bara' (bread in Welsh) and 'gwin' (wine). To the French, they were speaking gibberish, hence the verb.

The hand-pumped Morlaix beer, apart from being very different to all the other sparkling, light French beers, and is very similar to Brains Dark, brewed in Cardiff.

BUCCANEER

'Privateering' was the practice of the state commissioning privately-owned ships to attack enemy merchant ships. It came into its own with the sea-dog captains of the Elizabethan Age, men such as Drake, Hawkins, Frobisher and Raleigh. Legally sanctioned, it was fundamentally different from piracy, which preyed on all shipping, in that it focused upon enemy ships only. The Crown often sold privateering licences in return for a cut of the spoils. Many of the privateers who fought the Spaniards in the 17th century became known as buccaneers, from the French 'boucaniers', meaning sun-dryers of meat. The most famous and successful of all the buccaneers was a Welshman, **Henry Morgan** (1635-1688).

Henry Morgan was a cousin of the Morgans that owned Tredegar Park outside Newport. He was born the son of a gentleman farmer, probably in Llanrhymney. He set sail from Bristol at the age of twenty, bound for the West Indies to make his fortune. Morgan was an indentured servant in Barbados for three years. After another four years working in the sugar plantations he joined in 1662 a ship heading to Jamaica to plunder Spanish ships and various enemy-occupied coastal towns. In 1655 Jamaica had been seized from Spain to serve as a base for freebooting American and British privateers to operate against Spanish America.

Morgan was so successful that within two years his share of the booty enabled him to buy his own ship. Aged just twenty-nine, he now used Jamaica as his base and from there he harassed the Spanish on the American mainland and built up an enormous treasure trove. When the Spanish started attacking British ships off Cuba, the Governor of Jamaica asked Morgan to return and scatter the Spanish fleet. Morgan was then made Admiral of the Jamaican fleet of ten ships and five hundred men, because of his courage and success.

Well documented is Morgan's sacking of Puerto Principe (now Camaguey in Cuba) in 1668. In the same year, he looted and ransacked the largest city in Cuba, Porto Bello, and Maracaibo in Venezuela. Morgan followed this up by crossing the Atlantic and he plundered some of Spain's richest coastal cities, but was eventually chased into open waters by the main Spanish fleet. Morgan and his privateers decided to turn and fight, and nearly annihilated

the Spanish. On his return to his Jamaican base, Morgan had lost just eighteen men, and plundered a quarter of a million pieces of gold and silver coins, jewellery, silks, spices, munitions, weapons and slaves. Captain Morgan was just thirty-three years old, with a reputation that had attracted seafarers from all over the West Indies to join his flag.

After his sacking of Porto Bello in Panama, Morgan attacked a French ship. It appeared that the French had given 'notes of exchange' to an English ship previously, in return for provisions. These notes had not been 'honoured' when presented for payment in Jamaica. Morgan positioned his flagship, *The Oxford*, in a bay in south Haiti, waiting for a sighting of the French ship. When it appeared, he invited the captain and officers to dine with them. Over the meal, he rebuked them for their treatment of the English ship and imprisoned them. Morgan and his crew commenced carousing, firing guns into the air in their drunken dancing. Unfortunately, a spark of gunfire lit the powder magazine, and there was an explosion. Three hundred crew and the French prisoners were blown to bits.

Morgan and his officers were at the stern of the ship, and survived, being furthest away from the explosion. He returned to the site later, in *The Jamaica Merchant*, to try and salvage the ship, during which *The Jamaica Merchant* also sank. It now appears that *The Oxford* has been found, and salvage attempts have started.

Also in 1669, the Spanish Capitan Pardal swore vengeance upon Morgan. After making a small raid on a Jamaican village he left the following note pinned to a tree near the smouldering village hall: '*I, Capitan Manuel Pardal, to the Chief of Privateers in Jamaica. I come to seek General Henry Morgan, with two ships and twenty-one guns. When he sees this Challenge, I beg that he will come out and seek me, that he may see the Valour of the Spaniards'.* Within weeks, Pardal was caught near the east coast of Cuba and shot through the neck in battle.

On his return to Jamaica, Morgan was put in charge of thirty-five ships and two thousand men. Aged thirty five, he decided to break the power of Spain in the West Indies by attacking Panama, their largest and richest town in the Americas. Meanwhile, Britain and Spain had negotiated peace in London and orders were despatched to him to call off any attacks on Spanish colonies. Morgan ignored the orders, reached the mainland in 1670, and marched across the Isthmus of Panama towards the city. In the course of this devastating raid, Morgan and his men succumbed to the heat and disease as they hacked their way through the jungle, destroying every fort and church in their path. By the time he reached Panama, in January 1671, Morgan had only a half of his original two thousand men left, but he attacked the defending force of twenty thousand Spaniards with such venom that they fled the city. One hundred and fifty mules were needed to take the booty back to the ships. Morgan went on ahead of the other buccaneer captains. He left for the safety of Jamaica, with the greatest treasure proceeds in history.

The Spanish put a price on Morgan's head, and as the raid had occurred in peace-time, he was arrested and extradited to London in 1672. Luckily for him, the peace did not last and he was released after paying out a huge part of his treasure to the Crown. King Charles II knighted him and sent him back to Jamaica as Lieutenant Governor of the island, where Morgan died, a successful planter, at the age of fifty two in 1688. In 1685 the English publishers of the translation of Esquemeling's contemporary book, *The Buccaneers of America*, were sued by Morgan for calling him a 'pirate' and questioning his upbringing. This was the first ever recorded case of damages being paid and apologies being made for libel. Subsequent editions featured the publisher's apologies.

C

CADW

'Cadw' is the authority in charge of many of Wales' most precious historic monuments – others are in the care of The National Trust, or of various councils (e.g. Cardiff Castle). Cadw means 'keep' in Welsh, which is a wordplay upon preserving the past, and the central architectural feature (the keep) of the hundred of castles in Wales. A season ticket to 'Heritage in Wales' is essential if you wish to tour the following sites (telephone 01222 473708), as family tickets only cost £36 in 1997-98. Some of the sites are free to the public, but great savings can be made on visits to the major attractions.

Castles at: Beaumaris, Bronllys, Caernarfon, Caerphilly, Carreg Cennen, Castell Coch, Castell-y-Bere, Chepstow, Cilgerran, Coity, Conwy, Criccieth, Denbigh, Dolbadarn, Dolforwyn, Dolwyddelan, Dryslwyn, Ewloe, Flint, Grosmont, Harlech, Cydweli (Kidwelly), Laugharne, Llanblethian, Llansteffan (Llanstephan), Llawhaden, Loughor, Monmouth, Montgomery, Newcastle, Newport, Ogmore, Old Beaupre, Oxwich, Raglan, Rhuddlan, Skenfrith, Swansea, Tretower, Weobley, White Castle and Wiston.

Mediaeval Houses and Fortified Sites at: Caernarfon Town Wall, Carswell Old House, Conwy Town Wall, Denbigh Town Wall, Hen Gwrt Moated Site, Kidwelly Town Gate, Penarth Fawr Mediaeval House, Twthill and Tretower Court.

Roman Sites at: Caer Gybi, Caer Leb, Caerleon, Caerwent, Segontium, and Y Gaer near Brecon.

Religious Sites at: Basingwerk Abbey, Capel Lligwy, Carew Cross, Cymer Abbey, Denbigh Friary, Leicester's Church and St Hilary's Chapel, Derwen Churchyard Cross, Eliseg's Pillar, Ewenny Priory, Gwydir Uchaf Chapel, Haverfordwest Priory, Lamphey Bishop's Palace, Llangar Old Parish Church, Llanthony Priory, Maen Achwyfan Cross, Margam Stones Museum, Neath Abbey, Penmon Cross and Priory, Rug Chapel, Runston Chapel, St Cybi's Well, St Davids Bishop's Palace and Close Wall, St Dogmael's Abbey, St Non's Chapel, St Seiriol's Well, St Winifred's Chapel and Holy Well, Strata Florida Abbey, Talley Abbey, Tintern Abbey and Valle Crucis Abbey.

Post-Mediaeval and Industrial Sites at: Blaenavon Ironworks, Bryntail Lead Mines, Dyfi Furnace, Penmon Dovecote and Pont Minllyn.

Prehistoric Burial Chambers at: Barclodiad y Gawres, Bodowyr, Bryn Celli Ddu, Capel Garmon, Carreg Coetan, Din Dryfol, Dyffryn St Lythans, Lligwy, Parc le Breos, Pentre Ifan, Presaddfed, Tinkinswood, Trefignath, Tŷ Mawr and Tŷ Newydd.

Prehistoric Sites at: Caer y Twr, Castell Bryn Gwyn, Chepstow Bulwark Camp, Din Lligwy Hut Group, Holyhead Mountain Hut Circles, Llanmelin Wood Hillfort, Penrhos Feilw Standing Stones and Tregwehelydd Standing Stone.

FOOTNOTE:
Apart from membership of CADW, another worthwhile investment for those living and visiting the Cardiff

area is a family ticket to the National Museums and Galleries of Wales, including the brilliant Museum of Welsh Life at St Fagans. The cost is £32.50 for one year.

CAER

It used to be thought that this was derived from the Latin 'castra', or fort, but it appears to be original Welsh. The prefix denotes the site of a castle, fortified camp or the like. Many of Wales' hundreds of Iron Age hill forts are prefixed Caer, Din or Dinas. All signify an ancient fortified site, but more often Caer has Roman connections. The prefix of din or dinas usually refers to an even more ancient defended site. The Roman fort-towns of Carmarthen and Cardiff are derived from Caerfyrddin and Caerdydd. Caerlaverock Castle, in the South-West of Scotland, has the same origins. Y Gaer is the site of a Roman fort near Brecon. After Boudicca's rebellion, the Roman frontier moved further West towards Wales, with Cirencester (Corinium) fort being dismantled and Caerleon taking its place. Caerleon seems to come from 'caer legionis', camp of the legion.

Caerleon has the best-preserved Roman amphitheatre in Britain, for centuries thought of as King Arthur's Round Table, and was the headquarters of the Second Legion in Britain. According to Geoffrey of Monmouth, Arthur was crowned there. Marie de France, in *'The Lay of Sir Launfal'* wrote in the 12th century: *'King Arthur, that fearless knight and courteous lord removed to Wales, and lodged at Caerleon-on-Usk, since the Picts and Scots did much mischief in the land. For it was the wont of the wild people of the North to enter the realm of Logres* (England), *and burn and damage at their will.'*

Caerleon fort's walls still stand up to 12 foot high in parts, and it possesses the only Roman legionary barracks visible in Europe. The monumental bath complex was built on the scale of a mediaeval cathedral, and some of it is now exhibited under the cover of a purpose-built museum. It is the only legionary bath visible in Britain. Caerleon was built at the mouth of the River Usk, in AD75, as the strategic base for the conquest of South Wales, and for ease of reinforcement and access to its gold mines at Dolaucothi. The position was also chosen because it was close to Llanmelin hill fort, the capital of the Cetic Silures tribe, which controlled south-east Wales. The nearby fortified town of Caerwent has the best-preserved Roman walls in Britain, a mile in length around the village. In the 3rd Century, Cardiff (Caerdydd) took over from Caerleon as the Romans' South Wales HQ.

In a move reminiscent of the Normans with their Marcher Castles and Edward I's 'iron ring of castles', the Romans placed their largest legionary fort in Britain, for the XX Legion, on the far end of the Welsh borders from Caerleon, at Caer (Chester) in AD79. Chester has the largest amphitheatre in Britain. Its mediaeval city walls sometimes follow the line of the Roman walls. For two centuries Rome kept two of its three British legions on the Welsh borders, with around five thousand men in each legionary centre. Chester gave access to silver from Flint and copper from Anglesey.

After the defeat of Caradoc (Caratacus) in AD51, the Welsh tribes were still troublesome, and the small camp of Wroxeter (Uriconium), near Shrewsbury (Pengwern), on the River Severn was expanded to become home to the XIV and then the XX legions. It became the fourth largest Roman city in Britain. Because of the numerous Celtic hill-forts, it was not until AD78 that Wales was conquered, and the Romans could put in a road system.

There were also 30 Roman forts in Wales, such as Y Gaer, near Brecon, and the fully garrisoned Caerfyrddin (Carmarthen) and Caernarfon (the Roman Segontium). Probably each had around a thousand troops garrisoned there. At Caerfyrddin (Moridunum) there was a Roman town, possibly even bigger than Caerwent.

Another great Roman legacy was 'Sarn Helen', the Roman road that crossed Wales from Moridunum (Carmarthen in the south) to Segontium (Caernarfon in the north), 'Sarn Helen' was known as 'Helen's Causeway', but is probably a corruption of 'Sarn Y Lleng', 'Causeway of the Legion'. Newer roads follow some of it, but parts of Sarn Helen are just as laid down by Roman slaves almost two thousand years ago. A 'new' Roman road appears to have been discovered West of Carmarthen and the Roman network makes for some superb country walking.

By AD78, Wales was effectively under Roman control until AD390. Magnus Maximus (the fabled Macsen Wledig in the 'Mabinogion') had left in AD383 to try to gain the Imperial crown. He took the British legions with him, eventually dying in battle in AD388 against Theodosius. The Princes of Powys as shown on the standing stone, Eliseg's Pillar, traced their royal lineage and legitimacy back to Macsen Wledig.

CAPITAL

Cardiff is one of Europe's youngest capital city, being awarded the nomenclature against competition from Swansea and Aberystwyth in 1955. Machynlleth also had claims, being the site of Owain Glyndŵr's first Welsh Parliament (there is a permanent 'Celtica' exhibition at Machynlleth, with the latest audio-visual technology, recounting the history of the Celts. The Parliament House is open to the public).

Cardiff used to be the busiest exporting docks in the world, taken over for a short time by Barry, with all the valleys' coal pouring through.

The capital's Edwardian Civic Centre, in gleaming white Portland stone, features the National Museum, The Welsh Office, City Hall, Glamorgan County Hall, Cardiff University, Law Courts and Temple of Peace and is considered to be one of the finest in the world. The Museum contains superb Impressionist paintings, one of the finest collections anywhere, donated by the Davies sisters (see David Davies). St David's Hall is one of Europe's newest concert halls, with 1900 seats. The New Theatre is a nearby Edwardian gem. Across the road to the West of the shopping centre and civic centre is the magnificent Cardiff Castle, built on Roman remains, and South and East are Victorian shopping arcades, the old covered market, pedestrianised shopping areas and covered shopping malls. Visitors must explore the arcades – the Castle Arcade is the only three-storey one in Britain. In the heart of the City, Cardiff Castle was restored by William Burges, working for the Marquess of Bute. In the late 1870s he also restored Castell Coch, just North of Cardiff, known to many as 'the fairytale castle', a mock-mediaeval fantasy of spires in woodland that must be visited. This is on the site of an earlier castle belonging to Ifor ap Cadifor, Ifor Bach (Little Ivor), who scaled the walls of Cardiff Castle in 1158 to capture William Earl of Gloucester, his wife and son. Ifor, Lord of Senghennydd, refused to release them until the Earl promised to give Ifor back the lands he had seized. Huge eagles are said to guard Ifor's treasure at Castell Coch.

Just outside Cardiff is the Museum of Welsh Life at St Fagans Castle. This has been an example for the rest of the world to follow since its inception in 1946. Chapels, a cockpit, a toll-house, ancient farmhouses, a working woollen mill, farmworkers' cottages and many other historic buildings from all over Wales have been rescued and restored with original furniture. Even a Miners' Institute has been moved there and reinstated – a former heart of learning where colliers could gain access to thousands of that precious commodity, books, for a penny a week.

Craftsmen like potters, coopers and wood-turners can be seen working at the museum.

The European Council of Ministers met at Cardiff in June 1998, and the Rugby World Cup was held in the new stadium in 1999. This all-purpose £100 million stadium has a retractable roof, seats seventy-five thousand spectators and is the most modern sports stadium in Europe.

CARDIFF BAY

Europe's largest urban regeneration scheme is impounding the outfalls from the Taff and Ely rivers to create a 500-acre freshwater leisure lake with eight miles of shoreline. This is fronting an eight hundred metres 'Arc of Entertainment'. The Barrage built to link Cardiff and Penarth and keep the 14 metre tides out was completed in 1998. The new Inner Harbour area has a target of two-million visitors a year by 2000, and the Atlantic Wharf leisure complex cost £30 million. The whole project is taking over a sixth of the area of the capital, and costing over £2.4 billion. Baltimore USA was used as the model for this fabulous concept, but Cardiff's regeneration is far bigger and better. The new Bute Avenue will link up the city centre with the waterside at last. As well as housing and leisure facilities, the Bay area intends to build upon Cardiff's claim as 'the multi-media centre of Europe', with over three hundred companies based in the capital, using latest fibre-optic links across the site.

The avant-garde visitors' centre, a long elliptical silver 'Tube', was unfortunately designed only to be temporary. However, it has been so popular that a new home is being sought for it in Cardiff Bay, together with the million pounds necessary to relocate it.

CASTLES

The Normans, within the space of four years from 1066, had totally overwhelmed England. It took hundreds of years to do the same to Wales, with its tiny population. Even in 1405 Glyndŵr virtually reconquered Wales for the Welsh and invaded England. When William I laid waste to the North of England, the Normans had sent a message to the Welsh – resist or die. The Norman Marcher Lords built frontier castles along the border from which they moved slowly westwards, trying to hold on to fresh gains by establishing castles, garrisons, cruelty and institutionalised torture. In the early Middle Ages, it was realised that the main bases of Norman attacks on Wales, at Chester, Shrewsbury, Montgomery and Hereford, were too far back, leaving extended and vulnerable lines of communication. Therefore the Lords of the Welsh Marches slowly pushed forwards, consolidating gains by building castles. Edward I, who reigned from 1272-1307, at the same time fortified strategic sites along the Welsh coast that could be fortified by sea. In return, the Welsh princes also built around fifty castles.

Wales thus has the highest density of castles in the world. The formidable Chepstow Castle in Gwent, built in 1067, is the oldest dateable secular stone building in Britain, although Dinas Powys also has a claim to be the oldest stone castle.

King Edward I spent half of his crown's annual incomes in building the 'iron ring' of castles to isolate Snowdonia and the Princes of Gwynedd from the rest of Wales. **Beaumaris** was the final link in the chain, and although uncompleted, is probably the most sophisticated example of a concentric castle (with ring within ring defences) in Europe. The most technically perfect castle in Britain, it was built on a flat swamp, 'Beautiful Marsh' in Eastern Anglesey, where the high tides sweep around its walls. (If visiting Beaumaris, the Courthouse has been active since it was built in 1614, the oldest length of time in Britain. Trials were held in English, so the local jury had no chance of following proceedings, nor the defendant to a fair trial against English judges).

Caernarfon Castle was built as a symbol of English power in 1283 by Edward I after the defeat and death in 1282 of Llywelyn ap Gruffydd (Llywelyn the Last), the last native Prince of Wales.King Edward I also built substantial town walls. Perhaps the greatest of Edward's castles, it was meant as a royal residence and seat of government for North Wales. It is the finest example of military architecture in Europe, its main gate being designed for no fewer than six portcullises, with assorted 'murder holes' above them. The arrow slits were designed for three archers to fire in rapid succession. Its appearance, with the banded towers and eagles, was based upon Edward's experience of the Crusades, having seen the fortifications of Constantinople. The future (doomed) Edward II was born here in 1284, and Edward I created him Prince of Wales seventeen years later in Lincoln. In 1969 Charles Windsor was crowned Prince of Wales at the castle.

Conwy Castle and the town walls were completed in 1287, in a superb strategic position. Eight-towered Conwy was called *'incomparably the most magnificent castle in Britain'* in a 1946 British Academy report. Seductive curves in the castle walls led attackers to a literal dead end in the West Barbican, where missiles and molten lead could be poured down from the murder-holes and machicolations above. As the guidebook states, *'forced entry is a virtual impossibility'*. The mile of walls contain over 200 listed buildings, including the wonderful Elizabethan Plâs Mawr, and is the finest example of a town wall left in Britain, surviving with little alteration. Conwy thus is not only the best example of a mediaeval walled town in Britain, but it also has the finest example of an Elizabethan town house. Shakespeare was wrong when he placed Flint Castle as the place where Richard II was betrayed to Henry of Lancaster – it was at Conwy Castle in 1399.

Standing where the river Conwy enters the Menai Straits between Caernarfonshire and Anglesey, the castle is at the centre of many Welsh legends. The most beautiful is that of Arianrhod's son, Dylan eil Don in 'The Mabinogion' (after whom Dylan Thomas was named). This *'Son of the Wave'*, was at home in the seas, and was killed by his uncle Govannon. The Book of Taliesin tells us that the waves of Britain, Ireland, Scotland and the Isle of Man wept for him. The sound of the waves crashing on the beach is the expression of their desire to avenge their son. The sound of the sea rushing up the Conwy river was still known last century as *'Dylan's death-groan'*. A nearby promontory, Pwynt Maen Dulen, preserves his name.

Cricieth Castle, built by Llywelyn the Great, was captured from the Princes of Gwynedd, and refortified by Edward in 1283. **Flint Castle**, built between 1277 and 1280, has walls of the Great Tower that are twenty three feet thick (7m), possibly a world record. At **Rhuddlan Castle**, in the 'ring of iron', Edward canalised the River Clwyd to enable it to be supplied from the sea.

Harlech Castle, built on a spectacular site, played a key role in Glyndŵr's national uprising in the fifteenth century, and he held a parliament there as well as in Machynlleth. Harlech is probably the most stirring of the World Heritage Listed castles in Wales, completed in 1290 and once painted a daz-

zling white. Formerly on the coastline, it stands 200 feet up on a cliff overlooking Cardigan Bay, and was captured by Owain Glyndŵr in his rebellion 120 years later. In the Wars of the Roses, Dafydd ap Ieuan ap Einion held out for the Lancastrians for eight years to a Yorkist siege, inspiring the stirring song 'Men of Harlech'. 'Black William of Raglan' eventually took the castle, but Dafydd had responded to his summons to surrender by saying, *'Once I held a castle in France till all the old women of Cymru heard about it. Now I'll hold this castle till all the old women of France hear of it.'* On the point of starvation, they marched out with flags flying and music playing, having surrendered on honourable terms. It was the last castle to hold out against the Yorkists, and one of its survivors was the 12-year-old Lancastrian, Henry Tudor, later Henry VII. In the Civil War, Harlech was defended by Royalists under Colonel William Owen against the Parliamentarians. History repeated itself as it was the last Royalist castle to hold out, its fall ending the First Civil War in 1647. Aberystwyth Castle was another link in the 'iron chain', slighted by the Parliamentarians in the English Civil War.

After Edward's successful war against Llywelyn in 1277, he built the castles at Flint, Rhuddlan, Builth Wells and Aberystwyth, and upgraded some captured Welsh castles. The second uprising by Llywelyn in 1282 saw Edward hire the greatest castle builder of the age, James of St George d'Esperanche, to extend the ring of castles around Gwynedd. These great castles of Harlech, Beaumaris, Caernarfon and Conwy cost massive amounts from the royal purse. These last four links in the

Iron Ring of castles, including the defensive town walls of Conwy and Caernarfon, have been designated a World Heritage Listed Site. Each castle was integrated with a dependent town, a *'bastide'* as in France, populated by English settlers, where the Welsh were not allowed to trade or bear arms. Bastides were given economic and other liberties, in return for defending their lords' territories.

Huge **Norman Marcher Castles** such as Chirk, Ludlow and Chepstow controlled the Marches, or borders, with Wales. After five hundred years of the Welsh fighting back the Saxons, the Norman earls of Shrewsbury, Hereford and Chester then pushed westwards over Offa's Dyke. They embarked upon a massive castle-building programme to subdue the Borders and South Wales. Caerphilly and Pembroke were two of the most powerful castles in Europe. Beyond the new Norman territories remained those inhospitable mountainous parts of Wales, that are still the strongholds of the language and culture.

There are many **Welsh native castles** such as Dolwyddelan (where Llywelyn the Great was born in 1173) and Dolbardarn. Castell Dinas Bran was built by the Prince Madog ap Gruffydd Maelor of Powys, as a superb base overlooking Llangollen, to attack the English borders. They were often taken by the Normans and Plantagenets and refortified. Some changed hands up to six times in the course of wars. Castell y Bere and Dolforwyn Castle were built by Llywelyn the Great. Ewloe was started by Llywelyn the Great in 1210 and completed in 1257 by Llywelyn the Last. Narberth Castle in Pembrokeshire was the ancient home

of Welsh princes, and features as the 'Court of Pwyll' in the Mabinogion.

In **South Wales**, **Pembrokeshire** was a major base of Norman settlement, with many castles. **Pembroke Castle** keep is eighty feet high with massive walls twenty feet thick. Because of the ever-present danger of attack, many castles stand close to the sea or on navigable estuaries and rivers, for example Tenby, Manorbier, Pembroke, Carew, Upton, Benton, Picton, Haverfordwest, Newport, and Cilgerran. Another line of castles including Roch, Wiston, Lawhaden and Narberth gave a defensive frontier, the so-called Landsker that still defines the difference between the English place-name, English-speaking territory of *'Little England Beyond Wales'*, and the troublesome Welsh on the Preseli Hills and beyond. **Carew Castle** was the site of the last medieval-style tournament held in Britain, in 1507.

Along the South Wales Coast, Tenby (in Welsh 'Dinbych Y Pysgod', 'Little Fort of the Fish') has a castle, port and well-preserved thirteenth century stone town walls. The most famous remaining gateway of this gem of a seaside resort is the Five Arches.

Cardiff Castle, up until the Second World War, was the longest continually-inhabited building in Britain. Robert Curthose, William the Conqueror's eldest son and heir, was captured at the battle of Tinchegrai in 1106 by his younger brother, Henry I. He was incarcerated in Cardiff Castle for the remaining 28 years of his life. Owain Glyndŵr sacked the castle in 1404. It now features Roman walls, a Norman shell keep on a motte, and a restored mediaeval castle with eight acres of castle green. Lottery money has been allocated to improve visitor require-ments on this magnificent site.

Caerffili Castle (Caerphilly), is the biggest castle in Britain after Windsor, and was built mainly between 1268 and 1271, after Llywelyn II destroyed the previous Norman castle. 'Red Gilbert' de Clare, the Anglo-Norman Lord of Glamorgan, built it to defend his territories from Llywelyn the Last. Its thirty acres of water defences are scarcely equalled in Europe, featuring a flooded valley, with the castle built on three artificial islands. The east wall is effectively a huge fortified dam, and together with the west walled redoubt, defends the central isle. This central core has a double concentric circuit of walls and four gatehouses. The depth and width of the moat was controlled from within the castle. The concentric system of defences was copied by Edward I in building his 'iron ring' of castles around Gwynedd. Caerffili is the only castle in the world with full-size replicas of four different 'siege-engines'. On certain days they are demonstrated, with huge stones being hurled into the lakes.

Nevertheless, Caerffili fell in Glyn-dŵr's uprising. Its leaning tower, at ten degrees tilt, out-leans that of Pisa, and was possibly damaged during the Civil War. One of the most important fortresses in Europe, when Lord Tenny-son first encountered it, he exclaimed *'This isn't a castle. It's a whole ruined town.'*

In Gwent, **Raglan Castle**, built in 1432 by William ap Thomas, held out in 1646 for King Charles against the Roundheads. After three months it was taken, mainly because Fairfax joined the siege with large cannon. Although Harlech Castle fought on,

the fall of Raglan effectively marked the end of all Royalist hopes against Cromwell. The great 'Yellow Tower of Gwent' was partially demolished after the Civil War, and was so resilient to cannon that teams of workmen had to laboriously carry out the work.

THE NATURE OF CASTLES

Castles are remarkably complicated buildings. Even if the outer walls are breached, there is then little room to use a battering ram. As there are no inner ramparts, anyone climbing on top of a wall is a simple target for those behind the inner walls. Many were surrounded by water, to make undermining the walls impossible. An attacker had to get through the Barbi-can (the outer defence defending the main gate), over a drawbridge, through the gatehouse, portcullis and machi-colations, through a bailey, another gatehouse, another bailey and then into the Keep, which was often built on a steep motte, or mound. Even if the attackers succeeded in getting into a tower or the keep, he had to charge up stairs that 'went the wrong way'. The spiral staircases wind away to the right, so going up the sword arm is obstructed by the central pillar. In some castles, there are some staircases that go in the opposite direction, so if the defending force lost a floor, it knew the easiest way to retrieve it. Another interesting device was the placing of 'false steps' on the staircase, not of the same level of the normal ones. The attacking man-at-arms would run towards the defender, eyes on his sword, keeping his impetus up, but misplace his footing and fall, just where the defender expected him to. The wonderful atmosphere of Welsh castles derives from the fact that they were never showpieces like Windsor – they saw real action, and all have a different story.

CATHEDRALS

The foundation of the Welsh cathedrals predates all the earliest other British cathedrals such as Canterbury, Westminster and Winchester by about a century. The four ancient provinces of Wales each had a dominant Celtic tribe. Gwynedd, around Snowdon, was ruled by the Deceangli; Powys, the Berwyn Hills district, was controlled by the Ordovices; Dyfed and Ceredigion, around the Plynlimon Mountains, belonged to the Demetae; and the Silures ruled Morgannwg and Gwent, around the Black Mountains. Thus the four ancient dioceses of Bangor, St Asaph, St Davids and Llandaff are at the centres of these four ancient Celtic kingdoms.

After the druids were massacred in their stronghold of the holy island of Anglesey in AD61, and the Welsh tribes finally succumbed to Rome in AD78, the Celts seemed to have adopted Christianity quickly, with a flourishing Celtic church outlasting the Roman departure in the fourth century.

St David's Cathedral (Dewi Sant) is the oldest cathedral settlement in Britain, founded by St David in 550 and based on his monastic site. The ruined Bishop's Palace of 1342 stands next to the present cathedral, which was burned down in 645, ravaged by Danes in 1078 (when the Bishop Abraham was killed), burned again in 1088 and rebuilt from 1176 by Peter de Leia. By 1120, Pope Calixtus II had decreed that

two pilgrimages to St Davids equalled one to Rome, and three pilgrimages would equate to one to Jerusalem. Santiago de Compostela in Spain was given the same dispensation, showing the importance of St Davids. St Davids boasts that it is Britain's smallest city, if we take the definition of a city as a town with a cathedral. The tower collapsed in 1220, and the structure was damaged by earthquake in 1248. Relics of St David and his confessor St Justinian are thought to be in the Holy Trinity Chapel, with its wonderful fan-vaulted ceiling.

Its situation in the Vallis Rosina, a sheltered and hidden valley, reminds one of the siting of Llanilltud Fawr, Llancarfan, and other holy sites, with the ever-present threat of Irish, then Viking destruction and desecration.

St Asaph (Asaff Sant) is the smallest cathedral in Britain, and was destroyed twice since its foundation by St Kentigern (Mungo) in his monastery at Llanelwy in AD537. His student, St Asaf, succeeded as Abbot and became the first Bishop in 560 or 570, dying around 600. Kentigern had been a missionary from the Strathclyde Britons, and also evangelised Cumbria, another remaining stronghold of the Celts. Called Mungo (corrupted Gaelic for 'my love' in Scotland), he is buried in the crypt of St Mungo's Cathedral, Glasgow. St Asaph's Bishop William Morgan (with other Welsh Bishops) finished translating the Bible into Welsh in 1588, thereby ensuring the continuation of the Welsh language.

St Deiniol founded a monastic settlement at **Bangor**, named *Y Cae Onn* (The Ash Tree) in 525, and this became a bishopric in 546, the oldest in Britain. The present Cathedral fabric dates from the 13th to 15th centuries. The Cathedral was destroyed and rebuilt by the Normans in 1071, and subsequently damaged by King John, Edward I and Owain Glyndŵr in turn. Bangor Cathedral (*Eglwys Gadeiriol Bangor*) has the longest continuous use of any of Britain's cathedrals. It is the oldest diocese in Britain, predating Canterbury by 81 years. The oldest monastery in Britain was founded in 180 in Bangor-is-Coed. By the seventh century it had an establishment of two thousand monks, of which twelve hundred were butchered after the Battle of Chester in 613. They were praying for the Princes of Powys, defending Chester from the invading King Aethelfrith of Northumbria, and were massacred. The survivors fled to Bangor, which was a related Celtic foundation. The Battles of Chester and Dyrham effectively sealed off the Celts in Wales from other Western Celts, and made the border of Wales.

Llandaf Cathedral (Eglwys Gadeiriol Llandaf), on the Taf, just north of Cardiff, was founded by St Dyfrig (Dubricius) in the 6th century, and probably contains his tomb and that of St Teilo who is also credited with founding the see. Dyfrig is also said to have established the first monastery on *Ynys Enlli* (Bardsey Island) in 615, with three pilgrimages there being regarded as the equivalent of one to Rome. In 1120 Bishop Urban of Llandaf brought Dyfrig's remains back to Llandaf to improve the prestige of his bishopric. Llandaf has claims to be the oldest bishopric with a continuous history in Britain, as a religious settlement seems to have been there very quickly after the establishment of Christianity in Wales. The Norman Bishop Urban re-dedicated the cathedral to St Peter, but

Giraldus Cambrensis later referred to it as the church of St Teilo.

Owain Glyndŵr destroyed the neighbouring Bishop's Palace, and the cathedral was hit by a German aerial mine in the Second World War. However, Llandaf has been restored with a superb sculpture by Jacob Epstein of Our Lord in Glory spanning the nave. There is work by Dante Gabriel Rossetti inside, and the Llandaf Cathedral Choir School dates back to the 9th century, possibly the oldest in Europe. There is a lovely walk alongside the River Taf to Cardiff Castle from the Cathedral.

Just outside Aberystwyth, the fifth of the ancient bishoprics, Llanbadarn Fawr, has never achieved cathedral status, although it was founded in the 6th century. With a 13th century castle, Llanbadarn is said to have minted its own coins, and was a major centre during Owain Glyndŵr's rising. The National Library of Wales was founded here in 1907, and in 1963 *Cymdeithas yr Iaith*, (The Welsh Language Society), was started. After years of Liberal voting, this is now Plaid Cymru territory.

There are other major cathedrals in Brecon and Newport.

CAVES

Dan Yr Ogof, near Abercraf, has the largest showcave complex, in the largest system of underground caverns in Western Europe, twisting and turning for 9 miles under the Swansea Valley. A further 10 miles are believed to exist. Its Cathedral Cave is named after the main feature, the Dome of St Paul's, a 42 feet (13m) high chamber approached by a long passage. Half a mile of the 9-

mile system is open to the public, with spectacular stalactites, stalagmites and a Bone Cave. As well as the caves, there are shire horses, a ski slope, dinosaur models and self-catering chalets. In the Second World War, TNT and art treasures were stored here. Photographs show the Morgan brothers exploring the three underground lakes in coracles in 1912 (see Coracle).

Ogof Ffynnon Ddu, Black Well Cave, near Abercraf, is an area of limestone plateau, crags and caves cared for by The Nature Conservancy Council. Breeding birds include the wheatear and ring ouzel. Plants in the area include limestone bedstraw, mountain melick, autumn gentian, lily-of-the-valley, mountain everlasting and mossy saxifrage. Ogof Ffynnon Ddu is the deepest cave in Britain at one thousand and ten feet (308m) and is its second longest cave.

Ogof Daren Ciliau, in Mynydd Llangatwg, Gwent, has the largest passage in any British cave, measuring sixty-five feet high (20m) by sixty-five feet wide (20m) and one thousand, three hundred and twelve feet in length (400m). Its nickname amongst cavers is 'The Time Machine'.

On the Gower Peninsula, near Parkmill, is **Cathole Cave**, inhabited by Stone Age Man ten thousand years ago, where the bones of woolly rhinoceros and mammoth have been found. In 1823 at **Paviland Cave** on the Gower coast, was found the 'Red Lady of Paviland', along with flint tools and the bones of extinct mammals. The Lady, whose bones were stained red by the local soil, was later found out to be a young man. Also on the Gower coast, at Port Eynon, is the strange cleft of limestone cliff sealed by a massive windowed wall, known as Culver

Hole. Culver is Anglo-Saxon for pigeon, so possibly it was an ancient dovecote, later used for smuggling.

Ogof Craig y Dinas in West Glamorgan is said to be where King Arthur sleeps. There are three caves associated with him in Gwynedd, in Llanllyfni, Llanuwchllyn and Snowdonia, and also three in Glamorgan, at Llantrisant, Ystradyfodwg and Pontneddfechan. Also caves in Caerleon and the Vale of Tywi claim Arthurian connections. Owain Lawgoch is supposed to lie waiting to deliver Wales in caves at Llandybie and Troed-yr-aur.

CELTIC CROSSES

Celtic crosses abound throughout Wales, with collections in the National Museum at Cardiff, Llanilltud Fawr church and Margam Abbey. The tallest Celtic cross in Britain is **Maen Achwyfan** (the Stone of Lamentation) near Holywell. The fine cross erected to Meredydd, Prince of Deheubarth, near Carew Castle, shows typical Celtic knotwork designs. The Pillar of Eliseg states that King Eliseg freed Powys from the English and is dated around AD750.

In the North aisle of Llangadwaladr Church in Aberffraw, Anglesey is **St Cadfan's Stone**, probably 8th century. It reads *'King Catamanus (Cadfan) wisest and most renowned of kings.'* In St Cadfan's Church in Tywyn, the eighth century Cadfan stone in the church is almost certainly the earliest known example of written Welsh. This gives strong support to Welsh being Europe's oldest living language.

There are three fine Celtic stones in **St Iltud's Church, Llanilltud Fawr**

(Llantwit Major). These are the Houelt Cross, for Hywel ap Rhys, king of Glywysing, the St Illtud or Samson Cross, and the Pillar of Samson, all with Latin inscriptions. Nearly all Celtic crosses have marvellous Celtic knotwork designs. The cross of Houelt is translated as *'In the name of God, the Father and the Holy Spirit, Hoult prepared this cross for the soul of Res his father.'* Hywel ap Rhys, King of Glywysing, is recorded as dying in 886, which makes the cross late 9th century. The Pillar of Samson reads *'In the name of God Most High begins the cross of the Saviour which Samson the Abbot prepared for his soul and for the soul of Iuthahelo the king and Artmail (and) Tecan.'* This is also late 9th century. The tenth century Illtud Stone, or Cross-Shaft of Samson reads *'Samson erected this cross'*, *'(Pray) For his Soul'*, *'Of Iltyd'*, *'Of Samson the King'*, *'Samuel'* and *'Ebisar'* on different panels.

According to one tradition, in the ancient churchyard at **Nevern**, the weeping red sap from the old yew trees will dry up, when Wales regains its independence. Its 13 foot high Celtic Cross of St Brynach is probably 10th century, with 21 carved panels, each enclosing a different type of love-knot pattern of endless interlacing ribbon, the symbol of eternity. St Brynach was a friend of St David, founded seven churches, and is said to have gone to Carn-Ingli mountain to die alone in 570. Another stone near the gatepost has Latin and Ogham inscriptions. In the church is the Maclogonus son of Clutari Stone, again with Latin and Ogham carvings, and another beautifully carved cross. There is also an early cross-marked stone and an inscribed stone to *Vitiliani Emereoto*, Vitalianus Emeretus. Castell Nanhyfer, the nearby multiple-banked

promontory fort, is linked with this holy site of Nevern.

There are around 50 stones with Ogham script, a series of slashes, in Wales. One such in Llandudoch St Dogmael's Church in Dyfed, has inscribed on its face 'Sagrani Fili Cunotami'. This Latin inscription, matched against the Ogham carvings on the edge of the stone, enabled scholars in 1848 to decipher for the first time the Ogham code, left by Irish visitors.

CELTS

It seems that the Beaker Folk came to Wales around 2000BC, from the Rhine area, with metals, bronze knives and battle axes. By 1000BC, the Iron Age saw these peoples grouped around large hill forts for protection, with settled farming and extensive copper mines. These Celtai (Roman) or Keltoi (Greek) formed a huge organized culture and social structure that stretched from Ireland and Spain in the West to Anatolia and the gates of Thessaloniki in the East. The Celts sacked Rome in 389BC, but a lack of political unity amongst the tribes ultimately led to defeat by the Roman legions, and the Celtic languages in continental Europe were replaced by those stemming from Latin bases (with the exception of Brittany and Spain's Galicia region).

More Celts had settled in Wales from around 600BC, bringing the La Tene art style, iron weapons instead of bronze, coins and the language. The great Celtic tribes were the Silures and Demetae in the South-East, the Cornovii in Mid-Wales and the Deceangli and Ordovices in the North. Tacitus recorded the submission of the Deceangli near

Chester, which gave us the first written record of Wales. The tribes had all submitted to Rome by AD78, but Roman rule had ended by AD390. After incursions by the Irish, during these Dark Ages, most of the energies of the native Celts were spent in fighting off the Ango-Saxon threat from the East.

The Battle of Dyrham near Gloucester, in 577, cut off the Celts in Wales from those in the West Country, especially Cornwall. The Battle of Chester in 616 effectively cut off the Welsh Celts from those of Cumbria. Thereafter, Wales was a single nation, with its princes and kings fighting constantly against not only Mercians but also Viking and Norse Invaders until the Norman Invasion in 1070. The Goidelic Celts were effectively pushed into Cornwall, Wales, Cumbria/The Lake District and South-West Scotland.

'Celtica' is a theme attraction at Machynlleth, telling 3,000 years of Celtic history with audio-visual displays, and recreations of Celtic homesteads in its 'corridor of time'. The design is the brainchild of John Sutherland, who created the Jorvic Centre at York, one of Britain's top tourist attractions. There is a recreation of a Celtic village in Wales in the first century, an 'Otherworld' and a 'magical forest' that intertwines Welsh legends and Celtic beliefs.

Parts of the Celtic Calendar survive:

November 1 – New Year's Day – the first day of Winter, when the goddess Cailleach made the ground hard, by hitting it with a hammer.

December 18 – the day of Epona, the goddess of horses.

December 21 – the longest night.

December 31 – Feast of Oimelc. Every years the Winter Hag, Cailleach, sends her dragon to kill the lamb of Brigit

of Spring. Each year the lamb wins, and celebrations are held – this is the real origin of the present New Year's Eve festivities.

January 25 – Dwynwen's Day – love tokens were exchanged.

February 1 – Imbolc – the start of the lambing season, which was also known as Ogronios – the Time of Ice.

March 21 – Alban Eiler day – the days begin to be longer than the nights.

April 30 – the Eve of Beltain – along with Oimelc, the greatest night for drinking.

May 1 – Beltain – the first day of Summer – the cattle were driven from shelter onto the grass meadows for grazing. Two bonfires were lit to represent the life-giving sun, and the cattle forced to pass between them, to protect them from evil.

June 20 – Midsummer's Eve.

June 21 – the Longest Day. Celts could stay up all night (the 'death-watch') and see the spirits of those who would die in the coming year.

July 14 – Well Day – when wishes could be made at sacred wells.

July 31 – Feast of Lughnasadh – women choose husbands, sometimes for trial marriages. There was a festivity for the gods. Crops were ripening, and the Celts wanted to ensure their safe gathering in.

September 21 – nights grow longer than days.

October 31 – Eve of Samhain – the spirits of the dead roam the land.

A CELTIC RIDDLE:
In come two legs carrying one leg,
Lay down one leg on three legs,
Out go two legs, in come four legs,
Out go five legs, in come two legs,
Snatches up three legs, flings it at four legs
And brings back one leg.

CENTRE FOR ALTERNATIVE TECHNOLOGY

A pioneering 'village of the future' near Machynlleth, which has had over a million visitors since its foundation in 1975. Styling itself *'Europe's leading eco-centre'*, it educates and entertains all ages. There is a water-powered Cliff Railway, wave power displays, water and wind turbines, solar power and organic gardens.

CHAPTER

A ground-breaking experiment, now copied all over the world. In Canton, Cardiff, two decades ago a huge, old, disused school was taken over as an Arts Centre. There are practising craft-workers, painters, sculptors, acting and dance troupes, a progressive cinema, theatre workshops, rock bands, bars and a restaurant.

CHOIRS

One of the most spine tingling events for a Welshman is to hear the National Anthem sung by a choir, or at the Millennium Stadium before a rugby international. *Mae Hen Wlad fy Nhadau* ('The Land of My Fathers'), was written by Evan James and his son James in Pontypridd last century, and a Goscombe John statue commemorates them near the famous Edwards Bridge.

Welsh language hymns, sung by male voice choirs, are the expression of pacifist rebellion against constant attack upon the Welsh language and customs. Most choirs are in what used to be the industrial South of Wales – The Treorchy Male Voice, The Pen-

dyrus, The Cwmbach Male Voice, The Morriston Orpheus, Dunvant, Dowlais are all famous. Rhos Choir in North Wales is also well-known; there used to be 50 pits around the Wrexham area. Most choirs were sustained by miners and steel workers. Now the pits have gone, it is sadly more and more difficult to get the men or the quality in the 300 remaining choirs.

CHRISTIANITY

From around AD250 Irish raiders were attacking the Western and Northern coasts of Wales. At this time of the relative peace of the 'Pax Romana', the Celtic Deisi tribes were spreading Christianity throughout South Wales. Irish attacks continued, and after the Romans left in AD390, the British tribes in Wales were being increasingly pressed by invasions of other British fleeing the Anglo-Saxon-Jute threats from England in the East. During these Dark Ages, there was the 'Age of the Saints' in Wales. The priests and monks were drawn from the higher strata of society, from the families of chiefs and princes, and some were more warrior than saint. There was an upsurge at this time in Ireland also, and Welsh and Irish monks took their message to Scotland, Cornwall, Brittany and parts of Europe.

The huge church at Llanilltud Fawr (the great church of St Illtyd) has been Anglicised into the English Llantwit Major. It is the site of the first Christian College in Britain and can claim to being the first university in Europe, instead of Bologna, where St Paulinus tutored St David. St Patrick and St David were also taught by St Illtud here around AD500. It was said that this great monastic school had over 2000 students, including kings, princes, Taliesin, Gildas and saints like St Paul Aurelian and St Samson, who became Archbishop of Dol in Brittany. This college-monastery is said to have lasted for over seven-hundred years, until the Norman conquest of the Vale of Glamorgan. The nearby town hall was a mediaeval guildhall, and next to it, the Old Swan Inn is thought to have been a banking house of Iestyn Gwrgan, the last Welsh prince of Glamorgan.

The Celtic Church was well-established, and sending missionaries all over Europe, by the time that St Augustine came from Rome to Dover in 597 to reintroduce the Christian faith to pagan England. Welsh monks had evangelised their Celtic cousins in Ireland, Brittany and Cornwall, but had wanted nothing to do with converting the hated Saxon invaders. In turn, Breton and Irish monks evangelised the continent of Europe. In his *A History of the Anglo-Saxons*, R. H. Hodgkin states *'it was a consolation to them to think that the invaders who had stolen their lands, and slain their clergy, were heading straight for hell-fire and an eternity of punishment.'*

The Welsh Church obviously did not want to be ruled by the new authority of Canterbury, with its Roman habits and allegiances. They disagreed with the date of Easter, on the type of tonsure, how to conduct baptisms, and the distancing of the priesthood from the laity. Easter was as agreed at Arles in 314, not the later date decided by the Roman church which adopted the Table of Dionysius. The Celtic-Welsh monks preferred to follow the ideas of the British monk Pelagius, whose doctrine of self-determination was the greatest theological controversy of the

fifth century. Pelagius from Usk had possibly first preached his 'heresy' from Castell Caereinion Churchyard – his doctrine that man was free from God's will, ruthlessly exterminated by the Roman church, appears to be returning to doctrinal favour at long last. The early Catholic church had formulated a doctrine whereby only the church could absolve man of his sins, preferably with money being transferred to the church treasuries. Any bypass of this profitable system simply had to be proscribed.

Augustine of Rome had landed in Kent in 597, and gradually the Saxons went over to Christianity. According to The Venerable Bede, no friend of Welshmen, Augustine invited the Welsh bishops to meet him in either 602 or 603 on the banks of the Severn, in England. His haughtiness was found distasteful by the Welsh representatives – he did not rise to meet them, so they would not acknowledge him as their archbishop, feeling that he would be even more contemptuous of them if they submitted. Although Augustine's mission to England was successful, the Celtic Christians of Wales kept their distance from these new Romanised converts. Saint Augustine gave his blessing to the Saxon armies, saying that *'if the Welsh will not be at peace with us, they shall perish at the hands of the Saxon'.* The Saxon Bede, a holy man in history, recorded with relish the victory of Aethelfrith over the Welsh at Chester in 613, including the murder of all the monks at Bangor-is-Coed. This battle helped formalise the Anglo-Welsh border for the first time, and soon the Welsh were cut off from fellow Celts in the North and the West of England.

In the second half of the seventh century, St Aldhem of Wessex complained that the Celtic Christians across the Severn not only declined to join in any act of worship with the Saxons, but would throw any scraps of food left by the Saxons to dogs and pigs, and refused even to eat off the same dishes until they had been thoroughly scoured with cinders or sand. The Welsh Celtic Church was not formally united with the Catholic church for two-hundred years, and did not accept all its strange practices for another six centuries. Easter was not altered to the Roman date until 768, and the use of married clergy persisted until 1138.

In 1091 a Breton was appointed by the Normans to be Bishop of Bangor, followed by a Norman Bishop of Llandaf (Urban) in 1107 and another Norman at St David's in 1115 (Bernard). The Welsh church, despite the best efforts of Giraldus Cambrensis, succumbed to the Norman Catholicism of Canterbury in 1203. Norman bishops controlled Welsh sees, and Norman priests took over many churches. It is a wonder that the language survived this influx of influence.

The translation of the Book of Common Prayer in 1551, and of the New Testament in 1567 by William Salesbury, and the translation of the entire Bible in 1588 secured the survival of the language (see Language). About this time, John Penry of Cefn Brith, Powys, was calling the Anglican bishops *'soul murderers'*, and he was hanged for treason in 1593. This saintly Christian's four daughters were named Sure Hope, Safety, Comfort and Deliverance.

In 1639 the first Nonconformist chapel in Wales was established, the so-called *'Jerusalem of Wales'*, at Llanvaches in Monmouthshire. It was followed in 1649 by the first Baptist chapel at Ilston in Gower, and also by 1649 the Quakers had established their prayer meetings. Because of relentless persecution by the established church, over 2000 Welsh Quakers had emigrated to Pennsylvania before the 1689 Act of Religious Tolerance.

A governing elite had taken over the churches by the 18th century. Between 1714 and 1870 no Welsh-speaking bishops were appointed to a Welsh see. One Bishop of Llandaf lived in the remote Lake District of England, and one Bishop of Bangor probably never entered Wales, but placed his nominees in all the livings in his see.

Hywel Harris led the Methodist Revival in Wales from 1735, and founded a religious settlement, *'The Connexion'*, at Trefeca near Talgarth. The members farmed the land and lived a strictly communal life in the 18th century, the precursor of many modern movements in Christianity. This revival swept Wales, and originated independently of English Methodism, following the strict doctrines of John Calvin rather than the teachings of John Wesley. The established Church of England soon came to be seen as the church of the gentry and of 'the English', whereas the common people went to 'chapel'. The power of the spoken word and the fervour of hymn singing hit a strong chord with the Welsh, allied to a natural hostility to an established church, with absentee English placemen as rectors.

Thus the first Methodist chapel was built at Groes Wen, near Caerphilly, in 1742. The Methodists really kick-started the Nonconformist Revival into the force it became, entering nearly everyone's lives. Before long, the Welsh church wanted separation (once again) from the Church in England – Disestablishment. With over 5000 chapels, more than in England and Scotland combined, the movement was a great force in preserving the Welsh language. (The separatist movement also gave us the longest 'natural' word in the English language – *'antidisestablishmentarianism'*).

The downside of this revival was the Calvinist suppression of popular music and dance, self-denial being the answer to this life's cares, and the constant competition for men's souls betwteen the different sects of Baptists, Methodists, Calvinist Methodists etc. With their separate chapels, there came to be more places of worship per head of population in Wales than any other country in the world.

That wonderful poet, Idris Davies, summed up many of his countrymen's attitudes to the more strict sects in his poem 'Capel Calvin':

'There's holy holy people
They are in capel bach –
They don't like surpliced choirs,
They don't like Sospan Fach.

They don't like Sunday concerts,
Or women playing ball,
They don't like Williams Parry much
Or Shakespeare at all.

They don't like beer or bishops,
Or pictures without texts,
They don't like any other
Of the nonconformist sects.

And when they go to Heaven
They won't like that too well,
For the music will be sweeter
Than the music played in Hell.'

Llanfihangel-y-Pennant is the village of Mary Jones, the 16-year-old girl who walked barefoot over the mountains to Bala in 1800 to buy a Welsh Bible with all her savings. This event inspired the formation of The Bible Society, whose London headquarters still treasures and displays her Bible.

By the middle of the 19th century, 80% of the population belonged to a chapel, and by 1891 the Liberal Party controlled Wales, because of the Liberals' platform of anti-establishment policies and opposition to the landlords. In 1906 the Liberal Government passed a law disestablishing the Church of England in Wales.

CIVIL WAR

In the English Civil War, Oliver Cromwell's New Model Army was the element that swung the war towards the Parliamentary forces and led to the Inter-regnum. Cromwell was the son of Sir Henry Cromwell. Henry Cromwell's father was Richard Williams, a Welshman who took the name of his uncle and patron, Thomas Cromwell. Most of Wales stayed Royalist during the Civil War, with the notable exceptions of the soldier/politicians John Jones and Philip Jones. The former was one of the signatories of the death warrant of King Charles I, and was himself executed on the return of Charles II in 1660. The latter was conveniently absent on his Welsh estates around Fonmon Castle when it was time to sign, and prospered under both Cromwell and King Charles II.

The Battle of St Fagans effectively was the last in the Second Civil War. The mainly Welsh Royalists were routed by the Parliamentarians and two-hundred and fifty Welsh prisoners were despatched to Barbados as indentured slaves for the rest of their lives.

CLIMATE

Wales is warmed by the Gulf Steam, and has a similar climate to Eire and Brittany. The old joke is that *'if you cannot see the mountains, it's raining – if you can see the mountains, it is going to rain'*. As a result of this climate, described as 'temperate', Pembrokeshire produces the earliest new potatoes in mainland Britain.

Dale Peninsula in Pembroke sometimes lays claim to the highest sunshine levels in Britain, with an annual average over 1800 hours. It is also one of the windiest places in Britain, with wind speeds of over 100mph having occurred at least 5 times since the Second World War.

Llyn Llydaw in Snowdon has the highest recorded monthly rainfall in Great Britain, with 56.5 inches, 1436mm in October 1909, and 246 inches fell in 1922 in Llyn Glaslyn in Gwynedd, ten times the London rate. The peak of Snowdon is the wettest place in Britain, with an average of 180 inches per year (4500mm), and a record of 246 inches (6200mm) in 1922. In Cowbridge (Y Bontfaen) 2.9 inches of rain fell in half and hour in 1880 – Wales can be one of the wettest places in Europe.

The longest lasting rainbow ever recorded, visible for over 3 hours, was reported on the coastal border of Clwyd and Gwynedd on 14 August 1979.

Britain's greatest snowfall over 12 months was 60 inches, 1524mm, in the Denbighshire Hills, Clwyd, in 1947 (shared with Upper Teesdale).

The highest recorded earthquakes in Great Britain were both in Wales, in the Llŷn Peninsula, 19th July 1984, and in Swansea, 27th June 1906, both measuring 4.8 on the Richter Scale.

Apart from The Bay of Fundy in Nova Scotia, the Severn Channel experiences the greatest difference between high and low tides in the world. Chepstow in Gwent had a difference in tidal range of over 50 feet in 1883, and Barry and Cardiff Docks have regular ranges of around forty feet (13m). This allows for great expanses of mud flats to assist waders and other wildlife.

COAL

'Black Gold' originally referred to Welsh Black Cattle, when they were herded to England in the Middle Ages onwards. The discovery of vast amounts of the 'Black Diamond' or the other 'Black Gold' effectively changed the nature of much of Wales forever. The beautiful wooded valleys of Rhondda Fach and Rhodda Fawr were suddenly filled with tightly-packed terraced communities made up of workers from all over Britain and Ireland.

Since Mrs Thatcher's decision to rely on subsidised foreign coal rather than the most efficient coal producing industry in the world, employment in the coalfields has collapsed. There were only 28 pits still open at the end of the miners' strike in 1984.

There are now only three of the 28 pits left. Tower Colliery is the only deep pit left in Wales, with just 240 employees, and a very limited lifespan. There are two drift mines in Betws and Cwmgwili employing around another 220 men. There are some large-scale open-cast operations run by Celtic Energy, producing around 2.5 million tonnes per annum. It is a far cry from the 1930s when Wales produced coal for a third of the world's consumption, and there were over 65 pits in The Rhondda alone. In 1913, over 250,000 men worked underground; now there are just 1500 colliers including overground staff. The present total output of Welsh pits is around 3 million tonnes, compared to 57 million tonnes in the old days. Forty per cent of Welsh coal goes to one power station at Aberthaw, and at the time of any renewal of contract we may see a switch to subsidised imports from Poland, Vietnam, Colombia or South Africa. Cardiff and Barry shipped a world record 13 million tonnes in 1913; now nothing goes out.

The coal industry has been in decline since the change of propulsion from coal to oil in the shipping industry. As Home Secretary, Winston Churchill sent English troops to keep order in Tonypandy, an act that ensured his eternal unpopularity in the Welsh Valleys, despite his heroic role in the Second World War.

In August 1914, the South Wales Miners' Federation proposed an international miners' strike to stop the outbreak of war, and there continued to be an anti-war movement in the South Wales mining areas. A massive increase in food prices, coupled with record profits for coal-owners, caused a demand for a new wage agreement in 1915 which was refused, so the South Wales miners went on strike. They were opposed by the Government, coal-owners, Great Britain Miners' Federation and the national newspapers, and the government threatened to imprison any strikers. However, the strike was solid. The then Minister of Munitions, Welshman David Lloyd George, intervened and settled the strike, acceding to most of the demands of the South Wales Miners' Federation.

Disputes continued, however, and in 1916 the Government took over control of the South Wales Coalfield. A year later, all other coalfields were effectively nationalised by the state, and in 1919 a Royal Commission recommended the continuation of nationalisation, as being in the best interests of the state and miners. After appearing to accept the Report, the Government handed back control of the industry in 1921 to the coal-owners.

The coal-owners demanded lower wages, and on 1st April 1921, began a lock-out of the million miners in Britain who refused to accept the new terms. After three months, the South Wales Miners' Federation accepted defeat, after not being supported by the Transport Workers and Railwaymen, who reneged on their promise of solidity with the miners.

In 1926, the miners refused to work an extra hour a day, coupled with large pay cuts of 16-25%. On 30th April 1926 those miners refusing the terms were locked out and the pits stopped producing. On 3rd May the General Strike, called by the TUC, began. The mood in South Wales was almost revolutionary at this time and when the TUC called off the strike just nine days later, the Welsh were left to fight on alone. Almost a quarter of a million men stayed away from the pit-heads. Police were called in from outside Wales to keep order, until the starving miners were forced back to work at the end of 1926. The effects on that South Walian generation solidified a feeling of 'us against the world' for decades. Once again, we return to Idris Davies to sum up the mood of the times, in a verse from 'Gwalia Deserta':

'Do you remember 1926? That summer of soups and speeches,

The sunlight on the idle wheels and the
*   deserted crossings,*
And the laughter and cursing in the
*   moonlit streets ?*
Do you remember 1926 ? The great
*   dream and the swift disaster,*
The fanatic and the traitor, and more
*   than all,*
The bravery of the simple, faithful folk?
"Ay, ay, we remember 1926," said Dai
*   and Shinkin,*
As they stood on the kerb in Charing
*   Cross Road,*
"And we shall remember 1926 until our
*   blood is dry."...'*

Between 1921 and 1936, investment fell in the industry, and 241 mines were closed in South Wales, with the number of working miners falling from 270,000 to 130,000. One company owned 80% of anthracite coal production in South Wales, so kept the screw tight on employment and wages. In Dowlais, 73% of men were without work. 500,000 people left South Wales between the wars, looking for work. Edward VIII had made a famous visit to the coal-mining valleys in 1936, telling the 200,000 unemployed miners struggling through the Great Depression, 'Something must be done. You may be sure that all I can do for you I will.' Within three weeks he had abdicated, never returning to Wales.

H. V. Morton, in *In Search of Wales*, 1932, reports a South Wales miner in the 1930s as saying:

'Some of the worst cases of hardship I've known have been in homes where the father was trying to keep six children on £2 5s. a week and was too proud to accept help off anyone . . . When you're on a shift you fall out for twenty minutes and eat bread and

butter, or bread and cheese which your wife puts in your food tin . . . One day we were sitting like this talking when Bill didn't answer . . . He'd fainted. So I lifted him and carried him to the pit bottom to send him home, but before I did this I gathered up his food tin. There wasn't a crumb in it ! He'd been sitting there in the dark pretending to eat, pretending to me − his pal − Now that's pride.'

In the 1960s seventy-four coal mines closed, and by 1985, only thirty-one were left. In 1996, only one deep pit, owned by the workers, is holding on at Tower. From 1948, with two hundred and fifty pits employing 113,000 miners, we have one deep mine, with just 240 colliers.

In the disastrous 1984 national miners' strike, the Welsh pits were the last to return to work. Maerdy, known as Little Moscow, was the last pit in the Rhondda, which closed in 1990. An Ogmore Vale collier defended the strike − 'Why on earth do they think we're fighting to defend stinking jobs in the pitch black? There are no lavatories or lunch-breaks, no lights or scenery . . . We're fighting because our community and our culture depends on it.'

Of course, coal has been a mixed blessing for Wales − it attracted people from all over Britain to the unspoilt Welsh valleys, who assimilated into the Welsh culture. It gave jobs, albeit dangerous ones. Miners' children were encouraged to 'improve' themselves and get into teaching rather than go down the pit. There is still a disproportionate number of Welsh people in British education at all levels. There were some terrible disasters, like the Senghennydd explosion. However, nothing in Welsh history hurt the nation as much as the Aberfan disaster of 1966. A coal slag tip, which the National Coal Board had been repeatedly warned was unstable, collapsed down a mountainside onto the village. The village primary school was drowned in black slurry, with one hundred and sixteen children and twenty-eight adults killed. A Disaster Appeal raised money for the remaining parents and the village, to build a new, smaller, school and make a memorial cemetery. £150,000 was taken out of the villagers' Disaster Fund by the Government to pay for the removal of the coal waste in 1967. In 1997, after thirty years' campaigning by Plaid Cymru, the Government repaid the money. However, they did not repay the £1.5 million it is worth now, but just the original £150,000.

The legacy of coal was that it changed South and North-East Wales and in two ways – the first is the obvious scarring of the landscape. Compare these two descriptions of the Rhondda Valley:

'The valley stretched for a distance of eight or ten miles between two nearly parallel lines of hills, broken by a succession of cliffs of singular beauty . . . The emerald greenness of the meadows in the valley was most refreshing . . . The air is aromatic with the wild flowers and mountain plants. A Sabbath stillness reigns . . . it is the gem of Glamorganshire.' – C. Cliffe 1847.

'The river Rhondda is a dark, turgid and contaminated gutter, into which is poured the refuse of the host of collieries which skirt the thirteen miles of its course. The hills have been stripped of all their woodland beauty and there they stand, rugged and bare, with immense rubbish heaps covering their

surface . . . The whole length of the valley has become transformed . . . the din of steel engines, the whirr of machinery, the grating sound of coal screens, and the hammering of the smithies proceed increasingly night and day, year in and year out. An unheard of wealth of industry and a great population have simultaneously sprung up together during the past sixty years . . . The industrial townships of this valley appear to be inseparably connected in one continuous series of streets of workmen's cottages to Pontypridd.' – Arthur Morris 1908.

So the valleys are scarred, but this population explosion in many ways reinvigorated Wales. Just from 1901 to 1910 the South Wales coalfield attracted 129,000 people, most from England. Wales was attracting immigrants from England, Scotland and Ireland at an annual rate of 4.5 per 1,000, almost as high as the new golden world of the U.S.A.

The history of Welsh coal mining can be glimpsed at today by visiting one of a number of mining museums. Big Pit, at Blaenafon, was sunk in 1860, but some galleries were worked for fifty years previously. It is now open as a mining museum, and the guided underground tour requires miners' helmets, and a three hundred feet (90m) drop in a pit cage to the coal seam.

Afan Argoed at Cymmer is the Welsh Miners' Museum, giving visitors an insight into the hardships of the old colliers and their communities. Little children pulled coal wagons 10-12 hours a day, 6 days a week, for two old pennies (less than one new penny) and were forced to repay one penny for the cost of their candles. Many ex-miners still suffer in agony from "The Dust" in their lungs, pneumoconiosis or silicosis, and in 1999 an historic legal judgement has led to compensation payments being made to surviving miners or miners' widows.

The Cefn Coed Colliery Museum in the Dulais Valley also simulates life underground, based at the Blaenant Colliery which was one of the last Welsh mines to close in 1990. The Rhondda Heritage Park is based around the former pits at Lewis Merthyr and Tŷ Mawr collieries in Trehafod.

COAST

Welsh Water is the only water company in the United Kingdom to practise full treatment on sewage effluent. As a result, Wales' beaches are becoming cleaner. Of all the bathing beaches in England, Scotland, Northern Ireland and Wales, only 45 are 'Blue Flag' beaches. Wales has no less than a third of these and the water company's aim is to raise this number of Welsh beaches to 50 by the year 2000. Wales has the cleanest rivers in Europe, and is on target to have the cleanest beaches.

The European 'Blue Flag' 1998 beaches are Rest Bay, Porthcawl; Port Eynon and Caswell Bay, Gower; Lydstep haven, Newgale, Tenby North and Whitesands, Pembrokeshire; Pwllheli, Barmouth, Abersoch and Dinas Dinlee, Gwynedd; and Llanddona and Llanddwyn on the island of Anglesey.

The only National Park based on coastline is that of Pembrokeshire.

CORACLES

The Romans described Celtic tribes using boats covered with skins, which have survived as the Irish 'curragh' or the Welsh 'cwrwgl' or coracle. With a basketwork frame, these one-man and two-man boats are extremely difficult to learn to handle, but ideal for netting sewin (sea-trout) and salmon when worked in pairs.

Dating from around the time of Christ, these primitive boats are used in the tidal Tywi river by twelve fishermen, with hereditary licences to net salmon. They are saucer-shaped replicas of the skin-covered boats used by the ancient Britons, which now use canvas stretched over wooden laths.

Designs and materials varied a great deal, depending upon the build of the fisherman and the type and flow of river – there are thirteen known different designs, Teifi, Tywi, Taf, Cleddau, Ironbridge Severn, Welshpool Severn, Shrewsbury Severn, Conwy, Upper Dee Llangollen, Lower Dee Bangor and Overton, Usk and Wye, Dyfi and Loughor.

The largest display in Europe of different types of coracles is in the Welsh Folk Museum at St Fagans. There is the National Coracle Centre, including nine varieties of Welsh coracle, and examples from Vietnam, Iraq, India and North America, at Cenarth Falls in Carmarthenshire. The best place to see these pre-Roman boats in action used to be on the River Teifi at Cenarth.

There is a coracle regatta every August in Cilgerran, near the craggy castle where Nest (Helen of Wales) was abducted by a Welsh prince from her Norman husband in 1109.

Coracle fishing is now only practised on three Welsh rivers, the Teifi, Tywi and Taf.

Salmon fishermen, in the four villages of Llechryd, Cenarth, Abercuch and Cilgerran on the Teifi, formed closed communities where particular reaches of the river belonged to each village. In 1807, Malkin wrote that there was *'scarcely a cottage in the neighbour-hood without its coracle hanging by the door'*.

The 1923 Salmon and Freshwater Fisheries Act effectively stopped all coracle fishing on the Severn, and restricted fishing severely on other Welsh rivers. Opposition from fly fisher-men and legislation has almost killed the craft – licences are not renewed, and generally with the death of a coracle man, the licence is withdrawn on that particular river. Only a few remain.

CRACHACH

Sean O'Neill gave an unbiased Irish view of this Welsh phenomenon in The Daily Telegraph in 1998. The 'crachach' *'is a university-educated, Welsh-speaking grouping with positions mainly in publicly-funded or recently-privatised bodies and service on the governing committees of universities, museums and charities.'* He goes on to name prominent Welsh people in positions of power, and quotes Dr. Deian Hopkin as saying *'Wales does not have that great, eminent, dominant, rich landed aristocracy that England has, so it has created a surrogate aristocracy, people who have rank and esteem depending on their contribution and role within Welsh society . . . In England, the dynastic link is often done by transfer of title or money. In Wales, there is a kind of cultural heritage handed on from generation to generation'*.

Crachach translates as *'petty gentry, conceited upstarts and snobs'*, and those outside its boundaries tend to dislike

it. Dr Kim Howells MP calls it *'the colonial class which runs Wales because they are born into certain families rather than because they are good at their jobs'*, deriding it as *'probably the most effective back-scratching organisation outside Sicily'*. Howells goes on to complain that *'it is dominated by a public school educated, Welsh-speaking elite. It has a very restricted membership but has grown over the last two decades as the result of the growth in Welsh language broadcasting, which offered a nice career structure, and the rising num-ber of quangos'*.

CRAFTS

Potters, wood-carvers, ceramicists, textile artists and painters exist in every corner of Wales. Welsh copper lustre pottery, of the type that used to adorn Welsh dressers all over Wales, is now only made in Aberthaw Pottery, Glamorgan. The owners learned about its manu-facture from the last surviving maker, just ten years ago. The oldest surviving pottery in Wales is at Ewenni, near Bridgend. It allowed its ancient bee-hive kiln to be moved to the Museum of Welsh Life, where the potter still makes the beautiful traditional *'wassail bowls'*.

At old Woollen Mills at Trefriw, Penmachno, Capel Dewi, Brynkir, Solva, Castle Morris, Dre-fach Felin-dre, Swansea Maritime Museum and at the Museum of Welsh Life, one can watch the processes of carding, spin-ning, dyeing and weaving to make traditional Welsh shawls, bed-covers and the like. There are also old work-ing flour mills open to the public at Pengoes and Llanddeusant (a working windmill), and a brochure on all these and more Welsh mills is available from the Welsh Mills Society, Y Felin, Ty'n-y-Graig, Ystrad Meurig, Ceredigion SY25 6AE.

From the sixteenth century, 'lovespoons' were carved out of a single block of wood, over the winter, by farmhands to give their sweethearts. The were also presented by young men to girls to try and start a relationship. The more difficult and intricate to carve, the more the lovespoon symbolised the maker's love. Some very intricate seventeenth century ones can be seen at the *Welsh Folk Museum* at St Fagans. Craftsmen throughout Wales will sell or make special lovespoons, which seem to have been the origin of the word 'spooning' so beloved by 1930s popular songwriters: *'then we will spoon, to my honey I'll croon, sweet tunes'* in *By the Light of the Silvery Moon*.

The most expensive lovespoons are those featuring wooden spheres in a long cradle, held by chain links. It may be that the love spoon represented an early type of engagement ring, or that its presentation and acceptance confirmed the beginning of a serious courtship. Certain symbols represent promises or wishes – triple spoons are a couple and a hoped-for family, a wheel is a willingness to work hard for a loved one, a key symbolises 'my house is yours', flowers mean courtship, and balls in a cage mean captured love or the number of children desired.

Another popular craft has been making 'corn dollies', which can be bought in many souvenir shops. Their origin is *Y Gaseg Fedi* ('The Harvest Mare'), celebrating the last sheaf of corn to be harvested. This last tuft of corn, symbolising the forces of natural growth, was plaited carefully, and a

contest followed where the workers took it in turns to shape it with their reaping hooks. The successful reaper then shouted a traditional rhyme (in Carmarthenshire the last line was *'I've got a little harvest mare'*). He then had to try to carry it to the harvest feast without it being soaked by women throwing water. If he succeeded, he sat in a place of honour and could drink as much beer as he wanted. If he failed, he was ritually scorned and was not offered beer. The harvest mare was kept in the house until the next harvest as a decoration. Over time they became more and more ornamental and complex.

CREMATION

Llantrisant in Mid-Glamorgan has a hill fort and provided the Black Prince's finest archers for The Hundred Years' War. However, its main claim to fame is its 19th century doctor/druid, Dr. William Price, who proselytised not just vegetarianism, nudity, and free love, but also the unhealthiness of socks, the potential dangers on the environment from rapid industrialisation, revolution, republicanism and radical politics. He refused to treat patients who would not give up smoking, and prescribed a vegetarian diet instead of pills. Born at Rudry, on 4th March 1800 he qualified as a doctor at the age of 21. He was the first doctor to be elected by a group of factory workers as their own general practitioner, being paid a weekly deduction out of wages paid at the Pontypridd Chainworks. This was the precursor of the miners' medical societies, which were, in turn, the origin of the National Health Service.

A skilled surgeon, he attended Chartist rallies in a cart drawn by goats. He was forced to escape to France (in a frock) to live in 1839, after taking part in the terrible Chartist Riots in Newport, and returned seven years later. He held druidic ceremonies at the rocking stone near Pontypridd, which were considered satanic by the local Methodists. He did not approve of marriage as it 'reduced the fair sex to the condition of slavery' and lived openly 'in sin' with his young housekeeper. This precursor of the Hippy Movement had a son when he was eighty-three, and named him 'Iesu Grist'(Jesus Christ). When in 1884 Iesu died, aged five months, Dr Price cremated him on an open funeral pyre. Price was dressed in flowing druidical robes and timed the event to take place as the locals were leaving their chapels.

The local population attacked him, rescuing the charred remains of the child, and the police arrested Price. The mob then went to find the mother, Price's young housekeeper, Gwenllian, but were deterred by Price's twelve large dogs. The doctor was acquitted after a sensational trial in Cardiff and cremation was legalized in Britain as a result. Another infant was born, named 'Iarlles Morgannwg', the 'Countess of Glamorgan' and in one of his many law-suits he called the child as assistant counsel to him. He issued medallions to commemorate his legal victory, and at the age of ninety had another son, again called Iesu Grist. At the age of ninety-three he died and was cremated in front of twenty thousand spectators at East Carlan Field, Llantrisant. This was the first legalised cremation (1893) and a ton of coal and three tons of wood were used to accomplish the mission. Price had organised the cremation himself, selling tickets in advance to the estimated twenty thousand people that later attended it. Llantrisant's pubs ran dry.

Price, with a long flowing beard and hair past shoulder-length, habitually wore only the national colours of red, white and green. On his head was a red fox-skin pelt, with the front paws on his forehead and the tail hanging down his back. His cloak was white, his waistcoat scarlet, and he wore green trousers – the colours of Wales. In 1838 he started building an eight-storey druidic temple, of which the gatehouses are lived in today.

Dr. Price's last dying act was to order and drink a glass of champagne before he moved on to his next destination.

He had dreamed of 'a golden age' when Wales would once again be ruled by Druids. His birthplace, the Green Meadow Inn at Waterloo, near Newport, was in the news in 1996. Discovery Inns wished to demolish it, to put up 13 dwellings. CADW, the historic monuments society in Wales, washed their hands of the matter, although the local community desperately wants to save this historic site.

CROMLECHAU AND STONE CIRCLES

CROMLECHAU
Wales has many stone circles and standing stones, some dating from the times of the pyramids, and has the highest density in Britain of dolmens, or cromlechs, groups of massive stones holding a capstone. The great Tinkinswood Cromlech, just outside Cardiff, was possibly the burial site for hundreds of people. Dating from 4000BC, its capstone of 40.6 tonnes is the largest

in Britain. A mile away, the ten feet (3m) high St Lythan's Cromlech, is also known as *Gwal-y-Filiast*, the 'Kennel of the Greyhound Bitch'.

Pentre Ifan, on the Preseli Hills, looks over Cardigan Bay, and is possibly the most revered Welsh site because of its situation. Made of the same Preseli bluestones as Stonehenge, its capstone is sixteen feet (5m) across. The inner circle at Stonehenge originally consisted of forty to fifty of these holy 'bluestones', each nine to ten feet high, two to three feet wide and weighing up to two tons each. Laboriously cut and shaped by flint, they were probably dragged down to ancient Narberth, rafted up the Bristol Channel, and dragged across to the Wiltshire Plains on rollers.

Anglesey's Bryn Celli Ddu is a 'passage grave' type of burial chamber, where a long passage leads to a central chamber with an upright stone, possibly used for sacrifices.

The impressive Neolithic Burial Chamber, Barclodiad-y-Gawres, at Rhosneigr, Anglesey, has inside it five standing stones ornamented with zigzags, spirals, lozenges and chevrons. The only parallel in the British Isles is probably New Grange in Ireland. The majority of these communal burial chambers, cromlechau, are found in Anglesey, with about fifty, and Pembrokeshire with forty five. They are similar to other megalithic monuments as far away as India. Excavation revealed a strange and ancient 'witches' broth' consisting of frogs, toads, snakes, mice, (sacred) hares, eels, wrasse and whiting. Other important Neolithic monuments are the Long House Cromlech at Trefin, Tŷ Isaf in the Black Mountains, and Capel Garmon near Llanrwst.

There are some fascinating burial

mounds left that have legends attached to them. Bedd Taliesin, the Grave of Taliesin, is on the slopes of Moel-y-Garn, near Talybont. Taliesin was a famous bard and warrior, perhaps a contemporary of Merlin. The barrow only consists now of a long stone slab and cairn, as many stones were removed for building. In the nineteenth century, local people tried to remove Taliesin's bones to re-inter them on a Christian burial site. During excavation, lightning struck the ground nearby, and the workers fled, never to try again.

Taliesin was also one of the seven warriors who survived Bran's invasion of Ireland. The story is recounted in the Mabinogion. Bedd Branwen (Branwen's Grave) is on the banks of the river Alaw, a mile north of Anglesey's Treffynon Church. This cromlech was excavated in 1813, and a Celtic urn, inside a stone chest, with the cremated bones of a woman were found. Her brother was Bran, who died when he attempted to bring her back from King Matholwch of Ireland. According to The Mabinogion, she died of a broken heart because of the destruction carried out in her name, at the place where the female bones were found. Local farmers carried away most of the stone for building after 1813, and now one large stone remains there, Carreg Branwen (Branwen's Stone).

STANDING STONES AND CIRCLES
Trelech, the Place of Stones, in Gwent, has three huge standing stones. Many Christian churches were superimposed upon earlier holy sites. Embedded in the porch of Corwen church is Carreg y Big yn y Fach Rewlyd (the 'Pointed Stone in the Cold Hollow'). At Maentwrog, Twrog's stone stands beside the church porch, as does Maen Llog out-

side Trallwng (Welshpool) Church. Llanaden and Old Radnor churches are also situated near sacred stones. Four standing stones form part of the churchyard wall at Yspyty Cynfyn.

Maen Huail (Huail's Stone) stands in St Peter's Square in Ruthin. Huail was killed by his brother King Arthur, either for killing Arthur's nephew Gwydre fab Llwyd (according to Caradog's 'Life of Gildas'), or for stealing Arthur's mistress (according to Elis Gruffydd's 'The Soldier of Calais' Chronicle). Huail was beheaded on this stone.

Standing stones and Celtic crosses are often associated with holy places (*llanau*) and saints in Wales. One Welsh treasure now in the British Museum in London is the stone from Llywel near Trecastle in Powys, with fifth century inscriptions in Ogham and Latin, and symbols and pictograms on three panels. A cast is now in Brecon museum.

On the Preseli Hills, Gors-Fawr stone circle has fifteen glacier boulders and two pointer stones. The Druid's Circle near Penmaenmawr has a diameter of eighty feet, and Llanaber in Merioneth has two stone circles of one hundred and twenty feet and one hundred and seventy six feet. An ancient stone avenue of one hundred and fifty feet leads into Llanrheadr ym Mochnant.

Many ancient monuments have been built over, ploughed over, broken up for building materials, or, like St Baruch's holy fifth century well on Barri Island, been ashphalted over to make way for a car park. Another act of vandalism (and there are thousands, even in this more enlightened century) happened to Sarn-y-Bryn-Caled Timber Circle near Powys Castle. Aerial photography showed a prehistoric ritual and funerary site on the floodplains of the Severn, and 1990s excavations showed it to be a huge timber double circle built c.2100BC, a possible prototype henge for Stonehenge. The Welshpool bypass now covers it.

CROMWELL

Morgan Williams of Llanishen, now a northern suburb of Cardiff, moved to London to become a brewer and inn-keeper. He married a daughter of Walter Cromwell of Putney. Their son Richard adopted his mother's name, as Thomas Cromwell was of great importance in Henry VIII's court. Richard Williams was made a baronet and Privy Councillor in 1527, and his sons and grandsons signed their names as 'Cromwell alias Williams'. In his early years so did his great grandson, Oliver Cromwell, who overthrew King Charles I and set up the parliamentary republic in Britain (see Civil War).

One unresolved mystery relating to Cromwell is in Jamaica. As well as the famous Cardiff Arms Hotel, named after the long-demolished Cardiff pub, there is a Great House on the massive Cardiff Hall plantation, surrounded by estates and beaches named after Llandovery. The mysterious builder of the Hall was supposed to have been a Welshman who was known as Captain James Blagrove, who fled Britain after trying to assassinate Cromwell. The Great House was built in 1789 for the Blagrove family. The house was built so it was hidden from pirates, and the actor Peter Finch later lived there.

CUSTOMS

Many Welsh folk customs died out during the 'reign of terror' of nonconformist righteousness in the nineteenth century, but it is interesting to comment upon one type of social control exerted on the community by a custom called **y ceffyl pren**, 'the wooden horse'. An effigy of a person who had offended the moral code was paraded on a wooden pole, and a noisy procession of people banging saucepans and chanting approached the house of the victim. A typical cause of such an event might be a potential mis-match in the age of two people about to be wed. Adultery was also often punished by the members of the procession tying the offending couple back to back and pelting them with rotten eggs. Mock courts were sometimes held last century, and in Llanfyllin, Montgomeryshire, a ceffyl pren was taken to the door of a husband and wife who quarrelled openly, and a traditional verse dialogue recited to the argumentative couple. It has been said that the Rebecca Riots (see riots) were an extension of the ceffyl pren as a means of keeping social norms intact.

Around New Year in Llangynwyd, the traditional **'Mari Lwyd'** ('Grey Mary' or 'Grey Mare') celebrations still involve rhyming and a roaming artificial 'horse', one with rather a different function to *ceffyl pren*. All over South Wales until this century, the Christmas and New Year saw people taking from door to door a horse's skull covered with a white sheet, and decorated with colourful ribbons. A man underneath the sheet could open and close the 'mare's jaw'. The party, often dressed up as Punch and Judy, Leader, Sergeant and Merryman, sang outside a house until they were permitted to enter, and the mari would chase any girls around the house, snapping its jaws. It seems now to be

only carried out in Llangynwyd, Glamorgan. In Tregatwg (Cadoxton), Barry, the custom was carried out on Christmas Eve until the early 1900s, as was **Sul y Blodau**, whitewashing and bedecking graves with flowers on Palm (Flowering) Sunday. Another Tregatwg custom was blocking the church exit of a newly-married man unless he gave everyone money for a drink to toast his health. With the influx of strangers to build Barry Docks (the population of Tregatwg and Barry rose from 500 to 33,763 between 1881 and 1911), this custom also atrophied. Records of 1892 show however, that a newly-wed 'Happy Billy' was dragged roughly along the graveyard of St Cadoc's Church, for refusing to acknowledge the local custom.

Wassailing and 'Hunting the Wren' were also carried out in this same time, from Christmas Eve to Twelfth Night, and may be associated with a pre-Christian fertility cult. Revellers called at houses, accompanied by a beautiful wassail bowl with looped handles. Once in a house, the bowl would be filled with warm spiced beer, and sometimes apples, and there would be ritual singing and dancing, wishing the family health and good crops and livestock. Wassailing was also celebrated on 2nd February, the Feast of Mary of the Candles, and on May Day, and typical ornamental bowls can be bought at The Museum of Welsh Life at Saint Fagans.

Hunting the Wren involved men in Pembrokeshire carrying a covered cage with a wren in it, the funeral 'bier' being covered with ribbons, to the house of a sweetheart of one of the men. They sang carols, and also visited other houses, where they drank beer. The ceremony was still carried out in the early 1900s, and is thought that originally the wren was sacrificed as a fertility rite for livestock and the land. Many old customs, such as the 'wren house', 'candlemass', 'hel solod' and the 'Mayor of Wakes' are described in Trefor Owen's *Pocket guide to The Customs and Traditions of Wales*.

Calennig was the custom of giving a New Year's gift. On New Year's morning children would go from house to house, carrying an apple or orange fixed on three short wooden skewers, and decorated with oats and holly. The children sang or chanted wishes of happiness for the New Year, and were given fruit or new pennies in exchange. The custom only just survives in a few rural areas and should be revived.

The last traditional **cadi ha** was seen in Holywell in the 1930s. This 'Fool', with a group of Morris dancers with equally blackened faces, carried the decorated 'summer branch' ('cangen haf') around the villages on May Day. Dressed half as a male and half as a female, the Cadi painted his lips, cheeks and around his eyes a vivid red.

An ancient Glamorgan custom practised in churchyards such as at Welsh St Donats, was 'raising the summer birch'. A birch branch was bedecked with ribbons by the ladies of the parish, and the men assisted them in lifting it up onto the churchyard cross on Easter Day. The birch was guarded for four days and nights against surrounding villages, and it was a disgrace for a parish to lose its birch. Any parish that retained its birch and captured another was held in great esteem, and broken bones were commonplace in some encounters.

CYMANFA GANU

A singing festival, the first of which was held in Aberystwyth in 1830, has been a major feature of Nonconformist worship in Wales. By the end of the nineteenth century chapel choirs were often performing full oratorios at Christmas and Easter.

CYMRU

The Welsh word for Wales is Cymru. The Welsh people are Cymry, and the adjective Welsh is Cymraeg. The words come from the Brythonic Celtic 'Combrogi', meaning fellow-countrymen, and is also the origin of the word Cumbria, when the Celts in Wales were cut off from those in the north of England (see Language).

D

DANCE

The strong non-conformist religion revival with its Calvinist overtones, that swept through Wales in the eighteenth and nineteenth centuries, almost exterminated folk music and dancing. However, Lady Charlotte Guest and others in the nineteenth century collected and published collections, and folk dance is seeing a resurgence, with 'Twmpath Dawns' being held more regularly.

As early as 1703 Ellis Wynne had attacked the evils of dance, worried about the effects of the closeness of the sexes and the effects of alcohol. By 1791 the Reverend Thomas Charles was commenting that '*The revival of religion has put an end to all the merry meetings for dancing, and singing with the harp, and every kind of sinful mirth, which used to be so prevalent among young people here. And at a large fair, kept here a few days ago, the usual revelling, the sound of music, and vain singing, was not to be heard in any part of the town.*' These revels were largely replaced by open-air preaching festivals.

In 1714 Rhys Prydderch, a minister in Carmarthenshire, wrote a list of the twelve major sins, which included cock fighting, long hair and sorcery. However, the *first* sin he considered was *dawnsio cymmyscedig* (mixed dancing).

Edward Jones in 'Bardd y Brenin' (The King's Bard, 1802), referred to the influence of the religious revival, 'The Great Awakening' upon dance and music: '*The sudden decline of the national Minstrelsy, and Customs of Wales, is in great degree attributed to the fanatick impostors, or illiterate plebeian preachers, who have too often been suffered to overrun the country, misleading the greater part of the people from their lawful Church; and dissuading them from their innocent amusements, such as Singing, Dancing and other rural Sports and Games, which heretofore they had been accustomed to delight in, from the earliest time . . . The consequence is, Wales, which was formerly one of the merriest, and happiest countries in the World, is now become one of the dullest.*'

Welsh folk dance was extremely exacting and complicated, as Richard Warner commented in 'A Walk Through Wales' in 1799, '*Men and women individually selected us to dance. As the females were very handsome, it is most probable we would have accepted their offers, had there not been a powerful reason to prevent us – our complete inability to unravel the mazes of a Welsh dance. 'Tis true there is no great variety in the figures of them, but the few they perform are so complicated and so long, that they would render an apprenticeship to them necessary in an Englishman.*'

Traditional Welsh dance falls into two categories, of which one is 'stepping'. Similar to Irish dancing, there is film of this dance in The Museum of Welsh Life, and stepping competitions between two men at a time were very popular. Clog and step dancing were also known as 'jigs and hornpipes'. There has been a renaissance in the dance and excellent 'steppers' of all ages can now be seen in eisteddfodau. Because of the energetic nature of the heel and toe clogging, with high leaps and Cossack-style dancing, dancers or 'jiggers' often followed each other individually at wakes and revels until the instrumentalists were too tired to play.

The second type of dance is 'folk dancing', which survived the Nonconformist attack by the thinnest of threads. To know the history of Welsh dance is to realise how important it is to preserve the Welsh language. The Llanover Welsh Reel was recalled in 1918 by Mrs Gruffydd Roberts, daughter of Thomas Gruffydd, the last harpist at Llanover Court. He was employed there from 1844 until his death in 1888. The reel was then revived by local schoolchildren, and for many years was regarded as the only genuine Welsh folk dance. However, the publication of the old Llandagfan dances in 1936 gave fresh impetus, along with many people researching the dances before time and memories ran out.

Then Mrs Margretta Thomas of Nantgarw, born 1880, remembered her childhood at local Sunday school tea parties, and dancing at homes and Caerphilly and Tongwynlais Fairs. (She also remembered when 'stepping' was popular in the Long Room in the local tavern). Her daughter, Dr. Ceinwen Thomas, painstakingly committed these memories of tunes and dances to paper. Now, only since 1954 we have the 'Nantgarw Dances' forming part of all folk dance group repertoires. They include the Flower Dance (with a beautiful costume), the Dance of St John's Eve, Rali Twm Sion, the Grasshopper Dance, Caerphilly Fair, the Snowball Dance and the Ball Dance. Dawns y Pelau (the Ball Dance) is spectacular, with each man and woman holding a multicoloured ball on elastic string, and each ball is decked with long ribbons in the national colours of Red, White and Green.

Mrs Thomas said of the present dancers '. . . they've a long way to go before they can dance the way the old people danced. The boys dance too much like women, you see. They're not muscular enough. The boys years ago would jump higher than the women, and because they were so energetic, the women looked more feminine.' Her family came to regard dancing as a one-way ticket to hell and damnation. Her husband's grandfather, Ifan Tomos, a well-known 'stepper' until his conversion in 1859, used to 'run past the tavern in the dark when he heard the harp and dancing outside, because the urge to join in was well nigh intolerable.'

Many of the dances were performed at *taplasau haf* or *mabsant*, assemblies of dance and song held most weekends in the summer months. For many centuries the most popular festival in Welsh calendars was the *gwylmabsant*, a wake or revel associated with the feast day of the parish saint. Work could be suspended for days. These in time were replaced by *twmpathau*, which often took place after the taverns shut, and so were disapproved of by 'respectable' folk. The feast days of local saints are still celebrated across all the towns and villages of Brittany, and these also feature processions in local constume – 'pardons', with folk music and dance following. It may be that some Celtic-Welsh dances can also be rescued from the Breton traditional dances.

Cwmni Dawns Werin Canolfan Caerdydd, Cardiff's Welsh dance troupe, has toured America and Japan in the last twenty-five years, and Nantgarw, Bridgend and Brynmawr also have flourishing dance societies. The Welsh Folk Dance Society, Cymdeithas Ddawns Werin Cymru, publishes dance pamphlets and books on the subject.

DAVID DAVIES

Born the eldest of nine children, in Llandinam, in mid-Wales, a wonderful statue of David Davies is placed outside the Docks Offices in Barry. His is the story of our only major Welsh industrialist of the nineteenth century. His father ran a small saw-mill, and Davies' nickname from working there stayed with him all his life – *Dai Top-Sawyer*. Later, as a contractor then financier, he took part in the building of seven Welsh railway lines, thereby earning another soubriquet, *Davies the Railway*. In 1865, he bought mineral rights in the heavily-wooded Rhondda Valley, looking for coal. He sank the two deepest coal shafts ever made at that time, anywhere in the world.

Running out of money, he addressed the workers, saying that he only had a half-crown piece left (about twelve pence in modern money), and could not afford to pay them any more wages. A man shouted *'We'll have that as well'*, and he threw him the coin. The men promised to work just one more week without wages, and in March 1866 a coal seam was found at the unheard-of depth of 660 feet – it became one of the richest in the world.

Tired of delays and charges at the Scottish Lord Bute's Cardiff Docks, Davies built a railway line to Barry, and built the most modern docks in history by 1889. Barry became the busiest port in the world, shipping coal everywhere. His Ocean Coal wagons rolling down to the Docks gave him his third nickname, *Davies the Ocean*. A Liberal MP and philanthropist, his grand-daughters Gwendoline and Margaret were responsible for the bequest of Impressionist Art that made The National Museum of Wales at Cardiff the envy of many other European museums. (Incidentally, the Marquis of Bute became the richest man in the world through his control of Welsh coal, docks and shipping).

His grandson David Davies, first Baron Llandinam, was the major benefactor of the first Welsh university and the National Library of Wales at Aberystwyth, as well as a chain of hospitals across Wales. A close ally of David Lloyd George, Baron Llandinam strongly supported The League of Nations, and erected the Temple of Health and Peace in Cardiff. He also founded the New Commonwealth Society and campaigned strongly for an international police force.

DRUIDS

The Celtic social hierarchy was headed by the Druids, masters of ritual, legend and astronomy, with attendant poets, seers and warriors. The Druids were the link between the people and around four thousand gods. Druids also appear to have acted as judges and doctors, receiving twenty years of oral instruction before they were admitted to the order. This priesthood practised a naturalistic religion, with focus on sacred groves and springs. The word 'druid' derives from an ancient word 'drus' meaning oak tree ('derw' is the Welsh for oak). The Roman Pliny recorded the rite where mistletoe was cut from the sacred oak tree with a golden sickle. ('Natural History XIV') Because mistletoe rarely grows on oaks, this obviously called for a special ceremonial occasion. *'They choose groves of oak for the sake of the tree alone, and they never perform any sacred rite unless they have a branch of it. They think that everything that grows on it has been sent from heaven by the god himself. Mistletoe, however, is rarely found on the oak, and when it is, is gathered with a great deal of ceremony . . . if possible on the sixth day of the moon.'*

The most important place for British druids was a wooden shrine, or sacred grove, on the holy island of Anglesey, known to the Romans as Mona, and to the Welsh as Môn. This island seems to have been important across Europe as the holiest site for all Celts, and this is possibly why the Romans were so focused upon destroying it. Tacitus described the attack on this last stronghold in AD60: *'The enemy lined the shore in a dense armed mass. Among them were black-robed women with dishevelled hair like The Furies, brandishing torches. Close by stood Druids, raising their hands to heaven and screaming dreadful curses. This weird spectacle awed the Roman soldiers into a kind of paralysis. They stood still – and presented themselves as a target. But then they urged each other (and were urged by the general) not to fear a horde of fanatical women. Onwards pressed their standards, and they bore down their opponents, enveloping them in the flames of their own torches. Suetonius garrisoned the conquered island. The groves devoted to Mona's barbarous superstitions he demolished. For it was their religion to drench their altars in the blood of prisoners and consult their gods by means of human entrails.'* ('Annals XIV, 30')

The druids acted as arbiters in disputes, and had freedom to move anywhere, as they were sacred. As they represented the cohesive driving force behind Celtic power, the Romans knew that they had to destroy the order and its sacred shrines. Perhaps Roman literature was sensationalist propaganda – the divination by entrails

scenario does not seem to fit with the druidic role of educating bards and minstrels. However, druidic laws forbade them to commit their knowledge to writing, so we mainly have Roman sources to rely upon. Julius Caesar made it evident that Gaelic Druids had massive political and judiciary power, officiating at sacrifices, teaching philosophy and religion, and settling all disputes. Only responsible to the Archdruid, they did not have to pay taxes or undertake military service. They instructed the children of the upper classes, so reinforcing their hold upon society. It also seems that they believed in reincarnation, the spirit passing to another life.

Julius Caesar reported the importance of British Druidism to their Celtic counter-parts across the continent of Europe: *'The druids officiate at the worship of the gods, regulate public and private sacrifices, and give rulings on all religious questions. Large numbers of young men flock to them for instruction, and they are held in great honour by the people. They act as judges in practically all disputes, whether between tribes or individuals; when any crime is committed, or a murder takes place, or a dispute arises about an inheritance or a boundary, it is they who adjudicate the matter and appoint the compensation to be paid and received by the parties concerned . . . All the druids are under one head, whom they hold in the highest respect . . . The Druidic doctrine is believed to have been found existing in Britain and thence imported into Gaul; even today those who want to make a profound study of it generally go to Britain for the purpose. The Druids are exempt from military service and do not pay taxes like other citizens. These important privileges are naturally attractive: many present themselves at their own accord to become students of druidism, and others are sent by their parents and relatives. It is said that these pupils have to memorise a great number of verses – so many, that some of them spend twenty years at their studies . . . A lesson they take particular pains to inculcate is that the soul does not perish, but after death passes from one body to another; they think that this is the best incentive to bravery, because it teaches men to disregard the terrors of death. They also hold long discussions about the heavenly bodies and their movements, the size of the universe and of the earth, the physical constitution of the world, and the power and properties of the gods; and they instruct the young men in all these subjects.'* (S. A. Handford's 1951 translation).

Druids advised their kings and also helped villagers with fortune-telling, and instructing them when best time to plant crops. They placated the gods of nature by throwing valuables and animals into wells and lakes. Many Celtic treasures have been found this way, and the custom of bending and throwing swords and daggers into water survived in Wales until the nineteenth century, where bent pins were cast into holy wells. In 1868, in Cevennes in France, animals and valuables were still being offered up to a lake in an ancient Celtic festival.

DUNES

Merthyr Mawr, a 'picture postcard' thatched hamlet near Bridgend, leads on to a wonderful dune system with the remains of Candleston Castle. The dunes are used by athletes for stamina training. From the highest dunes one can look down on the ruins of Ogmore Castle, guarding the ford with stepping stones over the river Ewenny. To jump off the top of the Great Dune, Europe's second highest at two hundred feet (61m), is still an inspiring experience for all ages. From Merthyr Mawr to Aberthaw (Aberddawen) runs fourteen miles of the lovely Glamorgan Heritage Coast.

The fifteen hundred acres of dunes in the National Nature Reserve at Kenfig (Cynffig) are home to five hundred species of flowers, which is a third of the total number of species of British flowers. Orchids such as the Pyramidal Orchid are fairly common because crushed shells have given an almost chalky quality to the soil on the dune 'slacks'. Ninety-five per cent of Britain's population of the Fen Orchid can be found here amongst the Burnet Roses, Sea Lavender and Sea Holly. A huge swathe of sand dunes protected most of the South Wales coast in the past. 'Blowouts' among the remains of these dunes have created ideal conditions in the slacks for rare species which survive extreme conditions.

The sands have been encroaching since the 9th century, covering Kenfig Village and its castle. The Normans built the castle and town around 1150, and by 1181 it was recorded that 24 ships lay in its harbour. By 1281 there were 142 burgesses living there, but by 1485 the site with its church, grange and castle had been virtually obliterated by sand dunes. Kenfig Medieval Borough is a scheduled monument of national importance. It has never been built upon or redeveloped, and is being slowly uncovered by archaeologists. The 'Town Hall' occupies the upper room of a local inn (see Beer and Pubs), and is symbolic of a site that had parliamentary representation up to 1832.

Kenfig Pool is home to many rare species of dragonfly, and the crumbling remains of Sker House, which features in R. D. Blackmore's 'The Maid of Sker' are a short walk away. Sker House was also famous for its ship-wreckers in centuries past. The Pool has all three types of swan, plus goldeneye, teal, redshank and sometimes the very rare bittern, while the peregrine falcon, and merlin can be seen over the dunes. Nearby Kenfig Beach is a well-kept secret as it is only accessible by foot.

Oxwich Dunes stretch for three miles next to Oxwich Beach on the Gower Peninsula. The Burnet Rose is common here, as on other Welsh dunes. The Common Restharrow, a pink and white vetch-type plant, is so-called because its tough underground roots used to slow down the old horse-drawn ploughs and harrows. There are Dune Early Marsh Orchids, Sea Spurge, Sea Rocket, the rare Yellow Whitlow Grass, and Sea Holly here. The seaweed used for laverbread dishes, Porphyra Umbilica, grows at Oxwich, and the inland marshes support colonies of wigeon, sedge and reed warblers.

Also on the Gower Peninsula, there can be seen pyramidal orchids in the Port Eynon dunes. These are sweet-smelling in the hours of light to attract day moths and butterflies, but emit a foxy odour at night to deter nocturnal moths. Also here are Yellow Whitlow Grass (a Gower speciality which flowers in March), spring squill, spurges, golden samphire and rock rose. The headland has the remains of the great Salt House, a mansion destroyed by storms some three hundred years ago, and a short walk takes one to the mysterious Culver Hole, a walled-up fissure in the cliffs possibly used for smuggling, and

definitely as a mediaeval pigeon/dovecote. Manx Shearwaters, Sanderlings, Gannets and Ringed Plovers can be seen in the vicinity.

Next to the seven mile stretch of Cefn Sidan Sands, near Burry Port is Pembrey Country Park and sand dunes. The dune slacks here include Marsh Helleborine, Fen Orchid, Dune Orchid, Autumn Lady's Tresses, Adder's Tongue, and thirty-two species of butterfly. Goshawks, crossbills and siskins can also be seen. Nearby at Burry Inlet, ponies graze on the salt marshes, and the cockle pickers scrape the sands to expose live cockles. Those that pass through a three-quarter inch mesh are collected, washed, sacked and then taken to be boiled and sold locally, for instance in Swansea or Neath Markets, or bottled or canned in vinegar or brine. The delicacy Marsh Samphire, also known as Glasswort, grows here. Nearby Ffrwd Fen features real rarities such as marsh-pea, floating club-rush and frogbit, and bitterns and marsh harriers can sometimes be seen in winter.

The dunes at the Dyfi National Nature Reserve, at Ynyslas on the Northern Borth Sands, attracts naturalists from all over Europe. On the same site, there are sand dunes, estuarine mudflats, salt marsh and raised bog habitats. On the shingle beach, there are sea beet, sea campion and scurvy grass. Towards the dunes, there are sea rocket, prickly saltwort, and little mouse-ear. In the dune slacks, many species of orchid thrive. In the raised bogs, there are bog-myrtle, and bog mosses. Birds in the area include bar-tailed godwit, shelduck, greenshank, ringed plover, and Greenland white-fronted geese.

Morfa Duffryn, at Llanbedr near Harlech, is a system of calcareous dunes, slacks and salt-marsh, with whimbrel, ringed plovers, marsh orchids, green-flowered helleborine, seaside centaury, sea-spurge and houndstongue. Morfa Harlech is a similar environment, cared for by the Nature Conservancy Council, and supports polecats, rare butterflies and orchids .

Newborough, in Gwynedd, dates from the uprooting of the Beaumaris population for Edward I to build his castle. Up until the 1920s the village was mainly involved in weaving baskets, mats and ropes from the marram grass upon the massive sand-dune complex of Newborough Warren. Now a National Nature Reserve, the six hundred acres are home to Soay Sheep, red squirrels and goldcrests, the latter living in the plantations of Corsican and Monterey Pine. The renowned bird artist Charles Tunnicliffe lived here from 1945 until his death in 1979. Scarce plants such as round-leafed wintergreen and grass-of-Parnassus can be found here.

E

EDUCATION

Born in 1510, Robert Recorde of Tenby, the son of Thomas Recorde of Tenby and Rose Jones of Machynlleth, went to All Souls College. His invention of the 'equals' sign (=) revolutionised algebra, and his mathematical works were translated and read all over Europe. He died in 1589.

John Dee, the gifted Elizabethan polymath, is covered in the 'Magic' section – he also published versions of Robert Recorde's work.

Possibly the most learned Welshman was Edward Lhuyd (1660-1709), from Glanfred, near Llandre (Llanfihangel Genau'r-glyn). The first noted taxonomist of zoology, he transformed Oxford's Ashmolean Museum, and also revised the 1695 edition of Camden's 'Encyclopaedia Britannica'.

Jesus College, Oxford's first Protestant foundation, was founded in 1571 by Dr. Hugh Price of Brecon, mainly for the needs of Welshmen, and its first Principal was Dr David Lewis from Abergavenny (died 1584). It became even more strongly identified with Welsh education after its re-endowment by Leoline Jenkins of Cowbridge (Y Bontfaen), in 1685.

Traditionally, the sons of the gentry were sent to England to study until the monastic school at Abergwili was removed to Christ College, Brecon, and was granted a royal licence in 1541. The reason given was that the 'people of Carmarthenshire knew no English'. Among the new Tudor Grammar Schools set up were those at Cowbridge, Margam, Ruthin, Caerleon, Bangor, Llanrwst, Presteigne, Carmar-then, Wrexham and Beaumaris. 'They exercised a strong Anglicising influence'. Haberdashers School in Monmouth was also granted a licence to educate.

Teaching was the traditional route away from the mines and steelworks for many Welsh children – not the traditions of engineering or medicine of the Scot. However, the almost forgotten Thomas Andrew Walker, of Caerwent, built the fantastic Severn Railway Tunnel and the Manchester Ship Canal in Victorian times.

Robert Owen founded the first infant school in Britain, in New Lanark (see Owen), and Kurt Hahn (the founder of Gordonstoun and Salem schools) set up the first United World College in St Donat's Castle, on the Glamorgan coast.

The religious revivals of the eighteenth century used Bishop Morgan's wonderfully pure Bible translation and kept the language alive. The dark side of Nonconformism was its hatred of enjoyment – dance, drink and association with the opposite sex. It altered the Welsh psyche from extrovert and carefree to a zealous and pious fear of God. However, all meetings were in Welsh, as were the group discussions that followed. There was a boom in religious books printed in Welsh. The 1846 Report that told the English government what it wanted to know, that the Welsh were illiterate and uncouth peasants because of their language, had the exact opposite effect in Wales. Welsh thrived, with evening educational classes being held after chapel and work on Sundays. Wales had a grammar school system that took the brightest working-class children. Despite language restriction in schools, the Welsh people had saved enough money from their pathetic wages to build the University of Wales at Aberystwyth in 1871.

Griffith Jones had started the 'circulating schools' around 1737, giving the Welsh opportunities for literacy. By the time he died in 1757, it was estimated that 160,000 people had learned to read, out of an estimated population of 480,000 (in 1750). This percentage of literate Welsh people was probably higher than any other European nation of the time, despite the grinding poverty. The Miners' Institutes of the 19th century assisted this literacy, with their wonderful library collections. One has been shifted, stone by stone, to the Museum of Welsh Life at St Fagans. The major contribution that Jones made was to save the life of the Welsh language – he taught the nation to read, and imbued it with a sound knowledge of Bishop Morgan's wonderful Welsh translation of the Bible.

David Rhys Davies (1835-1928) features in 'The Guinness Book of Records', for having taught as a pupil teacher, teacher and finally headmaster for a total of 76 years in Wales

EGYPT

One of Wales' ubiquitous Herberts, George Edward Stanhope Molyneux, Earl Caernarfon, financed Howard Carter's excavations of the royal tombs in Thebes from 1907. He died shortly after the discovery of Tut'ankhamun's intact tomb, thereby starting off 'the Curse of the Pharaoh' myth.

EISTEDDFODAU

Eisteddfodau is the plural of Eisteddfod, the great 'Meeting of Bards'. There are traditions of an eisteddfod at Ystum Llwydiarth held by Taliesin in 517, of one under Maelgwn Gwynedd on the banks of the Conwy River in 540, and of 'Y Bardd Glas' held by Geraint in the 9th century, when 'cynghanedd' was established as a verse component.

The first authenticated eisteddfod was held in Cardigan Castle by Lord Rhys, in 1176, but the present form of eisteddfod is an early nineteenth century recreation, thanks to Iolo Morganwg. The mediaeval meeting of the bards called the Eisteddfod was revived as a means of attracting patronage for Welsh cultural activity. At first the competitions were confined to the traditional poetry composition (the strict Welsh form known as cynghanedd) and harp playing, but today choirs, bands, acting, recitation, fiction writing and painting can also be included. The 1176 date gives Wales the right to claim the oldest European festival, one with both poetic and political overtones.

Thomas Pennant described the eisteddfod of Lord Rhys: '*In 1176, the Lord Rhys, prince of South Wales, made a great feast at Christmas, on account of the finishing of his new castle at Aberteifi, of which he proclaimed notice through all Britain a year and a day before; great was the resort of strangers, who were nobly entertained, so that none departed unsatisfied. Among deeds of arms, and variety of spectacles, Rhys invited all the bards of Wales, and provided chairs for them, which were placed in his hall, where they sat and disputed and sang, to show their skill in their respective faculties: after which he bestowed great rewards and rich gifts on the victors. The bards of North Wales won the prizes; but the minstrels of Rhys's household excelled in their faculty. On this occasion the Brawdwr Llys, or judge of the court, an officer fifth in rank, declared aloud the victor, and received from the bard, for his fee, a mighty drinking-horn, made of the horn of an ox, a golden ring, and the cushion on which he sat in his chair of dignity.'* Among the rivals for the bardic crown were Owain Cyfeiliog, Prince of Powys, and Hywel ap Owain Gwynedd, whose poems survive today. Hywel's more famous brother was Prince Madoc, the legendary discoverer of America.

The most important of the early eisteddfodau was at Carmarthen in 1451, where men from Flint won all three main prizes, for poetry, singing and the harp. It was here that Dafydd ap Edmwnd first laid down the rules for 'strict metres' of poetry. Henry VIII commissioned eisteddfodau, as did Elizabeth I. The Tudors remembered their Welsh roots. Queen Elizabeth I, knowledgeable of her Tudwr-Welsh heritage, had made the Eisteddfod into a kind of test for bards, to sort out the real poets from the rest. At the 1568 Eisteddfod commissioned by Elizabeth, the prizes were small silver models – a harp for the harpist, a crwth for the fiddler, a chair for the poet and a tongue for the best singer. The 6-inch high harp has survived in the possession of the Mostyn family.

The Owain Glyndŵr Hotel in Corwen was originally a monastery, then a coaching inn, dating from at least 1329. There are claims that here was held the first Eisteddfod, to which the general public were admitted, in 1789. Sloping floors and ancient beams make this a wonderful stop for a few nights.

In 1858, the Llangollen Eisteddfod, the first 'modern' eisteddfod, lasted four days and it was the first to which crowds were brought in excursion trains. 'The Telegraph' reported the Eisteddfod as *'a national debauch of*

sentimentality', and 'The Times' called it *'simply foolish interference with the natural progress of civilisation and prosperity – it is a monstrous folly to encourage the Welsh in a loving fondness for their old language.'* This was at the time when children heard speaking Welsh in school were beaten, so organisation and participation in the event was extremely courageous. To celebrate poetry, literacy and past achievement was *'uncivilised'*, according to the then London press.

In 1955, a young unknown called Luciano Pavarotti sang with his father's choir from Modena, at the **Llangollen International Eisteddfod**. It is said that his hearing Tito Gobbi sing at Llangollen, combined with the acclaim and the award of first prize, were the spurs that made him decide to make singing his professional career. In July 1995 he returned to give a free, and triumphal, performance, ending the night in tears in front a rapturous audience. Local ladies had made flower displays for the stage, only to learn that Pavarotti was allergic to flower pollen. Shortly before the performance, they had to pinch off all the pollen-bearing anthers, and spent one hundred and fifty pounds upon hair lacquer to spray on the flowers and prevent any pollen interfering with the maestro's performance. He enjoyed the sweet so much at the post-concert banquet at the Bryn Hywel Hotel, that he secretly had another four sent up to his bedroom.

Started by Harold Tudor in 1947 in an attempt to bring peoples together after six years of war, Llangollen is the place to see scores of national costumes and enjoy the most varied dancing and singing in Europe, probably the world. Over twelve thousand international participants come as folk singers, choirs, dancers, groups and instrumentalists, with one hundred and fifty thousand visitors descending on this town of just four thousand people, making it a marvellous cosmopolitan affair. Bryn Terfel was the star presence in 1996, and Montserrat Caballe appeared in 1997. The European Centre for Traditional and Regional Cultures (ECTARC) is based in Llangollen, with revolving performances and displays featuring the cultures of all the EU states.

In the **Royal National Eisteddfod**, all proceedings are conducted in Welsh, the first language for 500,000 of the 2.7 million Welsh population, with a simultaneous translation service. There is no permanent site, and the Eisteddfod rotates between North and South venues every year, and is always commemorated by a permanent circle of standing stones. This is Wales' biggest single annual event, and the ceremonies are carried out by a Gorsedd of Bards, an association of people interested in Welsh arts and music. The two important ceremonies are the Chairing and the Crowning, when each winning poet in different styles is chaired or crowned in attendance by other poets or writers. The Chair (see the entry on Literature for Hedd Wynn) is the symbol of authority. The Welsh for 'cathedral' is literally the 'church of the chair', *'Eglwys Gadeiriol'*.

There are many other eisteddfodau in Wales, from schools to villages, one of the largest and best being at Pontrhydfendigaid in Mid-May. A remarkable event happened in 1957, when Paul Robeson, the black American singer and champion of human rights, had been invited to attend the Welsh Miners' Eisteddfod. He was denied his passport because of the Communist witch-hunt of Senator Joe McCarthy, so a telephone link-up was made and recorded. The record opens with a message from the miners' president, the late Will Paynter, and is followed by a reply by Robeson, who then sings several songs and ends his performance with a message to the eisteddfod. The Treorchy Male Voice Choir sings Y Delyn Aur and the link-up ends with the audience singing 'We'll Keep A Welcome'. This historic recording has been on sale since the 1996 Miner's Eisteddfod at Bridgend.

Carlo Rizzi, The Welsh National Opera's Musical Director, puts into perspective the role of eisteddfodau in Welsh culture: *'To me, the Urdd Eisteddfod for young people is a wonderful opportunity for youngsters in Wales to try their skills and forge their characters, giving them the chance to exchange experiences. The renaissance of the Welsh language, with more and more young people speaking it, is another factor which is important in all this. For me it is a very strange experience to attend the eisteddfodau and hear everyone speaking Welsh, even though I have been learning the Welsh language and can now hold conversations in it (perhaps having a Welsh-speaking wife has something to do with this). The language is an indication of the strong will-power of the Welsh people to maintain their own identity. Maintaining this identity also means maintaining their own music. Wales has so many beautiful songs, my favourite being Myfanwy by Joseph Parry. Also, I think that the Welsh National Anthem is one of the finest national anthems.'*

This **Eisteddfod Genedlaethol Urdd Gobaith Cymru** alternates between south and north Wales and is the largest youth festival in Europe. It includes rock music, to help keep minority languages alive, and is open to performers and groups from all over Europe.

It may well be that Wales is the only country whose national festival is devoted solely to the arts.

EMBLEMS, FLAGS
AND CRESTS

Upon St David's Day, 1st March, the daffodil or leek is worn by Welsh people everywhere to announce their Welshness. They are also prominent during Eisteddfodau and at rugby internationals, especially massive home-made leeks. According to the Wales Tourist Board, '*On the evidence of Shakespeare, the leek was the recognised emblem of his day, and there is written evidence that it became the Welsh emblem considerably earlier. Entries in the house-hold accounts of the Tudor kings include payments for leeks worn by the household guards on St David's Day. According to one legend, the leek is linked to St David because he ordered his soldiers to wear them on their helmets when they fought a victorious battle against the pagan Saxons in a field full of leeks. It was more likely, however, that the leek was linked with the vegan St David and adopted as a national symbol because of its importance to the national diet in days of old, particularly in Lent.*' St David's own emblem is a dove.

The leek is a *cennin*, and the daffodil a *cennin Pedr* or Peter's leek. Perhaps people took 'pedr' to be interchange-able in the past, because the daffodil became an emblem after the leek, but it is difficult to attribute the reason.

The Welsh national flag is not fea-tured on the Union Flag (Union Jack) of the United Kingdom, which super-imposes the blue and white saltire of St Andrew, and the red and white crosses of St Patrick and St George. The British flag thus features representation from Northern Ireland, England, and Scot-land, but none from Wales. The Welsh Flag consists of two horizontal stripes, white over green, with a large red dragon passant. Green and white are the traditional Welsh colours, worn by the Welsh bowmen at the Battle of Crécy. The Red Dragon, one of the most ancient badges in the world, was brought to Britain by the Romans, who had copied it from the Parthians, and it was later used by both British and Saxon kings. Traditionally it was King Arthur's flag, and it was definitely the standard of Cadwaladr, from whom the Tudors were descended. Owain Glyndŵr adopted the red dragon of Cadwaladr as his standard and the national flag of Wales.

The word *draig* or dragon was used in Welsh poetry to symbolise a warrior or leader. Pendragon, as in Uther Pen-dragon, meant a head, or chief leader. A legend dates from the eighth century about a fight between a Red Dragon (*Y Ddraig Goch*) representing Wales and a White Dragon representing England foretelling the triumph of the red dragon. The red dragon of the Celts was their flag and symbol against the Saxons for 600 years after the Romans left Britain. The White Dragon of the Saxons was last seen in battle against the Normans at Hastings in 1066.

Y Ddraig Goch, was widely accepted as the oldest flag in the world at the international conference of flag makers in South Africa in 1987, according to the President of the Flag Institute. Flag-maker Robin Ashburner makes the point that it is the only flag to have remained unchanged in the last 1,000 years, '*the Welsh will be the only people to enter the next millenium with the same flag as they entered the current one*'. Denmark also claims the oldest flag, dating from 1219, but the 'father of flag science', or vexillology, Dr Whitney Smith of Mas-sachusetts, supports the Welsh flag. The dragon came from China via the Romans, and when the Western Roman Empire was set up, the dragon symbol was used by the local chiefs in Britain. It was the Welsh symbol long before Offa built the dyke between the Saxon and Welsh kingdoms.

The Welshman Henry Tudor invaded England, through Wales, to end the Wars of the Roses. With the 'Red Dragon of Cadwaladr' as his standard, his smaller army defeated and killed the last Plantagenet king Richard III, at Bosworth Field. Henry used as his livery colours green and white, and on these colours his retainers painted the red dragon. When Henry became Henry VII of England in 1485, he decreed that from henceforth the Red Dragon should be the official flag of Wales. Henry even set up the official herald's position of Rouge Dragon Pursuivant to protect the flag. For a time the Dragon coexisted on the English Crown's royal crest with the Lion, but was replaced by the Unicorn of the Scottish Stuarts on the accession of James I in 1603. Thus neither the Welsh flag nor the Welsh emblems of daffodil and leek appear in a united British context.

There was no red rose of Lancashire during the Wars of the Roses, and the White Rose of Yorkshire was one of Edward IV's badges. It seems to have been Henry Tudor's idea to amalgamate the two into the Tudor Rose when he ended the wars and married Elizabeth of York. Henry VII balanced his Greyhound emblem of Richmond and Lancaster on the Tudwr royal arms, with the Red Dragon of Wales and Cadwaladr. To him the dragon showed his 'Trojan' descent and gave his kingship a legitimacy distinct from the houses of Lancaster and York.

A few years back, a Welshman used to attend rugby internationals in a fantastic Red Dragon outfit, complete with tail. On one occasion the dragon was arrested by an English policeman for urinating in a public place!

The Welsh crest of three white feathers and the motto 'Ich Dien' were adopted by the Black Prince at the Battle of Crécy, copied from the decorations of the blind King of Bohemia, who died in a cavalry charge which was wiped out by Welsh archers. The crest has been that of the Prince of Wales since the fourteenth century, and is on the Welsh international rugby shirt.

The Flag of St David, a gold cross on a black background, is gaining in popularity in West Wales, much like the black and white stripes of Finistere are becoming more prevalent in the Breton-speaking part of North-West France.

Although the flags of the princes of Gwynedd were red and gold dragons, it seems that their soldiers wore green and white, as an *englyn* of Llywelyn I's time states, '*There is a host in Rhosfair, there is drinking, there are golden bells. There is my lord Llywelyn and tall warriors follow him; a thousand, a host in green and white.*' Green and white may come from the colours of the leek, and these are also the colours which the Black Prince's Welsh troops wore at Crécy in 1346, a hundred years after Llywelyn. D. L. Evans commented that they were '*the first troops to appear on a continental battlefield in national uniform*'.

ENTERTAINERS

Music and poetry are the mainsprings of Welsh entertainment, from the days of the bards and travelling harpists through to male voice choirs and more recently poets and rock groups (see Eisteddfod, Harp and Rock Music). In Welsh legend, the inventor of vocal music was said to be Gwyddon Ganhebon.

Entertainers from Wales include the old music-hall star from Cardiff, 'Two-Ton' Tessie O'Shea, Terry Jones (of Monty Python), Rolf Harris, the Australian all-rounder with Cardiff parents, the former 'Goon' Harry Secombe and comedians Griff Rhys-Jones, Paul Whitehouse and the unforgettable Tommy Cooper. It is also thought that the brilliant Harold Clayton Lloyd, the American film comedian who died in 1971, had Welsh parentage.

EXPLORERS

Mention has already been made of Madoc (Prince Madog ab Owain Gwynedd), and the Lewis-Clark expedition that opened up the American West (see America and Madoc).

There is a remarkable quartet of Welshmen who flourished around the end of the sixteenth century. The almost unknown **Martin Llewellyn** (c.1565-1634) was the first British cartographer, who spent his last thirty-five years as the steward of St Bartholomew's Hospital. Only in 1975 were rediscovered the sixteen charts drawn by Llewellyn, covering the area from the Far East, including New Guinea and Japan, to the Cape of Good Hope. The charts are over fifty years earlier than any other known map-maker, and each are around three feet by two feet, in black ink and four colours. It appears that he was a survivor of the two-year trading expedition from 1597-1599 by the Dutch Cornelis de Houtman, and his son stated that the maps were 'drawn in his own hand and according to his own observations'. The Oriental volume of 'The English Pilot', thought to be the first English chart of the eastern seas, was not published until a century later.

From 1612-1613, **Sir Thomas Button** (1577-1634) of Duffryn House, near Cardiff, led an expedition looking for Henry Hudson. In his attempts to discover a North-West Passage to Asia, he explored Hudson Bay, where Button Island is named after him, and is called 'The First White Man in Manitoba'. He proved that there was no elusive 'North-West' Passage from Hudson Bay to the Pacific Ocean. He named New Wales, Nelson River and Button's Bay. He later suppressed Irish pirates attacking British shipping.

Admiral Sir Robert Mansell (1573-1656) of Margam also explored northwest routes to Asia, and Mansell Island is named after him. A close friend of James I, he led an expedition against the corsairs of Algeria in 1620, releasing forty English merchant captains. His days as Treasurer of the Navy (1604-1618) were notable mainly for the increase in his private fortune. Mansell also ran a famous glassware shop in London, and is known for the quote: '*An optimist is one who makes opportunities of his difficulties; a pessimist is one who makes difficulties of his opportunities.*'

In 1631-32, **Thomas James** (c.1593-1635) of Abergavenny charted Hudson Bay, again searching for the elusive passage, and James Bay recalls his efforts. He also named Cape Henrietta Maria and wintered at Charlton Island exploring the coast. A 1633 account of his voyage has been suggested (along with Captain Shelvocke's 1719 voyage) as the inspiration for *The Rime of the Ancient Mariner*.

Sir William Edward Parry (1790-1855) was in command of five expeditions to the Arctic. In 1818 he volunteered for the Ross Arctic expedition, and commanded the 'Alexander'. He took the 'Hecla' to search for the North-West Passage in 1819, and in 1821-23 spent another two seasons in the Arctic, in the 'Fury'. He took the 'Fury' and 'Hecla' to the Arctic again in 1823-25. In his last expedition in the 'Hecla', he tried to reach the North Pole on sledges from Spitzbergen in 1827, reaching further North than anyone had done before. Only unexpected ice conditions prevented his success, decades before the Pole was reached. He became a rear-admiral and hydrographer of the Navy. His grandson Sir John Franklin Parry (1863-1926) also became an admiral, and Navy hydrographer and surveyed the coasts of Borneo and China.

Sir Henry Morton Stanley, of *'Dr Livingstone, I presume'* fame, was born in Denbigh, and one of his claims to fame was killing five Africans with four shots from his elephant rifle when attacked. He had loaded the gun with explosive charges as a precaution. Born in 1841 in Denbigh, he was the illegitimate son of John Rowlands and Elizabeth Parry, and was brought up as John Rowlands in St Asaph's workhouse. He went to sea as a cabin boy in 1859, was befriended by Henry Morton Stanley of New Orleans, and took his benefactor's name. He fought on both sides in the American Civil War, and in 1867 joined the *New York Herald*. As its correspondent, he travelled to Abyssinia and Spain, and was told by his editor to find Livingstone in 1869. He found Livingstone at Ujiji in 1871, (described in *How I Found Livingstone*) and explored Lake Tanganyika. His further explorations are detailed in *Through The Dark Continent* and *In Darkest Africa*. He traced the course of the River Zaire (Congo) to the sea between 1874 and 1877, and established the Congo Free State (Zaire) 1879-84. Stanley charted much of the unexplored African interior between 1887 and 1889 when he led an expedition to relieve Emin Pasha (Eduard

Schnitzer). Stanley Falls, Stanley Pool and Stanleyville have now been renamed Boyoma falls, Pool Malebo and Kisangani. Between 1874 and 1877 he carved out a huge colony in Central Africa for his friend and employer, King Leopold of Belgium. This poor Welsh urchin ended up a celebrated explorer, MP and with the Grand Cross of the Order of the Bath, dying in 1904.

In 1909, **Sir T. W. E. David** of Saint Fagans led the Shackleton Antarctic Expedition's team, the first to locate and reach the magnetic South Pole, just 100 miles from the true South Pole.

In the expedition to the South Pole one of Captain Scott's ill-fated team to die with him was Petty-Officer **Edgar Evans** from Rhosili, Gower, where there is an evocative memorial. Another Evans, Edward, was second-in-command and brought the expedition home from the Antarctic. In World War I this naval commander was in charge of 'HMS Broke', when with 'HMS Swift' it encountered six German destroyers off the Dutch coast. In the ensuing night battle, Evans ordered the Broke to ram a German ship, sinking it, and fierce hand-to-hand fighting took place as it closed with another German destroyer. This enemy ship was also sunk, along with another, and the German navy fled from the engagement. Captain Edward Evans was awarded the DSO and known until his death in 1975 as 'Evans of the Broke'.

Dr Dafydd Rhys Williams, whose family comes from Bargoed, sent Welsh messages to the BBC television programme 'Wales Today' in April 1998 from the space shuttle Columbia. He also took a Welsh flag and Gareth Edwards' fiftieth rugby international cap on the shuttle, which orbited the earth at twenty-five times the speed of sound.

F

FALKLANDS

Welshman Simon Weston is the visible face of the Falklands to Wales and many throughout the world. The agonies he suffered from his burns and later operations were recorded for posterity. Forty-three Welsh Guards died on Sir Galahad, even though its captain had been implored to disembark the soldiers from his sitting duck target for Exocet missiles.

The only Victoria Cross won in the Falklands campaign was by Welshman Colonel H. Jones, awarded posthumously in 1982, having led his troops to capture an Argentine machine-gun emplacement.

FASHION

The current Scottish kilt was only invented a century ago, and there is a movement to wear the Welsh kilt, a development of the *Brycan*. The Brycan was a length of hard-wearing wool, two yards by six, that served as the Celt's dress by day and blanket by night. When hunting or in active pursuits, the brycan was belted at the waist to kilt (tuck) up the folds – the resulting skirt falling to the knees was the kilt in its embryonic form. In February, 1961, Kenfig Hill Rugby Club announced that they would adopt the kilt for social occasion, the Archdruid of Wales gave his blessing and the Welsh Tourist Board began to devise a suitable kilt for Welshmen – it was plain and dark green in colour, to be worn with same colour stockings with a white fringe. Gad-y-Gwlan, based at Chapter in Cardiff, make black and bottle-green kilts from Welsh wool for around £90.

Welsh costume, with the tall 'stovepipe' hat for women, is an adaptation of eighteenth century peasant dress. Traditional colours of women's woollen shawls and skirts varied between areas, but were usually a mixture of black, brown, white and red. Men wore plain woollen breeches and waistcoats, with heavy black shoes. Llanuwchllyn, near Bala, was the last place where the national costume, of tall beaver hat and a scarlet cloak, was regularly worn by ladies going to market and religious services.

William Coxe, in his 1801 'An Historical Tour in Monmouthshire', tells us of a typical scene in Pontypool marke: *'It was a pleasing amusement to mix in these crowded meetings, to observe the frank and simple manners of the hardy mountaineers, and endeavour, in asking the price of their provisions, to extort a Saxon word from this British progeny. The women were mostly wrapped in long cloth coats of a dark blue or brown colour; all of them wore mob caps neatly plaited over their forehead and ears, and tied above the chin; several had also round felt hats like those worn by the men, or large chip hats covered with black silk, and fastened under the chin. This head-dress gives an arch and lively air to the younger part of the sex, and is not unbecoming.'*

There is a clog-maker in the Welsh National Folk Museum at St Fagans. Itinerant clog-sole makers used to roam the sycamore woods in Wales, sending soles in vast numbers to the clog factories of Northern England. In Wales, each village once had its clog-maker, shaping the thick wooden soles and cutting the leather uppers to make long-lasting footwear for the villagers.

Laura Ashley was Welsh and her British factory is at Carno, Powys. However, nearly all the fashionable garments in her international chain of shops are manufactured outside the UK, in the Far East. David and Elizabeth Emmanuel, the designers of Lady Diana Spencer's wedding dress were Welsh, as was Mary Quant, who changed the face of world-wide fashion with her 1960s mini-skirts. Tommy Nutter was another famous designer of men's suits and shirts in the 1960s through to his death in 1992. Jeff Banks, the designer, is from Glamorgan.

FESTIVALS AND SHOWS

For details of over fifty arts festivals, from jazz to classical music, children's events or drama, please write to 'Festivals of Wales', Red House, Newtown SY16 3LE, or telephone 01686 626442. The Eisteddfodau have been covered under a previous heading.

Brecon Jazz Festival – early August, attracts major talents from all over the world to one of Europe's major music events.

Cardiff Festival – late September, early October. This is one of the UK's largest themed festivals, with music, the arts, drama, literature and opera events.

Cardiff Singer of the World competition is a massive, week-long televised festival of music and song, with inter-national opera singers and potential stars.

Cardiff Street Festival, last week in July, first week in August – includes the Butetown Carnival and a party/rock concert down Cardiff Bay.

Cricieth Festival in mid-June, featuring Celtic music, art and theatre.

Excalibur Celtic Festival, in Swansea and the Gower area, including sports competitions and music events, in the first two weeks in September.

Gregynog Festival – classical music in a country house setting in the last week in June, with major performances at Gregynog Hall, near Newtown.

Gŵyl Werin y Cnapan – A massively popular Celtic music and folk festival, second weekend in July, in Ffostrasol near Newcastle Emlyn.

Hay Festival of Literature – usually in the last week of May/early June, this attracts top writers to the Book Capital of Europe.

Llandrindod Wells Victorian Festival – a week towards the end of August, where everyone dresses in Victorian costume and we return to the life of a century ago.

Llangollen International Music Eisteddfod, is the second week in July – see Eisteddfod entry.

Llanwrtyd Wells runs all sorts of festivals, including Drovers' Runs – see the Marketing entry in this book.

Machynlleth Festival – around the same time as Llandrindod Wells – a mainly classical and chamber music event, with a 'pop' fringe and guided walks.

New Quay on the Dyfed coast has a marvellous New Year's Eve Festival, where nearly everyone in the town dresses in fancy dress to usher in the New Year, dancing in the streets after pub-crawling the evening away.

Pontardawe Folk Music Festival – in late August, with ceilidhs, folk music and traditional dancing.

Royal National Eisteddfod – first week in August – see Eisteddfod entry.

Royal Welsh Agricultural Show – at Builth Wells around the third week in July, a memorable experience.

Swansea Cockle Festival – a seven-day food festival celebrating local produce is held in October.

Swansea Festival of Music and Arts – similar to Cardiff's festival, in October. The 50th anniversary took place over three weeks in October 1998.

Swansea Festival of Sea Shanties is held in May in the Maritime Quarter.

Vale of Glamorgan Festival – for a week in early August, modern classical music.

FLIGHT

On 26th July, 1998, 'The Sunday Times' carried a long feature *'Welsh airman beat Wrights to the skies'*. Andrew Alderson wrote that Welsh carpenter, Bill Frost, flew in the summer of 1896:

'Until now, history has credited the Wright brothers with conquering the skies. But new evidence suggests that their famous flight was not the first. Seven years before them, Frost is said to have set off in a "flying machine" from a field in Pembrokeshire and stayed in the air for 10 seconds.

Newly discovered documents reveal that Frost, from Saundersfoot, Pembrokeshire, applied to register a patent for his invention – a cross between an airship and a glider – in 1894.

It was approved the following year and detailed how the invention was propelled upwards by two reversible

fans. Once in the air, the wings spread and are tilted forward "causing the machine to move, as a bird, onward and downward." A fan is used to help the aircraft "soar upward", while the steering is done by a rudder at both ends.

Crucially, locals in the Welsh seaside resort insist that the aircraft was built and flown within a year of the patent being approved. Yesterday experts on both sides of the Atlantic believed that the name of William Frost, not the Wright Brothers, deserves pride of place in aviation record books as the first pioneer of manned, sustained and powered flight.

Historians, descendants and a former neighbour of Frost are convinced that only his modesty – in failing to acclaim his role or having a photograph of the flight – meant his achievements went unacclaimed.

Roscoe Howells, the historian and writer, used to be a neighbour of Frost in Saundersfoot and heard an account of the flight from the inventor himself. "He became airborne, so he said, and I would never believe that Bill Frost was a liar or romancer," said Howells. "His flying machine took off, but the undercarriage caught in the top of a tree and it came down into a field. If he hadn't caught it in the tree, he would have been right over the valley over Saundersfoot and it would have been death or glory."

Frost's flying machine was 31 feet long and made of bamboo, canvas and mire mesh, with hydrogen-filled pouches to attain "neutral buoyancy".'

The later flight by Orville Wright in 1903 lasted just 12 seconds. Alderson describes Bill Frost as a carpenter and builder on the nearby Hean Castle estate, who was a deacon of the chapel and founded the local male voice choir:

'His determination to fly his aircraft after the initial flight was defeated by bad luck and lack of money. Although he repaired his machine after hitting the tree, it was later ripped from its moorings and damaged by gales, apparently in the autumn of 1896.

He later travelled to London and tried to get funding from the government's war department. According to Frost's descendants, he received several approaches from foreign governments for the rights to his patent, but refused on the grounds of patriotism. The revelations about Frost's design and flight have been uncovered by Jill Waters, a producer, and Patrick French, a presenter, for BBC Radio 4's Flying Starts.

"The Wright Brothers had the benefit of independent witnesses, log books full of technical data and, most important, photographic evidence," said French. "Yet there are compelling reasons for thinking that the first person to fly was Bill Frost." In an interview given in 1932, three years before his death, Frost described himself as "the pioneer of air travel". Then aged 85 and blind, he spoke of his lack of funding after the war department dismissed his efforts, arguing "the nation does not intend to adopt aerial navigation as a means of warfare".

Jeff Bellingham, a British-born mechanical engineer now living in Minnesota, first discovered Frost's invention after reading Howells's local history book and deciding, on a whim, to see if the inventor had a patent. Today, a century on, there is a new race. Bellingham intends to build a replica, first a quarter-size and later a full-size one, of Frost's aircraft. "I believe it will fly and that afterwards people will acknowledge history books are wrong," Bellingham said.'

FOOD

'If you want at all times to be merry, eat saffron in meat and drink, and you will never be sad. But beware of eating too much, lest you should die of excessive joy'. The Physicians of Myddfai.

Because of the climate, oats were the staple diet of Welsh people in the past, with *cistiau styffylog* (great wooden 'oatmeal chests') being important items of furniture in most houses. There were many varieties of oatmeal dishes served with milk or buttermilk, such as *bwdram, picws mali, llymru, siot, sycan blawd* and *brywes*. In the 1890s, the typical diet of a hill farmer had not changed much for centuries, with bruised oatmeal cake and buttermilk to start the day, bread and butter and tea, and bacon and potatoes for dinner. There was *sycan blawd* (steeped oatmeal, boiled and served with fresh milk) for tea, and oatmeal porridge, or bread and cheese and buttermilk for supper. *Bara-llaeth* was a mixture of hot milk and bread, sometimes thickened with egg. *Stwnsh rhidans* is a popular mash of swede and potato. Cardiganshire's staple dish was its version of the famous Welsh *cawl*, a broth of vegetables and bacon, reheated and added to daily. Potatoes also were added, to fit with the *bwyd llwy* ('spoon food') tradition of Welsh eating, where meat was of less importance than dairy produce.

Cawl is still popular in the winter all over Wales, and 'lobscaws' was a derivant of cawl made with any leftovers from meals. This was the staple diet of the poor Welsh families who flooded into Liverpool from north Wales, looking for work in the nineteenth century. From this we have the slang for a Liverpudlian – a 'scouser'. 'Lobscouse' was the popular name on sailing ships for the broth that was served from the galley.

Cawl dates from prehistory, formerly a mutton broth with any available vegetables thrown in, and a winter favourite for all Welsh mothers to give their families in pre-central heating days. Neck of Welsh lamb is browned and then brought to the boil in lamb stock, and peas, broad beans, leek, carrot, onion, turnip and parsnip are added. The dish is seasoned, covered and left to cool for up to three hours. Cauliflower florets and shredded lettuce can be added twenty minutes before the end of cooking time, and the dish is served with crusty bread. Welsh lamb is used in many dishes, often minted or with thyme. In days gone by, the cawl cauldron was just topped up on a daily basis, and reheated for weeks on end.

The best-known cheese in Wales is Caerphilly (*Caerffili*), a soft, crumbly and slightly tart, white cheese which used to be very popular down the pit when Wales had coal miners. This farmhouse cheese was cheap, as it was made from skimmed milk only, and fed to farm workers. When mixed with beer (and sometimes mustard) and toasted on bread, it makes the traditional Welsh Rarebit. The story is that the real name of this should be 'Welsh Rabbit'. In past centuries, many of the staff serving in the rich mansions of England were Welsh. While the lords and ladies upstairs were eating rabbit, the servants downstairs were making

do with cheese on toast, Welsh rabbit. The Welsh always had a passion for roasted cheese, *caws pobi*, which became a national dish back in Tudor times.

Flavoured cream cheeses, such as those with marigolds, were popular as treats in Tudor and Stuart times, and a creamy 'Normandy-type' cheese was made in the 18th century, known as Newport Cheese. Sage cheese was made using sage and spinach juice. Cheese is now being made again in Caerphilly. *Y Fenni* is a marvellous cheddar-type cheese, flavoured with beer and mustard seeds. Unpasteurised cheeses such as Llangloffan (red, and garlic-flavoured) are also very popular, despite the attempts of the EU to close down all non-standardised food producers. Caerfai near St Davids makes organic traditional Caerffili, with one variety having leeks and garlic added. Cwm Tawe offers a pecorino-type cheese made from ewes' milk, and Llanboidy offer a cheese with laverbread. Pen-y-Bont makes four pound wheels of goats' cheese. From Teifi Farmhouse Cheese, there is a superb and mature unpasteurised nettle cheese. The St Ivel – Unigate creamery at Merlin's Bridge, Haverfordwest, produces ten per cent of all the UK's cheese.

Probably the most evocative South Wales meal ingredient is laver (*Porphyra umbiliculis*), a local lettuce-type seaweed – laver bread (*bara lawr*) is a mixture of laver and oatmeal fried, preferably in bacon fat, to make a delicious starter, or served as part of a traditional breakfast with pork sausage, egg and bacon. Laver is extremely nutritious because it is high in protein and iodine and contains vitamins B, B2, A, D and C. It is also low in calories.

Local cockles, mussels, king and queen scallops, lobster and leeks appear in many Welsh restaurant dishes, along with locally caught fresh salmon, superb sewin (sea trout) and other trout.

Glamorgan Sausages are a superb vegetarian combination of spices and local cheese. Eggs are beaten with mustard, parsley, thyme and seasoning, and are added to a cheese and breadcrumb mixture. 'Sausages' are rolled, dipped into beaten egg, and fried in oil until golden brown.

Another lovely vegetarian speciality is Anglesey Eggs, *Wyau Ynys Môn*. This features leeks, mashed potatoes, butter, eggs, cheese, milk, breadcrumbs and nutmeg.

Bara brith has always been popular, bread with dried fruit (softened overnight in hot tea) in it, to accompany afternoon tea. Welshcakes, *Pice ar y Maen*, are small flat pancakes of sugared dough, and just about every Welsh mother always had some on hand. Until the 1950s, most households had one of the heavy, flat, iron bakestones used for cooking them. Lardy Cake is also popular, a very moist and heavy fruit bread, delicious with a hot drink. A Glamorgan speciality is *teisen lap*, a long 'cut and come again' cake made with currants and nutmeg.

According to 'The Guinness Book of Records', Bernard Lavery of Llanharry holds no less than fifteen World and five UK records for growing fruit and vegetables, including the world records for a cabbage (124 lbs), marrow (108 lbs), courgette (65 lbs), celery (46 lbs), cucumber (20 lbs) and parsnip (171 inches). His British records are for pumpkin (710 lbs), squash (504 lbs), watermelon (36 lbs), melon (18 lbs) and carrot (11 lbs).

Wales is an excellent place for mushrooming with its clean air and fresh climate – the world record for a total fungi spore count was established near Cardiff in 1971, with 161,037 spores to the cubic metre.

Wales is famous for its lamb, regarded by many as the finest in the world. Mountain lambs feed off pure grass and sweet herbs such as wild thyme. From Cardigan and Gower there is Saltmarsh lamb.

Similarly, beef from the Welsh Black Cattle is highly regarded.

Wales, being a coastal nation, supports small fishing fleets, but a considerable quantity of the catch, particularly lobster and other shell fish, are exported to France and Spain.

Wales also boasts a number of highly praised food markets. Swansea's 'Covered' Market has been acclaimed a number of times in the 1990s as Britain's best food market.

One should end this section with a word of praise for the Welshwoman who single-handedly brought English cooking into the 20th century, Elizabeth David (1913-1992). Born Elizabeth Gwynne, her early works (*Mediterranean Food* 1950, *French Country Cooking* 1951 and *Italian Food* 1954) brought the attention of the British to such exotic substances as olive oil, previously only sold in chemists. Versed in the history of gastronomy, her scholarly books have influenced three generations of chefs to the extent that good British restaurants now rival their equivalents anywhere in the world.

G

GAMBLING

Richard (Beau) Nash was born in Swansea in 1674, educated at Carmarthen (Caerfyrddin) Grammar School and Jesus College, Oxford, and supported himself in London as a gambler. He moved to Bath in 1705 and established The Assembly Rooms, drawing up a polished code of etiquette and dress for society, and chiding The Prince of Wales upon occasions. As Master of Ceremonies, this dandy dictated society manners, bolstered by his income from the gaming rooms. The Gambling Laws of 1740-45 deprived Beau Nash of his source of income, but from 1758 until his death in 1761 the Corporation of Bath gave him an allowance of ten guineas a month in recognition of his services in building up Bath as a spa resort.

GARDENS

Owned by The National Trust, **Gardd Bodnant** (Bodnant Garden), overlooking the River Conwy and Snowdonia, is one of the finest gardens in Europe, with 100 acres (40 hectares) of magnificent trees, shrubs and flowers.

The beautiful **Duffryn Gardens**, near Cardiff, have been sadly neglected owing to council cuts in funding over the years, and have been sold to a hotel chain with Duffryn House. Hopefully, the public will still have access at a reasonable fee. Some of its fine collection of acers are being moved to the new National Botanic Garden of Wales, being conceived at Myddleton Hall, Carmarthenshire.

Gardd Powys (Powis Garden) has formal and informal gardens in the grounds of Powis Castle. This National Trust property was originally built by the Welsh princes of Powys. Many of the collection of Indian treasures of 'Clive of India' are displayed there. These are probably the most famous of Wales's great gardens.

A 'Guide to the Historic Parks and Gardens of Wales' is available from The Welsh Historic Gardens Trust, Tŷ Leri, Talybont, Ceredigion, SY24 5ER, and a fascinating tour of Wales could be based on the booklet of sixty-three tourist attractions. Featured are Clough Williams-Ellis' Portmeirion, Humphrey Repton's Plas Newydd, Gwydir castle, Bodelwyddan Castle, Erddig Hall, Chirk Castle, Nanteos Mansion, Llanerch-aeron, Stackpole, Margam and Tredegar Park, among many other superb days out.

GHOSTS

There are hundreds of ghosts reported across Wales in its castles, ruined mansions and priories.

Possibly the earliest poltergeist infestation in Wales or Britain for that matter was reported by Geraldus Cambrensis. Reference is made in his *Itinerary through Wales* to an 'unclean spirit' that appeared in a house in Orielton. Dirt and 'other things' were thrown, a noise was heard.

Ghosts and other spectres have been sighted in, amongst myriad places, Llanina House, Aberavon, Plas Mawr in Conwy, Roch Castle in Haverfordwest, Plas Newydd in Llangollen, St Donat's Castle in Llantwit Major, St Michael's Church in Monkton, and Bush House in Pembroke.

Probably one of the most famous hauntings is that of Tintern Abbey by the phantom monk. The story appears in Lord Halifax's famous *Ghost Book* (1937) having previously been privately printed in 1910. The ghost transpired to be a Saxon soldier who had been killed fighting for Henry II. He had been hurriedly buried without a Mass. He communicated by indicating letters to the writer's wife and laboriously they realised he wished Masses to be read and he would feel 'infinitely' easier. Masses were said and ten years later at a seance the ghost again communicated to two psychic women: 'Very many thanks for the Masses said.' The two ladies claimed at the same time they saw a figure of a bearded, middle-aged and handsome man dressed in strange close-fitting clothes of grey material.

There are tales galore of hauntings in Welsh churches, castles, houses and even streams, caves and mountains.

GLYNDŴR – OWAIN AP GRUFFYDD – LORD OF GLYNDYFRDWY (c.1353-c.1416)

For some Welshmen, Millennium Day will be 16th September, 2000, Glyndŵr's Day, six hundred years since a company of nobles gathered in his manor at Glyndyfrdwy to proclaim Owain Glyndŵr Prince of Wales.

No other Welsh leader is referred to simply by his surname. Owain Glyndŵr is the Welsh leader 'sans pareil',

the name a rallying cry for all things Welsh. The group of people who regularly set alight to English holiday homes in remote areas of Wales from the 1960s to the 1980s called themselves *Meibion Glyndŵr*, 'The Sons of Glyndŵr'. Glyndŵr not only lit up Wales with a united rebellion against overwhelming odds, but also his mysterious disappearance from history left an unbeaten feeling in Welsh hearts. He was the last *Mab Darogan*, 'Son of Prophecy' for the Welsh bards, before Henry Tudor (Tudwr or Tudor) took the English crown in 1485 from the last of the Angevins, Richard Plantagenet.

There are numerous Welsh legends about Glyndŵr's birth. They include the fact that his father's horses were standing in blood up to their fetlocks in their stables, and that the baby would cry at the sight of a weapon, and only stop when he could touch it. The legends are referred to in Shakespeare's 'Henry IV, Part I':

> '. . . At my birth
> The front of heaven was full of fiery
>   shapes;
> The goats ran from the mountains,
>   and the herds
> Were strangely clamorous to the
>   frighted fields.
> These signs have marked me
>   extraordinary,
> And all the courses of my life do show,
> I am not in the roll of common men.'

Glyndŵr could trace his heritage back to Rhodri Mawr, who was head of the royal houses of Gwynedd, Powys and Deheubarth. He was born around 1353, and some say he was educated at Oxford. It is known that he studied for seven years at the Inns of Court in Westminster. Later he became squire to the Earl of Arundel and Henry Bolingbroke, later Henry IV. Fluent in Latin, English, French and Welsh, he served King Richard II in his 1385 Scottish campaign. He also may have fought on the Continent for the English King, but records are incomplete. Aged around forty-five, after a life of service to the crown, it appears that he returned to Wales to retire to his great family estates at Glyndyfrdwy (an area of the Dee Valley, between Llangollen and Corwen), and at Cynllaith on the other side of the Berwyn Hills. (Glyndyfrdwy means valley of the river Dee, and was shortened to Glyndŵr, meaning valley of water). At Sycharth, in Cynllaith, was Glyndŵr's chief house, protected by moats, with nine guest rooms, resident minstrels and bards, fishponds, deerpark, dovecot, vineyard, orchards, mill, wheat fields and peacocks. His income from his estates, around £200 a year, had enabled this faithful servant of the English Crown to settle down in 1398 with his wife Margaret, and nine or so children.

But just four years later, in 1402, the English had burnt down both the manor houses at Sycharth and Glyndyfrdwy, of this fifty year-old nobleman. It is difficult to describe the desolation Glyndŵr must have felt about the destruction of Sycharth, in particular. All that is left is the moat, in one of the most beautiful parts of Wales. His family bard Iolo Goch, who died about 1398, has left us a full description, which ends:

'Seldom has there been seen there
Either a latch or a lock,
Or someone playing porter,
No lack of bountiful gifts,
No need, no hunger, no shame,

No-one is parched at Sycharth.
The best Welshman, bold leader,
Owns this land, Pywer Lew's line,
Slim strong man, the land's finest,
And owns this court, place to praise.'
(Translated by Joseph Clancy)

The year of 1399 had been the turning point in Glyndŵr's existence. King Richard II had sailed to Ireland when he heard that the exiled Henry Bolingbroke, son of John of Gaunt, had landed in England. Richard returned via Milford Haven and made for Conwy, choosing Wales as his base for a battle. However, he was met by Henry Percy, Earl of Northumbria, who assured him that Bolingbroke meant no insurrection, but just wanted to inherit his father's lands and title. Richard rode to Conwy Castle to listen to Bolingbroke's request, but was ambushed, forced to 'abdicate' in favour of Bolingbroke, who then became Henry IV. King Richard was spirited away to Pontefract Castle and disappeared from history. Richard's royal baggage train, still at Conwy, was seized by Henry's troops, but then 'liberated' by local Welshmen, who recognised treason when they saw it. Henry IV therefore was not over-enamoured of the Welsh, and it also appears that Glyndŵr might have been a squire to Richard II, as well as to Bolingbroke. Owain Glyndŵr had also in the past fought for King Richard and Henry Bolingbroke was obviously dubious as to his loyalty to an usurper.

King Richard's abduction and murder ruined Glyndŵr's idyllic existence after just one year of retirement. His income from his estates was around two hundred pounds a year, but in 1399 Reginald Grey, Lord of Ruthin, stole some of his Glyndyfwrdwy lands.

Glyndŵr was legally trained, and decided to fight Grey with a lawsuit in the English Parliament. A proud and loyal man, of royal blood, extremely tall for his times, he wore his hair down to his shoulders against the prevailing fashion of cropped hair in London. His case was dismissed with the comment *'What care we for barefoot Welsh dogs!'*

Even Shakespeare referred to Glyndŵr as a brave and cultivated man:

'. . . a worthy gentleman,
Exceeding well read, and profited
In strange concealments, valiant as
* a lion,*
And wondrous affable, and as bountiful
As mines of India',

and he gives Glyndŵr these lines:

'For I was trained in the English court,
Where, being but young, I framed to
* the harp*
Many an English ditty lovely well
And gave the tongue an helpful
* ornament.'*
('Henry IV, Part I)

We can see that Owain Glyndŵr was not the type of man to be thrown out, and treated like a dog, by an ignorant French-speaking English Parliament. The new king, Henry IV, now raised taxes in Wales, and his aggressive (and illiterate) Marcher Lords like Grey urged him to settle the growing unrest there. Henry was preoccupied with Scotland, however, and instructed his barons to offer free pardons to lawbreakers, hoping to defuse the situation. Lord Grey offered a pardon and a position as master forester to Gruffydd ap Dafydd, who had stolen some of his horses. The Welshman gave himself up,

as requested, at Oswestry, but was lucky to escape alive.

He sent a letter to Grey about the betrayal:

'I was told that you are in purpose to let your men burn and slay in any land which succours me and in which I am taken. Without doubt as many men as you slay for my sake will I burn and slay for yours. And doubt not that I will have bread and ale of the best that is in your Lordship.'

Lord Grey sent a copy to the Prince of Wales, the future Henry V, together with a copy of his reply to Gruffydd, threatening him:

'I hope we shall do thee a privy thing, a rope, a ladder, and a ryng (noose), high on gallows for to hang. And thus shall be your ending.'

Grey could not be trusted. He desperately wanted more land in Wales. When Henry IV summoned each noble to bring a quota of men to fight in Scotland, Grey did not pass on the message to Owain Glyndŵr. His absence from the army, just after the Parliamentary slighting, would hurt Glyndŵr's standing further in Henry's eyes. Henry's army was badly beaten. The king now allowed Grey leave to proceed against his *'treacherous subject'*, Glyndŵr.

Lord Grey decided that a frontal assault was unlikely to succeed, and therefore arranged a meeting to discuss Glyndŵr's grievances. Glyndŵr agreed, but knowing Grey's record, asked for only a small band of men to accompany the Marcher Lord. Grey agreed, and arrived to open discussions at Sycharth. Luckily, Iolo Goch was told of a much larger band of Lord Grey's horsemen, hidden in the woods outside the house, waiting for the signal to attack. Iolo Goch entertained the host, and singing in Welsh alerted Glyndŵr to the threat. Owain made an excuse and fled his beloved Sycharth to his other estate, further west at Glyndyfrdwy, just before Grey's troops arrived.

Here on 16th September 1400, Glyndŵr took the 'Red Dragon' of Cadwaladr and Wales as his standard. Aged almost fifty, he was proclaimed Prince of Wales, by Welshmen flocking to Glyndyfrdwy. Students from Oxford and Cambridge, labourers, noblemen and friars came to support him, resenting English wrongs. On 18th September, Glyndŵr's small, poorly armed force rode into Lord Grey's base of Ruthin, looted the fair and fired the town. No-one was killed, but fourteen rebels were captured and hanged. Glyndŵr's band soon learned about fast-moving warfare. By 24th September, they had fired and looted Denbigh, Flint, Hawarden, and Rhuddlan, and were moving on to Welshpool. However, the Sheriff of Shrewsbury had raised men from the Border and Midlands, and beat Glyndŵr's little force decisively on the banks of the Vyrnwy River. On 25th September, Henry IV arrived in Shrewsbury with his army, and dismembered Goronwy ap Tudwr, a local nobleman, sending his limbs along the Welsh borders to Chester, Hereford, Ludlow and Bristol, as an example to those thinking of supporting Glyndŵr.

Glyndŵr was now in hiding when his aggrieved cousins, Goronwy ap Tudwr's kinsmen on Anglesey, Gwilym and Rhys Tudwr, started a second rebellion. Near Beaumaris, at Rhos Fawr, the Tudwr army was defeated but managed to melt away before it was destroyed. Henry IV then destroyed Llanfaes Abbey, as its Franciscan monks had supported the Welsh rebels. Henry marched to the coast at Mawddwy and returned to Shrewsbury. The small Welsh army watched him all the way, not strong enough to face the Plantagenet force. Henry offered a pardon to Glyndŵr's brother, Tudwr, which he accepted. However, Owain Glyndŵr was excluded from terms, and all his lands given to the Earl of Somerset, John Beaufort. It looked as if Glyndŵr's days were numbered at the end of the year 1400.

The Marcher Lords were allowed to take any Welsh land that they could by force of arms or subterfuge. On top of this, in 1401, the English Parliament passed laws that no Welsh person could hold official office, nor marry any English person. The Welsh could not live in England, and had to pay for the damage caused by the 1400 rebellions. This racial purity enforcement enraged the Welsh of all classes.

Glyndŵr was back now at Glyndyfrdwy, isolated with few supporters, as Gwynedd had accepted the royal pardon. Other noble Welsh families sent envoys to King Henry, complaining about the brutality and taxes of the Marcher Lords. However, the situation looked bleak until the Tudwr brothers once more decided to change the rules of the game. They emerged from hiding in their Anglesey stronghold. While the garrison of Conwy Castle was at church outside the walls, on Good Friday 1401, two of their men posed as labourers, gained access to the castle and killed the two gatekeepers. Gwilym and Rhys Tudwr, with a band of just forty men, fired the town and took control of Conwy Castle. Henry Percy, nicknamed Hotspur, controlled north Wales, and needed to get them out of the castle. After weeks of negotiations, the Welsh were starving. Both sides agreed to a sad compromise. The Tudwrs were guaranteed free passage back to Anglesey upon the giving up of some of their force. Gwilym selected them in their sleep – they were later drawn, hanged, disembowelled and quartered while alive by Hotspur, their remains being scattered about Wales as a warning against further rebellion.

Many Welshmen again started returning from England to Wales, and were backed by supporters of King Richard (by now probably dead) with donations to the Welsh cause. A man called William Clark had his tongue pulled out for daring to speak against Henry IV, then his hand cut off for writing against him, then he was beheaded. By May 1401, another small band of men had joined Glyndŵr, but he was routed by Hotspur near Cader Idris. He was forced to move South to the slopes of Pumlumon and raised his standard again where Nant-y-Moch reservoir now corrupts the land. With around four hundred men only, he rode down to loot and burn Llandrindod Wells, New Radnor, Cwmhir Abbey and Montgomery. Welshpool resisted and Glyndŵr returned with the remains of his little band (just one hundred and twenty men, according to Gruffydd Hiraethog), to the safety of the Pumlumon (Plynlimon) foothills and caves.

Unknown to him, an army of fifteen hundred Flemings from the settlements in south-west Wales – the 'Englishry' south of the Preseli Hills – was marching to exterminate this threat to their livelihoods. They surrounded him and charged downhill at Glyndŵr's trapped

army at Hyddgen on the Pumlumon foothills. Glyndŵr's army knew that they either died there and then, or would be slowly disembowelled if captured. The incentive was enough, and they halted and reversed the Flemings' charge. News spread all over Wales that the Welsh had won a real battle at last.

Hotspur, disillusioned by a lack of support from Henry in Wales, now took his north Wales peace-keeping army back to Northumberland. This was Glyndŵr's opportunity to traverse all Wales, hitting Marcher Lord possessions and those of their sympathisers. These years are described by Sir John Wynn in his 'History of the Gwydir Family': *'beginning in Anno 1400, continued fifteen years which brought such a desolation, that green grass grew on the market place in Llanrwst . . . and the deer fled in the churchyard'. In 1400 Owain Glyndŵr came to Glamorgan and won the castle of Cardiff and many more. He also demolished the castles of Penlline, Landough, Flemingston, Dunraven of the Butlers, Tal-y-Fan, Llanbleddian, Llanquian, Malefant and that of Penmark. And many of the people joined him of one accord, and they laid waste the fences and gave the lands in common to all. They took away from the powerful and rich, and distributed the plunder among the weak and poor. Many of the higher orders and chieftains were obliged to flee to England.'*

The king saw that Wales was turning to Glyndŵr, and that his Marcher Lords could not control any parts of the country. In October 1401, Henry marched to Bangor in north-east Wales, then west to Caernarfon in Gwynedd, then south, looting the abbey at Ystrad Fflur (Strata Florida) near Aberystwyth. Henry carried on to Llandovery, butchering any Welshman he caught, while Glyndŵr's men picked off his outriders and made constant assaults on his baggage train. At Llandovery, Henry publicly tortured to death Llywelyn ap Gruffydd Fychan for refusing to betray Glyndŵr's whereabouts.

While his supporting bands harried the King's army, Glyndŵr unsuccessfully attacked Caernarfon and Harlech castles. Facing a professional army with mere volunteers, and holding no castles of consequence, Glyndŵr made overtures to the Scots, Irish and French for desperately-needed assistance against their mutual *'mortal enemies, the Saxons.'* He even asked Hotspur to try to arrange a peace with Henry IV. The King was inclined to agree, but Lord Grey hated Glyndŵr, and Lord Somerset wanted more Welsh estates, so they agreed to use peace talks as a device to capture Glyndŵr. Fortunately, Hotspur, an honourable northerner, refused to be part of this treacherous charade.

The year 1402 started off well for Owain Glyndŵr. On 31st January, he appeared before Ruthin Castle, challenging Grey to fight. Grey was captured, trussed up and carried away to be imprisoned in Dolbadarn Castle. Perhaps Glyndŵr should have killed the man who was the cause of all his troubles, but he immediately ransomed him for £10,000. Some money was raised immediately, and his son was given in surety for the rest. Raising this ransom effectively ruined Grey, who signed an agreement never again to attack the man he had made an outlaw. (If positions had been reversed, the Norman Lord Grey would have tortured Glyndŵr before hanging, drawing and quartering him. The Welsh did not believe in such bestiality. We can also see that when Glyndŵr captured Lord Mortimer in battle at Pilleth on 22nd June, Mortimer eventually married

Glyndŵr's daughter in captivity, and died fighting for him against the English.)

Soon after, Glyndŵr survived an assassination attempt by his cousin, Hywel Sele of Nannau, probably on the orders of King Henry. An arrow was deflected by the armour under his jerkin, and Hywel Sele was killed and placed in a hollow oak tree. Throughout the rest of the year, Glyndŵr ravaged north Wales (leaving alone Hotspur's estates in Denbigh), and then moved against Powys, controlled by the great Marcher Earls, the Mortimers.

On St Alban's Day, 22nd June, at the Battle of Pilleth (near Knighton), Edmund Mortimer's English knights and Herefordshire levies charged uphill at Glyndŵr's army. Mortimer's Welsh archers poured volley after volley of deadly arrows into the English charge, apparently in an unrehearsed expression of support for Glyndŵr. (Much of western Herefordshire and Worcestershire was Welsh-speaking at this time). Up to two thousand of Mortimer's troops were killed on the slopes. Rhys Gethin, Rhys the Fierce, had drawn up his men hidden behind the top of the hill, so Mortimer had underestimated the Welsh force of four thousand, as well as having been unable to control his Welsh archers. Mortimer was captured in the battle, but Henry IV accused him of treason and would not ransom him. Hotspur, Mortimer's brother-in-law, was incensed that a villain like Lord Grey could be ransomed, whereas Henry had set his mind against the innocent Mortimer.

In Shakespeare's 'Henry IV Part I', a horrified courtier recounts:

'. . . the noble Mortimer,
Leading the men of Hereford to fight

Against the irregular and wild
Glendower,
Was by the rude hands of that
Welshman taken;
A thousand of his people butchered,
Upon whose dead corpse there was
such misuse,
Such beastly, shameless transformation
By those Welsh women done, as may
not be,
Without much shame, retold or
spoken of.'

Forget this propaganda against Welsh women – after this event Henry IV passed legislation banning English men marrying Welsh women. Who would have wanted to marry such harridans if the stories of such atrocity were true?

Glyndŵr at last had freedom to do whatever he wanted – he attacked and burnt Abergavenny and Cardiff, and the ruins of his sacking of the Bishop's Palace at Llandaf in Cardiff can still be seen. He besieged Caernarfon, Cricieth and Harlech castles. This forced Henry IV to totally ignore his Scottish problems and assemble three armies, totalling a massive one hundred thousand men, on the Welsh borders. The bards had been singing of Glyndŵr's supernatural powers, and during Henry's advance into Wales, appalling weather conditions forced all three armies to return to England by the end of September. It was thought at the time that Glyndŵr could command the elements, and well as possessing a magic Raven's stone that made him invisible. Even the English troops ascribed magical properties to this guerrilla partisan. Again, this is referred to in Henry IV, Part I:

'Three times hath Henry Bolingbroke
made head

Against my power. Thrice from the
banks of the Wye
And sandy-bottomed Severn have
I sent
Him bootless home, and weather-beaten
back.'

A 1402 entry in 'Annales Henrici Quarti', the English recording of the times, reads that Glyndŵr *'almost destroyed the King and his armies, by magic as it was thought, for from the time they entered Wales to the time they left, never did a gentle air breathe on them, but throughout whole days and nights, rain mixed with snow and hail afflicted them with cold beyond endurance.'*

In 1402, the imprisoned Edmund Mortimer married Owain Glyndŵr's daughter, Jane. Mortimer's nephew, the young Earl of March, had a far better claim to the English throne than Henry IV, and no doubt Glyndŵr was hoping that Henry Bolingbroke would be killed and Wales made safe with an English king as an ally. His big problem was that Hotspur captured the Scots leader, the Earl of Douglas, at the battle of Homildon, securing England's northern border. With his Scottish problems solved, this allowed Henry IV to plan to finally subdue Wales. Glyndŵr, on his part, wanted complete control of Wales before Henry struck.

In 1403, Owain Glyndŵr kept up his blockade of the northern Welsh castles, while attacking Brecon and Dinefwr and trying to displace the Flemings from Pembrokeshire. Glyndŵr's able lieutenants were the three Rhys's; Rhys Gethin (the Fierce), Rhys Ddu (the Black), and Rhys ap Llewellyn. The latter had real reason to hate the invading English – it was his father, Llewelyn ap Gruffydd Fychan, who had been slowly killed in front of

Henry IV at Llandovery in the dark days of 1401, for refusing to lead him to Glyndŵr. Later in 1403, a Welsh army was beaten at Laugharne by Lord Thomas Carew. Glyndŵr also sadly learned of the deliberate demolition of his manors and estates at Sycharth and Glyndfrdwy by the Prince of Wales, Henry of Monmouth, who later won undying fame at Agincourt.

Hotspur, meanwhile, wanted to ransom the Earl of Douglas, but Henry demanded him as a prisoner to secure the ransom. Coupling this insult with the argument over Edmund Mortimer's ransom, Hotspur allied with Edmund Mortimer, Douglas and Glyndŵr to form an army near Chester. At the bloody Battle of Shrewsbury, Hotspur was killed, despite the havoc wrought by his Chester archers. This tragedy happened before he could link up with Glyndŵr. Henry then went to Northumberland to suppress a small uprising by Hotspur's father, Earl Percy of Northumberland. Glyndŵr ravaged Herefordshire in Henry's absence.

The enraged King Henry now passed legislation that any Welshman found in any border town would be executed. He marched through south Wales to Carmarthen, but like the previous invasion, Glyndŵr did not come to the party. Henry returned to England and within a week Glyndŵr had taken Cardiff, Caerphilly, Newport, Usk and Caerleon. Some French troops were assisting Glyndŵr by now, and his army had grown to at least 10,000 men-at-arms.

By 1404, Owain Glyndŵr's main focus was the taking of the seemingly impregnable 'Iron Ring' of castles in north Wales. He won over the starving Harlech garrison by pardons or bribes when it had only sixteen men left. The great castles of Cricieth and Aberystwyth then fell, and at Machynlleth, in The Parliament House, Owain Glyndŵr held his first Parliament. Envoys came from France and Spain, and an ambassador was sent to France. Dafydd ap Llewelyn ap Hywel, Davy Gam ('squint-eyed') tried to assassinate him here for Henry IV, and was surprisingly imprisoned rather than cut to pieces. (Davy Gam later was knighted by Henry V as he lay dying at Agincourt). Another Welsh Parliament was held in Dolgellau in 1404.

Glyndŵr now took a small army to again pillage Herefordshire, but the Earl of Warwick captured his standard at Campstone Hill near Grosmont Castle. Glyndŵr just escaped capture. Fortunately, the English did not pursue the defeated troops, which regrouped and beat Warwick at Craig-y-Dorth, three miles from Monmouth, and chased them back into the fortified town. Glyndŵr was in the south-east awaiting a French invasion fleet of 60 vessels under the Count of March, who for some reason never landed. Glyndŵr returned to his court at Harlech. In Anglesey, Owain's forces were now beaten at the battle of Rhosmeirch, and also lost Beaumaris castle.

In 1405, Rhys Gethin burned Grosmont Castle in Monmouthshire, but was then decisively beaten by Prince Henry, using Welsh archers. Glyndŵr sent his almost identical brother, Tudur, and his son Gruffydd to restore the situation by attacking Usk Castle where Prince Henry had established himself. In the battle of Pwll Melin, two miles away, Tudur and Abbot John ap Hywel of Llantarnam were killed. Gruffydd ab Owain Glyndŵr was imprisoned in the Tower of London in disgusting conditions until he soon died. Three hundred prisoners were beheaded in front of the citizens of Usk, as an example *pour les autres*.

After the Welsh defeats at Grosmont and Usk, Henry now offered a pardon to those who renounced the rebellion, and thereby regained full control of south-east Wales. He then gathered an army of forty thousand at Hereford to advance into mid and north Wales. Another English force took Beaumaris and control of Anglesey in the far north. At this time, Archbishop Scrope of York led a rebellion in the north of England. Henry diverted his forces to Shipton Moor where he beat back the northern rebels. This gave Glyndŵr some breathing space, and he gathered ten thouand men in Pembrokeshire to wait for an invasion fleet of one hundred and forty French ships. Around five thousand Frenchmen arrived at Milford, joined with Glyndŵr and sacked the English/Fleming town of Haverfordwest, but could not take the castle. They next looted Carmarthen and then took over Glamorgan, leaving Glyndŵr back in control of most of Wales.

In August 1405, he moved on to attack England, its first invasion since 1066. Henry raced to Worcester to face the threat of Glyndŵr, who was camped on Woodbury Hill. There were some skirmishes, but Glyndŵr had no lines of supply, so he retreated back to Wales, following a scorched earth policy. Henry's starving army was forced to call off the pursuit, freezing as the bitter winter took hold. Again, the terrible weather was blamed upon Glyndŵr's supernatural powers. This had been Henry's fifth invasion of Wales and still Glyndŵr seemed untouchable.

In 1406 a treaty was made between the dead Hotspur's remaining Percy family of Northumberland, Earl Mortimer and Glyndŵr. This 'Tripartite Indenture' divided England and Wales between the three Houses, with Glyndŵr possessing Wales and gaining a 'buffer zone' on its borders. At his second Machynlleth Parliament, Glyndŵr wrote to Charles VI of France, asking for recognition, support and a 'Holy Crusade' against Henry for pillaging abbeys and killing clergymen. In turn, Glyndŵr promised the recognition by St Davids of the French-based Pope Benedict XIII. (Welsh Parliaments were also held in Pennal, Harlech and Dolgellau). Glyndŵr also asked Papal permission to place two universities, one each in north and south Wales, to build a future for his country. This letter was signed *'Owain by the Grace of God, Prince of Wales'* and is in the French National Archives.

However, Henry IV was wasting away through syphilis or leprosy, which enabled his son Henry, the 'English' Prince of Wales to take control of the Welsh campaigns. He beat a Welsh army, killing yet another of Glyndŵr's sons in March, and retook South Wales, fining the landowners heavily to support his thrust into north Wales. North Wales, being fought over for five years, had neither financial nor manpower reserves to support Glyndŵr, but he still held around two thirds of the land in Wales and castles at Aberystwyth and Harlech. At his time, he almost disappears from history except for bardic references of him roaming the country.

In 1407, Prince Henry beseiged Aberystwyth Castle with seven cannon. One, 'The King's Gun' weighed four and a half tons. Rhys Ddu held out and Henry returned to England. Glyndŵr reinforced the castle, while England unfortunately signed a peace treaty with France. In this year, Owain's great ally, Louis of Orleans, was murdered in mysterious circumstances in Paris. It may have been the work of English spies.

In 1408 Glyndŵr received another blow. His ally, the old Earl of Northumberland, Hotspur's father, was killed at the Battle of Braham Moor by Prince Henry's forces. The Prince then re-entered Wales, bombarded Aberystwyth into submission, and by 1409 had also taken Harlech, Glyndŵr's last bastion, capturing his wife and family. Edmund Mortimer, the former enemy who became his son-in-law in captivity, died (probably of starvation) in Harlech, fighting for Glyndŵr. Owain had just managed to escape from Harlech as the besiegers moved in. It must have been a difficult decision to leave his family there, while he tried to round up support rather than be cornered. A sad footnote has been the discovery noted in John Lloyd's 1931 book *Owen Glendower*. He *'left behind him in the castle one little personal relic which has recently been unearthed in the course of excavations, viz. a gilt bronze boss from a set of horse harness, bearing the four lions rampant which he had assumed as prince of Wales'*. The four lions rampant, counterchanged in gold and red, were the ancient arms of the princes of Gwynedd. Glyndŵr was more a descendant of the Houses of Deheubarth and Powys than Gwynedd, but he had needed that provenance, that in effect died out with the vicious assassination of Owain Lawgoch, to be accepted throughout Wales.

The last gasp of Glyndŵr's revolt occurred near Welshpool Castle when a raiding party under Phillip Scudamore, Rhys Tudwr and Rhys Ddu was

beaten and the leaders captured. After the usual revolting, slow, barbarous executions, Scudamore's head was placed on a spike at Shrewsbury, Rhys ap Tudwr's at London, and Rhys Ddu's at Chester.

In 1413, the Plantagenet Prince of Wales succeeded as Henry V, and in 1415 offered a pardon to Glyndŵr and any of his men. In 1416, he tried again, through Glyndŵr's remaining son Maredudd, who himself accepted a pardon in 1421. It thus appears that Glyndŵr was still alive a few years after his last recorded sighting. Gruffydd Young, in the Council of Constance in France, was still working for Owain Glyndŵr in 1415, stating that Wales was a nation that should have a vote in ending the papal schism. Glyndŵr would have been around sixty-five years old at this time, having spent his last fifteen years in constant warfare against the English crown.

Some say Owain died in a cave in Pumlumon (Plynlimon), where it all started, mourning the death of all but one of his six sons. Others believed he ended his days with his daughter Alice and her husband John Scudamore in Golden Valley in Herefordshire. The present owner of the Great Hall of Kentchurch, Jan Scudamore, has been besieged with people asking permission to search her estate for the remains of Glyndŵr.

Many identify him with Sion Cent of Kentchurch (see Magic), a poet, magician and mystic whose grave can still be seen, half in and half out of Grosmont church. Other stories have him dying at Monnington Court, near Kentchurch, at Monnington-on-Wye in 1415, in the deep oakwoods of Glamorgan and on a mountain ridge in Snowdonia. The bards raided Arthurian legend to put him sleeping with his men in a cave to be awakened again in Wales's hour of greatest need. One bard stated that Glyndŵr, *'went into hiding on St Matthew's Day in Harvest (1415) and thereafter his hiding place was unknown. Very many say that he died: the seers maintain that he did not '*.

Glyndŵr's greatest problem had been that he was up against the greatest soldier of his age, Harry of Monmouth, who within a few years was to win at Agincourt with Welsh archers, and be recognised as the future King of France. Henry cut his teeth against a massively under-resourced Glyndŵr, who had no incomes to pay his troops and relied on volunteers against a vastly superior professional force. However, Owain could still point to a career where he set up his own law-courts and chancery, tried to form the first Welsh universities, summoned parliaments, sent envoys to foreign courts and nominated bishops. However, this last battle between the 'Welsh' Prince of Wales and the 'French-Plantagenet' Prince of Wales could have only one ending.

Repressive laws were enacted after the rebellion to stop any future threat from Wales to the English crown. No-one with Welsh parents could buy land near the Marcher towns, own weapons, become citizens of any towns or hold any offices. In lawsuits involving a Welshman and an Englishman, the Englishman decided the verdict and the sentence. Gatherings of Welsh people were forbidden, and an Englishman marrying a Welsh woman became legally Welsh, forfeiting all his rights of citizenship. No Welshman could be a juror. These and many more impositions, on top of the already harsh

regime of the Statute of Rhuddlan of 1282, ensured Harri Tudwr great popular support in his move to gain the crown of England in 1485.

Massive taxes were raised to pay for the invasions of the two Henry's, but Welshmen were not allowed to help each other to harvest their fields, causing major food shortages. If merchants of any towns were robbed in Wales, and the property was not returned within a week, they could retaliate upon *any* Welshman that they could seize.

Richard Sale's excellent book, *Owain Glyndŵr's Way* gives the background to Wales, details of Glyndŵr's life, and a description of the long-distance footpath that commemorates the man. The best summary of Glyndŵr is by the noted English historian, G. M. Trevelyan . . . *'this wonderful man, an attractive and unique figure in a period of debased and selfish politics'*. The French historian, Henri Martin, calls Glyndŵr a man of courage and genius. Most English encyclopaedias do not mention him – one of the truly great, principled and forward-thinking men in British history. Welsh schools have not taught the history Glyndŵr in any depth whatsoever, for over a hundred years, but his name still inspires Welshmen all over the world.

J. E. Lloyd puts Glyndŵr into proper perspective in the Welsh national psyche:

'Throughout Wales, his name is the symbol for the vigorous resistance of the Welsh spirit to tyranny and alien rule and the assertion of a national character which finds its fitting expression in the Welsh language . . . For the Welshmen of all subsequent ages, Glyndŵr has been a national hero, the first,

indeed, in the country's history to command the willing support alike of north and south, east and west, Gwynedd and Powys, Deheubarth and Morgannwg. He may with propriety be called the father of modern Welsh nationalism.'

Although Glyndŵr had briefly won political, cultural and ecclesiastical independence, before final defeat and the harshness of the laws of a revenging English king, the wars had been a personal disaster for him. His closest brother Tudur had died at the Battle of Pwll Melyn in 1405. His son Gruffydd was captured there, and spent the remainder of his years imprisoned in the Tower of London and Nottingham Castle. Glyndŵr's wife, two daughters and three grand-daughters were taken into imprisonment after the fall of Harlech Castle. His son-in-law, Edmund Mortimer, with a good claim to the English crown, died at Harlech. Mortimer's wife, Owain's daughter, died in prison with two of her daughters. Her son Lionel, Owain's grandson and a claimant for both Welsh and English crowns, died. Owain Glyndŵr's closest lieutenants and comrades-in-arms, Rhys Ddu, Rhys ap Llewelyn, Rhys Gethin and Phillip Scudamore had been tortured to death.

It appears that only one relative survived the carnage, his son Maredudd, who had hidden with him when the rebellion was crushed. When Maredudd ab Owain eventually accepted the King's pardon upon 8th April, 1421, it had been twenty years and six months since Owain Glyndŵr had proclaimed himself Prince of Wales. These two decades of fighting against overwhelming odds, of reclaiming Cymru from the Normans, are neglected in all British history books. This British hero has been excised from the history of Britain even more effectively than William Wallace was.

Glyndŵr had no funeral elegy from the bards – he was probably a broken man – but in Welsh mythology his disappearance from history, rather than his capture and execution, gave the poets and gives the nation a hope for the future – Glyndŵr is the Welsh hero par excellence. This is a story of culture, humanity, nobility, treachery, courage, bitter defeat, glorious resurgence and a mysterious finale.

It was not until 1948 that a Parliamentary Act, declaring Glyndŵr to be a proscribed traitor, was repealed.

GOLD

Romans mined in Wales for copper, lead, iron and gold. Gold-mining in Dolaucothi, near Pumsaint in Carmarthenshire is of European importance in the history of prehistoric and Roman technology, and two major aqueducts represent the highest and lowest of nine hydraulic systems. The Celts first found gold here, and the Romans exploited the site by open cast and gallery workings. It was the most technologically advanced mining site in Europe. A seven mile aqueduct was channelled along the hillsides to bring water from the rivers Cothi and Annell. The water was stored in tanks cut into the rocks, from which it was sluiced to remove top soil, wash crushed ore and drive simple machinery.

About a hundredweight of gold a week was extracted by slaves, to send to the imperial mints at Lyons and Rome. Visitors to the site can see the strong-room where gold was stored, a cavalry station and the remains of a

Romano-Celtic temple, and also go on an underground tour. It is the only place that we know the Romans mined gold in Britain, was one of the Empire's main sources of bullion and was so important that they built a fort, where the Dolaucothi Arms Hotel now stands. Work stopped around the second century, until an Australian reopened some of the galleries in 1870, and they were worked until 1939.

The wedding rings of the British royal family are traditionally made of Welsh gold, which commands a price premium to the public because of its rarity. Dolgellau became Wales' answer to the Klondike in the nineteenth century, when gold was found in the hills above Bontddu on the Mawddach Estuary. Earlier the Cistercian monks at Cymer Abbey on the Mawddach had found small gold deposits in the 13th century, and the Romans also found evidence of gold in the area. About 20 small mines were working in the area until the onset of World War One.

At the Welsh Gold Visitor Centre, near Dolgellau, you can chip away at rocks, but will usually only find iron pyrites, 'fool's gold'. This Gwynfynydd Mine, in Snowdonia National Park, (reopened in 1981) is the only mine still producing pure Welsh gold, just a few ounces a day. Welsh gold is more precious than platinum, because of its rarity and difficulty of extraction. Two tons of ore produce just one ounce of gold. Ordinary gold costs £250 a ounce, platinum £650, and Welsh gold £750. It has a slight variation in colour to other gold.

Near Pont Dolgefeiliau in Coed y Brenin, Ganllydd, are a nineteenth century abandoned engine shed and old gold workings, next to the beautiful waterfalls of Pistyll Cain and Rhaeadr Mawddach.

GRAVESTONES

In St Andrews Church in Presteigne is a gravestone marking the death in 1805 of Mary Morgan, a seventeen year-old sentenced to death for the murder of a new-born illegitimate child. The jury included the child's father, and the unanimous verdict meant that the girl was executed before the arrival of a reprieve from London. The original gravestone accusing her of *'sin and shame'* still stands, but the good people of Presteigne put another gravestone facing it, engraved *'He that is without sin among you, let him first cast a stone at her'*, from the Gospel of St John.

In the beautiful ruins of Strata Florida Abbey, near the resting place of the bard Dafydd ap Gwilym, is a Georgian tombstone to the amputated left leg of Henry Hughes, the rest of whom emigrated to America.

Montgomery's churchyard contains 'The Robber's Grave'. John Davies was hanged in 1821 for sheep-stealing. He was the bailiff on Oakfield Farm to a wealthy widow, but Thomas Pearce wanted to marry her, and Robert Parker coveted the farm. They framed him, and he protested his innocence. From the scaffold he cursed his accusers, predicting that for 100 years no grass would grow on his grave. Records show that the prophecy was true. Soon after his death, Pearce became an alcoholic and died in a quarry explosion and Parker died of a wasting disease. A man who planted a rose bush on the bare earth died soon after.

On the gravestone of R. J. Lloyd Price in Bala (see Whisky, Marketing) is chiselled a 'thankyou' card to the race-horse Bendigo. It won the Cambridge-shire Stakes and restored much of Squire Price's fortune.

In Carmarthenshire, the tiny church of Castell Dwyrain near Llanfallteg is decaying. The gravestone to a former rector is in a railed enclosure and reads:

> *"Richard Bowen Jones"*
> *Born 1811 Transferred 1887*
> *Here lie the remains of a*
> *"Classical Ass"*
> *The accursed of his sons by the*
> *name of "Jabrass"*
> *In the earth he is Ammonia and*
> *Trisophate of calcium*
> *On earth a "Home Demon"*
> *and a "Ferocious Old Ruffian".*

The English language was not a majority language in Monmouthshire in 1736, which may be an explanation for the following gravestone to one Philip Stead in Mitchell Troy:

> *Life is unsartain*
> *and deth is so shuer*
> *sin is the wound*
> *& Christ is the cuer.*

The ten ton 1879 stone slab that covers the Vaynor grave of Robert Crawshay, the vicious owner of Merthyr Ironworks, pleads 'GOD FORGIVE ME'. Perhaps he realised the terrible suffering he inflicted on his workers. In the same graveyard is a sad epitaph to a rejected lover:

> *Here lies the body of Gruffydd Shon*
> *Covered here with earth and stone*
> *You may sweep it up or leave it alone,*
> *It will just be the same to Gruffydd Shon.*

There is also a plaque to Catherine Morgan, who lived to one hundred and six, and died in 1794:

> *She was born in the third year*
> *of the reign of King James II*
> *and lived under seven reigns.*

The marvellous Norman Ewenni Priory Church has a tablet to David William, the village blacksmith, who died in 1742:

> *'My sledge and hammer lie decay'd*
> *My bellows too have lost their wind*
> *My fires extinct, my force allay'd*
> *My vice is in the dust confin'd*
> *My coal is spent, my iron's gone*
> *My nails are drove, my work is done.'*

GRUFFYDD AP CYNAN (1055-1137)

From Gruffydd ap Llywelyn ap Seisyllt's death in 1063, there was almost per-manent fighting between the Welsh princes. The laws of Gavelkind meant that kingdoms and princedoms were constantly being broken up between all male heirs, legitimate and illegiti-mate. Gruffydd ap Cynan, grandson of Iago of Gwynedd, landed in Anglesey from Ireland to reclaim his lands from Trahaiarn, in 1075. (His father had died fighting with Gruffydd ap Llywelyn against Harold of Wessex in 1063, when Gruffydd ap Cynan was just eight years old). He defeated Trahaiarn at the Battle of Waederw and recovered Mer-ioneth as well as Gwynedd, but there was a revolt against him because of the conduct of his Irish mercenaries. Gruffydd tried again in 1076, but was forced off Anglesey. In 1081, he re-turned once more, allying himself with Rhys ap Tewdwr to try and heal the land after the depredations of the Earl of Chester and vicious Robert of Rhuddlan.

The carnage in Wales only relented with the victory of Rhys ap Tewdwr (of the royal house of Deheubarth), and Gruffydd ap Cynan (of the royal house of Gwynedd) at the battle of Mynydd Carn in 1081, when Trahaiarn was killed. William the Conqueror, on a pilgrimage to St David's in 1081, recognised Rhys ap Tewdwr's right to Deheubarth.

However, in his attempts to gain the throne of Gwynedd, Gruffydd ap Cynan was captured by Hugh the Fat, Earl of Chester and held as a prisoner in chains at Chester for twelve years. Hugh the Fat had bribed Meirion Goch to bring Gruffydd to a meeting in 1082, where peace might be arranged between the Welsh and Normans.

In 1094, the Earl of Chester had ordered that Gruffydd be displayed in chains at Chester market place so the people could see the fall of the great Prince of Gwynedd. In the bustle of the market, he was rescued by Cynwrig Hir. A blacksmith knocked his chains off and the small rescue party managed to escape to Aberdaron, and sail back across to Ireland. Gruffydd soon returned to Wales, with his fellow prince, Cadwgan ab Bleddyn. He ravaged parts of Shropshire and Cheshire, and defeated the Normans in the woods of Yspwys. William II (William Rufus) invaded Wales in 1095 to restore order, but the Welsh retreated to the hills, and William returned to England. In 1096, Gruffydd defeated Norman armies at Gelli Trafnant and Aber Llech. William led another fruitless invasion in 1097 against Gruffydd and Cadwgan.

In 1098 the earls of Chester and Shrewsbury campaigned against them, and invaded Anglesey, but Gruffydd and Cadwgan fled to Ireland. Norman cruelty led to a fresh revolt, and just then the Scandinavians descended upon Anglesey. The earls were beaten on the banks of the Menai River by the force led by Magnus Barefoot, King of Norway, who personally killed Red Hugh, the Earl of Shrewsbury. Gruffydd now moved to restore and consolidate his Gwynedd power base as the Normans retreated, reigning over Anglesey, Caernarfon and Merioneth.

In 1114, King Henry I invaded with three forces; in South Wales under Strongbow; in North Wales under Alexander of Scotland, and a force under himself against Powys. Gruffydd submitted to him, and promised to give up Gruffydd ap Rhys, another patriotic leader, in order to keep the peace, but Gruffydd ap Rhys quickly fled to Aberdaron. A boat then took him to the safety of the great forest of Ystrad Tawy in Deheubarth. Gruffydd ap Rhys was the son of Rhys ap Tewdwr, the co-victor of Mynydd Carn. The Chronicles tell us that Gruffydd quietly sent a messenger to Pembroke Castle to warn Nest that her brother's life was in danger. Gruffydd ap Rhys later married Gwenllian in Ystrad Tawy (see Gwenllian), and later held a great eisteddfod at Cardigan. The Chronicle of the Princes called him *'the light, and the strength, and the gentleness of the men of Deheubarth'*.

Gruffydd ap Cynan ruled Gwynedd quietly until 1121, when he moved with King Henry quickly to take over Powys, which was riddled with internal disputes. He later took over Deheubarth. His sons Owain and Cadwalladr cemented his grip on most of Wales. Gruffydd ruled over a peaceful Wales until his death in 1137. The work of some poets of his time is preserved in

The Black Book of Carmarthen, and the court poetry of his bard Meilyr survives. His biography was written just twenty years after his death, declaring Gwynedd to be the 'primus inter pares' ('first among equals') of Welsh kingdoms. Gruffydd was buried in Bangor Cathedral to the left of the high altar, and his son, the heroic poet-prince Owain Gwynedd succeeded peacefully.

His daughter Gwenllian was executed by the Normans after the battle of Maes Gwenllian (see Gwenllian). Her son, The Lord Rhys (see Rhys ap Gruffydd) fought with Owain Gwynedd against the Normans, and took over leadership of Welsh resistance upon his death. Thus Gruffydd's descendants carried on the fight for Wales for sixty years after his death, to the death of Rhys ap Gruffydd in 1197. Just thirteen years after this, Welsh leadership had passed to Llywelyn the Great, of the House of Gwynedd. In 1485, Gruffydd ap Cynan's descendant, Henry Tudor, became the first Welsh King of England.

GRUFFYDD AP LLYWELYN AP SEISYLL (1007-1063)

Royal succession was important in Welsh history. Cunedda (c.440 AD) established the main tree of descent, dividing Wales between his eight sons, whereby Meirion received Merioneth, Ceredig had Ceredigion (Cardiganshire) etc. In line from Cunedda were Maelgwn Gwynedd (died 547), Cadwaladr ap Cadfan (defeated by Offa of Mercia in 634), Rhodri Mawr (who united Wales against the Norse invaders, and died in 878), Hywel Dda (who established the Laws, and died in 950), and Gruffydd ap Llywelyn, killed by Harold before Hastings).

Maredudd ap Owain ap Hywel Dda had briefly recreated the Kingdom of Wales from 986 to 989, after the schisms that followed his grandfather's death around 950. Later, Llywelyn ap Seisyll ruled Gwynedd from 1018 to 1023, and had beaten the Prince of Deheubarth to establish himself as King of Wales. Llywelyn's mother, Angharad, was a great-grand-daughter of Hywel Dda. Llywelyn was killed in 1023, through the jealous treachery of Madog, Bishop of Bangor.

Anarchy again restarted upon his death, with all the Welsh princes reasserting their independence. His son, Grufydd ap Llywellyn, was also Maredudd's grandson (on his mother, Angharad's side), but had to flee to France, where he stayed for sixteen years.

Brut y Tywysogion ('The Chronicles of the Princes') records that between 950 and 1100 twenty-eight Welsh princes met violent deaths and four were blinded. In a hundred years, nearly fifty Welsh rulers were tortured, incarcerated, murdered or slain in battle. Wales was racked by internal warfare and invasions by the Mercians until Gruffydd returned from France, and beat Earl Leofric (Lady Godiva's husband) at Rhyd y Groes (near Welshpool) on the Severn in 1038. In 1039, he killed Iago ab Idwal to regain Gwynedd and gain Powys. He ravaged Cardigan and carried off the wife of its prince Hywel ab Edwin.

Gruffydd then gathered forces and won a battle at Pencader in 1041 to control Cardigan, and one at Newport in 1044 to gain South-East Wales, Gwent. Also in 1044, he killed Hywel ab Edwin at the battle of Carmarthen, when Hywel had allied with Danes to gain his revenge. With control of South Wales, Gruffyd now turned aggressively on the Saxon invaders. In 1052 he crushed the Saxons and their Norman mercenaries near Leominster. He caused the death of Gruffydd ap Rhydderch to gain Deheubarth in 1055. Gruffydd was now master of almost all of Wales.

The year 1055 was eventful. Harold of Wessex, son of Earl Godwin, ensured that the Earldom of Mercia went to his brother. The deposed Earl, Leofric's son Aelfgar, allied with Gruffydd and Gruffydd married his daughter, Ealdgyth. The allies burned Hereford, and Gruffydd took possession of Whitford, Hope, Presteigne, Radnor, Bangor-Is-Coed and Chirk, beating a small Saxon army. These lands, across Offa's Dyke, had been in Saxon possession for three-hundred years until the border stabilised. Bishop Leofgar of Hereford assembled a mixed force of Norman settlers and Saxon-English. He crossed the Dyke, but was killed by Gruffydd and his army destroyed in 1056. Gruffydd had settled his court at Rhuddlan, an area heavily settled by Mercians, and from north-east Wales now re-conquered large parts of the Earldom of Chester over Offa's Dyke, including much of Flintshire and Denbighshire.

In 1056-1057 Gruffydd drove Cadwgan ap Meurig out of Morgannwg, to control the last princedom. Gruffydd ap Llywelyn became the only Welshman ever to rule over the whole of Wales. From 1057 until his death in 1063, the whole of Wales recognized his kingship. In the same year, Aelfgar needed Gruffydd's help to regain Mercia again, and in alliance with the Viking Magnus Barefoot's fleet, they triumphed. However, Harold of Wessex, one of the greatest generals of the time, had been occupied defeating MacBeth in Scotland and uniting Wessex, Mercia, East Anglia and Northumberland for eight years before he unfortunately turned

the Saxon war machine of the House of Godwinson against Gruffydd.

Gruffydd's brutality against rival Welsh families was well-known – he defended it *as 'blunting the horns of the progeny of Wales so they do not wound their mother'* (see Walter Map's *De Nugis Curialum* of 1180). As such, when Harold and his brother Tostig of Northumbria attacked by land and sea, much support faded away and the other royal houses saw the opportunity to reclaim their princedoms of Deheubarth, Morgannwg, Powys and Gwynedd. It was winter, and Gruffydd's 'teulu', or bodyguard, had returned to their lands for the winter, not expecting any attack. Harold feinted to attack from Gloucester, and raided the south Wales coast with a fleet based in Bristol. Harold made a long forced march with lightly armed troops to the North (similar to his superb march from the Battle of Stamford Bridge in Yorkshire to Hastings three years later). Most of Gruffydd's forces were separated from him, in the South. He had been caught out by the fast-moving Saxons.

Harold struck so rapidly at Rhuddlan, Gruffydd's seat of government, that Gruffydd only just escaped by sea. He was pressed back towards Snowdon, and a reward of three hundred cattle offered for his head. He was killed by one of his own men, Cynan ap Iago (according to the Ulster Chronicle the son of Iago, who had been killed by Gruffydd). The king's death on 5th August 1063 had been made possible by the treachery of Madog, the very same Bishop of Bangor who betrayed Gruffydd's father, Llywelyn, forty years earlier.

Gruffydd's head was carried to Harold, who married his widow and made Gruffydd's brothers his regional commanders in Wales. Harold refused to pay the traitor Madog, and his ship was sunk carrying him to exile in Ireland. Harold did not annexe any Welsh land, and in part because of this victory, he was elected King of England over the claims of Edward the Confessor's nephew and rightful heir. Soon the Saxon enemy was to be replaced by a far more powerful force – the Normans.

The Welsh Chronicles, lamented Gruffydd as the '. . . *head, shield and defender of the Britons . . . the man erstwhile thought invincible, the winner of countless spoils and immeasurable victories, endlessly rich in gold and silver and precious stones and purple apparel.'* The Anglo-Saxon Chronicle recalls Gruffydd ap Llywelyn as '*King over all the Welsh race.'*

GWENLLIAN (1098-1136)

Sister of the great Owain Gwynedd and daughter of the warrior Gruffydd ap Cynan, King of Gwynedd, Gwenllian was born in 1098, when Wales was under unceasing attack from the Normans. Owain Gwynedd had succeeded his father in leading the Welsh defence against the Marcher Lords, and Gwenllian married Gruffydd ap Rhys ap Tewdwr and lived in Dinefwr, with her four sons, Morgan, Maelgwn, Mareddud and Rhys. On New Year's Day, 1136, her husband joined other Welsh forces in an attack upon the Norman invaders.

Gruffydd ap Rhys was away in North Wales, trying to gain assistance from Gwenllian's father, Gruffydd ap Cynan. Maurice de Londres, the detested Norman Lord of Cydweli (Kidwelly) attacked the Welsh in South-West Wales. Gwenllian led the few defenders that were left in the area,

although her youngest son, Rhys, was only four years old. Giraldus Cambrenis stated that '*she marched like the Queen of the Amazons and a second Penthesileia leading the army'*. In 1136, Gwenllian led her army against the Normans at Cydweli. A Norman army had landed in Glamorgan, and was marching to join the force of Maurice de Londres. Gwenllian stationed her rapidly assembled volunteers at the foot of Mynydd-y-Garreg, with the river Gwendraeth in front of her, and Cydweli Castle just two miles away. She sent some of her forces to delay the oncoming invasion force, but it evaded them and her remaining army was trapped between two Norman attacks.

One son, Morgan, was killed, another, Maelgwn, imprisoned, and towards the end of the fighting, Gwenllian was captured and executed, over the body of her dead son. She had pleaded for mercy, but beheaded on de Londres' express order. The battlefield is still called Maes Gwenllian, a mile from the castle, and a stone marks the place of her death. She left a 4-year-old son, to be known as The Lord Rhys, (see Rhys ap Gruffydd) the grandson of Rhys ap Tewdwr who was slain by the Normans at Brycheiniog in 1093, and the nephew of the great Owain Gwynedd. Her daughter Nest married Ifor ap Meurig, the Welsh hero who scaled the walls of Cardiff Castle to kidnap Earl William and regain his stolen lands (see Heroes).

Dr Andrew Breeze (*Mediaeval Welsh Literature*) believes that the author of *The Four Branches of the Mabinogion* (see Mabinogion) is Gwenllian, around 1128, making her the first British woman author. The battlefield has still not been fully explored, and should be preserved as a heritage site.

H

HARP, HORNPIPES AND CRWTH ('TELYN, PIBGORN A CRWTH')

The harp is the national musical instrument, and is traditionally used to accompany *penillion* singing – a complex web of sound where the harp counters with a different melody to the singer. The words sung are a pattern of alliteration and rhyme, chosen from poems written in the ancient *cynghanedd* form. This *canu penillion* (singing of verses) or *cerdd dant* (art of string) has existed for over a thousand years.

Different types of harp used are the large Gothic, the Grecian (Orchestral) Harp, the small Harp and the very difficult Triple Harp with three sets of strings. One can see harp makers exhibiting at the National Eisteddfod, and the annual festival, *Gŵyl Cerdd Dant*, ensures the continuation of the old tradition. Until the sixteenth century, the harp (*y delyn*) had the highest social status of any instrument in Welsh culture, but its close associations with dance made it offensive to puritanical non-conformists by the eighteenth century (see Dance). There was still a harpist employed at Llanover Court until his death in 1888. The massive concert pedal 'Welsh' Harp came over from Austria in the seventeenth century, ousting in popularity the authentic portable Welsh harp, that had been described by Giraldus Cambrensis in the twelfth century.

Before the Nonconformist fever, the harp was often used with a *pibgorn* (pipe) and *crwth* (Celtic violin). There was also a primitive Welsh bagpipe, the *pibacawd*. From over eight centuries ago, Giraldus Cambrensis gives us the following description in his *The Journey Through Wales*:

> 'Guests who arrive early in the day are entertained until nightfall by girls who play to them on the harp. In every house there are young women just waiting to play for you, and there is certainly no lack of harps. Here are two things worth remembering: the Irish are the most jealous people on earth, but the Welsh do not seem to know what jealousy is; and in every Welsh court or family the menfolk consider playing on the harp to be the greatest of all accomplishments.'

The Laws of Hywel Dda, codified around 940-950, specify that each master must employ a *pencerdd* (chief musician) and give him a harp, pibgorn and crwth. These traditionally accompany dancing until the eighteenth century, when the harp and fiddle became the main accompaniment. The pibgorn was last commonly played by Anglesey shepherds in the early 1800s. The crwth was originally plucked like a lyre but from the eleventh century played with a bow (with some plucking). The last Welsh crwth player, or 'crowther', travelled through Anglesey in the eighteenth century. Crwths, pibgorns and harps can be seen at The Museum of Welsh Life in Saint Fagans.

A famous 1612 manuscript by Robert ap Huw notates traditional harp music, using five scales, and no-one has yet interpreted it correctly – Wales' own Rosetta Stone. This is in the British museum, and part had been copied from an earlier manuscript of the Elizabethan harpist, William Llewelyn. Arnold Dolmetsch has transcribed it, believing that it is 'the only source of knowledge of the polyphonic music of pre-Christian civilisations'. Gustave Reese, the American author of *Music of the Middle Ages*, states that *'if the contents of the manuscript are as ancient as have been claimed, that fact would revolutionise both our notions concerning the development of music in medieval Europe, and the general belief that the concept of harmony as a system governing musical combinations from the vertical standpoint did not make itself felt with any radically great strength until the seventeenth century.'* He admits that the older part of the manuscript contains the twenty-four measures of Welsh string music, mentioned in even older Welsh manuscripts.

Wales's most famous harpist was David Owen (1712-1741), born at Y Garreg Wen farmhouse near Borth-y-Gest in Gwynedd. He used to play the harp at *nosweithiau llawen* ('happy evenings', informal gatherings for music and songs). Carrying his harp home one night from Plas-y-Borth, he lay down and slept, to be woken by the sound of a skylark, whereupon he composed the famous *Codiad yr Ehedydd* (The Rising of the Lark). On his deathbed, aged only twenty-nine, he woke and described a dream to his mother where he had been listening to a beautiful song, accompanied by two white doves. He noted the song, and asked his mother to sing it at his funeral. This was the haunting *Dafydd y Garreg Wen* (David of the White Rock), the

favourite piece of music of Carlo Rizzi. His family and friends sang the tune all the way of the funeral procession from his farmhouse to Ynys Cynhaearn Church.

HARRI TUDUR – HENRY TUDOR – HENRY VII OF ENGLAND AND WALES (1457-1509)

The Welsh supported the Lancastrian cause in the Wars of the Roses, and many died in the slaughter at Mortimer's Cross in 1461. One of the Welsh captains, Owain Tudur (Owen Tudor), was captured and beheaded by the Yorkists, and his head placed on the steps of Hereford Cathedral. Here *'a mad woman combed his hair and washed away the blood from his face, and got candles and set them round his head, all burning, more than a hundred.'* This may have been an act of clairvoyance, because Owain Tudur's grandson, Henry, founded the Tudor dynasty that united England and Wales. Henry's father, Edmund, died in Yorkist imprisonment in Carmarthen just three months before Harri Tudur was born in 1457.

Born in Wales, of royal Welsh descent, one of Henry's ancestors was Llewelyn the Great's Justiciar, Ednyfed Fychan, whose heraldic arms were three severed Saxon heads. Brought up by a Welsh nurse, Henry Earl of Richmond was lucky to be alive, even before he raised the Red Dragon of Cadwaladr upon Bosworth Field. Harri Tudur was only fourteen in 1471, the year that the Lancastrian King Henry VI was murdered and his son Prince Edward killed. Suddenly Harri was the prime Lancastrian claimant to the English crown in the continuing Wars of the Roses. His uncle Jasper Tudur (the Earl of Pembroke) only just managed to help him flee to Brittany, then still a country independent of France, and with a similar language to Welsh. Mayor Thomas White of Tenby hid young Henry in cellars which can still be seen. The new English King Edward IV asked for Harri to be handed over, but died soon after and was succeeded by Richard III of York, who killed Edward IV's two sons, the 'princes in the Tower'.

In 1483, Harri Tudur pledged his band of followers that he would marry Edward IV's daughter Elizabeth of York and thus unite the warring Lancastrian and Yorkist factions. His own lineage went back through his grandfather Owain's marriage to Catherine, widow of Henry V, to the Royal Houses of Gwynedd and Gruffydd ap Cynan, and that of Dinefwr and Rhys ap Tudur.

In September 1484, Harri barely escaped with his life as he was warned that a group of Breton nobles were going to take him to Richard III. He crossed the border into France, and with the Earls of Oxford and Pembroke, the Bishop of Ely and the Marquis of Dorset, prepared to invade Britain. He borrowed money from France, and with two thousand mainly Welsh, Breton and French troops, landed near his birthplace in Pembrokeshire. Tudur moved through Wales gathering support. Rhys ap Thomas gathered the men of Deheubarth and met Henry at Shrewsbury. So did the men of Gwynedd under Richard ap Hywel of Mostyn. While pleading his cause at Mostyn, King Richard's men from nearby Flint Castle arrived and Tudur had to escape by a back window. A stained glass commemoration panel in Mostyn Hall can be seen, and Henry presented

the family with a silver bowl and ewer after the Battle of Bosworth, which can still be seen.

Many Welshmen believed that Harri was the promised 'mab darogan', 'son of prophecy', to free Wales from the English. Glyndŵr's rebellion had paved the way for this nationalist upsurge. The Lancastrian forces crossed the Severn near Shrewsbury, finally meeting Richard's numerically superior army at Bosworth Field in Leicestershire. This was one of the strangest battles in history. From the west, Henry's force, watched by Richard's mounted scouts, had moved from Lichfield to Leicester, and was making its slow progress towards Bosworth Field. It had swollen from 2,500 to 4,500 soldiers on its journey across Wales. The Earl of Shrewsbury brought 500 men to the scene. From the east of England, Lord Norfolk's loyalist army of 4,000 men was approaching in the opposite direction. Percy of Northumberland was bringing Richard's 3,000 troops from the north. Richard with 6,000 followers was hurrying from the south, and another two armies of the Stanley brothers also arrived at the same time. Of the six main armies, three were uncommitted at the start of the battle.

Yorkist armies under the Stanley brothers had pledged to assist Richard III, mainly as Lord Stanley's son was held hostage by Richard, but held back from the battle. The battle was started by the Earl of Oxford attacking the Duke of Norfolk's army. Lord Thomas Stanley led his 4,000 men towards Northumberland's position on a nearby hill. Oxford's force were soon beaten back. Around half an hour into the battle, Richard could see Henry and Jasper Tudur, with the standard of the

Red Dragon, on the slopes behind Oxford's tired forces. Richard took a great gamble. At the head of a hundred men, he charged across to this position, passing William Stanley's army. The Red Dragon was cut down, and the standard-bearer, Sir William Brandon was killed. In the melée, part of the army of 2,500 men under Sir William Stanley charged to help Henry. Lord Stanley held his 4,000 men back. Equally, the army supporting Richard under the Earl of Northumberland refused to engage the Lancastrian army, watching the battle develop. Richard and his small force was quickly overwhelmed and Richard killed. The forces of the Lancastrian Earl of Richmond, Henry Tudur, eventually overcame the rest of the Yorkist army of Richard III. Rhys ap Thomas was said to have been knighted on the battlefield for killing Richard of York with his great battle-axe, and supposedly put Richard's crown on Henry's head.

Richard's death effectively ended the battle, and Henry's marriage and diplomacy effectively ended the Wars of the Roses. A Yorkist invasion force mainly composed of Irish and Germans was bloodily defeated in 1487 at Stoke. The impostors to the throne, Perkin Warbeck and Lambert Simnel were dealt with. By the standards of the age he was extremely merciful to the defeated Yorkists, with few of the executions that had followed previous battles. Despite several threats to the crown, Henry Tudur laid the basis for a stable constitutional monarchy. By the cunning Treaty of Etaples, he took money from the French in return for not fighting them. He built trade and alliances, and under his Royal Commission John Cabot reached Nova Scotia in 1497.

Aged only fifty-two, Henry Tudur died in 1509, leaving a peaceful country, full treasury and an uneventful succession. The *'founder of the new England of the sixteenth century'*, Francis Bacon called him *'a wonder for wise men'*. The great historian G. M. Trevelyan pointed out the influence of Bosworth Field and the Tudors: *'Here, indeed, was one of fortune's freaks: on a bare Leicestershire upland a few thousand men in close conflict foot to foot . . . sufficed to set upon the throne of England the greatest of all her royal lines, that should guide her through a century of change down new and larger streams of destiny.'*

Henry's success had been largely due to Welsh support, and the emissary for Venice reported to the Doge that: *'The Welsh may now be said to have recovered their independence, for the most wise and fortunate Henry VII is a Welshman.'* And Francis Bacon commented that *'To the Welsh people, his victory was theirs; they had thereby regained their freedom.'*

Henry VII had brought up his eldest son and heir, Arthur, as a Welsh speaker. Arthur was married with great ceremony to Catherine of Aragon in 1501, cementing the Spanish alliance. Arthur's untimely death gave the nation Henry VIII and changed the course of British history. Without him Britain would probably still be a Catholic country. Henry VIII's daughter Queen Elizabeth I oversaw the greatest flowering of culture, in the British Isles, under this Tudor dynasty. For the first time Britain became a real player on the world stage in the arts.

Elizabeth I was called a *'red-haired Welsh harridan'* by the English historian A. L. Rowse, and under her thirteen of the sixteen bishops appointed to Welsh sees were Welsh – the exact opposite of

Norman-Plantagenet policy. Her chief minister, William Cecil, Lord Burghley, was descended from Dafydd Seisyllt of Welsh-speaking Ergyng (now Hereford-shire), who accompanied Henry VII to London as a guard-sergeant. Henry VII's personal bodyguard was the origin of today's 'Beefeaters' at the Tower of London. This 250-strong 'Yeomen of the Guard' was formed of Welshmen in 1485.

HEROES

The Welsh hero par excellence is Owain Glyndŵr. Apart from Glyndŵr, there are separate entries in this book on Prince Madoc (see America and Madoc), Gruffydd ap Cynan, Gruffydd ap Llewelyn, Hywel Dda (Hywel the Good), Llewelyn the Great, Llewelyn the Last, Owain Llawgoch (see Assas-sination), Owain Gwynedd, Rhodri Mawr, Rhys ap Gruffydd (The Lord Rhys) and the semi-mythical Arthur. Wales also has both the greatest pirate and greatest buccaneer that the world has known, Black Bart Roberts and Captain Henry Morgan.

Wales was never completely sub-dued by the Romans. Two of their four British legions were stationed on the borders, at Deva (Chester) and Isca Silurum (Caerleon). Isca was built, with Venta Silurum (Caerwent) to keep the Silures down, while Caerfyrddin (Carmarthen) was the heartland of the Demetae tribe. In AD78, Tacitus re-marked that it was necessary to exter-minate almost *'the entire race'* of the Ordovices of mid-Wales and Gwynedd. When the British Catuvellauni tribe of the south-east of England, based around Colchester, were defeated by Aulus Plautius in AD43, their leader

fled to the Silures of south-east Wales. This was **Caradog** (the Caratacus of Roman history), our first Celtic hero identified with Wales. Caradog led a series of attacks by the Silures against the new Roman provinces in AD47 and 48. Tacitus recorded that Scapula received the submission of the Deceangli of north-east Wales on the River Dee in AD49, enabling him to pressurise the Silures. In the same year a fort was established at Gloucester, with others at Usk and Clyro.

Caradog continued resistance, with a joint alliance of Silures and Ordo-vices, but was defeated in AD51, his wife and children captured, and he fled to Queen Cartimanuda of the Brigantes in north-east England for support. She chained him and handed him over to the Romans. Caradog's father had been Cunobelinus (Shakes-peare's Cymbeline), the strongest of the Brythonic kingdoms of England, but the first to be attacked by Rome. The site of Caradog's last stand against Rome is still not known, but it appears to have been in the north-east of Wales, near the upper River Severn. Tacitus describes this last battle thus:

'He chose a spot protected by high, rocky hills, and in the place where the hills were less steep he built a rampart of large stones piled on top of each other; a river flowed through the plain, its fords and shallows of uncertain depth. Ostorius was very surprised by the fearless attitude of the Brythons and the spirit which permeated the whole army. He saw a river to cross, a fence of stakes to throw down, a high slope to climb, and every part defended by a great number, but the Roman soldiers were impatient to attack. The sign was given. The river was crossed without

much difficulty. The struggle by the fence of stakes was stubborn, but the Brythons had to yield at last and they fled to the tops of the hills. They were followed eagerly by the Romans. The legionaries and not only the light military pushed their way to the top of the hill after firing a shower of spears. Since the Brythons had neither breastplates not helmets, they could not continue to fight. The legions carried all before them. The victory was decisive.'

Caradog was marched in chains with his brother, wife and daughter in the triumphal procession for the Emperor Claudius in Rome. Such captives were always publicly executed as enemies of Rome, but Caradog's proud bearing and speech to the Tribunal is again recorded by Tacitus:

'To you the situation is full of glory; to me full of shame. I had arms and soldiers and horses; I had sufficient wealth. Do you wonder that I am reluctant to lose them? Ambitious Rome aims at conquering the world: does the whole human race then have to bend to the yoke? For years I resisted successfully: I am now in your hands. If vengeance is your intention, proceed: the scene of bloodshed will soon be over, and Caradog's name will fall into oblivion. If you spare my life, I shall be an eternal memorial to the mercy of Rome.'

Uniquely, Caradog was pardoned by the Emperor Claudius, and after seven years' captivity is said to have been allowed to return to his base at St Donat's, near Llanilltud Fawr. It is thought that his daughter Eurgain married a Roma (Lucius Fawr), and

brought back Christianity to Wales, founding a monastic settlement called Cor Eurgain in Llanilltud Fawr (see Llan and Christianity).

The Silures kept fighting after Caradog's capture, and defeated the Twentieth Legion in AD52. In AD57, Nero ordered that Anglesey, the chief centre of British discontent, be taken, and Tacitus descibes the burning of the sacred Druidic groves. The Iceni then rose under Buddug (Boadicea), preventing the Romans from finishing off the conquest of Wales. From AD69-78 there was another great push against the Silures and the Ordovices, by Julius Frontinus, then Julius Agricola. Three of the four Roman legions were now opposed against the Welsh borders. The XX Legion was at Uriconium (Wroxeter), the XX Augusta Legion at Isca, and the XX Adiutrix Legion at Deva. The Silures were beaten by AD 75, and the Ordovices almost slaughtered out of existence by AD84. There had been at least thirteen separate campaigns against Wales and its borders between AD48 and 79, which explains the multiplicity of Roman villas, forts, fortlets, marching camps, roads and civil ruins dotted over much of Wales.

Cadwallon Lawhir (Long-Handed), Cadwallon ab Einion Yrth ap Cunedda, finally took the Isle of Anglesey from the Irish that his father had been fighting. The decisive battle was fought at Cerrig y Gwyddyl near Trefdraeth in Anglesey. Usually the Celtic tribes rode to battle and fought dismounted. Cadwallon ordered his army to tie their horses' fetlocks together so there could be no quick escape.

Maelgwn Gwynedd, Cadwallon's Lawhir's son, consolidated North Wales around 550, and opposed Ida the Flame-bearer of Bernicia, and also fought Saxon armies. Called Maelgwn Hir (the tall), he was also referred to sometimes as 'Island Dragon' for he controlled Anglesey. He gave land at Holyhead to St Cybi, and supposedly gave land to St Deiniol to start the monastery at Bangor which became a cathedral. There is a folk tale that he and the other chiefs should meet in Cardigan Bay and sit on their thrones, waiting for the fast tide of the river Dyfi to come in. The greatest chief would be he who held his place the longest. Maelgwn had a special wooden chair made, which floated, and proved he was the greatest prince of North Wales. The sands of the mouth of the river Dyfi have always been called Traeth Mael-gwn. The bard Taliesin (see Bards, Taliesin) described Maelgwn's terrible death from the Yellow Plague. He took refuge in a church near his castle at Deganwy, but fearing enemies had to see if any were approaching *'and Mael-gwn Gwynedd beheld the Yellow Plague through the keyhole of the door, and forth-with died.'*

The Christian **Cadwallon** was the greatest military and political leader of Wales after the time of his grandfather Maelgwn Gwynedd. He later defended Gwynedd against attacks by Edwin of Northumbria, but had to flee to Ireland for seven years. In 632, Cadwallon made a pact with Penda of Mercia, who may have been a fellow-Briton rather than a Saxon, and attacked Edwin at Heathfield, possibly near Doncaster in 633. Edwin was killed and North-umbria subdued. He beat off Osric, Edwin's son in the following year. However, a year later at Hexham, Aethelfrith's son Oswald killed Cad-wallon in 635. Cadwallon's son, Cad-waldr joined forces with Penda of Mercia in 642 and avenged his father, killing Oswald at the battle of Maser-field. However, in 655 the Mercians and Welsh were beaten at Winwaed-field by Oswin of Northumbria, and Cadwaladr died in 664. This was the end of Welsh attempts to recover the North of England from the Danes.

Another hero well known to Welsh children is **Ifor Bach**, 'Little Ifor'. Ifor ap Meurig, Lord of Senghennydd, attacked Cardiff Castle when Henry II was invading West Wales. In 1158, he scaled the walls of the considerable Norman motte which can still be seen inside the grounds of the castle. Ifor Bach captured Earl William of Glou-cester, his wife and eldest son, and took them back towards Caerphilly, holding them until the Earl promised to give back the lands he had stolen from the Lordship of Senghennydd. This was an amazing feat, for Cardiff was a Norman town. Ifor and his small force had to scale the Roman walls, then get into the high keep, which still exists, and get out alive. There were one hundred and twenty men-of-arms and numerous archers stationed in the castle. Ifor's wife was Nest, a grand-daughter of Rhys ap Tewdwr, and a sister of the Lord Rhys. Their great grandson, Llywelyn Bren, was to be executed for trying to regain his birth-right.

'The Chronicles of the Princes' tell us of **Iorwerth ab Owen**, a descendant of the princes of Gwent, who control-led the lands around Caerleon. Rhys ap Gruffydd had given King Henry II free passage to cross Wales and invade Ireland in 1171. Henry took Caerleon from Iorwerth and installed a garrison. Iorwerth retook the ancient fort, and told the Normans to follow their king to Ireland. He then burnt the site so that the king would never want it again. In 1172, Henry returned, offering a pardon and the return of Iorwerth's lands. He invited Iorwerth to meet him for a peace treaty, and gave safe conducts for him and his sons. The Welsh leader was well aware of Henry's practice of blinding hostages, and sent just one son Owain, bearing gifts. Owain was killed, so Iorwerth crossed the Wye, attacking Gloucester, burning Hereford, and returned to Caerleon and rebuilt the town. His brother-in-law Seisyllt ap Dynwal captured Abergavenni Castle, and another kinsman Seisyllt ap Rhirid took the king's castle at Crickhowel (Crug Hywel), killing the garrison. In 1175, the Normans attacked suddenly and retook Caerleon from Iorwerth and his surviving son Hywel. However, The Lord Rhys arbitrated, and it was restored to Iorwerth soon after. Iorwerth was the only Welsh chieftain who escaped from the treachery of William de Braose, where Seisyllt ap Dunwal was murdered (see Treachery). He then forced the Norman Marcher Lord to flee from Abergavenny back to Brecon, trying to avenge this massacre of seventy unarmed Welsh noblemen.

In 1287, Prince **Rhys ap Maredudd** was wronged by the new Justiciar of South Wales. Rhys had been loyal to King Edward I, but rebelled to take back his former royal home of Dinefwr Castle. He then overcame mighty Carreg Cennen Castle and Llandovery. He swept south through Carmarthen, then north to take Llanbadarn Castle. English armies totalling twenty thousand men were sent to take him, and he was beseiged in Dryslwyn Castle for three weeks by twelve thousand of them, before continuing a running fight through Cardigan and Newcastle Emlyn. Driven to the hills, he was captured in 1291, and tortured and executed in the same barbarous manner as Dafydd, the brother of Llewelyn the Last.

In 1294, a national rising was planned as Edward I was to sail to France. The leaders were Morgan in Morgannwg, Cynan in Brycheiniog, Maelgwn in Ceredigion and **Madog ap Llywelyn** in Gwynedd. Madog was the son of the last of the lords of Meirionydd, and a direct descendant of Owain Gwynedd. In one day, Caernarfon castle was captured, there were attacks on Debigh Castle, Castell y Bere, Cardigan Castle and Builth Castle. The Sheriff of Anglesey was killed, an army under Lord de Lacey was crushed in the Vale of Clwyd, and large parts of the country returned to the Welsh. Cardigan Castle was taken, and in Ceredigion, Morgannwg and Brycheiniog, castles and manors were sacked. Madog pronounced himself Prince of Wales. Unfortunately, prevailing winds meant that Edward had not sailed, and he brought his French invasion force up to Conwy.

Madog moved south, looking for support from Powys, when he was attacked by the Earl of Warwick at Maes Maidog, near Caereinion in 1295. Warwick had used the King's funds to hire Glamorgan and Gwent longbowmen, who broke the back of Madog's small army. Five days later, the King's forces came on the remnants of the exhausted Welsh army and slaughtered 500 of them in their sleep. Madog, Morgan and Cynan were eventually caught and executed using the normal barbaric Angevin methods.

Llewelyn Bren, a cultured, dignified nobleman, led a rebellion in 1314 with his five sons against the cruelty of Lord Payne de Turberville of Coity Castle, the Norman Lord of Morgannwg. Turberville advocated the expulsion of Welshmen from his Glamorgan lordship. Hugh Despenser had appointed Payne Turberville of Coity Castle to be Custodian of Glamorgan. Sir William Berkerolles of East Orchard was Despenser's sub-lord, given full powers over the estates of Llywelyn Bren. This had been done to evict Bren from his rightful possessions across Glamorgan. The Normans found it far easier to subdue these flatter and richer southern parts of Wales, where reinforcements from the sea were available during their slow and uneven conquest. However, Berkerolles owed Llywelyn Bren his life, as Llywelyn had previously protected him in a Welsh attack, where thirteen Norman soldiers on Berkerolle's bodyguard were killed. Bren's estates had been taken while he and his two sons were imprisoned in the Tower of London. Llywelyn appeared before the King and barons at Lincoln Parliament on 28th January, 1316 because he had tried to restore Glamorgan to the Welsh.

He received a full pardon on 17th June, 1317 and returned to recover his estates, which had been taken over by the local Norman lords. He returned to his base of Castell Coch, which the Normans had taken, and they refused to hand it over. Gathering around a thousand supporters, he scaled the castle walls and started another revolt. He destroyed the castles at Sully, Barry, Old Beaupre, Kenfig, West Orchard and possibly East Orchard. Thousands of Welshmen attacked Cardiff, Caerleon, Llantrisant and the Vale of Glamorgan, but Llewelyn made the grave mistake of trying to besiege the enormously powerful Caerphilly Castle for nine weeks. King Edward II sent two armies against him and he was cornered near Ystradfellte. To save his followers, he surrendered knowing his fate, saying *'It is better for one man to die than for a whole population to be killed by the sword.'* He knew that Edward needed his men to fight against the Scots, and in 1318 he endured the usual drawn-out death by hanging and disembowelling that was regarded as just punishment. There is no known record of Welshmen torturing or killing prisoners in this way. Hugh Despenser, the new Lord of Glamorgan, had insisted on this disgusting execution of this rightful heir to most of Glamorgan. It appears that when Llywelyn surrendered to the Earl of Hereford, he was released. Despenser then captured him, killed him, and took over the rest of Glamorgan and some of Gwent.

Llywelyn Bren was executed at Cardiff Castle on the order of Despenser to Berkerolles, whose life Bren had previously saved. He was hung drawn and quartered, according to Despenser on the orders of King Edward II, but Despenser had received no such authority from the King. He wanted Bren out of the way, and had made Berkerolles execute him to distance himself form the unlawful event. Thus Despenser was executed himself near the Black Tower of Cardiff Castle and is said to be buried in the adjoining Greyfriars Monastery ruins, alongside Llywelyn Bren. The full charge against Despenser reads *'That he did wrongfully adjudge Llywelyn Bren, causing him to be beheaded, drawn and quartered to the* discredit of the King and contrary to the laws and dignity of the Crown'. Bren's widow attacked the castles of Cardiff, Caerphilly and St Quintin's after his death. Berkerolles was judged innocent in the tragic affair, and kept his castle at East Orchard.

HEROINES

The Celtic Queen **Buddug** (Budigga, Boadicea) led her Celtic Iceni warriors against the Romans in the east of Britain. After King Prasutagus had died, he left his kingdom to two daughters with the Emperor of Rome as co-heir. This was the usual practice for a client-king of Rome. While the governor of Britain, Suetonius Paulinus, was fighting in Anglesey, the procurator, Decianus Catus took over the Iceni kingdom. Buddug protested, and was flogged and her daughters raped. The Iceni rose instantly, and destroyed Colchester. With the Trinovantes, the Iceni then almost annihilated the IX Legion on their march on London. Buddug took London and then St Albans (Verulanium). Tacitus recorded that 70,000 civilians and soldiers died in this wave of attacks. Paulinus hurried back with 10,000 hardened troops and overcame the Celts.

Apart from the tales of Gwenllian and Jemima Nicholas (see Invasions), there is a remarkable story from The Crimean War. **Betsi Cadwaladr** was born at Pen-rhiw farm near Bala in 1789. She was known as Beti Cadwaladr or Beti Pen-rhiw. She joined the service of a rich Liverpool family aged just fifteen, and travelled with them over the Continent. As they could not say 'Cadwaladr', she called herself *Elizabeth Davis*. Bitten by the travel-bug, she

left their service and worked on ships travelling to the West Indies, Australia, Tasmania, China, India, Africa and South America. She is accredited in saving a ship by lowering the sails while the crew cowered below decks. She met the missionaries William Carey and Bishop Heber in India, and John Davies in Tahiti. Reginald Heber was astonished to find that she was the daughter of the poet Dafydd Cadwaladr.

Betsi returned to London to live with her sister, and was accepted by Guy's Hospital to train as a nurse, in her fifties at the time. In September 1854, at the age of sixty-five, she read in 'The Times' about the terrible Battle of Alma in the Crimean War, and that hundreds of British troops were dying from cholera and the intense cold, as well as untreated wounds. She just missed Florence Nightingale's first group, but joined the second to go to Scutari. The wounded had to be taken in ships, with unattended wounds, across the Black Sea to Scutari. She was one of the very few women who actually nursed in the war. Nightingale only visited there twice, not nursing but only organising the Scutari hospital. Betsi did not like the set-up and wrote a personal letter to Lord Raglan asking to nurse at the front line in Balaclava. He granted permission, and Betsi took a troopship to the base hospital there. As she said, '*By the time the wounded soldiers get across the Crimea to Turkey and the Scutari hospital they are dead. I want to be there close to the battlefield*'. Her work saved hundreds of lives. She supervised the feeding of the wounded men and their medication.

Her bedroom was rat-infested, unsanitary and not even rain-proof. She took eleven other nurses with her, and took charge of the kitchens by day and the wounded at night. When her health broke under the deplorable conditions, many soldiers and officers came to thank her in person for saving their lives, before she returned to London. Betsi's true opinions of the saintly Florence Nightingale were said to be unprintable, and she left after another quarrel with the haughty and imperious woman. Betsi died in poverty in 1860, and leaves behind no gravestone, just a two-volume autobiography of her adventures *Autobiography of Elizabeth Davis* in 1857.

Remarkable women feature strongly in Welsh history. **Nest**, known as the Helen of Wales, was daughter of the King of Deheubarth, mistress to Henry I of England, married Gerald de Windsor, the Constable of Pembroke, and was abducted by Owain ap Cadwgan, son of the Prince Cadwgan of Powys. Her other romantic liaisons were legion, and she features in many dynasties across Britain.

Catrin o Ferain, Katherine of Berain, of the 16th century was later called *Mam Cymru*, the Mother of Wales, because of her vast numbers of descendants. A grand-daughter of Henry VII, she allegedly had six wealthy husbands, killing five of them by pouring molten lead in their ears as they slept. She buried them in Berain orchard. The story is that the sixth locked her up and starved her to death. In Lloft y Marchog (the Knight's Bedroom) at Berain are irremovable stains of blood on the wall, where Catrin is supposed to have attacked her second husband, Sir Richard Clough. A more dispassionate reading of history reveals that she was born Katheryn Tewdwr in the mansion of Berain,

Llanefydd in 1534 and died in 1591. She married four times, all to men influential in Welsh affairs, and had six children, so founding several dynasties of the Welsh upper classes. At the funeral of her first husband, John Salesbury of Lleweni, Denbigh, she was led out of the church by Maurice Wyn of Gwydir, who asked her to marry him. She politely declined, as she had already accepted a proposal from Richard Clough on the way to the funeral. Her third husband was Maurice Wyn of the famous family of the 'Princes in Wales' at Gwydir, and she predeceased Edward Thelwal, of Plas y Ward, Ruthin, her fourth husband.

Thomas Pennant, the Flintshire scholar who corresponded with the eminent Linnaeus, and with Gilbert White of Selborne, kept fascinating diaries of his travels through Wales, Ireland and Scotland. *A Tour of Wales*, (1773-1776) recently republished by David Kirk, Carreg Gwalch, is a fascinating assemblage of three volumes to which we are indebted the following information. **Marged uch Ifan** was an Amazonian woman who lived near Llyn Padarn, and played the fiddle, made harps and built boats. She was also the local blacksmith, a well-known wrestler and a champion hunter. Pennant noted that *'At length, she gave her hand to the most effeminate of her admirers, as if predetermined to maintain the superiority which nature had bestowed on her.'*

Anna Harriette Leonowens (1834-1914) is better known as the tutor to the royal children in Siam. How much 'The King and I' with Yul Brynner replicates the true story is a matter of debate. Her real name was Margaret Landon, and she was born in Caernarfon. In her story, she wrote: '*the Romans had not stamped the love of freedom out of our Welsh hearts, nor could the English do that in the centuries that followed.*' She had sailed to Bombay aged fifteen to join her mother and stepfather. She married but her husband died early, leaving her with three infants, when she saw the advertisement to be the Governess to the children of King Rama IV.

HILLFORTS

Wales has the highest concentration of Iron Age Hillforts in Britain, and probably Europe. Only the West Country, especially the Celtic stronghold of Cornwall, rivals it.

One of the largest Iron Age hillforts in Wales is that of **Garn Goch**, near Llandeilo in the foothills of The Black Mountain, best approached from the village of Bethlehem, which itself is famous for its Christmas postmark service.

Tre'r Ceiri Iron Age fort on the Llŷn Peninsula has around 150 dry-stone hut circles, and 15 foot thick and up to 12 foot high defensive ramparts. It is the largest iron age fort in North-West Europe.

Carn Ingli Iron Age hillfort, upon the slopes above Newport, Pembrokeshire is impressive. In legend, St Brynach communed with the angels here, and it is associated with the Celtic goddess Arianrhod. It is also on a ley line from Pen Dinas through **Carreg y Gof** (Rock of the Smiths) with its five Iron Age burial chambers. Recently volunteers have been asked to sleep on Carn Ingli in order to analyse their dreams. It is a strange, evocative place.

In Dyfed, **Castell Henllys** Iron Age Fort recreates the living conditions of two millenia ago on an ancient site. Nearby, Newport's Carreg Coetan Arthur capstone is supposed to mark Arthur's burial site (one of many in Wales).

Din Lligwy on Anglesey is a small, well-preserved Romano-British settlement with a group of huts surrounded by a defensive wall. Nearby is a ruined Norman chapel.

Twmbarlwm hillfort, north of Newport, Gwent is the scene of a legend featuring a battle between the wasps and bees. The druids are also supposed to have had a court there, hurling the bodies of the guilty into the valley below it, which is still called Dyffryn y Gladdfa, the valley of the burial ground.

Llanmelin Hillfort, near Caerwent, may be the site of King Arthur's base – it was the tribal centre of the Celtic Silures, who were moved two miles away to Venta Silurum (Caerwent) by the Romans. It has a remarkable horned earthwork entry system, and its proximity to Caerwent, Caerleon and its 'round table' of Arthurian legend lend the site some credence. Within a few miles are many other hillforts, Y Gaer (Tredegar Fort) and Stow Hill in Newport, Wilcrick Hill, Twmbarlwm and Lodge Hill in Caerleon being the most notable.

A line from Llanmelin through Caerleon to Coed-y-Defaid fort (and Ffynon Oer) outside Bassaleg takes one to an area anciently known as Maes Arthur (Arthur's field). The line then goes on to Coedkernyw, where the present church is on the site of one dating from the 6th century, founded by Glwys Cernyw, a son of Gwynlliw Filwr (the Warrior). (Another son of Gwynlliw was Catwg, Cadoc, the saint who founded Llancarfan monastery). Kernyw was the name once given to the coastal area between Chepstow and Cardiff, long before Cornwall was known as Kernyw in the 10th century. (see Arthur).

In the Welsh Triads, Gelliweg in Cerynw is given as one of Arthur's three principal courts in Britain. Llanmelin used to be named Llan y Gelli (the church of the grove) – Chris Barber and David Pykitt, in *Journey to Avalon*, make a very strong case for Llanmelin being Arthur's court of Camelot.

HIRAETH

This is an almost untranslatable word meaning *'a deep, deep longing for home'*. To some extent this is why Wales has retained its distinct identity despite being so close to England. Emigrants from Elihu Yale onwards return home when their work is done, on a far greater scale than the Irish or Scottish. Welsh communities of expatriates overseas, except in Patagonia, hardly exist. Some 430,000 Welshmen left in the 1930s Great Depression, but it appears a far higher proportion returned after the war than did the Scots, Irish or English.

The wonderful actor-director Kenneth Griffith is a man with a deep social conscience, as evidenced by his documentary on India's Untouchables. At 73, he caught what he calls a *'whiff of mortality'* travelling to Britain from India, and was *'suddenly overcome by an irresistible yearning to be home'*. Although he had left Tenby aged 13, and had no family left there, he headed straight there and booked into a hotel overlooking North Beach. *'Griffith has recently found himself making the journey quite often, On one such visit, he*

was out walking along the North Cliff, admiring the view, when he was approached by a passer-by. Doubtless, the stranger was going to say "I know who you are. You're that actor fellow", he thought with resignation. *Sure enough, the elderly man began, "I know who you are",* but went on to say, *"I can see your grandfather's features in your face". The actor's eyes fill with tears at the memory of that seafront meeting.'* (Alan Road, 'The Times Magazine', 17th August 1996).

Possibly the best example of the hold that Wales has on its people is the rate of emigration in the nineteenth century. Twenty-six times as high a proportion emigrated from Ireland, due mainly to the terrible Potato Famine, but also the proportion was four times bigger from England and seven times bigger from Scotland. Most Welsh leave only as far as England to work, and then a very substantial proportion returns, many to retire.

Between 1921 and 1936, 140,000 jobs disappeared from South Wales mining and Welshmen had to traverse the world to feed their families. The feeling of 'Hiraeth' is wonderfully summed up by R. J. Barker in his 1936 'Christ in the Valley of Unemployment:

> *'I preached at Nanticoke, a Pennsylvanian mining town, and three parts of the congregation were made up of Welsh men and women who had heard me preach in South Wales in the previous seven or eight years. I went to see one old miner, a native of the Rhondda. He had lost his sight as a result of working in the mine . . . I can still see that pathetic figure standing at his door as I went down the road after bidding him farewell. His last words to me were "weep not for the dead! weep for the living, who will never see their native land again".'*

HOLY GRAIL

One of the Thirteen Treasures that Merlin had to guard was the Dysgl of Rhydderch, a sixth century King of Strathclyde. It was a wide platter, that *'whatever food are wished for thereon was instantly obtained'*. This was also a description of the drinking horn of king Bran the Blessed, in which one received *'all the drink and food that one desired'*. Ceridwen's cauldron contains all knowledge, and she gives birth to Taliesin. The Cauldron of Diwrnach would give the best cut of meat to a hero, but none to a coward. Bran also had a cauldron in which dead men could be revived. The cauldron of the Celts seems to be a precursor of the Grail, or cup of the Last Supper.

The cup used by Jesus Christ at the Last Supper was supposed to have been brought by Joseph of Arimathea to Glastonbury, and from there to Ystrad-fflur (Strata Florida Abbey). When Henry VIII dissolved the monasteries, the last seven monks are supposed to have taken the cup into the protection of the Powell family at Nanteos near Aberystwyth, the descendants of Edwin ap Gronw, Lord of Tegeingl. A tradition says that the fragment of the wooden bowl remaining inspired Wagner to write *Parsifal*, and visitors are showed to the music room where Wagner worked on the opera. Fiona Mirylees, the last Powell heiress, placed the treasured *cwpan* in a bank safe in Herefordshire, as the Powell family left Nanteos Mansion in the 1960s. The remaining ancient fragment is about four inches across, made of olive wood. So little is left, because supplicants used to wish to take a tiny splinter home with them.

HUNGARY

Janos Arany wrote *A Walesi Bardok* in 1867, the most famous Hungarian poem. 'The Massacre of the Welsh Bards' commemorates a fictional event. After the death of Llywelyn the Last by treachery in 1282, King Edward I ordered the bards to celebrate his victory in song. To a man they refused, so he slaughtered them. Instead they chose death by singing of the death of Welsh independence. This would have been entirely in character with this French-speaking King of England, but did not occur. It is intriguing that another country caught between more powerful neighbours, has such an acute empathy with the Welsh position.

HUNGER STRIKE

After the Government went back on a promise to give Wales its own television channel, the Welsh Nationalist leader Gwynfor Evans announced his hunger strike. He foresaw that the survival of the language now depended upon television, a lesson only now being learned in Eire. While demonstrations and graffiti erupted all over Wales, Gwynfor had a last photograph taken with his family. He expected to die, but the government eventually made funds available. With the foundation of S4C, Sianel Pedwar Cymru, he achieved his aim.

HWYL

Hwyl is a fervour, a passion, a feeling of invincibility, that the Celts had when they charged naked into battle against the Romans. (This was more sensible than it sounds, as the blue dye woad, in which they painted their bodies, has been found to have antiseptic and healing effects). Often it occurs amongst the crowds supporting the Wales national rugby team, particularly when the match is against England

Hwyl can also be experienced at eisteddfodau, cymanfa ganu and at the remarkable times when dozens of Welsh choirs congregate to sing in The Royal Albert Hall. Tremendous *hwyl* was also injected by the old nonconformist preachers, moving the parishioners nearly to tears.

HYWEL DDA – HYWEL THE GOOD OF DEHEUBARTH – HYWEL AP CADELL AP RHODRI AP MERFYN BACH (890-950)

In AD918, it appears that Hywel ap Cadell ap Rhodri Mawr ruled Dyfed, and in 920 took over Seisyllwg when his brother Clydog died, so his lands covered the kingdom of Deheubarth, South-West Wales from the rivers Dyfi to the Tawe. He made a pilgrimage to Rome in 928, and then from his power base in Deheubarth, this grandson of Rhodri Mawr added Powys and Gwynedd to his kingdom, to largely reunify Wales in 942. In *Brut y Tywysogion*, Hywel was described as '*the chief and most praiseworthy of all the Britons.*'

The only Welsh king to earn the epithet *Dda*, 'the good', he peacefully unified much of Wales by inheritance, marriage, alliances and diplomatic relations with Alfred the Great of Wessex. Upon the death of Idwal Foel of Gwynedd at the hands of the Saxons, Hywel drove out Idwal's sons and took over Gwynedd and Powys. He led no invasions into England, and coexisted peacefully with Aethelstan upon his succession after Alfred's death. It had helped that Alfred's chief advisor, Asser, was a former monk at St David's. Hywel understood the power of his larger neighbour, despite strong calls from the bards to ally against them. He had seen the death of Idwal and witnessed the final extinction of the Brythonic kingdom of Cornwall, and wished to keep Wales intact. Hywel Dda's quiet diplomacy helped give Wales another three centuries of independence against its larger neighbour.

The assembly called by Hywel in 930 at Y Hendy Gwyn (Whitland) was one of the first of its kind in Britain. In 942 the assembly finally established a legal code for all of Wales, *Cyfraith Hywel*, codifying the common laws of all the different kingdoms. This legislation was only destroyed in 1536 with the Act of Union with England, where laws based upon the right of the individual of any sex were replaced by laws based upon male supremacy, property ownership and class structure solidification.

Welsh Law gave precedence to the woman's claim in any rape case; marriage was an agreement, not a holy sacrament, and divorce was allowed by common consent, with an equal share of land and possessions; illegitimate children had the same rights as legitimate children; there was equal division of the land between all children upon the death of parents. (This last law contributed to the strife among Princedoms and Kingdoms – everyone had a claim somewhere, and most tried to rebuild what their parents had – the Normans were clever at playing off one heir against another and gaining in the long run). Under Hywel's Laws, farming was a communal affair (reminiscent of Robert Owen eight hundred years later), and the man did not have unrestricted control over his wife as a possession, unlike all the other 'civilised' European countries.

In the Celtic Church, as well as outside, there was a tradition in Wales that women had a real social status – a woman's rights to property under Cyfraith Hywel were not granted in English law until 1883. A woman also had a right to compensation if her husband hit her without any cause. In English law, the woman was the property of the husband, a chattel, whereas a divorced Welshwoman received half the property. It is typical of the Laws that the queen had special privileges – there is no mention of a queen in early English, Irish or Germanic laws.

Doctors were liable for the death of patients unless the family had agreed to the course of treatment. Contracts were stronger than legislation in civil disputes. In criminal procedings, recompense by the offending family network, and reconciliation, took precedence over revenge. The laws tried to achieve social harmony. The rate of execution in 'primitive' 12th century Wales was proportionately less than a quarter than that endured under modern English law in the 19th century. Under the entry upon 'Riots' we can see that the sentence given to the leading Welsh Chartists in 1839 was that they should be 'hung, drawn and quartered' – this was for asking for democracy.

For theft there was no punishment whatsoever if the purpose was to stay alive. Up to the late 18th century, children were hung in England for stealing a lamb.

Children were of equal status – the law of Gavelkind meant shared inheritance amongst all children – a civilised and socially unique method of preventing massing of power and lands. Even more advanced was the law that illegitimate children received all the rights, including inheritance, of family offspring – 'Cyfraith Hywel' states that the youngest son has equal rights to the oldest, and also that *'the sin of the father and his wrongdoing should not be set against the son's right to his patrimony'*, so illegitimate children had equal rights. A boy came of age at 14, free of parental control, and a father could be chastised for hitting him after this age. A girl came of age at 12, and like the boy could decide whether she wished to stay in the father's household. She could not be forced into marriage, nor arbitrarily divorced. Rhiannon, in the Mabinogion story of Pwyll, Prince of Powys, refuses to marry, saying *'every woman is to go the way she willeth, freely.'*

Professor Dafydd Jenkins has noted that aspects of Hywel's laws, that were superseded by English law in 1536, are being reintroduced as enlightened reforms in the 1990s, such as reparation to the victims of crime. Compensation of the victim was more important than punishment of the offender. For damage unwittingly done, redress had to be made. Even for murder, the Welsh state was active in seeking compensation for the victim's family, to remove the need for vengeance and feud. Obviously, the far-extended Welsh family-clans exerted pressure on their members to toe the line, as if any of them offended, all had to pay something. All the checks and balances were in place under this system to make society enforce its own social code.

Unlike many societies, there were no

differences in morality requirements for the sexes. A Welsh woman could heavily fine her husband on an increasing scale for adultery, and also divorce him for it. A woman could even divorce her husband for *'stinking breath'*. She had property rights not given under English law until the Married Woman's Property Act of 1870. In France and the rest of Britain, wife-beating was a recognised right of the husband. In Wales there had to be a definite, very serious offence, and then the punishment was limited to just three strokes of a rod. The Welsh have possibly been the most civilised race in the world in their attitudes towards women from the Dark Ages of the fifth century to the present day.

Hywel's death in 949 or 950 saw the resumption of Viking attacks, and the laws of gavelkind meant that princes fought against princes with no national unity until the accession of Gruffydd ap Llewellyn in 1039. There were ninety years of murder and mayhem and internal power struggles against a background of Saxon, Mercian and Norse invasions. But the Laws lived for six-hundred years, and their ethos of human equality is slowly replacing the property-based spirit of English laws.

The finest book upon what was the finest legal framework in history is by Dafydd Jenkins, *Hywel Dda, The Law*.

FOOTNOTES ON THE LAWS

1. There is a tradition that the tribal laws and customs were codified by Dyfnwal Moelmud long before Hywel, but the earliest manuscripts date from the 12th and 13th centuries, extracts made by practising lawyers, the earliest from the time of Llewelyn the Great.

There were slight differences between North, West and South Wales, known as the Venetian, Dementian and Gwentian Codes, and they stayed in force in entirety until Edward I's Statute of Rhuddlan in 1283, and many provisions remained until the period of the Tudors in the 16th century.

2. Many Welsh laws and traditions are noted in the ancient 'Triads', expressions where objects are grouped in threes. We know of nothing similar in any other country, and some of these sayings may date back to the time of the Druids, who committed the old laws to memory. Triads are found in the oldest Welsh manuscripts such as the *Mabinogion*, bardic poems, the 12th century *Black Book of Carmarthen*, ancient versions of the Welsh Laws, and the 14th century *Red Book of Hergest*. Examples are:

> *Three things a man experiences through litigation: expense, care and trouble.*
> *Three things which canot be hidden: love, hatred and pride.*
> *Three things not easily restrained are the flow of a torrent, the flight of an arrow, and the tongue of a fool.*
> *Three things a good liar must have: a good memory, a bold face, and a fool to listen.*
> *Three things that will take a good man unawares: sleep, sin and old age.*
> *The strength of a bard is his muse, that of a judge is his patience, that of a lawmaker his patriotism.*

3. The amazing fact that the laws were written in Welsh as well as Latin helped ensure that the language thrived. To keep a culture, history, laws, literature, religion, language and community must intertwine and be respected. These Welsh laws, first written down over

a thousand years ago, according to Saunders Lewis fashioned: *'lively forms of the mind of every poet and writer in Wales until the sixteenth century, and also directly influenced the shape and style of Welsh prose. This implies that the language had already reached a philosophical maturity unequalled in its period. It meant that it had a flexibility and positiveness which are the signs of centuries of culture. This means that there is a long period of development behind the prose of the (Cyfreithiau Laws).'*

4. From the Laws, we find that Welsh kings had a servant called a 'Foot-Holder'. This anti-stress kit consisted of a man holding the king's feet in his lap, from the moment the king sat down to eat in the evening, until he went to bed. At this time, the king had no power, as he was no longer king while his feet were off his kingdom. He could therefore relax, and not have to make any decisions, while his power passed to the 'Foot-Holder'. The 'Foot-Holder' could now grant pardons to criminals, arbitrate in disputes and the like.

I

INVASIONS

The last invasion of British soil was a Franco-Irish force in 1797 at Carreg Wastad Point, near Fishguard. A forty-seven year old cobbler, Jemima Nicholas ('The Welsh Heroine') single-handedly captured fourteen French soldiers. The force surrendered in The Royal Oak Inn in the centre of Fishguard, which still retains mementoes of the time. In recognition of Jemima's bravery, the government awarded her a handsome pension of £50 a year, which she drew until her death aged 82.

When the first of four French warships was spotted from the now-ruined fort overlooking Fishguard Bay, a single shot was fired from one of the cannons that still are in position. The fort only had three live rounds, so it fired a blank, but it persuaded the captains to withdraw to Carreg Wastad, a steep headland. There disembarked the four-teen-hundred strong 'Legion Noire', 'The Black Legion', mainly made up of convicts.

The English Captain Thomas Knox, commander of the part-time local militia, The Fishguard Fencibles, was attending a ball at Tregwynt, just six miles away, when he heard of the landing. He with all the guests, took to their horses and carriages and set off in haste for the relative safety of Haverfordwest.

The drunken invaders looted and raped their way inland, desecrating Llanwnda Church. At Bristgarn Farm, a grandfather clock still has bullet holes in it, made by a Frenchman when he was startled by the clock's sudden chiming. A force led by Lord Cawdor was outnumbered three to one, but accepted the surrender of the invaders at the Royal Oak Inn, in Fishguard. It is said that the French had misjudged the strength of the defending forces as they mistook Welsh women in their red cloaks and tall black hats as 'Redcoat' soldiers.

Fishguard is the only Battle Honour earned on British soil, awarded in 1853 to The Pembrokeshire Yeomanry in recognition of the defeat of the French Landing. The unit has merged and is now called 224 (Pembrokeshire Yeomanry) Squadron, Royal Logistics Corps (Volunteers). Thus it is now the only Territorial Army unit with a 'battle honour'.

The most interesting and long-lasting effect of this invasion was that the run it caused on the Bank of England. Investors panicked and wanted to recover their gold sovereigns from the Bank, which was forced, for the first time, to issue paper bank-notes, to the value of £1 and £2. It seems symbolic that the printing of all the UK's money is now carried out in Wales at The Royal Mint in Llantrisant.

INWARD INVESTMENT

Wales has the cheapest labour force in the United Kingdom. This, combined with the fact that the Japanese call the Welsh *'the gentle folk'*, has attracted many multinational companies to set up in Wales. Apart from Japanese electronics companies, Cardiff and Swansea have attracted many companies in the financial services sector. Admiral

Insurance, according to a spokeswoman, *'wanted an easy-to-understand accent and one that makes customers feel good about the company. The Welsh accent scored quite high – far higher, in fact than other regional accents'*. The company employs six-hundred people in Cardiff selling insurance over the telephone, and is expanding to offer another three-hundred jobs in Swansea. A survey by the then Coopers and Lybrand (quoted in 'The Times', 1st January, 1997) praised the flexibility of the Welsh workforce. The top fifty inward investors said that *'their workforce bear requirements for productivity and willingness to train*. Sony said *"We are the most flexible, productive and profitable site in Europe".'*

After British Steel, Sony is the biggest single (private) employer in Wales, closely followed by Matsushita-Panasonic. Tokyo even has a *Clwb Hiraeth*, set up by Japanese who had worked in Wales and are nostalgic for the country.

In 1998, there were over four-hundred overseas companies based in Wales, one hundred and seventy nine from Europe, one hundred and thirty seven from America and forty-five from Japan. These have created seventy thousand jobs, a third of all manufacturing jobs in Wales.

Despite the relative 'success' of inward investment compared to the rest of the United Kingdom, Wales is constantly dropping back in living standards, and now is the poorest part of the U.K.

The average household in Wales now has a lower gross weekly income than Northern Ireland. Recent statistics show that a Welsh home now has only £282 per week to live on, compared to £375 in England.

ISLANDS

Ynys Môn – Anglesey, the sacred island of the Druids, was home of the princes of Gwynedd, who had a palace at Aberffraw. Signs announce it to be *Mam Cymru*, the 'Mother of Wales', and over seventy per cent of its people have Welsh as their first language. It was the last place to fall to the Romans in Wales, to Suetonius Paulinus in AD 61, when he exterminated the Druid movement and their sacred groves. Traditionally the granary of Wales, it allowed the Princes of Gwynedd to survive constant attacks by the English. Ynys Mon is 261 square miles (676 sq. Km), and is Wales' largest island.

Off Eastern Anglesey is **Puffin Island** (**Priestholm** or **Ynys Seiriol**), with the site of a monastic settlement founded by St Seiriol in the sixth century. Puffins actually nest there, with razorbills and guillemots, and cruises are available from Beaumaris. Rats are becoming a problem for the birds that live in the burrows there. Penmon Priory on the nearby mainland has a remarkable dovecote, and was founded by the St Seiriol and St Cynlas. Ynys Seiriol is a Site of Special Scientific Interest and covers 78 acres (38 hectares). From Penmon Point, one can often see grey seal, and birdlife includes grasshopper warbler, stonechat and lesser whitethroat.

Off Western Anglesey is **Holy Island**, **Ynys Gybi**, with Trearddur Bay, connected by road and rail with the main island. Ynys Gybi is Wales second largest island, at 28 square miles (73 sq. Km). It is a Site of Special Scientific Interest (SSSI). Just off the island, South Stack is a major seabird colony, a small islet with guillemots, fulmars, razorbills and puffins nesting on ledges.

Next to Llanddwyn Bay in Anglesey,

a four mile sandy beach backed by dunes, there is **Ynys Llanddwyn, Llanddwyn Island**, barely attached to the mainland, a nature reserve with breeding shags and cormorants, with a holy well. Spring squill, golden-samphire, dune helleborine, butterwort and meadow saxifrage grow in the dunes. It is 70 acres (28 hectares), and an SSSI.

The Grade I listed church of St Cwyfan near Aberffraw, the court of the princes of Gwynedd, is now cut off by the tide for much of the day. (St Cwyfan is the fore-runner of today's name Kevin, and the old Gaelic was Coengen). It used to be on the mainland, but much of this north-west coast slid into the sea, and the church is half its former size. The legends of *cantre'r gwaelod*, the flooded lands, abound in this area.

Bardsey Island, Ynys Enlli can be reached from Aberdaron in a two mile sea trip. A monastery was founded there in 615 by St Cadfan. An important pilgrimage site since the 6th century, and the reputed burial place of Merlin, three pilgrimages were equivalent to one to Rome. A fourteenth century stone house, *Y Gegin Fawr* ('the Big Kitchen') in Aberdaron was where pilgrims rested and ate their last meal before crossing the treacherous waters. In a rock at the foot of Mynydd Mawr facing Enlli is a well called *Ffynnon Fair* ('Mary's Well') and the pilgrims used to walk down *Grisiau Mair* ('Mary's Steps') to drink the sacred water and say their last prayers before setting off from Porth Meudwy ('Hermit's Port') to the island. Many came here to die. St Deiniol, who founded the monastic site at Bangor, is also supposed to be buried there. Apart from the remains of an abbey and some Celtic crosses, there are many

nesting seabirds such as Manx Shearwaters, choughs, fulmars and guillemots on the island. Two types of dolphin and leather-backed turtles can sometimes be seen. Wales greatest living poet, R. S. Thomas, was minister at the twelfth century Church of St Hywyn, a nephew of Arthur, in Aberdaron, until he retired in 1978. The church had been founded in the 6th or 7th century. Ynys Enlli is an SSSI, and is the sixth biggest Welsh island, with 498 acres (201 hectares).

This most holy of Welsh islands was given to St Cadfan by Einion, King of Llyn. Saint Dyfrig and Saint Deiniol were buried here in the 6th century, and Saint Beuno in the 7th. In 1781, Thomas Pennant wrote of the its 'halo of sanctity' when being rowed to visit the island: *'The mariners of Aberdaron seemed tinctured with the piety of the place: for they had not rowed far, but they made a full stop, pulled off their hats, and offered up a short prayer . . .'*

Farming and fishing supported a population of a hundred until 1925, when there was a mass emigration. Its leader, Love Pritchard, had been declared unfit for military service in World War I because he was too old. In a fit of pique, this acknowledged 'King' of Enlli declared the island a pacifist enclave. The title of King probably went back to the Middle Ages when it was held by the Abbot, and then taken over by the islander who represented the islanders to the landlord, then Lord Newborough. The islanders were usually very late in paying their rents, despite which Lord Newborough had donated a crown to Love Pritchard. In response to the authorities' fears that the king and his Enlli subjects would side with the Kaiser, a boatload of police appeared, and took away everyone of military age. In 1925, the King of Enlli led a mass exodus of farmers and their families, leaving only half a dozen people behind.

Wynford Vaughan Thomas recounted a visitor's recollection of a 1910 meeting with Love Pritchard at suppertime:

> '*His Majesty sat in his grandfather's chair eating supper which consisted entirely of crabs and beer. On one side of the chair was a collection of good-sized crabs among seaweed in a wooden pail; on the other side an equally big pail of beer. The King was smoking but every now and then he reached down into the left-hand pail, pulled out a crab, put it on the back of his left hand and brought his right fist down on it with a crash. He took out the insides of the crab, dropped them in the beer, and swallowed the lot with one gulp.*'

Now there are only thirteen people living one the island, who have introduced Welsh Black Cattle to add to the sheep which have been there for generations. More than three hundred and fifty species of lichen have been recorded in the pure environment of the island, and four thousand pairs of Manx Shearwaters nest in grassland burrows. Unusually, several pairs of little owls breed in disused burrows. Grey seals can also be seen here.

The Welsh name for Bardsey, Ynys Enlli, means 'Isle of the Currents', and the two mile crossing, even by motorboat, has been known to take two hours, but its former name, Ynys Afallach, has been associated with Merlin and Avalon. Merlin hid his treasure on the island, and Arthur was rowed there to be healed after his last battle with his cousin Mordred (see Arthur, Merlin, Saints, Thirteen Treasures).

Porth-Oer, near the Aberdaron crossing to Bardsey Island, features the strange phenomenon of 'whistling sands', with the granularity of the sands causing whistling or squeaking noises when one walks on them.

Cardigan Island, off Gwbert, is noted for its vernal squill, Atlantic seals, seabirds and an unusual breed of Viking Soay sheep, which are chocolate-coloured. Black-backed gulls, fulmars and shag breed here. It is the property of the West Wales Naturalist Trust. It covers forty acres (16 hectares) and is an SSSI. When thick white mists roll in from the Irish Sea, Cardigan people used to say '*The children of Rhys Ddwfn will be coming to market today.*' Far out in Cardigan bay lie the Cormorant Isles (*Ynysoedd Mulfrain*), invisible to all but those who have eaten a certain herb from a small patch of ground near Cemaes (magic mushrooms?). The children of Rhys Ddwfn have lived on the islands for centuries, and come to the mainland to buy corn for their bread, but no-one has ever seen them.

Mochras, or **Shell Island**, off Llanbedr, is cut off at high tide, and has around two hundred different types of shells on its beaches.

Near St Davids, *Dinas Island* is not an island but a 'necked' promontory suitable for superb bird-watching, with several useful nearby pubs for the serious walker.

Ramsey Island, **Ynys Dewi** ('David's Island') is linked with St Justinian, and lies just off St David's Head. The fourth largest island in Wales, it has been a Royal Society for Protection of Birds sanctuary since 1992. Atlantic grey seals, red deer, kittiwakes, fulmars, guillemots, razorbills and birds of prey populate the island, where accommodation is available for a life-enhancing experience. Manx Shearwaters are re-populating the island, with the disappearance of the rats that took over their burrows, and choughs have always nested there. It has been farmed since mediaeval times, and the tide race between Ramsey and the mainland sometimes runs at ten knots. Its two hills, Carn Llundain and Carn Ysgubor rise up to 446 feet (135m) and 323 feet (100m) respectively, and it is an SSSI.

The following three islands can be visited by boat from Martin's Haven in Pembrokeshire: **Skomer** has a Viking name, and is 722 acres (292 hectares) of superb bird-watching territory. Puffins, razorbills, guillemots, storm petrels, shearwaters, kittiwakes, shags, fulmars as well as grey seals are here, and it is carpeted by wild flowers. Peregrine falcons, choughs and little owls can also be seen. It rises two hundred feet from the Broad Sound, which separates it from *Skokholm*, two miles away, and is a National Nature reserve. Wales' third largest island at 722 acres (292 hectares), it is home to the unique Skomer Vole and one of the most important seabird sites in Britain. The vole is almost tame and can be picked up. Skomer is an SSSI.

Nearby, the island of **Skokholm** had Britain's first bird observatory in the seventeenth century, and rare Manx Shearwaters nest here, along with puffins, storm petrels, razorbills, guillemots and oystercatchers. The shearwater population of 195,000 pairs on Skomer and Skokholm is internationally important. The world's largest colony of this burrow-nesting bird homes in to its burrows at night. The call of the returning birds, greeted by their mates in the burrows, is unearthly and goes on until three in the morning.

Skokholm island is composed of Old Red Sandstone, and visiting birds include wryneck, great skuas, hobbys, black terns, hoopoes, bluethroats, firecrests and Lapland buntings. Skokholm is 263 acres (106 hectares), Wales seventh largest island, an a SSSI.

Further out is the island of **Grass-holm**, **Gwales**, which has the second largest colony in the world of Gannets, 60,000 screaming dive bombers constantly vanishing into the seas. Grassholm is owned by the Royal Society for Protection of Birds. Ronald Lockley had returned to Wales in the mid-1930s to take out a lease on Skokholm, and pioneered studies of the puffin, shearwater and stormy petrel. His work helped gain recognition for the need for the Pembrokeshire Coast and islands to become a National Park. A first bird observatory was established on the island by Lockley in 1933. Petrels and Shearwaters, like Puffins, live in burrows, but only fly into them at night. Shags, Razorbills and Guillemots also breed on this 22 acre (9 hectares) lump of basalt rock.

Six miles off Grassholm is the Smalls Lighthouse, first built in 1776. In the vicious winter of 1800-1801, one of the two lighthouse keepers died. The survivor understandably did not want the decomposing body in either of the two small rooms. He therefore made a makeshift coffin and lashed it to the rails outside. It was all of three months before he could be relieved. After this, there were always three keepers. The present lighthouse was built in 1861, 126 feet high, and assembled and shipped from Solva in pieces to the Smalls reef.

Thorn Island, off Dale has a fort that used to hold a garrison of a hundred men. The buildings were converted into a hotel, and it is currently for sale. Thorn Island is just 8 acres (3 hectares). The world hopscotch championship has been held for the last seven years there. The film 'Whisky Galore', based on a story by Compton Mackenzie, seems to have been inspired by the wreck of the 'Loch Shiel' on Thorn Island in 1894. When the boat broke up, its cargo of bottles of whisky and barrels of gunpowder started to drift into Angle Bay. Some looters carted away the barrels, thinking them to be full of whisky. Women packed the legs of their bloomers with bottles, knowing that the Customs and Excise men would not dare to look there. Three people died, two from alcoholic poisoning and one from drowning while trying to gather the whisky. Nearby **Sheep Island** has an Iron Age fort.

Gateholm, **Goat Island**, can be reached at low tide from Marloes sands, and has a Romano-British village of hut circles and deer. It is 20 acres (8 hectares).

Caldey Island, or **Ynys Pyr**, can be reached by boat, sometimes with rusty old wartime amphibious vehicles (DUKW's) transferring you to the island off the boat. It was settled by Celtic monks in the 6th century, and in 1136 Benedictine monks built a priory. There is now a monastery of Reformed Cistercians, and one can buy their perfumes, honey and cream, wander around the 600 acre island and its old buildings, or just chill out on the beach that faces Tenby. The 14th century St Illtud's Church is now the oldest British church in Catholic hands. At 500 acres (203 hectares), it is the fifth largest island of Wales. The adjoining 20 acre *St Margaret's Island* was once connected to Caldey by causeway, and is a nature reserve with breeding cormorants.

Burry Holms off Rhosili Bay can be reached at low tide, and there is an Iron Age settlement and remains of a 12th century church. At Worm's Head off Rhosili you can see Devil's Bridge, an arc over the sea, and Blow Hole, where the tide rushes through. Rhosili headland has golden and rock samphire, rock sea lavender, and kittiwakes, razorbills, shag, fulmar, puffins and shearwaters can be seen. In winter, there are common scoters and purple sandpipers.

Barry Island, **Ynys y Barri**, was connected by a breakwater to the mainland in the 1880s, to build David Davies' coal docks and break Cardiff's stranglehold on the coal trade. Before World War I Barry was the busiest dock in the world, out-exporting Cardiff, but it is now a funfair and promenade with an excellent sandy beach between twin promontories.

Barry was once Wales eighth largest island at 170 acres (69 hectares). Not many visitors know that the swimming pool at Cold Knap, next to the Island, is one hundred and thirty yards long, the second longest in Europe. From Barry and nearby Penarth throughout the summer months, the Waverley offers cruises in the Bristol Channel. This is the only surviving ocean-going paddle steamer in the world.

Sully Island can be reached at low tide from Swanbridge, where the lovely Captain's Wife pub has been turned into a theme-pub for children. There is sea-holly, and the remains of an iron-age fort on the Eastern end. Some Viking raiders were trapped here and killed a millenium ago. It is an SSSI and is 28 acres (11.3 hectares).

In the Bristol Channel, **Flat Holm** is a Welsh island, used by Viking raiders and as a cholera hospital in the past. From Lavernock Point on the nearby mainland, the first conversation was heard by radio waves. Marconi had stationed his assistant, George Kemp, on Flat Holm three miles away. The first words were, unsurprisingly, *'Are you ready?'*. The eighth biggest island, it measures 95 acres (38 hectares), and daily boat trips run from the Flat Holm Project offices in Barry Docks, subject to weather conditions. It is an SSSI, like 13 other Welsh islands. *Steep Holm*, the near neighbour to Flat Holm, is English, and it is said that the knights who murdered St Thomas a Becket fled there to hide, and are buried either there or on Flat Holm.

Other notable Welsh islands are Ynys Feurig*, Bishops and Clerks*, The Skerries (*Ynysoedd y Moelrhoniaid*), St Tudwal's East and St Tudwal's West, Middleholm* (Midland Island), Ynys Gifftan* and Ynysoedd y Gwylanod*. (*denotes an SSSI). There are over twenty other Welsh islands which are under 5 acres (2 hectares). Of the dangerous Bishops and Clerks, George Owen wrote in the seventeenth century that *'they preach deadly doctrine to their winter audience.'* St Tudwals isles were the haunts of pirates as were Flat Holm and Enlli.

K

KINGS AND QUEENS OF ENGLAND

England's greatest dynasty, the Tudors, were Welsh, and this was when Britain was first recognised as a player among the European powers. The Elizabethan Age saw the greatest flowering of literature in British history. Britain's greatest statesman of the times, Lord Burghley, was a Cecil from Wales (the original name was the Latin Sextilius, later Cymricised to Seisyllt, and later Anglicised to Cecil).

The Norman Mullock Bridge in Pembroke has an intriguing story. The Welsh prince Rhys ap Thomas had given an oath to Richard III that no enemy would enter Wales except *'over my bellie'*. He met the future King Henry VII at Dale, crouched under the bridge when Henry passed over (thus fulfilling the pledge), and accompanied him to the fateful Battle of Bosworth Field.

Wales gave England its only golden dynasty of monarchs. Unfortunately, Henry VII's son Arthur, brought up a Welsh-speaker, and in Welsh ways, died young and his brother Henry VIII succeeded. Henry married Arthur's widow, Catherine of Aragon. Henry VIII's Act of Union between England and Wales in 1536 tried to make the two countries indissoluble, with Wales being governed upon English lines. The Act proceeded to deal a hammer blow to the language: *'from henceforth no Person or Persons that use the Welsh Speech or Language shall have or enjoy any Manner of Office or Fees within this Realm'*.

It is ironic that a Welsh king did most to Anglicise Wales. He was brought up at the English court, and subject to English influences, unlike his elder brother Arthur, brought up as a Welsh-speaking Welshman. The survival and popularity of the Welsh language, almost half a millennium years later, is a remarkable story of native stubbornness that has helped keep the concept of the Welsh nation and identity intact.

Henry VIII's daughter Margaret married James IV of Scotland, who was killed by Henry's forces at the battle of Flodden Field. However, their son became James V of Scotland when just thirteen months old. His daughter Queen Mary was the mother of James VI of Scotland, who became James I of England, founding the Stuart dynasty. Thus the Welsh can claim that the Stuart Royal Family was partly Welsh. Henry's other daughter Mary was betrothed to the future Hapsburg Emperor, Charles V, but eventually married the aged King Louis XII of France.

FOOTNOTE:
It is accepted that only one of Henry VII's grandparents was Welsh, but he was brought up as Welsh by his Welsh uncle Jasper Tudur, in Wales, and chose Wales as his point of invasion of England. His army was Welsh and he was considered the *mab darogan* to free Wales from English rule. Certainly he was thought of as a 'Welsh' king at the time, and Elizabeth I also was extremely sympathetic to Wales and its people.

L

LAKES

Its mountainous environment and regular rainfall has given Wales over four hundred natural lakes, and caused fifty-seven dams and ninety reservoirs to be built, many supplying the English North-West and Midlands.

The Snowdonia lakes have links with Arthurian legend. *Bwlch y Saethau* ('The Pass of the Arrows'), was where the treacherous Mordred fought the King; the black boat that carried the dying Arthur away sailed across Llyn Llydaw to the Isle of Avalon, Bardsey Island; Merlin threw the crown jewels into the fishless lake, Llyn Cwmglas near Llanberis, and Sir Bedivere threw Excalibur into Llyn Ogwen or Llyn Llydaw.

Lake Bala (Llyn Tegid) is the largest natural lake in Wales, being four miles long. A fish said to be unique to Bala and a couple of smaller Gwynedd lakes, a relic of the ice age, is the gwyniad. This white fish of the salmon species hides in the deep waters and allegedly has never been caught by a rod and line, but is sometimes found washed up on the shoreline. Red-breasted mergansers and goosanders breed here, in one of the best fishing lakes in Britain. Plants include globeflower, Welsh poppy, shoreweed and floating water-plantain. Tegid Foel and his wife, the Celtic corn goddess Cerridwen, in legend lived on an island in the middle of the lake.

The deepest lake is **Llyn Cowlyd** at 229 feet (70m), while the 'bottomless' **Llyn Glaslyn** is only 127 feet deep. Glas can mean either blue or green in Welsh, and the peacock hues of Glaslyn are probably caused by mineral deposits. Wales' highest lake is *Llyn-y-Cwrt* in Snowdonia, at 2500 feet (762m).

The beautiful **Trawsfynydd** lake has the terrible scar of a derelict nuclear power station. The station stopped generating electricity in 1991, but the site clearance is not scheduled until 2136. This will cut the costs of decommissioning from £700m to £200m. It appears that the private company, BNF Magnavox intend to 'entomb' the station as an abandoned 'safestore'. They applied for planning permission in 1998. However, the nuclear waste will be above a complex geological area where the rocks are fractured to a depth of 80 metres, and also just 19 miles from the epicentre of Britain's strongest earthquake in July 1984. The structural integrity or design of this 'safestore' cannot ever be guaranteed in this spectacular area of the Snowdonia National park.

A first-century Belgic Celtic feasting tankard was found in the lake. Made of yew staves, encased in bronze, it is complete and the most beautifully ornate of the only three found in Britain.

Tal-y-Llyn, near Dolgellau, is a large natural lake under Tal-y-Llyn Pass, with the great bulk of Cader Idris brooding over it. Common sandpipers and dippers can be seen in the summer here. In June 1963, on the slopes of Nant Cader just above Tal-y-Llyn lake, two picknickers noticed some pieces of sheet bronze half-hidden under a great boulder. They were part of a tightly packed bundle of bronze sheets, that had been hammered down for re-melting. The hoard has mounts for two shields, some plaques ornamented with double human figures which probably adorned shields, and other artefacts. The pieces date from around the time of Christ.

The nine-mile long **Elan Valley lakelands** were the first of Mid-Welsh reservoirs, built between 1892 and 1903 to supply Birmingham and the English midlands, over seventy miles away. The lakes form the basis of a 45,000 acre (18,200 hectare) estate of open mountains, rivers and woodlands surveyed from above by the Red Kite.

A great find of Celtic treasure was made in **Llyn Cerrig Bach**, Anglesey, of bronze and iron artefacts from the 2nd century BC to the first century AD. This hoard, with its chariot-fittings, horse-harnesses, swords, shield bosses, spearheads, trumpet, cauldrons, sickle and manacles for slaves or prisoners of war, may be a relic of the Druids' last stand, described by Tacitus. These intriguing finds can be seen in the National Museum of Wales. The hoard was found during the construction of a runway in 1942, as a peat bog was dredged. The first find pulled up by a harrow was an iron chain. It was so strong that it was used to pull a tractor out of the mud, before its true nature was ascertained – a slave-gang chain of iron with neck shackles. Another hundred and fifty Iron Age objects were found, all thrown into the waters as offerings to gods.

Llyn Efernwy (Lake Vyrnwy) was built from 1877 to supply Liverpool's water, and the Welsh village of Llanwddyn, with its population of four hundred and forty, was forcibly moved to new houses down the valley to accommodate its construction. The heather moors around the lake are the most extensive in Wales. An enormous variety of other habitats has led to the siting of over one hundred and forty species of birds in the vicinity, including the great grey shrike, hawfinch, nightjar, quail, osprey and goshawk. There are also unusual plants such as globeflower, club mosses, lesser twayblade, southern marsh orchid, heath spotted orchid and greater butterfly orchid. There are dozens of species of butterfly, moth and dragonfly, and crossbills, merlins, whimbrel, woodpeckers, long-eared owls and brambling make this a birdwatcher's paradise. Red and black grouse have also been seen here.

Llyn Mawr, near Newtown, has quillwort, yellow water-lily, marsh cinquefoil, sundew, marsh lousewort, butterwort and the northern marsh orchid. Bird include goosander, Greenland white fronted goose, wigeon, goldeneye and whooper swan.

Llynnau Cregennen, Cregennen Lakes, near Cader Idris, are superbly situated with views over Cardigan Bay, and in the care of the National Trust. Bog plants such as water lobelia, marsh cinquefoil, quillwort, shoreweed and marsh St John's wort can be seen here.

Llyn Cau, below the summit of Cader Idris, supposedly bottomless, is said to contain a monster that seized a swimmer in the 18th century. It is a very cold and deep corrie lake, where can be found rare species such as brittle bladder fern, saxifrages and green spleenwort. This is a good place for spotting ravens and peregrine falcons, and merlins can also be seen here.

Near Llanbedr, the small lake **Llyn Cwm Bychan** is near the Roman Steps, an ancient pack-horse route between Harlech and Bala.

Near Llanberis, **Llyn Padarn** has the rare freshwater char in its depths.

Llyn Clywedog, near Llanidloes, is another supply of water for the Midlands. Its 237 feet (72m) dam is the tallest concrete dam in Britain.

Nant-y-Moch reservoir on the slopes of Plynlimon traps the headwaters of the River Rheidol, to provide power for the Rheidol hydro-electric scheme.

North of Pontrhydfendigaid are the **Teifi Pools**, mountain lakes that form the headwaters of the River Teifi.

Llyn Brianne was completed in 1973 to supply Swansea with water, and the Brecon Beacons has a series of lakes and reservoirs supplying Cardiff and the Valleys.

The drowning of Welsh valleys to supply water to England caused a major dispute when **Llyn Celyn** was built, along the Trywerin River, to supply Cheshire and north-east Wales. All Welsh MPs except one voted against the bill to flood the village but the House of Commons voted in favour. In 1965 a valley, village and chapel, Capel Celyn, were destroyed. A simple slate memorial was erected in 1971 commemorating those resting in the graveyard. It reads:

'Under these waters and near this stone stood Hafod Fadog, a farmstead where in the seventeenth and eighteenth centuries Quakers met for worship. On the hillside above the house was a space encircled by a low stone wall, where larger meetings were held, and beyond the house was a small burial ground. From this valley came many of the early Quakers who emigrated to Pennsylvania, driven from their homes by persecution to seek freedom of worship in the New World'.

Bosherston Lakes, also known as Bosherston Lilyponds, are three long fingers of water dammed in the 18th century to make a country estate, complete with an iron age camp on one of the peninsula. The ponds have a marvellous display of lilies and unusual birds and the area is one of the most important for otters in Britain. Nearby are the wonderfully sheltered beaches of Broad Haven (not to be confused with the beach and village of the same name in North Pembrokeshire) and Barafundle Bay. St Govan's sixth century chapel is in a cleft in the nearby rocks. Legend links Govan with Gawain, of Arthurian Round Table fame.

Llyn Eiddwy in Dyfed features in the prophecy by Merlin – if it ever dries up, Carmarthen will suffer a catastrophic disaster.

Llys-y-Fran reservoir near Haverfordwest, is a haven for wildlife as it is the only large (187 acre, 76 hectare) expanse of fresh water, in this area of Pembrokeshire. There is a seven mile perimeter path, and the park supports polecats, Whooper and Bewick swans, goldeneye, wigeon and Siberian white-fronted geese. Nearby is a *Tŷ Un Nos* (literally house one night – see Architecture), a small thatched cottage erected in a day. In old Welsh custom, any building erected on common land between sunset and sunrise, belonged forever to the builder.

Llyn Bwch is the largest natural lake in Radnorshire, near Builth Wells, and is an important winter site for wildfowl. Teal, dunlin and sandpipers can be seen here.

Marloes Mere, near Marloes Sands in Dyfed, is flooded in winter, and home to large flocks of wigeon, with pintail ducks, shovelers, teal, jacksnipe, snipe, peregrine falcons, buzzards and merlins also present.

Llangors Lake (Llyn Syfaddan) in

Powys is said to be the largest natural lake in South Wales. Nearby is the 6th century church dedicated to St Paulinus (St David's tutor) and a Viking burial stone. The legend, that the lake covers a lost city, can probably be attributed to the fact that a small artificial island in the lake is the only known Welsh site of a *crannog*, a defensible fort used by lake dwellers. It may be at this royal crannog that Aethelflaed captured the king's wife and thirty-three other persons in 916, according to The Anglo-Saxon Chronicle. He sent an army into Wales to Brecenanmere, the old English name for the lake (Brecknock Mere). It was probably the wife of Tewdwr ap Elised, King of Brycheiniog (Breconshire) at the time, who was taken. High quality textiles from the period have been excavated in the silt on the site.

There may also be a crannog in **Llyn Fawr** in Northern Glamorgan – here was found the 2500-year-old Celtic hoard of two great bronze cauldrons, an iron sickle and a massive sword, unique in Britain in its resemblance to Hallstatt weapons.

Llyn Y Fan Fach, near Llanddeusant, in The Black Mountain, carries its legend of The Lady of the Lake. She rose from its waters and married a local farmer on the condition that if he struck her three times without good cause she would return to the lake. They had sons with magical healing powers. Inevitably, the farmer struck her three times and she returned to the lake. Nearby Myddfai was the home of the *Physicians of Myddfai* in mediaeval times, a family who were celebrated throughout Wales for their cures, a curious inter-tangling of mythology and fact with the Lady of the Lake. Rhiwallon and his three sons were physicians to Rhys Gryg, Lord of

Dinefwr, who died in 1234. Their folk remedies were recorded in mediaeval manuscripts dating from the thirteenth century, and collected and published in book form in 1861. The last descendant of these physicians was said to be John Williams, doctor to Queen Victoria. Higher up on the Black Mountain lies the larger **Llyn y Fan Fawr**.

The largest pike caught in Britain, a 46lb 13 ounce (21.2kg) monster was landed at **Llandegfedd Lake** in 1992. This reservoir near Pontypool is excellent for spotting wintering wildfowl such as goosander, great crested grebe, terns, pochard, teal and wigeon.

Kenfig Pool (Pwll Cynffig) is also said to be the largest natural lake in South Wales, the centre of a fabulous eco-system of sand dunes leading to the sea. A half-buried castle is in the dunes, and the whole site is a superb nature reserve, with 90% of Europe's Fen Orchid population and the odd wintering bittern. Unfortunately, locals use this precious site to allow their dogs to roam, disturbing nesting birds. The site of the mediaeval town may be unique in Britain, as it has never been built upon. Slow progress (because of lack of funds) is being made in its archaeological excavation.

LANGUAGE

The Welsh word for Wales is Cymru. Y Cymry is the Welsh people, Cymro is a Welshman, and Cymraes a Welshwoman. Cymreig is the adjective for all things Welsh and Cymraeg means the Welsh language. Cymry, fellow-countrymen, gave the relic Celtic population in Cumbria their name. (Cymry derives from the Brittonic 'Combrogi', meaning fellow countrymen). The British being pushed back to the west of England and Wales by successive invaders thus called themselves a Celtic word, 'Cymry' to form a common bond. Romans Latinised Wales as Cambria. Sais, the Welsh for Saxon, has come to mean Englishman, and the English language is 'saesneg'.

'Lloegr', the old Welsh name for England, came to be used in French and British literature as 'Logres', the realm of King Arthur. The Saxons that settled in Britain, pushing the Celtic Britons into the Western peripheries, adopted the collective name of 'Engle' or 'Engisc', which Latin writers termed 'Angli' ('Angles'). These English invader-settlers called the native British 'foreigners', 'wallas', 'wealh', 'wylisc' or 'walsci', and called the Welsh language 'weallas', which became known as Welsh. The name Wales is therefore Saxon. So the Welsh became unwanted strangers in their own land at a very early date. The settling English called the settled Celts alien, a habit that they kept up through the centuries as they conquered other, more exotic lands.

Wales has a common root with 'Walloon' in Belgium, 'Wallachian' in Romania, 'Walachian' in Greece, 'Vlach' in Romania and 'Valais' in Switzerland – foreigners in one's own lands. French-speaking Walloons are known to the Flemish Belgians as 'Waalsch'. In German or High-Dutch, the world welsch means foreign, and to them, the Italians were the 'Welsch' or 'Walsch'. Slavs also call Latins 'Vlachy', 'Wallachs' or 'Wlochy'. In turn, these assorted Vlachs and Wallachians in the Balkans call themselves 'Romani', 'Rumeni' (Romanians) or 'Aromani' (Romans).

The Celtic-British province of 'Cerniw' was suffixed with the same root ('wal'), making 'Cornwall', the Welsh-speaking tip of the West Country. Cornish for Cornwall is 'Kernow'. Welsh settlers pushed from the West of England and Wales in the fifth and sixth centuries to settle the province of 'Cornouaille' in Western Brittany. Perhaps 'Wal' and 'Gaul' were the same word, with Wal being the shortened form of 'Gwal'? The Celtic root 'gal' means land of the Gauls or Gaels. Wales is 'Pays de Galles' in French, 'country of the Gauls'. Portugal, Galicia (in Spain and Poland), Galloway, Calais, Caledonia, Donegal, and Galatia have the same origins. Whatever the entymology, Welsh is a term meaning foreigner, which is a fairly strong reason to refer to ourselves as Cymry, rather than Welsh.

Taliesin and Aneirin were writing in Welsh around 600, and as John Davies writes in his superb *History of Wales*: '*This was a bold act for, throughout the territories that had been part of the Western Empire, the Latin of Rome was the sole written medium, and hardly any attempts were made to write Latin's daughter-languages, French, Spanish and Italian, until after 1000.*' Unfortunately, the disappearance of paper from Europe and the expense of parchment means that most surviving Welsh from this period is in the form of marginalia on religious parchments. There was a cell containing Welsh manuscripts at the fort in Tenby around 880, but the only surviving literature consists of later copies.

Welsh is spoken by about 20% of the population as a first language, with around 70% in its heartlands of North and West Wales. Compared to Erse (Irish) and Gaelic (Scots), it is surviving, partially because of the 1967 Welsh language Act, and partially because of S4C, *Sianel Pedwar Cymru*. This Welsh television channel produces twenty-two hours of programmes a week, including the 'soap opera' set in the Valleys, *Pobol Y Cwm* ('People of the Valley'). BBC's Radio Cymru also broadcasts in Welsh for twelve hours a day, and 'Y Cymro' is a weekly newspaper in the Welsh language.

The Welsh language is one of, if not the, oldest living language in Europe, belonging to the Celtic family of languages rather than the Germanic (Dutch, German) or Latin (French, Italian, Spanish) groups. Welsh comes from the Brythonic form of Celtic, which existed in Britain before the coming of the Angles, Saxons and Jutes in the 4th and 5th centuries AD. Brythonic, or P-Celtic, gave us Welsh, Breton and the nearly extinct Cornish language. Goedelic, or Q-Celtic, is the origin of Scottish and Irish Gaelic and the extinct Manx language. (There is no Q in Welsh, and the form mac, of son of, in Scots and Irish Gaelic is replaced by map, or ap, in Welsh.)

Welsh has been used as a written language since AD600, 300 years before French and German were first written, and over 600 years since the first English (semi-recognisable to today's reader) occurred in Chaucer's Canterbury Tales and the like. What we would recognise as Modern English dates from nearer Shakespeare's time around 1600.

Apart from modern electronics terms, the only significant intruders to the Welsh language were borrowed from the Romans in the years to 500, e.g. *porth* for door or gateway (porta) and *ffenestr* for window (fenestra), which demonstrates the antiquity of the language. Around a thousand words were derived from Latin, e.g. *llyfr* (liber, book), *pysgod* (piscis, fish), *eglwys* (ecclesia, church), *mur* (murus, wall,),

milltir (mille, mile), *cyllell* (cultellus, knife), *melys* (mel, sweet or honey), *ceffyl* (caballus, horse), *perygl* (periculum, danger) and *pont* (pons, bridge).

There are 28 letters in the Welsh alphabet, with the following consonants being added to the English alphabet : ch (pronounced as in loch), dd (as the th in then), ff (as in off), ll (as in Loch Lomond, running the ch and L together), and th (as in teeth). The consonants j,k,v,x and z do not exist in Welsh, but k and z appear in Cornish and Breton. All consonants are pronounced 'hard' phonetically. Note that c is always hard, as in cat, never soft as in proceed, and that f is also hard, as in of, not off. Also g is like the g in garden, not George, and h is always pronounced as in hat, not left silent as in honest.

The vowels are a (as in hat), e (as in bet), i (either pronounced as in hit or like the e in me), o (usually as in hot), u (pronounced ee), w (pronounced oo, either as in book, or room), and y (pronounced as the u in understand or as ea as in tea).

It was a Welshman, Sir William Jones, serving as a judge in Calcutta, who *'made the epoch-making discovery that the main languages of Europe are closely related to the principal languages of India. Jones saw the link between the classical Latin and Greek and ancient Sanskrit. It subsequently turned out that many modern Indian languages formed part of the same family as their counterparts in Europe, namely the Romance, Celtic, Germanic, Baltic and Slavonic groups'* (*Europe – A History* by Norman Davies).

THE SURVIVAL OF THE LANGUAGE
The Act of Union with England of 1536 stated that *'No person or persons that use the Welsh speech or language shall have or*

enjoy any manor, office or fees within the realm of England, Wales or other of the king's dominions upon forfeiting the same offices or fees unless he or they use and exercise the speech or language of English'.

This Act of Henry VIII, son of the Welsh King Henry VII, also stated that English was to be the only language used in the courts of Wales, causing vast areas of land to be taken from monoglot Welshmen by English litigants. This was yet another step by England to rid itself of the oldest and once dominant native language of Britain, following the laws from the Statute of Rhuddlan in 1282 and those passed in the early fifteenth century during and after the Glyndŵr Rising. For a period after 1549 English was the language used in church services, all law and administration and its mastery was the only method for a Welshman to rise in life. As Gwynfor Evans said, it was the English language that made Englishmen out of the Brythons, Angles, Saxons, Danes and Normans that made up their nation. From 1536 until today it has been used to try and make the Welsh into Englishmen.

The turning point in the survival of the Welsh language was the translation of The Bible into Welsh. The preacher William Morgan ministered in Llan-rhaeadr-ym-Mochnant, and by 1588 had completed the translation, with three other clergymen working over 25 years. His most able assistant was the brilliant Bishop Richard Davies of Abergwili. One of Morgan's precursors in religious translation, William Sales-bury (Salebury, Salusbury), was said to be a former privateer, a profession at which the Welsh have gained some international renown over the centuries. Morgan said that *'Religion, if it is not taught in the mother tongue, will lie hid-*

den and unknown'. The Privy Council decreed that a copy should be placed in every Welsh church. 'Y Beibl' stan-dardised the different types of prose and dialects of the time into the Welsh of today.

The Bible moved the people towards a standardised national language based on the speech of the North and North-west of Wales, but there are still four recognizable dialects: y Wyndodeg (Ven-edotian) of the north-west; y Bowyseg (Powysian) of north-east and mid-Wales; y Ddyfydeg (Demetian) from the south-west; and Gwenhwyseg (Gwent and Morgannwg) in the southeast. Today's dialects interestingly coincide with today's major and oldest bishoprics, which are based on the old Welsh princedoms, which were themselves founded from the ruling Celtic tribes in the area. Thus the dialects date back two-thousand years.

In 1621, John Davies wrote: *'It is a matter of astonishment that a handful of the remaining Britons, in so confined a corner, despite the oppression of the Eng-lish and the Normans, have for so many centuries kept not only the name or their ancestors but also their own original lan-guage to this very day, without any change of importance, and without corruption.'* (*Antiquae Linguae Britannicae*).

Building on the Welsh Bible was Griffith Jones (1683-1761), Rector of Llandowror, Carmarthenshire. His cir-culating schools made Wales the most highly literate country in Europe. By 1757, with a third of the population being able to read, and the main read-ing being, of course, the family Bible (see Education). The emphasis upon the importance of the Bible and read-ing is another factor in keeping the language alive.

One problem in the survival of Welsh

was the appointment of Englishmen to Welsh bishoprics and clericships, with Welsh being excluded from church services, to which Lewis Morris referred in a letter in 1764: *'What can you expect from Bishops or any other officers ignorant of a Language which they get their living by, and which they ought to Cultivate, instead of proudly despising. If an Indian acted thus, we would be apt to Call him Barbarous. But a Scot or Saxon is above Correction'*. This was written to Evan Evans, a Welsh poet-curate who could not obtain a living in Wales, only a curacy under an absentee English rector.

In 1766, a seventy-year-old, ailing English monoglot was given the living of Trefdraeth and Llangwyfan in Anglesey. Only five of the five hundred parishioners spoke any English. In 1768 the churchwardens brought a case of unfitness against him on the grounds that he spoke no Welsh. In 1773 Canterbury decided in their favour, but the English rector kept the job. The argument used by the rector's counsel in court was that:

'Wales is a conquered country, it is proper to introduce the English language, and it is the duty of the bishops to endeavour to promote the English, in order to introduce the language . . . It has always been the policy of the legislature to introduce the English language into Wales . . . The English language is, by act of parliament, to be used in all courts of judicature in Wales, and an English Bible to be kept in all the churches in Wales that by comparison with that of the Welsh, they may the sooner attain to the knowledge of English'.

In 1846, an inspection was carried out of the Welsh-speaking Nonconformist schools, by three English barristers and seven Anglican assistants. Their report became known as *'Brad y Llyfrau Gleision'* (*'The Treason of The Blue Books'*), as it called standards deplorable, blaming the Welsh tongue *'the language of slavery'*. The language condemned the Welsh to intellectual backwardness, encouraged depraved sexual habits, and had produced *'no Welsh literature worthy of the name'*. As well as criticising the dirtiness, laziness, ignorance, superstition, promiscuity and immorality of the Welsh, it lamented the effects of the Nonconformist religion and stated *'The Welsh language is a vast drawback to Wales and a manifold barrier to the moral progress and commercial prosperity of the people. It is not easy to over-estimate its evil effects.'*

English papers then reported that the Welsh were settling down into savage barbarism, with the habits of animals. Chambers Edinburgh Journal of 1849 stated that the use of the Celtic tongue was a *'national discredit'*. In 1852, the Inspector of Schools announced that it was *'socially and politically desirable'* that the language be erased. English-only Board Schools were imposed to hasten the decline of Welsh. By 1847, only three out of 1,657 day schools in Wales taught any Welsh. By 1899, Welsh was being examined in only fifteen out of 1,852 elementary schools. The effects were dramatic. It looked as if the language could never recover from this official onslaught. In 1801 Meirionydd (Merioneth) was totally Welsh-speaking, closely followed by Gwynedd. By 1881 just 12% of the population spoke only Welsh. By this year only Anglesey had significant strength in Welsh speakers, where for 40% it was their sole language. The process of Anglicisation had been quickly accelerated by the disgusting 'Welsh Not' (see entry), which had been hung around the necks of Welsh speakers in many schools for half a century.

The English poet and schools inspector, Matthew Arnold, declared in 1855 that the British regions must become homogeneous . . . *'sooner or later the difference of language between Wales and England will probably be effaced'* . . . an event which is (yet again) *'socially and politically desirable'*. In 1865 'The Times' called the language *'the curse of Wales . . . the sooner all Welsh specialities vanish off the face of the earth the better'*.

At the same time the prominent Welsh industrialist, David Davies (see David Davies) was saying that Welsh was a second-rate language – *'If you wish to continue to eat barley bread and lie on straw mattresses, then keep on shouting "Bydded i'r Gymraeg fyw am byth"* (May the Welsh language live forever, the chorus of the National Anthem). *But if you want to eat white bread and roast beef you must learn English !'*

In years to come, older people used to boast of how many times they had been caned for wearing the 'Welsh Not' at the end of the day. The 1870 Education Act made the English school system compulsory in Wales. Many children refused to speak English, so learned nothing at school, for instance Sir Owen M. Edwards, a distinguished educationalist of the early 1900s, who would have remained semi-literate but for the Welsh-speaking Sunday schools.

In 1871 a number of people led by the Liberal MP, Osborne Morgan, petitioned the Lord Chancellor to appoint just one Welsh-speaking judge, as the majority of Welsh people spoke mainly Welsh, and there were substantial monoglot communities. The Lord Chancellor replied that *'there is a statute of Henry VIII which absolutely requires that legal proceedings in Wales shall be conducted in English, legal proceedings had been in English for 300 years, and, moreover, the Welsh language is dying out . . . probably the best thing that can happen for Wales is that the Welsh tongue should follow the Cornish language into the limbo of dead languages.'*

A rallying call, broadcast by Saunders Lewis in 1962 led to the founding in 1963 of *Cymdeithas yr Iaith Gymraeg*, the 'Society for the Welsh Language'. By various methods of civil disobedience, it forced the English Parliament to pass the Welsh Language Act in 1967, giving equal status to the Welsh language for the first time since 1536.

As recently as 1965, a Mr. Brewer-Spinks tried to enforce an 'English Only' language rule at his factory at Blaenau Ffestiniog. Three staff resigned, and he only rescinded the rule after a meeting with The Secretary of State for Wales. In 1970, Dafydd Iwan, the Welsh folk singer and nationalist, was imprisoned for refusing to pay a fine for defacing English road signs. Twenty-one Welsh magistrates paid his fine to release him. Later, Gwynfor Evans's intended hunger strike forced the English government to give Wales its own Welsh-language media and help the survival of the language.

The percentage of people speaking Welsh has dropped from 54.4% in 1891 to only 18.7% in 1991. According to the 1992 Welsh Office survey, 70% of the Welsh-speaking households they surveyed were childless. The last monoglot Welsh speakers seemed to have died out in the mid-twentieth century.

Of the eight former Welsh counties, the largest were Dyfed, Powys and Gwynedd, with 27.8%, 24.4% and 18.6%

respectively of the area, making up over 60% of Wales. The percentage of the population who speak Welsh in these areas is high – 61%, 20% and 44%. Gwyneddd is solidly Welsh except for the Aberconwy holiday home area with 36%. Powys has been under threat since the war with non-Welsh people moving into the counties of Brecon, Montgomery and Radnorshire. Certain other areas have a high proportion of Welsh speakers, e.g. the Lliw Valley in West Glamorgan with 37% and Glyndŵr in Clwyd with 40% (Owain Glyndŵr's homeland).

The main danger is the mobility of people in modern times, especially into the main Welsh-speaking areas. For instance, in the 1991 Census, only 67% of Gwynedd's population was born in Wales. For Powys it was only 61%, and for Dyfed 75%. In the non-Welsh 'industrialised' counties of Gwent, Mid, South, and West Glamorgan, the Welsh native birth statistics are much higher, at 82%, 89%, 78% and 87%. This is the main pressure on the language, as more and more people come to this relatively safe, inexpensive and unspoilt area of the United Kingdom to retire. The proportion of Wales' inhabitants aged over 60 has trended as follows:

Percentage of population aged over 60
1871 1901 1931 1961 1981 1991
8%   7%   11% 18% 21% 23%

As we have seen with Welsh folk dance, it hung on by a thread in the memory of one old woman. There are now similar fears for the language. According to a 1997 report by *Cymdeithas yr Iaith Gymraeg* only 21 villages and towns will be able to be classified as Welsh-speaking by 2001. This report takes 75% of Welsh speakers as mean-

ing a Welsh community. Most of such communities will be clustered at the end of the Llŷn Peninsula beyond Porthmadog, and in Caernarfon and Blaenau Ffestiniog, with Llangefni the only Welsh-speaking community in Anglesey. The report blames English immigration, attracted to rural Wales by house prices which remain low while those in the South-East of England rise rapidly.

Even the strongholds of the Princes of Gwynedd are now threatened, and there is disagreement with the quango known as The Welsh Language Board, which believes that the language is safe, because of the number of new learners in south-east Wales. The report's authors point out that they *'feel very strongly that, if it is to survive, the Welsh language must keep its community base, its foothold as a community language. Otherwise we would go the way of the Irish, with lots of speakers on paper, but which does not exist as a community language except in a very few areas . . . The Welsh language will not survive unless there is an environment where people can communicate through Welsh, can live their lives through Welsh, rather than as individual Welsh speakers'.*

LAWS – *see Hywel Dda, Hywel the Good*

LEADERS

From the Kings of Ceredigion and Ystrad Tywi, Gwynedd, Powys, Gwent and Morgannwg, and Dyfed, one leader emerged to control Wales. Descended in direct line from the Kings of Gwynedd and Powys, *Rhodri Fawr* of Powys (Rhodri the Great), married Angharad of the royal lineage of Ceredigion and Ystrad Tawe and united the nation.

The great Houses of Gwynedd, Deheubarth and Powys emerged to be the focal points of resistance against fresh waves of invasion. *Hywel Dda* of Deheubarth (Hywel the Good), Rhodri's grandson, codified the ancient laws of Wales. One of Hywel's descendants, *Gruffydd ap Llewelyn*, was the only Welshman to unite *all* of Wales and throw the Saxons back over Offa's Dyke, but was killed in battle by Harold Godwinson of Wessex, the future King Harold Godwinson (of Hastings and 1066 fame).

Owain Gwynedd of the House of Gwynedd, a descendent of Hywel, briefly reunited Wales after years of anarchy. Owain's nephew, *The Lord Rhys*, Rhys ap Gruffydd of the House of Deheubarth, whose mother was Gwenllian of the House of Gwynedd, took control, before *Llywelyn Fawr* (Llewelyn the Great of Gwynedd) rose to dominance. *Llywelyn Ein Llyw Olaf* (Llewelyn Our Last Prince, of Gwynedd), Llywelyn Fawr's grandson was the last Prince of Wales to be acknowledged by the English.

The heroic *Owain Glyndŵr*, with descent from the Houses of Powys, Deheubarth and Gwynedd, was the last man who united most of Wales, and invaded England. *Owain Llawgoch* (see Assassination), the last direct descendant of the House of Gwynedd, was a leader in exile. *Harri Tudur* became the first of the Tudor dynasty of British kings, Henry VII. All of these men, who kept fighting to keep Wales united, are described individually in the book.

Welsh heroes, except for Harri Tudur, have a history of fighting superior external forces and constant internal ones. The Celts are ultra-parochial and still tribal. They do not like being governed by anyone, but will rally against a common cause. We saw it against Rome, and the Saxons, Normans and Plantagenets. We see it today. To Cardiff rugby supporters, the traditional enemy has always been Newport, just seven miles away. To Swansea, it is either Llanelli or Neath, again close by. However, when it comes to choosing the national team, there are cries from Cardiff and Newport that there are not enough East Wales players in the team, but to Swansea, Llanelli and Neath there are not enough West Wales players. When it comes to playing England, all differences are suspended for the afternoon, and the nation holds its breath and prays for a Welsh victory.

LITERATURE

(Poetry has a separate entry)

The earliest extant poem in Welsh is *Y Gododdin* by Aneirin (see Poetry), written in Strathclyde in Scotland and describing a Celtic war party's defeat at the Battle of Cattraeth (Catterick) in Yorkshire.

Gildas, the 6th century historian, studied at Llanilltud Fawr (Llantwit Major), but wrote in Latin. He died in 570 and was the first writer of history in Britain. His *De Excidio et Conquestu Britanniae* shows the resistance of fifth century Britons against the Anglo-Saxons. After his wife died, he had become a monk, and his account is the only contemporary British version of history from the invasion of the Romans, (in the first century), until his own time.

Nennius lived around 830 and was a pupil of Elfodd, Bishop of Bangor. His *Historia Britanorum* gives us information upon the fabled Arthur, who as 'dux bellorum' after the death of Hengist led the Britons against the Saxons in twelve battles. He drew strongly upon Gildas's work.

In the ninth century Asser's *De Vita et Rebus Gestis Alfredi* gives us the story of Alfred burning the cakes. A monk of St David's, he joined King Alfred's household in 885 and studied with him for six months a year, until his death, whilst Bishop of Sherbourne in 910. He also wrote a chronicle of history from 849 to 887.

The superb illuminated manuscript, *The Llandaf Charters*, with Welsh annotations in its margins, was stolen from the Cathedral and renamed 'The Gospel of St Chad' in the seventeenth century. This important part of Welsh heritage now is shown off in pomp in Litchfied Cathedral in England.

From around 930, *Armes Prydain*, a great poem of lament, asked for an alliance between Brittany, Wales and the Norsemen of Dublin to throw the hated Saxons out of the British Isles. Hywel Dda is castigated for his accommodating stance towards Athelstan of Wessex, in this *Prophecy of Britain*.

Annales Cambriae is a set of 10th century Welsh annals, giving extra information upon Arthur and his times, including the Battle of Badon in 518 and the fatal Battle of Camlan in 539 where both Arthur and Mordred were killed. Written about 960, the pedigrees of the Welsh royal families in this document are invaluable for understanding early Welsh history.

Around 1050 to 1150, the stories known as *The Mabinogion* (see Mabinogion) were first written down, possibly by Gwenllian, as they are remarkable in their female view of events. Four Welsh documents ('The Four Ancient Books of Wales') are truly outstanding

pieces of mediaeval literature, of international importance. They were all written down using far older material: 'The Black Book of Carmarthen', dating from the third quarter of the twelfth century; 'The Book of Aneirin', written in the late thirteenth century; 'The Book of Taliesin', from the fourteenth century; and 'The Red Book of Hergest', also fourteenth century. In The Red Book are to be found Welsh translations of 'British Chronicles', the famous 'Triads', ancient poems of Llywarch Hen, and the priceless Mabinogi stories.

The oldest surviving manuscript in Welsh, *Llyfr du Caerfyrddin* ('The Black Book of Carmarthen') dates from around 1250. About fifty years later , in the scriptorium at Ystrad Fflur (Strata Florida Abbey), *Llawysgrif Hendregadredd*, the collection of mediaeval Welsh poetry was collected.

Geoffrey of Monmouth 'established' a lineage for Britain dating from the Trojans and created the Arthurian basis for future romances. The Breton, Geoffrey of Monmouth, born around 1090, was schooled in Monmouth's priory. At Oxford, he was entrusted with translating a very old manuscript from the original British language into Latin. From this and other sources he compiled his *History of the British Kings* (c.1135), which refers to Cymbeline and Lear, the departing Romans and the flourishing of Arthur in the Dark Ages. This *Historia Regum Britanniae* became an instant success across Europe. Its translation into French ensured the mythology of Arthur spread across the continent. He traced ancestry from Cadwaladr in 689 back to Brutus, the great-grandson of Aeneas of Troy, nineteen hundred years of history, and described the Anglo-Saxon invasions of Britain. Probably an Archdeacon of

Llandaff, he moved to St Asaph in 1152 and died in 1155. According to him, London was founded by the Trojans as New Troy, Troynovant, which accounted for the Celtic tribe of Trinovantes in the South-East of England.

In mediaeval times, Walter Map (1140-1210), a border Welshman who became Archdeacon of Oxford, was highly regarded. Chaucer refers to his *Courtiers' Trifles* (*De Nugis Curialum*) in the 'Canterbury Tales'. Map also wrote 'Lancelot', but only some of his writings survive.

Giraldus Cambrensis (Gerald de Barri, Gerald of Wales, 1146-1223) has left valuable writings, and also desperately tried to ensure the independence of the Church of Wales against the supremacy of England. Born in Manorbier Castle, a son of Nest (the 'Helen of Wales'), he was rejected twice for the Archbishopric of St Davids, once by Henry II and once by the Archbishop of Canterbury. He appealed to Rome, was outlawed and fled abroad to be held at Chatillon. Later pardoned, this Archdeacon of Brecon wrote important works on Ireland and Wales. His *Itinerarium Cambriae* ('Voyage through Wales') is a fascinating and sympathetic view of Wales and its people in mediaeval times.

The *Brut y Tywysogion* ('Chronicle of the Princes') of 1256 is probably the best sourcebook for Welsh history, linking the Llywelyns back to Cunedda, and detailing battles and geneologies.

In 1536, the Act of Union with England forbade the use of Welsh for official purposes, but only ten years later the first book printed in Welsh (in London) was written by Sir John Price (John Prys) of Brecon (*Yn y Llyfr Hwn*). Just a year later, William Salesbury published his *Dictionary in English and Welsh* in 1547.

The Act of Uniformity, 1549, declared that all acts of public worship had to be in English. Yet Salesbury published his *Kynniver Llth a Ban* in 1551, a translation of the main text of the Prayer Book. The indomitable Salesbury published another book in 1556 on *How to Pronounce the Letters of the British Tongue* (*Now Commonly Called Welsh*). In 1567 he translated the New Testament into Welsh, and in the same year Gruffydd Robert published a book on Welsh grammar from his exile in Milan.

The year of the Armada, 1588, saw the publication of Bishop William Morgan's masterful translation of the Bible into Welsh. With Salesbury's earlier New Testament, this saved the language more than any other influence. It was not until 1942 that the Welsh language was allowed to be used in court proceedings, and not until 1967 that Welsh appeared upon official forms, but Welsh still had no official status as a language. In 1993 its status was improved by a new Welsh Language Act, and now there are around 500,000 Welsh speakers in Wales, with 1,500,000 able to understand some Welsh.

Wales is a literary nation, with its background suffused by the Bardic poetic tradition – as Idris Davies says in 'Psalm':

> '*Make us, O Lord, a people fit for poetry,*
> *And grant us clear voices to praise all noble achievement . . .*
> *Make us worthy of the golden chorus*
> *That the sons of God have always yearned to sing.*
> *Make us, O Lord, a people fit for poetry.'*

The great French scholar Camille

Julian confirmed that Celtic unity was *'in the domain of poets rather than statesman'*. The progression and importance of poetry throughout Welsh society to the present day, including reference to wonderful ancient Welsh prose and verse such as 'The Mabinogion' and 'The Gododdin' are covered in the section upon Poetry. (See Bards and Poetry for early literature).

LITERATURE – PROSE

The writings of **Thomas Traherne** have been recently compared, in America, with those of the European philosopher-critics Martin Heidegger, Jacques Derrida and Jacques Lacan. Born around 1637, Traherne died in 1674. A devout man, his *Roman Forgeries* exposed the falsifying of ecclesiastical documents by the Church of Rome in the ninth century. His *Centuries of Meditations* includes the following lines:

> *'You never enjoy the world alright, till the sea itself floweth in your veins, till you are clothed with the heavens, and crowned with the stars: and perceive yourself to be the sole heir of the whole world, and more than so, because men are in it who are every one sole heirs as well as you. Till you can sing and rejoice and delight in God, as misers do in gold, and kings in sceptres, you never enjoy the world.'*

In *Meditations*, he was the first British writer to depict the experience of childhood. His writings were not discovered until 1903, and with *Centuries of Meditations*, his *Poems, Poems of Felicity* and prose work all anticipate the work of William Blake.

Sir Richard Steele (1672-1729) from Llangunnor, founded and co-edited 'The Spectator' with Addison, in which he wrote *'the noblest motive is the public good'*, and that *'there are so few who can grow old with a good grace'*. He founded 'The Tatler' in 1709, in which his comments included *'every man is the maker of his own fortune'*, *'reading is to the mind what exercise is to the body'*, *'let your precept be, Be easy'*, and *'these ladies of irresistible modesty are those who make virtue unamiable.'* Also a writer of comic plays, money troubles forced him to leave London in 1724 and he died in Carmarthen.

One of the most influential and original Welshmen in history was **Dr Richard Price** of Llangeinor (1723-1791), a dissenting minister and radical who, with his friend Joseph Priestley helped found the Unitarian Society. He influenced Mary Wollstonecraft, who wrote the important *Vindication of the Rights of Women*. His *Review of the Principal Questions in Morals* put an element of realism into the philosophy of the day, and was possibly the greatest of his theological and ethical treatises. A close friend of Benjamin Franklin, Price supported the American revolution, and *The Declaration of Independence* owes a great deal to his *Observations on the Nature of Civil Liberty*. This seminal work sold 60,000 copies and ran to twelve editions by the end of 1776. He argued that each community had the right to self-government, responsible only for carrying out their electors' wishes, and that denial of this responsibility constituted treason. How different to today, where MP's are only responsible to their lords and masters who dictate three-line-whip party policy. (See Philosophers).

He also drew up the first budget of the new American nation, and his expertise on demography and actuarial matters influenced the financial policies of William Pitt and Shelburne. Unwavering in his support for the American colonies, despite English opprobrium, he refused an offer of American citizenship. Price was also a great supporter of the French Revolution. His 1789 sermon celebrating their 'ardour for liberty', in *A Discourse on the Love of our Country* provoked Burke to write his *Reflections on the Revolution in France*. When Price died, he was officially mourned in France.

It is said that the magazine 'Punch' was conceived by its originator and proprietor, Henry Mayhew, when he was staying at the local pub in Erwood, Powys.

Mary Ann Evans (1859-1880), as **George Elliot**, wrote *Adam Bede, The Mill on the Floss, Silas Marner, Daniel Deronda* and the towering masterpiece *Middlemarch*. Her work was full of intense compassionate intelligence and she made a major contribution to the development of the novel.

Arthur Jones-Machen (1863-1947), from Caerleon, was hailed by Sir Arthur Conan Doyle as a *'genius'*, and John Betjeman stated that Machen's work changed his life. By 1894 he had translated the *Memoirs of Jaques Casanova* into twelve volumes of five thousand pages, and the translation has been reprinted seventeen times. Oscar Wilde had encouraged him to move into fiction, and his first major work, *The Great God Pan* scandalised Victorian society. It was published by John Lane at the Bodley Head, also in 1894. Oscar Wilde congratulated him on *'un grand succes'*, and the book, a sensational Gothic novel that mixed together sex, the supernatural and horror was quickly reprinted.

The reviews had been spectacular – 'The Manchester Guardian' called it *'the most acutely and intentionally disagreeable book we have yet seen in English.'* 'Lady's Pictorial' said *'this book is gruesome, ghastly and dull . . . the majority of readers will turn from it in utter disgust.'* 'Westminster' reviewed it as *'an incoherent nightmare of sex and he supposed horrible mysteries behind it, such as might conceivably possess a man who was given to a morbid brooding over these matters, but which would soon lead to insanity if unrestrained.'* 'The Daily Telegraph', however, said that *'the supernatural element is utilised with extraordinary power and effectiveness'*, and the 'Liverpool Mercury' stated *'the coarser novels of Edgar Allan Poe do not leave behind them the shudder one feels at the shadowed devil-mysteries of The Great God Pan.'*

His next major novel, his masterpiece, was set in Caerleon and London, tracing a boy's search for beauty through literature and dreaming, finally ending in a drug-induced depraved tragedy. *The Hill of Dreams* was called *'the most beautiful book in the world'* by the American aesthete Carl Van Vechten in 1922, and was named as *'the most decadent book in all of English literature'* by the French critic Madeleine Cazamian in 1935. It was said to be a work *'worthy to stand upon the shelf beside Poe and De Quincey.'* It is the book's *'prose poetry that distinguishes the book most of all from its contemporaries, giving it a potency and imperishability that most of the serious and acclaimed novels of the day, dealing also with the theme of the individual's spiritual pilgrimage, do not have.'* (*Arthur Machen*, Mark Valentine).

'He also wrote the story acclaimed as the greatest weird story ever written, The White People; and those vignettes collected as Ornaments in Jade, which are certainly among the finest prose poems ever written.' (Valentine, ibid). He also made a

scholarly case for the search for the Holy Grail being a remembrance of the lost liturgy of the Celtic church.

His influence was massive. A 'Spectator' article (29th October 1988) traced lines of descent of his thought through Alistair Crowley and the 'Golden Dawn' movement to L. Ron Hubbard and Scientology, to the Hippy Movement and the revival of interest in ley lines and magical stones, to the Neo-Romantic art of Ceri Richards and Graham Sutherland. John Ireland (1879-1962), the composer, dedicated work to him because of the 'life-changing' effect of Machen's work. The famous film director Michael Powell (1905-1990), known for his collaborations with Emeric Pressburger, had a similar experience reading Machen when aged 20. Two years before his death, Powell wrote *'It is fitting that I record now, many years later, in 1988, how much I owe him for the terror, pity and fantasy – how much we all owe the Wizard of Gwent.'* The biography of the noted American author Paul Bowles also recorded that Machen's books *'would remain in Paul's memory for a long time, with the themes markedly re-echoing in some of his later fiction.'*

Many other authors, including masters of the modern horror genre like Stephen King and Clive Barker acknowledge their debt to Machen, and he earned the respect and praise of such major literary figures as T.S. Eliot, D.H. Lawrence, Henry Miller, Jorge Luis Borges, H. G. Wells, Oscar Wilde, W. B. Yeats, Siegfried Sassoon, George Moore and John Betjeman. Machen is periodically revived as a master of imaginative writing – the time has come again, especially in his native land – our prophets are without honour.

An interesting aside on Machen's career is that he tried to boost morale and spread his supernatural beliefs, by propagating the 'Angel of Mons' story in the 'London Evening News' in August 1914. British soldiers had seen weird figures in the sky on their retreat from Mons in World War I. Machen suggested that it was Saint George leading Henry V's archers from Agincourt. His bowmen were 'replaced' in popular retelling and modern mythology by an angel, or flock of angels.

In 1934, the novelist **John Cowper Powys** (1872-1963) moved to Corwen for inspiration from the mountains, and wrote two of his finest works, Owen Glendower (1940) and Porius (1951). His first major novel had been 'Wolf Solent' in 1929, which Herman Hesse called *a 'cumbersome chunk of genius'*. In 1955 he moved to Blaenau Ffestiniog, where he died in 1963. Henry Miller praised him fulsomely, as did Simone de Beauvoir and Elias Canetti. He wrote *'We Aboriginal Welsh People are the proudest people in the world. We are also the humblest'*. A powerful but neglected novelist, his brothers Llewelyn and Theodore Francis also contributed to a notable literary outpouring from one family.

Cardiff-born **Howard Spring** (1889-1965) wrote many popular novels, including *O Absalom!*, later published as *My Son, My Son!*, and *Fame is the Spur*, detailing a Labour politician's rise to power. He achieved great popularity in the USA as well as Britain.

Richard Llewelyn's book *How Green Was My Valley* was a moving account of coal-valley life, made into the famous film by John Ford. Born Richard David Vivian Llewelyn Loyd at St David's between 1905 and 1907, he was a film director before writing a series of novels between 1939 and his death in 1982. His Anglophobe father refused to register his birth, instead insisting that it was written in the family Bible in true Welsh fashion, but the Bible was destroyed by a V2 bomb in 1944. When he joined the Welsh Guards, Richard Llewellyn gave two dates of birth in 1905 and 1906, but his widow believes he was born in 1907. He changed the David to Dafydd in later life.

Richard Arthur Hughes wrote *High Wind in Jamaica* (called *The Innocent Voyage* in the USA) which achieved worldwide success. He wrote plays, verse and some wonderful novels like *The Fox in the Attic* and *The Wooden Sheperdess* before his death in 1976. **Alexander Cordell**'s *The Rape of the Fair Country* is just one of his fine novels of Welsh suffering in the industrial revolution.

Saunders Lewis was a playwright, literary critic, novelist and poet, a writer in Welsh with a reputation across Europe, known for his contribution to the 20th century nationalist cause. He was nominated for the Nobel Prize for Literature. Idris Davies' poem tells us:

> '*Some may cavil at his creed*
> *And others mock his Celtic ire,*
> *No Welshman loyal to his breed*
> *Forgets this prophet dared the fire,*
> *And roused his land by word and deed*
> *Against Philistia and her mire.*'

Saunders Lewis is mentioned under the headings on language and Plaid Cymru – his *The Deluge 1939* begins:

> '*The tramway climbs from Merthyr to*
>   *Dowlais,*
> *Slime of a snail on a heap of slag:*
> *Here once was Wales, and now*
> *Derelict cinemas and rain on the*
>   *barren tips.*'

Jean Rhys (Ella Gwendolen Rees Williams 1890-1979), born in Dominica, was a chorus girl in London, a volunteer cook in the First World War and lived mainly in Paris, meeting Hemingway, Ford Madox Ford and Joyce, before returning to Britain. Her father was a Welsh doctor and her mother a Creole. The radio broadcast in 1958 of her *Good Morning, Midnight* of 1939, and *Wide Sargasso Sea* of 1966 rekindled wide interest in her early novels such as *Voyage in the Dark* and *After Leaving Mr. MacKenzie.*

Caradoc Evans (born David Evans, 1878-1945) from Llanfihangel-yr-Arth wrote short stories exposing the greed and hypocrisy of chapel-going West Walians. He was vilified for his play *Taffy* which also hit out at the narrowness of nonconformist bigots.

Kate Roberts (1891-1985) has been the most distinguished writer in Welsh in the twentieth century. Born near Caernarfon, she has been called 'the Welsh Chekhov'. **Emlyn Williams** (1905-1987), the playwright, novelist and actor, wrote the psychological thriller *Night Must Fall* in 1933, and often played the lead in his own plays. **Alun Richards**, born in 1929 at Pontypridd, has been a leading playwright, novelist and short story writer. **Bernice Rubens** was the first woman to win the Booker Prize, in 1970, and **Alice Thomas-Ellis** is a well-known novelist, but Wales is best known for its poetic rather than its prose tradition. (see Poetry). **David Hughes** won the WH Smith Literary Award in 1988 with *The Pork Butcher*, filmed as *Souvenir* in 1989.

T. E. Lawrence ('Lawrence of Arabia') of 'Seven Pillars of Wisdom' fame, was born at Tremadog, and only his birth there qualified him for a scholarship at Jesus College, Oxford's 'Welsh' college.

Many more fine writers are of Welsh descent – Jerome K. Jerome (who based the character of Harris in *Three Men in a Boat* on George Evan Jenkins), Harriet Beecher Stowe, Charles Kingsley (*The Water Babies, Hereward The Wake*), George Meredith and Mary Webb (née Meredith) spring to mind.

Last century, Matthew Arnold put the Celtic contribution to English literature in its rightful place: *'while we owe to the Anglo-Saxon the more practical qualities that have built up the British Empire, we have inherited from the Celtic side that poetic vision which has made English literature the most brilliant since the Greek'* (*The Study of Celtic Literature*).

FOOTNOTE:
Hay-on-Wye is the second-hand book capital of the world and annually hosts an important International Book Festival. There are over 20 bookshops, including even the old cinema and Norman castle being used as stores, and the largest shop, Richard Booth's, has half a million tons of books.

Booth declared 'home rule' for Hay in 1977, with himself as King. He appoints 'ministers' and hands out passports and car stickers to visitors.

LLAN

Many places with this prefix, meaning 'religious enclosure', are associated with very early Christian settlements, containing a church dedicated to a Celtic saint. Unfortunately, many of these churches were rebuilt and renamed by the Normans in the 11th and 12th centuries. Churches named after St Michael (Llanfihangel) or St Mary (Llanfair) thus are often on the sites of earlier foundations. There are still over 600 churches in Wales (and just over its present border) still dedicated to the original saints.

A monastic settlement was traditionally surrounded by an earth wall or rampart and a ditch – the area enclosed was known as a 'llan', and the name in later times became associated with a church. Thus Llanbadarn was founded by St Padarn, Llanilltud Fawr by St Illtud, etc.

Llanilltud Fawr (the great Church of St Illtud) is mentioned in the entry on Christianity, and made an immense contribution to history, but equally intriguing is Llancarfan, a few miles away, where seven small streams meet. Originally called Nant Carfan, it is the Carbani Vallis mentioned in the ancient Book of Llandaf, and was the seat of a famous Celtic monastery back in the sixth century. The church is dedicated to St Catwg (Cadoc). Catwg was born c.500 in Monmouthshire, possibly educated at Caerwent, and founded the monastery in 535. The monk Caradoc of Llancarfan was referred to by Geoffrey of Monmouth as a contemporary, and it has also been claimed that he wrote *Brut y Tywysogion* (Chronicles of the Princes).

In its hidden valley there are many wells, some of which were claimed to have healing powers, and nearby is the hill-fort known as Castle Ditches. Close to these Llanfeithyn Farm is said to have been the site of Catwg's monastery, where Dyfrig (Dubricius) was taught, and his name is attached to Dyfrig's Well. Also taught there were St Baruwg (Baruc – buried in the old chapel on Barri Island), and St Finnian of Clonnard. Llanvithyn (Llanfeithyn) had a chapel dedicated to St Meuthin and it became a grange attached to Margam Abbey in the twelfth century.

Nearby the ancient building, now a farmhouse, at Garnllwyd is also said to have been a monastic site, and hundreds of human bones have been found in an adjacent field. These three monastic sites are within a mile of each other, and only four miles from Llanilltud Fawr.

Llanilltud monastery was a centre of learning, perhaps from AD180, as Cor Eurgain, founded by Caradoc's daughter and her Roman husband on their return from the imprisonment of Caradoc (the hero Caratacus of the Silures) in Rome. In the sixth century, Illtud seems to have taken over the great monastery to train missionaries. Bologna claims to be the oldest European centre of learning, but Llanilltud Fawr (Llantwit Major) has a longer history.

LLOYD'S OF LONDON

In February 1688, 'The London Gazette' mentioned the Tower Street coffee-house, that Edward Lloyd from Wales had started. Soon after Lloyd began issuing a weekly bulletin, the forerunner of 'Lloyd's List', giving news about shipping and business. The coffee-house quickly became a meeting house and information service for all those interested in shipping insurance and commerce.

It grew into the world's largest insurance association, moving to the Royal Exchange, and issuing its first standard policy in 1774. Lloyd's still provides the point of contact between syndicates of 'names' (members who supply the capital), and firms of underwriters who share the cover on policies issued.

LLYWELYN FAWR – LLYWELYN THE GREAT – LLYWELYN AP IORWERTH AB OWAIN GWYNEDD (1173-1240)

Dolbadarn Castle was built by Llywelyn's father, Iorwerth, around 1170, and it was there (or Nant Conwy) that this last true Prince of Wales was born in 1173. He never claimed the title, but was content to be overlord of Wales, being recognised as Prince of Gwynedd and Lord of Snowdon. His grandfather was the great Owain Gwynedd.

Professor T. Tout has called Llywelyn *'certainly the greatest of the native rulers of Wales . . . If other Welsh kings were equally warlike, the son of Iorwerth was certainly the most politic of them . . . While never forgetting his position as champion of the Welsh race, he used with consummate skill the differences and rivalries of the English . . . Under him the Welsh race, tongue and traditions began a new lease of life.'*

Llywelyn gained possession of part of Gwynedd in 1194, when Richard I, The Lionheart, was King of England. Aged just 22, Llywelyn beat his uncle Dafydd at the battle of Aberconwy. On the death of his cousin Gruffydd in 1200, Llywelyn gained the rest of Gwynedd. Llywelyn wished to push out from his Gwynedd power base, to take over the kingdoms of Deheubarth (after the death of The Lord Rhys) and Powys. To help his plans, Llywelyn first allied with King John, who became King in 1199, and he married John's daughter, Joan in 1205. Equally, John wished to limit the ambitious Gwenwynwyn of Powys. Powys was traditionally the weakest of the three major princedoms of Gwynedd, Deheubarth and Powys, squeezed between the other Welsh houses and the English Marcher Barons. Llywelyn overran Powys while King John captured Gwenwynwyn at Shrewsbury. Llywelyn also pushed Gwenwynwyn's ally, Maelgwyn, out of Northern Ceredigion. Llywelyn then took the Marcher Earl of Chester's castles at Deganwy, Rhuddlan, Holywell and Mold. From this position of control of North Wales, Llywelyn ap Iorwerth could then assist John on his invasion of Scotland in 1209.

However, by 1210, King John saw Llywelyn as an over-powerful enemy, and with Gwenwynwyn and Maelgwn invaded Wales. Llywelyn, deserted by other Welsh nobles, fell back towards his mountain base of Gwynedd, trying a scorched earth policy to starve John's army. However, Llywelyn eventually was forced to sign an ignominious peace treaty that just left him Gwynedd. The lesser Welsh rulers had preferred an absentee overlord rather than a native Welsh ruler, but the situation changed when they saw King John build castles near Aberystwyth, near Conwy and in Powys.

This threat of subjugation reunited the Welsh under Llywelyn in 1212, and John's castles were attacked and taken. Pope Innocent III gave his blessing to the Welsh revolt, and King Philip of France invited Llywelyn to ally with him against the English. True to form, John hanged his Welsh hostages, including Maelgwyn's 7-year-old son. By 1215, Llywelyn had captured many Norman castles and was in control of Pengwern (Shrewsbury). Llywelyn joined the English barons at Runnymede, and his power was one of the major factors that persuaded John to sign the Magna Carta in that year.

At Llywelyn's Parliament at Aberdyfi in 1216, he adjudicated on claims from rival Welsh princes for the division of Welsh territories under his overlordship, and his decisions were universally accepted. This was probably Wales' 'first Parliament'. By 1218, Llywelyn had taken Cardigan, Cilgerran, Cydweli (Kidwelly), Llansteffan and Carmarthen castles, and was threatening the Marcher castles of Swansea, Haverfordwest and Brecon. John had died in 1216, and in 1218 Llywelyn's pre-eminence in Wales was recognised by the new English king Henry III, at The Treaty of Worcester.

However William, Marcher Earl of Pembroke, seized the castles of Carmarthen and Cardigan in 1223, as the English barons moved in concert to push Llywelyn back to Gwynedd. Hubert de Burgh, justiciar of England, pushed into Powys, but was beaten by Llywelyn at Ceri in 1228. Hubert consolidated his hold on Marcher Lordships and by 1231 Llywelyn was forced to go on the offensive, pushing down to South Wales and burning Brecon and Neath. Pembroke and Abergavenny were also taken. Henry III invaded Wales and was lucky to escape with his life when Llywelyn launched a night attack on Grosmont Castle. By the Peace of Middle in 1234, Llywelyn was once more recognised by the English as pre-eminent in Wales, calling himself Prince of Aberffraw and Lord of Snowdonia. As we have seen, he had to be conscious of the feelings of his subject rulers in the rest of Wales. It was almost a quarter of a century earlier, that they had turned on him to support King John.

At this height of his powers, *Annales Cambriae* records '*The Welsh returned joyfully to their homes, but the French* (i.e. the Norman-English), *driven out of all their holds, wandered hither and thither like birds in melancholy wise*'.

He had been very much helped in his dealings with the English through his marriage to Joan, the daughter of King John, and spent his later years building up the prosperity of Wales. Llywelyn helped religious foundations, and supported a great flowering of Welsh literature. The earliest known text of 'The Mabinogion' was written down, and the imaginative brilliance of the bards can still be read today. They praised the strength and peace their lord had brought Wales against the '*French*' king and his Norman barons. Dafydd Benfras said he was '*his country's strongest shield*', Einion ab Gwgan hailed him as '*the joy of armies . . . the emperor and sovereign of sea and land*', and Llywarch ap Llywelyn wrote '*Happy was the mother who bore thee, Who are wise and noble.*'

Aged sixty-eight, this great lord of Snowdon died as a monk at Aberconwy Abbey in 1240, worn out and crippled. Llywelyn ap Iorwerth ab Owain Gwynedd had inspired a revision of the 'Laws' of Hywel Dda, reorganized the administrative machinery of Wales, maintained cordial relations with the Pope and the English Church, and brought peace and prosperity to a united Wales. He had also ensured that Henry III recognised his son by Joan, Dafydd, as rightful heir. His remarkable diplomatic and military skills were celebrated by all the Welsh poets of the times.

However, Gruffydd, Dafydd II's elder brother, was still imprisoned in the White Tower in London. He died on St David's Day, 1244, trying to escape on a rope of knotted sheets. In 1245 Henry III reneged on his promises and again invaded Wales, but was defeated by Dafydd in the only significant battle at Deganwy, and retreated back to England. Upon the tragically early death of Dafydd ap Llywelyn Fawr in 1246, a new power struggle took place to control Wales, only to be resolved by Llywelyn the Last. Mystery surrounds Dafydd II's death. It may be that he was poisoned on Henry's orders.

Years later, Llywelyn's great stone sarcophagus was removed from Conwy Abbey, as King Edward I symbolically built his castle over the abbey. It went to the Gwydir Chapel in the Church of St Grwst in Llanrwst. The present Chapel is said to have been designed by Inigo Jones. However, Llywelyn's bones were not allowed to be taken away, and left under the new castle of Conwy. His bard, Dafydd Benfras, wrote this moving lament at his death:

'*Where run the white rolling waves*
Where meets the sea the mighty river,
In cruel tombs at Aberconwy
God has caused their dire concealment
  from us,
The red-speared warriors, their nation's
  illustrious son.'

'Annales Cambriae' refers to his death: '*Thus died that great Achilles the Second, the lord Llywelyn whose deeds I am unworthy to recount. For with lance and shield did he tame his foes; he kept peace for the men of religion; to the needy he gave food and raiment. With a warlike chain he extended his boundaries; he showed justice to all . . . and by meet bonds of fear or love bound all men to him.*'

Y LLYW OLAF – LLYWELYN THE LAST – LLYWELYN AP GRUFFYDD AP LLYWELYN FAWR (c1225-1282)

Welsh custom of 'gavelkind' meant that Llywelyn the Great's kingdom had to be divided among all his four male heirs, although Llywelyn had tried desperately for all the kingdoms to be united under his son Dafydd. Within a month of Llywelyn's death, in 1240, King Henry III moved against Dafydd, invading and reneging on his agreement, forcing him to surrender many of his father's gains. Dafydd yielded his elder brother, Gruffydd as a prisoner. Incarcerated in the Tower of London, Gruffydd died trying to escape, four years later. King Henry's treachery meant that Norman Marcher lords took Welsh territories, Gruffydd ap Gwenwynwyn took his realm back, and the king claimed the territories of Tegeingl, Carmarthen, Cardigan and Cydweli.

Llywelyn's father, Gruffydd, has a particularly tragic history – he was the illegitimate son of Llywelyn the Great, and was imprisoned as a hostage by King John from 1211-1215 after John defeated Llywelyn in battle. Then Llywelyn the Great saw Gruffydd as a problem for Dafydd's succession and locked him up in Deganwy castle from 1228-1234. From 1239 to 1241 both Gruffydd and his son Owain Goch were held by Dafydd in Cricieth Castle. Finally, after Dafydd's defeat by Henry III, poor Gruffydd was to spend his last three years in the Tower of London. So Gruffydd ap Llywelyn Fawr ap Iorwerth was imprisoned by King John for four years, by his father Llywelyn the Great for six years, by his step-brother Dafydd II for two years,

and then by King Henry III for three years, when he died trying to escape. From 1211 to 1244 Gruffydd spent fifteen of thirty-three years imprisoned. This sad history affected his son, Llywelyn ap Gruffydd in his view of Norman-Welsh relations, for the rest of his life.

Gruffydd's tragic death sparked the Welsh to react to Henry's overlordship. Assisted by Gruffydd's vengeful son, Llywelyn, Dafydd allied with all but two of the other Welsh princes (Powys and Gwynllwg). They attacked the Norman lands and regained the important border castle of Mold. Dafydd appealed to Pope Innocent IV for help, offering Wales as a vassalship in return for protection against the Norman-English. He called himself Prince of Wales, the first to use that title.

Henry III assembled an army at Chester and beat the Welsh on the banks of the river Conwy, slaughtering all the Welsh prisoners. An English army was recalled from Ireland to lay waste to Anglesey. Dafydd kept fighting from his Gwynedd fastnesses, and forced Henry to withdraw. One of the great tragedies of Welsh history is Dafydd's premature death in 1246, possibly from poisoning. Henry claimed all of Dafydd's land, because he had been promised it if Dafydd died childless. A Norman army now pushed up through the South, conquering Ceredigion, Meirionydd and Dyganwy.

The leaderless men of Gwynedd immediately accepted Llywelyn and his eldest brother Owain Goch as rulers of Gwynedd. (Owain had been imprisoned in the Tower of London with their father, Gruffydd). However, after three years of warfare, the brothers had reached a point where the starving population could no longer support an armed force, and sued for an armistice. In April 1247 they were confirmed as lords of Gwynedd uwch Conwy (that part of Gwynedd west of the Conwy river and north of the Dyfi) and the status of Gwynedd reduced to an English vassalship, conforming to the matters of status of an English lordship. In this year, Matthew Paris recorded that '*Wales had been pulled down to nothing*'.

In 1256, *Brut y Tywysogion* records that '*The gentlefolk of Wales, despoiled of their liberty and their rights, came to Llywelyn ap Gruffydd and revealed to him with tears their grievous bondage to the English; and they made known to him that they preferred to be slain for their liberty than to suffer themselves to be unright-eously trampled on by foreigners.*'

By 1255, Llywelyn ap Gruffydd ap Llywelyn Fawr, this grandson of Llewelyn the Great had won total control of Gwynedd. He had defeated and imprisoned his two brothers at Bryn Derwen. Poor Owain Goch, was incarcerated in Dolbadarn Castle for twenty years to ensure stability, but Dafydd escaped to England. ('Red Owen' thus spent twenty-three years incarcerated, eight more than his father). Llywelyn now pushed out all over Wales, beating back Henry III's army, while the men of Deheubarth beat royal forces near Llandeilo in 1257. The ruling houses of Powys, Glamorgan and Deheubarth acknowledged Llywelyn as their lord in 1258, as he had not only pushed the Normans out of Gwynedd, but also out of most of Wales. Until 1262 there was a fragile truce, but Llywelyn went back on the attack to gain more of Wales, first from Roger Mortimer, and then part of the lordships of Brecon and Abergavenny. In 1264, he allied with Simon de Montfort, who was now in control of England after beating the

king at Lewes. By the Pipton Agreement, de Montfort recognised Llywelyn, on behalf of the crown, as Prince of Wales and overlord of the other great men of Wales.

The English chronicler Matthew Paris wrote that '*the North Welsh and the South Welsh were wholly knit together, as they had never been before*', and praised the courage and vigour of Llywelyn, saying ' *Is it not better, then, at once to die (in battle) and go to God than to live (in slavery)?*' Later, King Henry III was forced, by The Treaty of Montgomery in 1267, to recognize Llywelyn as Prince of Wales, who in return recognised the suzerainty of the English crown. Llywelyn now had more control and influence in Wales than any prince since the Norman Conquest of England. However, where his relations with the devious Henry had always been poor, he was soon to come up against a new king of England who simply resented Llywelyn's very existence.

When Edward I succeeded to the English crown, Llywelyn, fearing the normal Norman-French treachery, did not attend the coronation. His father had died in London. Llywelyn also refused to pay tribute to Edward I and built a new castle and town, Dolforwyn, against Edward's wishes. Llywelyn had sent a letter to Edward in 1272, stating that '*according to every just principle we should enjoy our Welsh laws and custom like other nations of the king's empire, and in our own language.*' Llywelyn was declared a rebel in 1274, and Edward invaded. Edward and his barons used violence to provoke rebellions all over Wales which were brutally crushed, while he pursued and harried Llywelyn, even forcing him to move, starving, from his mountain stronghold of Gwynedd.

In 1277, Edward had 15,600 troops in Wales, and Llywelyn was humiliated with the Treaty of Aberconwy when he sued for peace. He was stripped of his overlordship granted at the Treaty of Montgomery. In 1278, King Edward felt secure enough to release Elinor de Montfort, the betrothed daughter of the great Simon de Montfort, from prison. He then attended her wedding to Llywelyn in Worcester Cathedral. (Years previously, Elinor had been captured with her brother, on her way to marry Llywelyn – the Plantagenets feared a dynasty that would be more popular than theirs).

However, after a peaceful interlude, Llywelyn's wayward brother Dafydd attacked Hawarden (Penarlag) Castle and burnt Flint in 1282, sparking off another war. Ruthin, Hope and Dinas Bran were quickly taken. Llywelyn had the choice of assisting his brother, who had been disloyal to him before, or supporting him. He fatefully chose the latter option, agreed at a Welsh 'senedd' ('senate') at Denbigh. Days before, Elinor had died on the birth of their first child, Gwenllian. Llandovery and Aberystwyth were soon taken as the revolt spread.

King Edward now assembled ten thousand soldiers at Rhuddlan, including a thousand Welsh archers. Navies with archers moved to the Dee and from Bristol. Other armies advanced under the Marcher Lords. The war first went well for the Welsh. The Earl of Gloucester was defeated by Llywelyn near Llandeilo, a force in Anglesey was smashed, and Edward was forced back from Conwy to winter in Rhuddlan. However, more English reinforcements, including fifteen hundred cavalry and Gascon crossbowmen arrived.

In 1282, a Welsh detachment of eighteen men was entrapped at Cilmeri, near Llanfair-ym-Muallt (Builth Wells). At this place on 11th December, Llywelyn was killed. His nearby leaderless army was then annihilated by Welsh bowmen in English pay. Llywelyn's head was cut off and sent to Edward at Conwy Castle, and later paraded through London with a crown of ivy, before being stuck up on the Tower of London. His coronet was offered up to the shrine of Edward the Confessor at Westminster Abbey. The *Croes Naid* of his ancestors, believed to be a fragment of the 'True Cross', and perhaps the Welsh equivalent of Scotland's Stone of Scone, was taken to Windsor Castle and vanished during the English Civil War.

There is no understanding of how Llywelyn came to be so far detached from his main forces in his Gwynedd stronghold. Edward had offered him exile and an English earldom in return for unconditional surrender. With his small band, Llywelyn had been waiting for someone at Irfon Bridge, but longbowmen suddenly appeared and cut them to bits. Llywelyn escaped, only to be speared by Stephen de Frankton, before he could reach his main forces. Archbishop Pecham of Canterbury had been negotiating between Llywelyn and Edward on the terms of an end to the war, and the documentation still exists.

According to Pecham's later letters, a document was found on Llywelyn inviting him to go to the Irfon Bridge, sent by the Marcher Lords. This document disappeared, and also a copy sent by the Archbishop to the Chancellor. It looks like Llywelyn was killed by Norman treachery – the treachery on the bridge is a recurrent theme in Welsh literature, and for centuries the inhabitants of Builth were known as traitors in Wales. ('Bradwyr Buallt', 'Builth Traitors' became a common term of abuse). Also according to Archbishop Pecham, de Francton's spear did not kill him, and Llywelyn lived on for hours, asking repeatedly for a priest, while his army was being slaughtered a couple of miles away. He was refused one, while his captors waited for the Marcher Lord Edward Mortimer to come to the scene. According to 'The Waverley Chronicle', he executed Llywelyn on the spot. Probably he also took possession of the letter in Llywelyn's pocket at this same time. It may have been that de Franckton was given a large farmstead at Frampton, just north of Llanilltud Fawr, in the now 'safe' Vale of Glamorgan, in return for keeping quiet.

The plaque on his roadside granite monument at Cilmeri simply proclaims *'Llywelyn ein Llyw Olaf'* – *'Llywelyn Our Last Leader'*. His mutilated body lies in the atmospheric remains of the Cistercian Abbey Cwmhir, (*Abaty Cwm Hir*) which had a 242 feet nave, the longest in Britain after York, Durham and Winchester Cathedrals.

On Llywelyn's death, his brother Dafydd III pronounced himself Prince of Wales, and survived for ten months, using guerrilla tactics against Edward's forces in Snowdonia. Dafydd ap Gruffydd escaped from Dolwyddelan Castle before its capture, probably moving down to Dolbadarn Castle. For a month he then operated from Llywelyn Fawr's former castle, Castell y Bere and the Cader Idris foothills. Just before four thousand troops under William de Valence reached there, he was forced back to Dolbadarn, as Castell y Bere was captured. The net was closing in on him. An army from Anglesey and a force of Basque mercenaries moved to encircle Snowdonia. Upon promise of pardon, some of his own men gave him up. After two-hundred years of struggle, the French-speaking Normans, with their Saxon troops and foreign mercenaries, had overcome the nation of Wales.

With Dafydd's capture, the English tried to destroy the dynasty of the Llywelyns of Gwynedd. Llywelyn's only child, the year old Gwenllian, was incarcerated for the rest of her life in Six Hills monastery in Lincolnshire. A recent plaque marks her possible resting-place. His nephew Owain was imprisoned for over twenty years in a cage in Bristol castle until his death. The other of Dafydd's sons, Llywelyn, also died in Bristol Castle. In 1317, Aberffraw, the traditional home of the Princes of Gwynedd, was obliterated by the English – the last of the Welsh royal palaces to be demolished.

The Prince of Wales, Dafydd III, was dragged by horses through the streets of Shrewsbury, and at the High Cross he was hung, drawn and the entrails ripped from his living body. His corpse was then quartered, and his joints distributed to York, Winchester, Bristol and Northampton for display. The representatives of York and Winchester disputed over which city should have the honour of receiving the right shoulder – it went to Winchester. Dafydd's head was led on a pole through the street of London, with a crown of ivy, to the sound of horns and trumpets. It was spiked on the White Tower in London, next to his brother Llywelyn's. Conwy Castle was symbolically built on the tomb of Llywelyn the Great. By 'The Statute Of Rhuddlan', in 1284, Edward finally and formally took control of Wales.

In 1282, Gruffydd ab yr Ynad Coch's magnificent elegy to Llywelyn tells us:

*'Great torrents of wind and rain shake
    the whole land,
The oak trees crash together in a wild
    fury,
The sun is dark in the sky,
And the stars are fallen from their
    courses,'*

and ends with:

*'Do you not see the stars fallen?
Do you not believe in God, simple men?
Do you not see that the world has
    ended?
A sigh to you, God, for the sea to come
    over the land !
What is left to us that we should stay?*
                (translated by Jeff Davies)

Because of the loss of independence of Gwynedd and Powys after a thousand years, Gruffydd wrote:

*'Oh God! That the sea might surge up
    to You, covering the land !
Why are we left to long-drawn
    weariness?
There is no refuge from the terrible
    Prison.'*

In 1294 a rebellion by Madog ap Llewelyn rose in revolt, but Edward defeated him, and the few privileges left to the Welsh in The Statute of Rhuddlan were rescinded. The bards longed for a 'Mab Darogan' to free Wales again – they had to wait a century for the great Owain Glyndŵr in 1400.

M

MABINOGION

This treasury of Welsh mythology consists of folk tales from the eleventh century and earlier, which were preserved by monks writing 'The White Book of Rhydderch' around 1300-1325, and 'The Red Book of Hergest' c.1400. These books are the source of much of the legend surrounding King Arthur, and the collection was first translated in full into English by Lady Charlotte Guest, and published between 1838 and 1849.

Lady Guest divided the tales into three volumes: the 'Four Branches of the Mabinogi', the 'Four Independent Native Tales' and 'The Three Romances', and added the story of Taliesin from another old manuscript. These stories are *among the finest flowerings of Celtic genius and, taken together, a masterpiece of mediaeval European literature'* according to Professor Gwyn Jones in his introduction to the Everyman edition. 'The Four Branches' are the Mabinogi proper, the stories of 'Pwyll', 'Branwen', 'Manawyddan' and 'Math'. There are two short stories, 'The Dream of Macsen Wledig', and 'Lludd' and 'Llefelys'. The other two stories are the incomparable 'Culhwch and Olwen', the earliest Arthurian tale in Welsh, and the romantic 'Dream of Rhonabwy'. The three Arthurian romances are 'The Lady of the Fountain', 'Peredur' and 'Geraint Son of Erbin'.

'The Dream of Macsen Wledig' commemorates the time of Magnus Maximus, the fifth century Roman leader of Britain (Dux Britanniarum) who took the British garrison with him to campaign across and gain most of the Western Empire of Rome. He was eventually defeated by Theodosius.

There is a theory that 'The Four Branches' were written by Gwenllian ferch Gruffydd, the Welsh heroine killed by the Normans outside Cydweli, making her the earliest known woman writer in Britain, save for five Anglo-Saxon nuns whose letters are preserved (see Gwenllian)

MADOC (1134 – c.1170)

Prince Madoc ab Owain Gwynedd is mentioned previously in the section upon America. Possibly born in Dolwyddelan Castle, he was smuggled to Ireland as a boy by his mother Brenda, daughter of the Lord of Carno in mid-Wales. Later in favour at his father's court, he married Annesta, a maid of honour at the court. According to legend, in the next three years he travelled to Ireland, Cornwall and Brittany, and in 1163 represented his father as emissary to the Lord of Lundy Island.

In 1169, Prince Owain died, and there was the likelihood of civil war between his many sons for the succession. Madoc and his brother Einion had three ships built, the flagship of the little fleet being the 'Gwennon Gorn'. Wood was felled from the great forest of Nant Gwynant in Caernarfonshire, and Viking practice was followed in the construction. The old stories state that stag horn nails were used instead of iron as they would not rot, and that the hulls were covered, like coracles, with cow hides tanned on oak bark. The ships were built at Abergele and they sailed from Rhos-on-Sea.

Madoc settled some of the company in America, and returned for his brother Rhiryd, Lord of Clochran in Ireland, as promised. Another band of settlers then left via Lundy, Rhiryd sailing in the 'Pedr Sant' (Saint Peter). An old stone found on Lundy Island read *'It is an established fact known far and wide, that Madoc ventured far out into the Western Ocean never to return'*. According to Indian legends, he went back to Wales a third time to bring more settlers, but never came back.

It may be that the two bands of settlers never met, because one story then takes the settlers heading up north-west and becoming the Mandan Indians, and another relates to a white settlers heading down to Mexico and Aztec territories. Hernando Cortez, who captured Mexico, mentioned Madoc, as did Montezuma, the King of Mexico. Montezuma, in his treaty with Cortez, stated that his light-skinned people came from a little island in the north. The buccaneering explorers Walter Raleigh and John Hawkins also mention Madoc in their writings. This uncle of Llywelyn the Great is commemorated with a plaque at Fort Morgan, Mobile Bay, Alabama: *'In memory of Prince Madoc, a Welsh explorer, who landed on the shores of Mobile Bay in 1170 and left behind, with the Indians, the Welsh language'*. Tom McRae ('The Inditer', on the Internet) looked with his uncle for two 'stone cauldrons' on Mobile Bay recently. His uncle had seen them as a child, when they were known as 'Viking Tarpots'. Very early ships carried stone pots for ballast and storing food. When they landed, the cauldrons were used to

boil resin from pine trees, to make pitch and 'caulk' the hulls of their ships.

On Columbus's return from his discovery of America, he stated that the people honoured a white man called Matec, and he wrote on his chart of the Gulf of Mexico *'these are Welsh waters'*. He also referred to one stretch of sea near the Sargasso as Mar di Cambrio (the Sea of Wales). For years, the early Spanish settlers in Nova Hispana (Florida) searched for the *gente blanco* who had reached America before them. One 1519 Spanish map labels Mobile Bay as Tierra de los Gales (Land of the Welsh). The Italian historian Peter Martyr (1459-1525) wrote about white Indians with brown hair, and said that Indians in Guatemala and Virginia revered 'Matec'. The Dutch writer Hornius argued in 1652 that America had been peopled by many races, with the Welsh as a major component. The stone forts around Mobile Bay cannot be explained by the Indians. The largest is on top of Fort Mountain in north-west Georgia, near the head-waters of the Coosa River whose waters flow into Mobile Bay.

A major boost to the Madoc legend was the return to Wales, after a missionary tour, of the Reverend Morgan Jones in 1669. He stated that he and some companions were captured by Indians who threatened to kill them. Jones turned to his fellow missionaries and told them, in Welsh, to prepare themselves for death. The Indians heard and understood him, welcomed the missionaries as cousins and set them free.

The explorer George Rogers Clark was told by Chief Tobacco's Son of the Shawnee Indians that white men had been killed at a battle, in the thirteenth century, on the Falls of the Ohio, near

Louisville Kentucky. The defeated colony moved on upriver along the Ohio, Missouri and Mississippi rivers. John Sevier, the founder of Tennessee, noted the old stone hill-forts from Mobile to Kentucky and Tennessee. Ancient Roman coins were found in these forts. He questioned Oconosta, who had been a Cherokee chief for sixty years, in 1782. Oconosta related the story of the white Indians escaping from hostility with local tribes, moving from the Carolinas down the Tennessee to the Ohio then up the Mississippi and Missouri. Oconasta related that *'they are no more White people; they are now all become Indians, and look like other red people of the country . . . He had heard his grandfather and father say they were a people called Welsh, and that they had crossed the Great Water and landed first near the mouth of the Alabama River near Mobile and had been driven up to the heads of the waters until they arrived at Highwassee River.'* The explorer-painter George Catlin thought that the Mandans were the lost Welsh tribe, as their women were fair-complexioned, with hazel, blue or grey eyes. Some of the men had beards, unlike other Indian tribes. They did not use canoes like neighbouring Indians, but round boats like coracles. Catlin also said that some of their words were identical to Welsh, and this before he found out about the Madoc story.

The Mandans, unlike other Indians, knew how to ride horses with bridles and saddles. Their lodges had once been oblong, rather than the circular ones favoured by native Indians. It was a matrilinear society, based upon agriculture, like the old Welsh society. Some beehive lodges are reminiscent of the styles used by Celts, as seen in the few Glamorganshire pigsties remaining. The Mandans had box-beds with skin curtains – box-beds with curtains were popular in Wales until 1800. Their rounded 'bull boats', made of skins and wickerwork, were almost identical to the Welsh coracles that have been used for the last two millennia. Anthropologists place their arrival on the Missouri at between 900 and 1400, the right time frame for Madoc's small band. The Mandans' legends said that they came from 'lower down' the Missouri. A string of strange stone 'forts' run down from their Heart River and Knife River territories down to Mobile Bay, on the Gulf of Mexico. Indians did not build forts, but Madoc was born in a castle. Up river from the Falls, at the mouth of Fourteen Mile Creek, a stone fortress once stood. In 1874, State Geologist E. T. Cox described the walled fortification on the 'Devil's Backbone' and drew a map of a pear-shaped enclosure. His assistant stated that a great deal of skill was necessary to build the walls without mortar. (The unique stone fortress was dismantled to build the Big Four Railroad Bridge. In 1898, a helmet and shield were found in Louisville, but were stolen. In 1799, six skeletons were unearthed in Jeffersonville, but have been lost.) The neighbouring Hidatsa tribe called the Mandans 'Gulf-people' because of their origins in the Gulf. These occurrences helped cement the connections between Madoc's settlers moving from Mobile and the Mandan tribe.

One of the first explorers to find the tribe, the French explorer La Verendrye in 1739, wrote *'The fortifications are not characteristic of the Indians . . . Most of the women do not have the Indian features . . . The tribe is mixed white and black. The women are fairly good-looking, especially the light coloured ones; many of them have* blonde or fair hair.' Many descriptions referred to the preponderance of brown and red hair, and blue eyes amongst the Mandans, and they were known as the 'white Indians' even by other Indian tribes.

The Mandans were almost wiped out by smallpox in 1781 when half the tribe died, and then in 1837 it decimated them to just a few dozen survivors. These were enslaved by the Arikaras, and now no Mandan-speakers survive. The remnants live on the Fort Berthold reservation in the heart of the USA, and their ceremonial grounds have been covered by the Garrison Reservoir (so there is definitely something in common with Wales). The Mandans worship 'the Lone Man', a white man who started the tribe, and his shrine is 'The Ark of the Lone Man', a holy canoe. Mandan cosmology also centres of a great flood – Madoc's lands in Wales bordered Cantre'r Gwaelod, the 'lowland hundreds' lost to the sea.

The late Gwyn Alf Williams, with his hatred of imperialism, was dismissive of Madoc in his 1979 book 'Madoc: the Making of a Myth', but one can only reiterate the final lines of his book, where he met a surviving Mandan, Ralph Little Owl:

'They came at last, those moments we had half-hoped for, half-feared, when a chill ran through us which was not the wind. Ronald Little Owl rehearsed the Mandan prophecies which had all come true, including one that old wolves would make the Missouri run backwards (as they have done). The last one, however, he would not tell us – "it would not be polite". The language? "When I die, the Mandan language will have gone." And the Lone Man? He bent his Asiatic face into the tele-

vision lights and said, "The Lone Man was the founder of our people. He was a white man who brought our people in his big canoe across a great water and landed them on the Gulf of Mexico." '

Just twenty years later, eight hundred years of history has been consigned to the realms of legend. A recent book by Dana Olson refers to the fact that a colony of Welshmen is mentioned in 'Walum Olum', the chronological history of the Delaware Indians:

'That the country north of the Falls of the Ohio and adjacent to the river was inhabited by a strange people many years before the first recorded visit of a white man, there can be no doubt. The relics of a former race are scattered throughout this territory, and the many skeletons found buried along the river banks of the river below Jeffersonville are indisputable evidence that a strange people once flourished here.'

According to Olson, there is:

'. . . additional and convincing proof that Prince Madoc founded the first recorded settlement in America and established in what is now Clark County, Indiana, the longest surviving colony (1170-1837) before widespread immigration brought other white men to this country.'

MAGIC

Mystical Wales is represented in its literature and in the Myrddin stories – Myrddin (Merlin) predates his inclusion in the Arthurian Cycle of stories.

Around 1240, some experts have identified the mysterious Siôn Cent with Owain Glyndŵr when he disappeared from history. This reclusive poet and scholar was also said to have been vicar of Kentchurch in Hereford (still Welsh until 1536) and Grysmwnt (Grosmont) in Gwent. Many supernatural happenings were attributed to him – could this have been a smoke-screen for Glyndŵr? He died at the age of *'at least one hundred and twenty'* and his grave exists half in the chancel and half in the graveyard of his church, supposedly because of a pact with the Devil. He is also said to have magically built the bridge over the River Monmow which has always been named after him.

Siôn Cent (see Poetry) was a master of the 'Dychan' ('satire'), and his poems sermonise against vanity and love of worldly things – these few lines are from 'Man's Vanity':

'After wine, the beloved kinsman
Will be put diligently into the earth
And his kin will mourn him for
    a while
As he is covered with a spade.
Cruel tormentor, does the man not
    know,
Grim task, that no border
Supports his house there, awful abode,
Except the earth alone?
And gravel presses against the cheek.'

Generations of the Harrieses, of Cwrt y Cadno near Llanpumpsaint, were revered as having magical powers. In the sixteenth century, one is supposed to have split a nearby megalith in two, near their village. In the eighteenth century, thunder in the Cothi Valley signified to locals that a Harries was consulting his chained and padlocked book of magic. Dr John Harries was the most famous member of the family.

The local conjuror or *cosuriwr* or *dyn hysbys* (wise man), was consulted by people up to the present century for investment advice or sickness remedies, often involving a large toad. One of these sorcerer-witch doctors was Huw Lloyd of Cynfal Fawr near Ffestiniog, who 'regularly met the Devil' on a rock in the Cynfal Gorge, known as Huw Llwyd's Pulpit.

John Harries and Huw Lloyd were the type of 'wise men' linked with black magic and medicine. Another type of recognised *dyn hysbys* was a renowned cleric such as Edmwnd Prys. The third category of *cosuriwr* were those who had 'inherited the gift' by belonging to a certain family. A well-known Llangurig family of wise men included Evan Griffiths of Pant-y-Benni, and Edward Davies of Y Fagwr Fawr, Ponterwyd. Learning from their families and books, they treated sick animals, and people came from all over Wales to receive a charm to protect their livestock. This took the form of a prayer written in a mixture of Welsh, Latin and English, the 'abracadabra' symbol and the zodiac signs. The prayer was corked into a bottle (*potel y dyn hysbys*), with the warning never to uncork it, and placed in the animals' barn. Some still remain in Welsh farmhouses, and there are examples in the Museum of Welsh Life and the National Library of Wales. Sometimes the evil spirit who troubled the farm was human, such as the local landowner or a troublesome neighbour, and similar protective charms were bought and bottled.

Mari Berllan Piter lived near Aberaeron, and her tumble-down cottage, Perllan Piter, is now covered by her orchard (*perllan*). It is now called 'The Witch's Cottage' and it is said that it is impossible to photograph it. She could change herself into a hare (sacred to the Celts, and protected by Saint Melangell) to escape from angry neighbours, who blamed her if any thing went wrong. Local farmers gave her gifts of flour and potatoes in return for not cursing their animals. When Dic y Felin, the local miller, refused to grind her wheat into flour, she made the mill-wheel reverse direction. When a young girl stole an apple from the witch's orchard, Mari put a spell on her that made her walk backwards all the way home. Mari died in 1896 and is buried in Llanbadarn Trefeglwys churchyard.

At Cefn Pawl near Beguildy was born Ieuan Ddu, John Dee, Black Jack, who became Elizabeth I's tutor, a man respected at court who was also a noted mathematician, astronomer, geographer and astrologer. It is thought that Shakespeare used him as the model for Prospero. 'John Dee' was better known back in Powys as a magician and practitioner of the Black Arts than as a court adviser to Queen Elizabeth. Born in 1527, he was a foundation fellow of Trinity College Cambridge in 1546, and moved to Louvain (Leuven) in modern-day Belgium because science and mathematics were better established there. He lectured at Paris when he was twenty three and returned to London to be taken into the heart of Elizabeth's court.

Dee claimed descent from Rhodri Mawr, and invented the term 'The British Empire' for Queen Elizabeth to prove her right to North America which had been 'discovered' by the Welsh prince Madog ap Owain Gwynedd. (i.e the Brythonic Celts, or the British, were the founders of her empire). He published the work of Euclid, and prepared an edition of Robert

Recorde's mathematical studies, Recorde being a fellow-Welshman and inventor of the 'equals' (=) sign.

The twin brother of Henry Vaughan (see Poetry), Thomas Vaughan (1621 – 1666) was also educated at Jesus College and became a 'natural magician' of repute, publishing several hermetic and alchemic treatises. He was involved in Rosicrucianism, and wrote *Magia Adamica* or the *Antiquity of Magic* in 1650. He had been a student of Henricus Agrippa, the occult writer described as an astrologer by Rabelais.

Richard Robert Jones (1780-1843) was known as 'Dic Aberdaron'. Uneducated, he learned fifteen languages, and travelled the countryside wearing a hare-skin hat, a ram's horn tied around his neck, and a cat at his side. It was said he could summon demons in the shape of piglets, which he called '*Cornelius's Cats*'. Reapers at Methlem farm near Aberdaron could not cut a field of thistles, but Dic's 'cats' stripped the field in minutes. He is buried in St Asaph.

In Mynydd-y-Gwair, in the hills north of Swansea, Harry Grindle Matthews supposedly worked on a secret weapon, a death ray, from 1934. He claimed that it could kill rats from a distance of sixty-four feet. Of course, he was known, and is remembered as 'Death Ray' Matthews. He had previously experimented in light-controlled boats, radio telephony from moving cars, sky projectors and in talking movies. In 1912, he demonstrated his 'aerophone', the world's first portable phone, to Queen Mary. A pioneer of talking films, he failed to persuade the British film moguls that 'talkies' were the future for the industry.

A biographer has stated that the reclusive inventor was also working on rockets, submarine detection and interplanetary travel, and that strange guests would suddenly arrive and disappear by private plane. It is rumoured that Goebbels visited him to see if he could ignite gunpowder at a distance using electromagnetism. 'Death Ray' disappeared in 1941, after destroying all his papers. He left behind a mysterious legacy. Some said that he was shot in the Tower of London for developing war weapons for Germany, and the National press featured his laboratory in the mountain mists.

A 1997 HTV programme, 'Home Ground', featured the strange story of a German Telefunken radio transmitter from the Second World War, set up for Morse Code use only. Capable of enough power to cover Europe, it was discovered in the basement of Telephone House, Swansea, having been impounded during the war. There were rumours of a German spy transmitting over a three day period before his arrest, and a major Luftwaffe blitz killed 347 people in Swansea during three nights in February 1941. The first wave of attacks knocked out the anti-aircraft guns operations room, and German pilots commented upon Swansea's lack of defences. Could 'Death-Ray' have been this German spy? Could his 'destroyed' papers resurface in the National Records Office, or secret service files, after sixty years' restriction under the Official Secrets Act? Matthews' strange disappearance and this bizarre transmitter story need further research.

MARCHES

After beating Harold of Wessex at the battle of Hastings in 1066, William the Conqueror saw the need to quickly subjugate the rest of Saxon England. To keep Wales in check, he appointed three powerful barons to hold the Welsh border against any invasion. He knew that the Welsh originally occupied England and had been pushed back by successive invasions of Saxons, Mercians, Angles, Danes, Jutes and the like. To hold the region east of Offa's Dyke, he appointed Hugh the Wolf (Hugh Lupus), also known as Hugh the Fat, as Earl of Chester. He was responsible for stopping any approaches from Gwynedd.

Further south, he made Roger of Montgomery Earl of Shrewsbury, to stop the Princes of Powys penetrating up the Severn Valley. William Fitz Osbern was made Earl of Hereford to stop the Princes of Deheubarth, Glamorgan and Gwent from entering England.

Thus was created the 'Marche', the mark or boundary that separated England from Wales. These Norman nobles had the right to do anything they wished in relation to their Welsh neighbours. They had carte blanche to take any land in Wales by any means possible, by lying, cheating, torture and war. The three earldoms were made 'Counties Palatinate' and the 'Marcher Lords' were promised that any Welsh land they took they could keep. They administered their own laws and taxes, and used a system of subsidiary Lords Marcher to invade Wales. It took seventy years to subjugate most of South Wales, compared to four years to occupy England. Not until 1420 did Wales finally succumb, after the Owain Glyndŵr rebellion. However, the territories of these lords was of increasing interest to the English crown, which slowly tightened its grip on the barons. With the Welsh Tudor dynasty, England

and Wales combined legally, and the days of these robber barons were ended.

MARKETING

In a small country, two-thirds the size of Belgium, with a relic population and language, famous only for the highest density of castles and sheep in the world, several attempts have been made to attract tourism by marketing 'scams'. Perhaps the Welsh were the first nation to realise that you have to sell the sizzle, not the steak.

Near Beddgelert (the grave of Gelert) a monument supposedly marks the burial-place of Gelert, the hound left by Llewelyn to guard his child. The poor dog, covered with blood, was killed by Llywelyn before he realized that Gelert had killed a wolf to save the child. The story was invented by the eighteenth century inn-keeper David Pritchard to attract tourists to this beautiful spot, where the River Glaslyn cuts through the Snowdon mountains. Pritchard is now reputed to haunt room 29 in the Goat Hotel. Gelert's Grave is a cairn in the field next to the church, but, in the words of Israel Zangwill:

> 'Pass on, O tender-hearted. Dry your eyes.
> Not here a greyhound, but a landlord, lies.'

Llanfairpwllgwyngyll ('St Mary's Church by the pool of white hazel trees') in Anglesey, was renamed by the local bard John Evans (Y Bardd Cocos, 1827-1895) as: *Llanfairpwllgwyngyllgogerychwyrndrobwllllantisiliogogogoch* (as above, but adding 'near the rapid whirlpool, by the red cave of the Church of Saint Tysilio'). Local tradesmen used it to publicise the village in the nineteenth century. British Rail used the concocted name when it reopened the railway station in 1973. Llanfair PG, as it is known across Wales, has another claim to fame in that Britain's first Women's Institute was established here, in 1915.

Not to be outdone, The Fairbourne Steam Railway at Barmouth has also invented a 'more commercial' station name for a station board sixty-four feet (19.5m) long, of: *Gorsafawddacha'idraigodanheddogledddollonpenrhynareurdraeth ceredigion* ('The Mawddach Station with its dragons' teeth on the Northerly Penrhyn Drive on the golden beach of Cardigan Bay' – the dragons' teeth are the remains of Second World War concrete defences)

It is good to see that Llanwrtyd Wells, which claims to be Britain's smallest town, is carrying on the tradition of niche marketing. Locals claim that they 'invented' pony-trekking in the 1950s. It stages off-beat events such as the annual 'Man versus Horse' Race over a hilly twenty-two mile course every June. Recently a man just failed to beat a horse for the £15000 reward. It also holds a Mountain Bike Festival including Bog-Leaping (August), the World Bog Snorkelling Championships (also in August), the Welsh International 4-Day Walk (September), The Drover's Walk in late-June following the old routes with a drover's inn re-opened for the day, the Welsh International 4-Day Cycle Race (October) and the Mid-Wales Beer Festival (November). The landlord at The Neuadd Arms Hotel enters into the spirit of things by holding the Mid-Wales Beer Festival in November, and by organising Real Ale Rambles. Upon December

31, 'The New Year Walk-In' is a torch-lit procession that seems to visit many of the pubs in the town.

Richard 'Beau' Nash (1674-1762) from Swansea, moved seamlessly from Oxford to an army commission to the Middle Temple to making a living from gambling, all before he was 30 years old. Then, by his fashion leadership, his influence on manners and improvements in streets and building, he made Bath 'the' fashionable holiday centre of its day. As Master of Ceremonies, he conducted public balls on a magnificent scale, with nobility flocking to 'take the waters' by day and to be entertained at night.

R. J. Lloyd Price, Squire of Rhiwlas near Bala, founded the Bala Whisky Distillery in the 1860s (see whisky). His entrepreneurial activities are recorded in an odd book of his called *Dogs Ancient and Modern and Walks in Wales*. Perhaps R. J. Lloyd Price was also covering his bets. Inside his book cover, Price advertised more of his enterprises, including: The Rhiwlas Game Meal; Rabbits for Profit and Rabbits for Powder; Welsh Whiskey; Rhiwlas Game Farm; and Fresh Laid Pheasants' Eggs. A plaque he placed on a house in Bala reads 'Home-made House – All Bricks and Slates Produced in Rhiwlas Estate'. He also organised the first recorded sheepdog trial on October 9th, 1873, which a plaque was erected to record near the field. (See Whisky, Gravestones).

Scotland spends four times as much as Wales upon marketing its country to overseas visitors. As a result, only 3% of visitors to the British Isles come to Wales, and Wales' share of the overseas tourist 'spend' is only 2%, as many are passing through on their way to Ireland.

MARX

Robert Owen (see Robert Owen) was a major influence upon Karl Marx and Freidrich Engels. Another Welshman, Richard Price (see Literature, Philosophers, America) influenced their thought, but Lewis Henry Morgan (1818-81) was hailed by them as giving independent confirmation of their materialist theory of history. His 'Ancient Society', a treatise upon the origins of the institutions of government and property, had followed pioneering studies on the North-American Indians from 1851-69. Morgan also appears to be the first author to argue that animals possess powers of rational thought.

MATHEMATICS

Robert Recorde of Tenby invented the equals sign (=) in 1550, and is commemorated in the parish church. He died a bankrupt, despite his book going into twenty-six editions in his lifetime. (See Scientists, Magic).

In 1706, William Jones of Llanfihangel Tre'r Beirdd, Anglesay, was the first person to use the symbol *pi* to denote the ratio of the circumference of a circle to its diameter.

MERLIN

Myrddin Emrys, after whom Caerfyrddin, Carmarthen, was named, is the Merlin of Arthurian legend. Merlin's Oak, a leafless stump held up by iron struts, stood in the centre of Caerfyrddin until 1958 when it was removed to assist more carbon and lead pollution by modern traffic. Merlin had prophesied that Carmarthen would fall with the death of the tree and with its removal 1,500 years of legend was also uprooted. Another of his prophecies was that a bull would go to the top of St Peter's Church in Carmarthen, and a calf was found at the top centuries later.

The most famous wizard in the world, he was in Welsh folk tales long before the Arthurian cycle where he appeared as Arthur's councillor, and foresaw the hero's downfall. He became known as Merlin because the Latinized form of Myrddin would have been Merdinus, linked to the Latin for dung, Merdus (or the French 'merde'). He was also a poet and a prophet, forecasting that one day the Welsh would once again take over the land of Britain and drive the Saxons out.

As a youth, Merlin was linked with Vortigern, King of Britain, who could not build a tower on Dinas Emrys. Merlin informed him that there was a problem because two dragons guarded an underwater lake. Recent archaeological excavation showed an underground pool. These red and white dragons were symbolic of the British against Saxon fight for Britain. In legend, he next advised Ambrosius Aurelius, the conqueror of Vortigern, to bring back the Giant's Ring of sacred stones from Ireland and erect Stonehenge. After the death of Ambrosius, his successor Uther Pendragon became besotted with Eigyr (Igraine), wife of Gorlois, so Merlin shape-shifted Uther into Gorlois and she conceived Arthur. After the Battle of Arturet, Merlin went insane and lived in the woods. He returned to advise Arthur. Welsh traditions say that he lies in chains in a cave

under Bryn Myrddin, Carmarthen, or in a cave near Dinefwr castle, or buried on Bardsey Island, where he took the 'Thirteen Treasures of Britain' (see Thirteen Treasures, Arthur). He is also thought to have been imprisoned in a pool in Britanny.

There were probably two Myrddins, one Myrddin Wyllt, a Celtic wizard who lived in the Scottish woods at the time of Vortigern, and Myrddin Emrys from Carmarthen, who lived at the time of Arthur.

The Breton link with Merlin and Arthur is interesting. There is a scenic tour in the 'Purple Country' of Broceliande, fifty-six miles of roads crisscrossing ancient sites and megaliths. The Barenton Spring is where Merlin first met Vivian the Enchantress. Merlin's Tomb is an old passage grave where he was imprisoned by Vivian. Also in the forest, the lake known as the 'Fairies' Mirror' is supposed to be used by Vivian to hold Merlin. Morgana le Fay imprisoned Arthur's unfaithful knights in The Valley of No Return. Comper Castle's lake is said to have been the home of Vivian, who brought up Lancelot under its waters, and the castle has an Arthurian exhibition. Paimpont Abbey celebrates the Welsh missionaries to Britanny.

Merlin left behind a set of prophecies for the next millennium after his death. Thomas Heywood's 1812 book *The Life of Merlin* links Merlin's prophecies through all the events in British history, for example the Gunpowder Plot:

'To conspire to kill the King,
To raise Rebellion,
To alter Religion,
To subvert the State,
To procure invasion by Strangers.'

MINERALS

(Coal and Gold have separate entries)

Wales has been systematically quarried for granite and road-building materials. Geologically, it has been blessed with minerals of value, which has often been of little benefit to the Welsh people.

In terms of rocks, Wales has the 650 million years old Pre-Cambrian strata in three main areas. These ancient rocks are found at the tip of the Llŷn Peninsula, possibly the most 'Welsh' and unspoilt part of Wales; at St David's Head, the most holy part of Wales for Christians; and finally in large parts of Anglesey, the religious centre and holy island for the Celts and Druidism.

The next oldest rocks, the volcanic Cambrian strata, form Snowdonia and the backbone of Merioneth and the Preseli Hills. The igneous Ordovician rocks in the Preselis are the famous mystical 'bluestones' that were transported to Stonehenge. Nearly all of Wales is composed of hard rock, over 200 million years old.

In four types of mineral production and technology, Wales was once the world leader – coal, copper, slate and iron-working. It was also important in lead-mining. Coal is mentioned in another entry, and for all these minerals (plus gold), Wales is a wonderful place to study and explore industrial archaeology. Wales is a small country, with no major cities covering its heritage as the leading world centre of the Industrial Revolution. Therefore, many major sites are either heritage centres, or surrounded by natural woodlands and wildlife. One, Blaenafon, may become a World Heritage Site.

COPPER

Apart from the gold in Dolaucothi, mentioned earlier, the Romans mined copper at Parys Mountain, near Amlwch in Anglesey. Before them, the Ordovices, a powerful Celtic tribe, exploited the source. This is now a red and yellow Martian landscape full of abandoned workings, but by the eighteenth century it had become the world's largest and most productive copper mine, following its rediscovery in 1768. Records at this time show that Amlwch had six thousand inhabitants and one thousand and twenty-five alehouses, surely some sort of world record for pubs, and the rock-bound inlet that is its port was one of the busiest in Europe. By the end of the 18th century, The Parys Mine Company employed twelve hundred men producing three thousand tons of copper ore annually.

The pollution in the harbour was so bad, that the iron hulls of ships did not corrode. When this was noticed, ships' hulls began to be sheathed in copper by their owners and boat builders, making another lucrative market for the mine. By the end of the 19th century, the mountain was worked out and left in the weird state we see today.

Also on the Great Orme in Llandudno, copper workings dating from the Bronze Age are open to visitors, showing how prehistoric men mined for copper. Bones aged up to four thousand years have been found, which were used as scrapers two hundred foot below the surface. Because the extraction process was simplified by a rock-softening process, known as dolomitization, this was once the most important copper mine in Europe, perhaps the world, before Parys Mountain took over. The Sygun Copper Mine near

Blaenau Ffestiniog, which was worked until 1903, has also been restored and is open to the public.

IRON AND STEEL

Nearly all the industrial heritage sites in Wales are in areas of real natural beauty and many have blended into their backgrounds. Saundersfoot, a lovely little seaside resort, used to be a coal exporting port for the South Pembrokeshire coalfield and in nearby Stepaside there are the remains of Grove Colliery and a 19th century ironworks, slowly being cleared from the woodlands that enclosed them by the Stepaside Heritage Project.

Near Pontneddfechan are abandoned gunpowder works and silica mines, in the woodland around the complex of waterfalls at Ystradfellte. A plaque on the wall of Tintern Abbey records the discovery and manufacture of brass, the alloy of zinc and copper, by Cistercian monks in 1568. As the Abbey was dissolved in 1536 by Henry VIII, the provenance and proof of this claim needs further research.

Blaenafon Ironworks opened in 1789, operating until 1900 and the remains, the best-preserved in Western Europe, are open to visitors. This historically important site includes a bank of blast furnaces, casting houses, water balance lift and workers' cottages, and is presently in the care of CADW (Welsh Historic Monuments). On the Forge site, a young Welshman called Sidney Gilchrist Thomas, with his cousin Percy Carlyle Gilchrist developed a new process of steel production in 1878. He used phosphoric ores, revolutionising steel manufacture by perfecting the 'Bessemer Process'. He sold the patent to a Scot called Andrew Carnegie, who then made multi-millions of dollars in the USA and elsewhere from what is known today as *'The Carnegie Process'*. Sidney Thomas's discovery vastly accelerated industrial expansion in Europe and America. Blaenafon is so internationally important in its archaeological remains that it may become a 'World Heritage Site'.

The Nantyglo site near Ebbw Vale features military round towers, built by ironmasters fearful of insurrection by their hard-pressed employees. There are heritage walks around the area. The old Clydach Ironworks near Neath lie in a gorge of native beech woods, now a National Nature Reserve.

Bersham Ironworks were important in the development of the iron industry. Here in 1775 a new method for horizontally boring-out cylinders was patented by John 'Iron-Mad' Wilkinson. The smooth circular bore enabled really accurate cannon to be manufactured for the American Civil and Napoleonic Wars. It also enabled the production of fine tolerance steam engine cylinders – James Watt was a customer – which speeded up the Industrial Revolution, with steam engines obsolescing water-powered production sites and replacing the horse and sail as methods of transport.

Merthyr was known as the 'iron and steel capital of the world' during the Industrial Revolution, and South Wales was producing half of Britain's iron exports by 1827. In 1831, Merthyr Tydfil had the largest population in Wales, surpassing Cardiff, Swansea and Newport combined. Iron masters such as Homfray, Guest, Hill, John Guest at Dowlais, and Richard Crawshay at Cyfartha controlled their mills with the proverbial 'rod of iron', and museums and Ynysfach Engine House recall these oppressive days.

Thomas Carlyle wrote to his wife this description of Merthyr in 1850:

'Ah me! 'Tis like a vision of Hell, and will never leave me, that of these poor creatures broiling in sweat and dirt, amid their furnaces, pits and rolling mills . . . The Town might be, and will be, one of the prettiest places in the world. It is one of the sootiest, squalidest and ugliest; all cinders and dust mounds and soot . . . Nobody thinks of gardening in such a locality – all devoted to metallic gambling.'

Antony Bacon's furnace at Cyfartha produced the rails for the earliest lines for Britain, America and Russia. Bacon retired in 1784, deeply worried by the fact that his works had supplied the iron for the guns that the Americans used in their War of Independence against England. Dowlais was the first plant in Britain to produce using the Bessemer process. All Merthyr's ironworks closed by the 1930s, Cyfartha having been the biggest foundry in Britain in 1800. Cyfartha had opened in 1765 and eventually closed in 1910. The other major ironworks at Merthyr, Dowlais, Penydarren and Plymouth, had opened in 1759, 1784 and 1763 respectively. Dowlais was the last to go in 1936.

All were owned by Englishmen, and the remains are evocative of a time when Merthyr was the world centre of the Industrial Revolution. William Crawshay built Cyfartha Castle, overlooking Merthyr, as a symbol of his dominance, in 1825. His son Robert, closed the works in 1874 rather than give in to worker demands for decent wages and conditions. He kept them closed until his death in 1879, causing

terrible hardships. On the huge stone slab covering his grave in nearby Vaynor, the inscription reads 'GOD FORGIVE ME' – God may forgive, but the Welsh remember still.

LEAD

Mid-Wales used to have several lead mines, and production peaked in the 17th and 18th centuries, leaving behind some intriguing industrial archeological sites. The Romans worked lead for its silver content, and at Llanymynych, Powys, it is said that the slaves never left the underground caverns. Cwm Ystwyth closed in 1916, so the site is fairly well-preserved, miles from anywhere. In the 1830s large increases in lead prices resulted in a boom and Llanidloes's Van Mines became the richest in Britain. Lead was found by chance here in 1862, two miles from the River Severn for easy transport, and by the 1870s a £5 initial capital share was worth £100. However, by 1878 the world price had fallen and by 1880 all the richest lodes were worked out. The remains are still impressive with the ore washing troughs, shaft chimneys and waterwheel still in evidence near the mounds of grey waste and Van Pool.

Near Ffrwd Fawr waterfall, the little village of Dylife once was populated by thousands of workers at a lead mine almost as rich as Van. Started before Van, production reached ten thousand tons per annum in the nineteenth century and there was a fifty foot waterwheel to drain the lower levels of the mine. The downturn in lead prices was even more disastrous than at Van because lead had to be taken by pack-horse many miles to Derwenlas. Sion-y-Gof, John the Smith, at these mines, suspected his wife of adultery and murdered her. For an alibi he also murdered his daughter, threw both bodies down a disused shaft and said that they had left him.

When the bodies were found, he was tried and sentenced to death. His body was to be gibbeted in an iron cage. As the only iron-worker in the village, he had to make his own cage, and he was hanged on Pen-y-Grocbren, The Hill of the Gallows. His body hung from the gallows in the iron gibbet cage until he rotted away, the gallows collapsed and the whole was buried with wind-blown soil. The story was thought of as a local myth, until in 1938, the cage was unearthed and the discoloured skull in its gruesome iron-piece is now in the Museum of Welsh Life at St Fagans, Cardiff.

Bryntail lead mines, near Llyn Clywedog, are also evocative ruins from the last century. A mile west of Ponterwyd in Cardiganshire is the Llywernog Silver-Lead Mining Museum, where one can follow a trail through a site that operated from 1740 to 1914. There is a 'panning shed' and an extended underground tour. This mining of silver-rich lead ore was a major rural industry in mid-Wales for two-thousand years.

Near Llyn Brianne, Rhandirmwyn means 'district of minerals', and this gorgeous countryside covers what was once one of Europe's largest lead mines. Minera Lead Mines near Wrexham have been restored to show visitors their 1820s hey-day. Bwlch-gwyn in Clwyd owes its existence to the lead mines worked during the 1840s (on the sites of previous Roman workings), and in Nant-y-Ffrith Valley are footpaths and the Milestones Geological Museum of North Wales.

SILVER
In 1637 a branch of the Tower Mint was set up in Aberystwyth, to coin locally mined silver. Near Cwm Einion (Artists' Valley, popular with artists last century), is Furnace, a historic metal-smelting site, dating from silver-smelting in the 17th century. Dyfi Furnace there is a well-preserved char-coal-fired blast furnace, with water-wheel, which was used for smelting iron between 1755 and the early nineteenth century. Silver was also mined near Llanidloes in the 17th century.

SLATE
The Romans used Welsh slate to roof Segontium in Anglesey, and Edward I used it extensively in his 'Iron Ring' of castles built to subdue the people of Gwynedd. During the Industrial Revolution, the Welsh slate quarries (like the coal mines and ironworks) were the world's largest producers. Slate dust, tuberculosis and long working hours made the miners' lives miserable – like colliers, they even had to buy their own candles from the quarry owners.

In 1900 the workers in Lord Pen-rhyn's Bethesda quarry went on strike for minor concessions, and stayed out for three years, Britain's longest-ever industrial dispute at the time. All managerial jobs had been given to the English or Scots, with very few going to local Welshmen, who had to become highly Anglicised to get on in the works. Welsh-speaking Welshmen did all the skilled work, grading and splitting the slate, but the management refused to recognise their union. Some men returned to work, because of the grinding poverty, but newspapers published their names, pubs and shops refused to serve them or their families, they were refused entry to chapel and stoned by furious strikers' wives.

Eventually the fabulously wealthy Lord Penrhyn, the former George Dawkins, who was spending the equivalent of millions of pounds on building Penrhyn Castle, took some men back on even less money. However, several hundred strikers were black-listed and refused work. The bitterness split the community into the 'bradwyr', traitors, who attended Anglican churches, and the betrayed, who went to chapel. This quarry was methodically exploited from the end of the eighteenth century, and developed into the largest and deepest (1410 feet) quarry in the world, employing three thousand five hundred men.

Blaenau's Gloddfa Ganol is now the world's largest slate mine, with forty-two miles of tunnels. You can visit the mine itself with its echoing caverns, dripping roofs and evocation of terrible working conditions. At the nearby Llechwedd Slate Caverns, one enters by electric train descending a steep 1:1.8 gradient to an underground lake, and there is an excellent mine tour and a heritage centre. The Chwarel Wynne Slate Mine in Glynceiriog, Clwyd, also offers guided tours through its eerie tunnels. In Gwynedd, the Dinorwig Slate Quarry near Llanberis was one of Wales' largest, employing over three thousand men. Upon its closure in 1969, it was preserved as the Welsh Slate Museum, with a huge fifty foot waterwheel. Corris also employed over a thousand men producing slate in its heyday, with a narrow-gauge railway taking the slate to Machynlleth. The Corris Railway Museum tells the story of the railway and the past workings at Corris. Near Harlech, the Old Llanfair Slate Caverns are also open to the public.

At the strange and atmospheric little harbour of Porthgain, which exported building stone, one can walk around the cliff point to 'The Blue Lagoon' at Abereiddi, a harbour quarried from slate and filled by the sea. The old slate workings here have some remarkable rare fossils.

TIN

Cydweli (Kidwelly) Industrial Museum is based at the site of its 1737 tinworks, one of Britain's largest, with huge rolling mills, steam engines and sorting and boxing rooms. Nearby is the superb 12th century Kidwelly Castle, a well-preserved concentric gem. Nearby Llanelli also concentrated on tin, and was nicknamed 'Tinopolis' in the nineteenth century. At this time Swansea had the largest nickel works in the world.

From 1730, tinplate was manufactured in Pontypool, breaking the previous German monopoly, and for many years Pontypool 'japanned ware' (such as teapots and serving trays) was famous, and is very collectable today. The first American ironworks, at Sagus River in Massachusetts, used Pontypool equipment.

In the mid-to-late 19th century, only the USA and the Ruhr rivalled South Wales a region of pure industrial power, with its vast outputs of coal, iron, steel, zinc, copper and nickel.

MONEY

The earliest form of money in Britain was sword blades, and the earliest Celtic coins were pure gold imitations of Phillip II of Macedon's saters, around 125BC. Later silver and potin (copper and tin) coins were minted.

The Romans introduced their own coinage, but *'after the fall of Rome, Britain showed the unique spectacle of being the only Roman province to withdraw completely from using coined money for nearly 200 years'*. (G. Davies, *A History of Money*).

Wales lagged behind the rest of the UK in readopting coins, using cattle (capital, chattels and cattle have a common root in linguistic development). The Welsh word "da" means good as an adjective, but goods or cattle when used as a noun. Fortunately, while fighting off the Anglo-Saxon threat, the Celts were spared the Danish method of enforcing poll tax in Ireland and parts of England. Non-payers had their noses slit, hence the expression *'to pay through the nose'*.

Coins were struck for Hywel Dda in the 10th century and possibly for Llywelyn the Great. The Royal Mint is situated in Llantrisant, and has its origins back in AD 287, making it the world's oldest company, according to 'The Guinness Book of Records'. It produces coins for over fifty countries. The Swan public house in Llanilltud Fawr was supposed to have been a mint for the last Welsh princes of Glamorgan (Morgannwg), and 'Mint Field' is the name of an adjacent house. Llanbadarn was also said to have minted coins for Welsh princes.

MONKS
WHITE, GREY AND BLACK

Fifteen abbeys and priories in Wales commemorate the Cistercian Order, the White Monks. The Grey Friars (the Franciscans) and the Black Friars (the Dominicans), had eight friaries in Wales by 1275. At this time, Llywelyn

the Last had cordial relations with all these foundations and the Cistercians commended him to the Pope in his dispute with the Bishop Anian of St Asaph.

One of the Norman Kings' first acts had been to introduce the Benedictine Order into Wales as their Marcher Lords expanded through the borderlands and south Wales. There were no Welsh monasteries following the Rule of St Benedict, a cohesive Latin influence on unifying European politics and Christianity, so the Normans sought to change the people's allegiance. In 1071, the Normans founded an abbey in the border town of Chepstow, and by 1150 had established seventeen monasteries in Wales. These monks owed their allegiance to higher monastic houses in England and the parts of France also held by the Normans. The Welsh *clasau*, the ancient monastic houses such as Llancarfan and Llantwit Major, were given to English monasteries at Gloucester and Tewkesbury, ending hundreds of years of the Celtic Church's independence from Rome. The first Welsh Bishop to succumb to Canterbury's rule was the Norman, Urban of Llandaf, who ruled the diocese of Glamorgan from 1107-1134.

By 1135, the monastic orders of Cluny, Tiron, Savigny and Citeaux all had houses in Wales. Priests also followed the Rule of St Augustine at Carmarthen, Llanthony, and Haverfordwest.

Basingwerk and Tintern were the first Cistercian settlements to be established, on the borders of Wales in 1131. Although the mother-church of the Cistercians in Wales was a Norman foundation, Whitland in 1140, and held its allegiance to Citeaux in France, these 'White Monks' were respected most of all the 'Latin' orders. In 1164, there was another Norman Cistercian foundation at Strata

Florida, Ystrad Fflur. However, with the growing influence of The Lord Rhys, Rhys ap Gruffydd, it seems that these were absorbed into the Welsh way of life. Many of their abbeys were in lonely, desolate places, and they were adopted by more Welsh princes as a replacement for the *clasau*. Strata Marcella was founded in Powys by Prince Wenwynwyn in 1170, Cwm Hir in Maelienydd in 1176, Llantarnam in Gwent in 1179, Aberconwy in Gwynedd in 1186, Cymer in Merioneth in 1198 and Valle Crucis in Powys Fadog in 1202. The monks followed a simple independent life, with a duty to the Abbot at Citeaux rather than to Rome or Normandy. All the Welsh princes tried to put a foundation in their territories. By 1212, King John was threatening to destroy Strata Florida because it *'harboured our enemies'*. The Hundred Years' War cut off links between Citeaux and its Welsh cells, so the Cistercians *'went native'*, identifying with their Welsh princes against the constant attacks by the Anglo-French. The Abbots of Aberconwy, Strata Florida, Whitland and Llantarnam were among Owain Glyndŵr's closest advisers in his war of independence, and a friar at Cardiff was executed for supporting his cause. The Abbot of Llantarnam, one of Glyndŵr's advisers, died fighting for him (see Glyndŵr).

By 1536, all but three of the twenty-seven monasteries of full status in Wales were dissolved. As John Davies says in his *A History of Wales*, *'Apart from the castles, the monasteries were the most splendid of all the buildings of medieval Wales; they were mercilessly vandalised at the time of the Dissolution and subsequently – a cruel blow to the architectural heritage of the Welsh'*.

The White Monks are commemorated with a network of paths connecting the ruins of their monasteries across Wales. This celebrated the 900th year of their foundation in 1099.

MOTORS

Charles Stewart Rolls, co-founder of Rolls Royce, came from Monmouth, the only town with a fortified gateway on a bridge in Britain.

Son of an MP, Charles Rolls had his first car at the age of nineteen, in 1896, when its speed was restricted by the need to have a man walking in front with a warning flag. It thus took him three days to drive home from his studies in Cambridge. From his days at Eton, he was besotted with engineering and had enrolled for a mechanical engineering degree at Trinity College. He was the first undergraduate and the fourth person in Britain to possess a car. He told friends of his ambition to have a car associated with his name, so that *'in future it might be a household word just as much as Broadway or Steinway in connection with pianos.'*

Rolls invented a bicycle for four, learned mechanical skills in the railway workshops at Crewe, obtained a third engineer's certificate so he could act as engineer on his father's yacht, and became an accomplished motor racing driver. After leaving Cambridge he opened his own car showroom in London, C. S. Rolls & Co., selling mainly French Panhards.

In 1904, he met Henry Royce, and was so impressed by his two-cylinder car that he financed the production of Royce's cars, ordering nineteen to sell in London, wanting to be able *'to recommend and sell the best cars in the world'*. In 1906, they formed Rolls-Royce Ltd., and their first car, the fabulous 6-cylinder Silver Ghost was available to the gentry. Royce was chief engineer, on a salary of £1250 pa, and Rolls took £750 and 4% of the profits as the technical managing director. Rolls publicised the cars by racing them, setting a record between London and Monte Carlo. He earned the dislike of Queen Victoria because she thought cars scared horses.

Living life at the maximum, and looking for fresh challenges, Rolls took up aviation. He became the first Briton to fly more than half-a-mile and made the first non-stop flight to France and back. However, on 12th July 1910, he achieved a more tragic first – he was the first British aviator to be killed in a plane crash. His Wright biplane broke up in an air display over Bournemouth and the wreckage was towed away by a Silver Ghost.

An exciting indigenous Welsh car manufacturer was Gilbern, based in Glamorgan in the 1960s and 1970s. These were super fibre-glass sports saloons and estates and there is a flourishing owners' club. The Gilbern Genie was popular and the classic Gilbern Invader features in Jeremy Clarkson's book featuring the fifty 'hottest' cars ever made.

Darrian Cars' GTI easily won the British GT championship in 1996, and its 180 mph successor looks like repeating the success, with a 0-60mph time of 3.4 seconds. These cars are built at Lampeter, with assistance from the design and engineering faculty at Swansea Institute. The medium-term focus is to build a car to compete in the Le Mans 24-hour race.

The World Land Speed record was broken by Welshman J. P. G. Parry Thomas on Pendine Sands in 1926, with a speed of 169 mph, in his twenty foot long 400 horse power 'Babs'. He built the car himself, using a V12 Liberty aeroplane engine. He beat Malcolm Campbell's year-old record by nineteen miles per hour. However, soon after, Campbell, in Bluebird, set 174 mph, and in 1927 Thomas skidded and overturned near the end of the measured mile, trying to beat the new record. He was decapitated by the chain driving the wheels and friends were so distressed that they buried the car on the spot. In 1969, Owen Wyn Owen dug up Babs from Pendine Sands and spent 16 years restoring the car to working condition.

The aluminium-bodied car is now the main exhibit at the recently-opened Museum of Speed overlooking Pendine Beach. Three world records were set consecutively at Pendine Sands in Wales, after world records set at Brooklands and Arpajon, and before Daytona and Bonneville became the venue for record attempts.

MOUNTAINS

Wales has one hundred and sixty-eight summits over two thousand feet high (610m) and fifteen summits over three thousand feet (914m). The fifteen peaks are all in Gwynedd, and in ascending order are Tryfan at three thousand and ten feet (917m), Crib Goch, Elidir Fawr, Carnedd Uchaf, Foel Fras, Y Garn, Yr Elan, Foel Grach, Pen yr Ole Wen, Glyder Fach, Glyder Fawr, Carnedd Dafydd, Carnedd Llywelyn, Crib y Dyysgi (Carnedd Ugain) up to Snowdon (Yr Wyddfa) at three thousand five hundred and sixty feet (1085m). In some spots in these Snowdonia mountains, snow does not melt in most summers, for example on the north faces of Carnedd Llywelyn.

Wales generally has a narrow fringe of lowland coastline, with several mountain ranges – The Brecon Beacons, The Black Mountains, The Clwydian Range, Snowdonia and the Preseli Hills. In the middle of Wales, rising up from Tregaron Bogs to Abergwesyn, is a plateau known as The Roof of Wales, or The Green Desert, a wilderness that is a sanctuary to rare plants, birds and animals.

Upon Anglesey, the highest point on the island, Holyhead Mountain, hardly counts as a mountain at seven hundred and twenty feet, but there are views of Ireland and The Isle of Man, as well as Caer y Twr, an old hill-fort, and the stone foundations of Cytiau'r Gwyddelod, a village dating back over seventeen hundred years.

Eryri is the massive mountain complex of North-West Wales. Its name comes from *eryr*, land of eagles. (In English, an *eyrie* is an eagle's nesting place). **Yr Wyddfa** (Snowdon), at three thousand five hundred and sixty feet (1085m), is the highest mountain in England and Wales. Yr Wyddfa refers to the now-vanished tumulus of one of King Arthur's victims, Rhita Gawr. Llyn Llydaw is supposed to be the lake where Sir Bedevere threw Excalibur when Arthur was wounded at Bwlch-y-Saethau (Pass of Arrows), in his last battle with Mordred. The ancient Celts often threw the weapons of dead chieftains into water, which was sacred, sometimes bending the swords first. Nearby Carnedd Ugain is the second highest mountain in England and Wales, and Crib Goch at 3023 feet and Y Lliwedd at 2947 feet are other high peaks in the Snowdon Range of 'Seven

Peaks'. Many arctic/alpine species grow in Snowdonia, and its cliff ledges support Welsh Poppy, Alpine Saw-Wort and globeflower. The rare rainbow leaf-beetle has survived in the area since the last Ice Age. The last glacier in Wales, in Snowdonia, melted about ten millennia ago.

Carneddau, Wales' second highest range of mountains, is also in Snowdonia, with the peaks Carnedd Llywellyn (3485 ft, 1066m) and Carnedd Dafydd (3424 ft, 1044m) being the highest. Carn Llugwy (3184 feet), Pen-yr-Oleu-wen (3210 feet), Foel Grach (3195 feet) and Foel Fras (3081 feet) are other major peaks in this range. Carneddau is wild scree area, with Snowdon Lily, globeflower, roseroot and mountain sorrel growing, and birds such as chough, ring ouzel and peregrine falcon can be seen.

Between Llanberis and Llyn Ogwen, the **Glyders** are a boulder-strewn range with the most difficult climbs in Wales being up Tryfan, a towering volcanic outcrop of 3010 feet (917m). The first successful Everest expedition trained here in the early 1950s. Glyder Fawr is 3279 feet, and Glyder Fach 3262 feet, separated by a mile long ridge covered with great stone blocks.

Opposite Capel Curig, Moel Siabod is 2860 feet, and Cynicht (2263 feet) has earned the name 'the Matterhorn of Wales' for its aspects from some directions.

The Arans stretch from Bala Lake to the Mawddwy River. Aran Benllyn (2901 feet), Aran Mawddwy (2970 feet) and Dyrysgol (2397 feet) are the most notable hills.

Near the sea, **Cadair Idris,** the highest mountain in mid-Wales, stands at 2927 feet (892m). The name means 'Chair of Idris', a giant skilled in poetry, philosophy and astronomy. It is said that anyone who stays the night on the summit will die, become mad or end up as a poet. There are two lakes on the bare summit area, Llyn y Gadair and Llyn Cau, and native trees in the foothills include wild cherry and wild pear. On the way up there is excellent bird-watching and from the peak sometimes Ireland can be seen.

The **Peaks of Ardudwy** stretch from Trawsfynydd to the sea, and include Llethr (2475 feet), and The Rhinogs (inland from Harlech) which is an inhospitable mass of moorland and rocks, with few paths or lanes. Rhinog Fach (2333 feet) is unsafe for the solitary walker, and Rhinog Fawr (2362 feet) is *'one of the most desolate and savage-looking places in Wales'.*

Pumlumon (Plynlimon) is 2468 feet (752m) in **The Cambrian Mountains** near Llangurig in Powys. Its foothills are the source of the Rheidol, Severn and Wye rivers. It is managed as traditional sheep-walk, and is covered with sheeps' fescue, heather, crowberries and bilberries. There is alpine clubmoss and starry saxifrage on the mountain. Birds include red grouse, ring ouzel, golden plover, common sandpiper, wheatear, whinchat and Greenland white-fronted goose. There are also red kites, short-eared owls, buzzards, merlins, peregrine falcons and kestrels.

Near Bala lies the range known as the **Berwyn Hills** – its highest summit, Cadair Bronwen, is 2575 feet, and is possibly the only place in Wales where you can pick cloudberries (a type of small orange blackberry). Other plants include cowberry, cranberry, cotton grass and starry saxifrage. On 23rd January, 1974, villagers in nearby Llandrillo heard a loud explosion and saw orange and blue lights floating over

Cadair Bronwen, leading to a report of a large circular glowing orange spaceship on the ground and strong UFO rumours.

The **Preseli Hills** is an unspoilt moorland range rising to Foel Cwmcerwyn at 1760 feet (536m), littered with prehistoric remains, from where Stonehenge's famous blue stones were dragged on rollers, and rafted, two hundred and forty miles to the World Heritage Site.

Near Abergaveny in Gwent stands the **Sugar Loaf Mountain** at 1955 feet (596m) and the **Skirrid Fawr** at 1596 feet (486m), the only mountain in the world to have a board game named after it. These are part of the **Black Mountains** in Gwent which lead across South Wales to the **Brecon Beacons**. The Beacons' highest peak is the Old Red Sandstone Pen Y Fan at 2907 feet (886m). The Brecon Beacons then merge into Fforest Fawr heading west, a moorland wilderness. This leads to The Black Mountain near Llandeilo, Carmarthenshire, where Fan Brycheiniog is the highest point at 2630 feet (802m).

The Black Mountains, south of Hay-on-Wye, are extensive moorlands, stretching to the English borders, with bilberry, crowberry, cowberry, purple moorgrass and heather. All three cottongrasses can be found here (common, hare's tail and broad-leaved), as can the beautiful globeflower, lesser skullcap, stag's horn firmoss, brittle bladder and the almost extinct bee orchid. Red grouse and peregrine falcons can also be seen.

The Brecon Beacons are made of limestone and Old Red Sandstone, and the plateau has a wide variety of habitats, supporting peregrine falcons, buzzards, wheatear, merlins and ring ouzel. Plants include globeflower, Wilson's filmy fern, green spleenwort, mossy saxifrage and purple saxifrage. Craig Cerrig Gleisiad, with its dangerous crags, has many rare Arctic alpines at the southern end of their range. There have been sixty bird species recorded there, including ravens, red grouse, peregrines, dippers, redstarts, tree pipits and merlins. The Welsh Poppy and parsley fern can also be found here. Illtyd Pools and Traeth Mawr, near Brecon, have many rare sedges and mosses.

Mynydd Du, The Black Mountain, at the head of the Swansea Valley, is upland limestone grassland, with many cave systems. There are two corrie lakes and a four mile escarpment of Old Red Sandstone. Notable plants include dwarf willow, Northern bedstraw, roseroot and cowberry. Craig y Cilau has important bat roosts, a superb range of birdlife, and unusual plants such as Angular Solomon's Seal, limestone polypody, Alpine enchanter's nightshade and brittle bladder fern.

The cliffs around Wales, for example along the Glamorgan Heritage Coast, are great viewing, but the *piece de resistance* is possibly **Elugig Stacks** in Pembroke, just off the coast, where you can watch guillemots, fulmars and razorbills flying around their nesting sites. (*Heligog* is Guillemot in Welsh.) Nearby is the famous Green Bridge of Wales, a grass-topped arc, attached to the cliff, through which the sea roars. Huntsman's Leap is a narrow cleft in two hundred feet (60m) high limestone cliffs on the same Castlemartin Peninsula. Near here on the flat grassy cliff top, you can look down into The Devil's Cauldron. This is a large deep hole eroded in the limestone, into which the sea pours through a narrow gap almost two hundred feet beneath one. There is

another Huntsman's Leap in the Old Red Sandstone cliffs near St Brides, also in Pembrokeshire. The highest sea cliff in England and Wales is at Ramsey Island, at over four hundred and fifty feet (137m).

Mount Everest was so named in 1865 after Sir George Everest of Gwernvale near Crickhowell, the former surveyor-general of India.

MUSIC

John Hughes, one of Wales best-known poets, was born in Llanarmon Dyffryn Ceiriog in 1832, and wrote verses to some old Welsh melodies, including the haunting *Dafydd Y Garreg Wen* ('David of the White Rock'). His Bardic name was Ceiriog.

Ann Griffiths was born in 1776, and converted to Nonconformism in the Pendref Congregational Chapel in 1796. She wrote seventy hymns in her small farmstead, Dolwar Fach, at Dolanog near Llanfyllin. She died tragically early at the age of twenty nine. Saunders Lewis called one of her hymns 'one of the greatest religious poems in any European language'. There is a memorial chapel in Dolanog, and she is buried in Llanfihangel-yng-Ngwynfa. One of her best-known verses is:

> *'Gwna fi fel pren planedig, O! Fy Nuw,*
> *Yn ir ar lan afonydd dyfroedd byw:*
> *Yn gwreiddio ar led, a'i ddail heb*
> *   wywo mwy,*
> *Yn ffrwytho dan gawodydd dwyfol*
> *   glwy'.*

> *'Make me as a tree planted, Oh! My*
> *   God,*
> *Sappy on the bank of the river of the*
> *   waters of life:*

Rooting widely, its leaves no longer
  withering,
Fruiting under the showers of a divine
  wound'.

Dr Joseph Parry was born in 1841 in
the now preserved terrace of skilled
ironworkers' cottages, Chapel Row,
in Merthyr. He wrote one of Wales'
favourite tunes, the lovely 'Myfanwy',
which is beloved by all Welsh male
voice choirs.

In 1856, the Pontypridd weaver
Evan James wrote 'Mae Hen Wlad fy
Nhadau', which soon became the Welsh
National Anthem.

There are many interpretations of
'Mae Hen Wlad' – perhaps the follow-
gives an insight into the Welsh psyche.
No other anthem celebrates its poets.
This has come down through generations from when the Celts placed their
bards higher in the social order than
their warriors.

Mae hen wlad fy nhadau yn annwyl
  i mi,
Gwlad beirdd a chantorion enwogion
  o fri;
Ei gwrol ryfelwyr, gwladgarwyr
  tra mad,
Dros ryddid collasant eu gwaed.

Gwlad, gwlad, pleidiol wyf i'm gwlad;
Tra mor yn fur i'r bur hoff bau
O bydded i'r hen iaith barhau

The old land of my fathers is dear to me,
Land of poets and singers, famous
  men of renown;
Its brave warriors, fine patriots,
Gave their blood for freedom.
My country, my country, I am devoted
  to my country,
While the sea is a wall to the pure
  loved land
O may the old language endure.

Translations of other verses are as
follows:

O land of the mountains, the bard's
  paradise,
With precipice proud, valleys lone as
  the skies,
Green murmuring forest, far echoing
  flood
Fire the fancy and quicken the blood
My country, my country, I am devoted
  to my country,
While the sea is a wall to the pure loved
  land
O may the old language endure.
For though the fierce foeman has
  ravaged your realm,
The old speech of Cymru he cannot
  overwhelm,
Our passionate poets to silence
  command
Or banish the harp from your strand.
My country, my country, I am devoted
  to my country,
While the sea is a wall to the pure loved
  land
O may the old language endure.

The best-known Welsh hymn writer
is probably the **Rev. H. Elfed Lewis**,
born at Cynwyl Elfed in 1860.

William Williams of Pantycelin was
renowned as Wales' finest poet, along
with Dafydd ap Gwilym. He was
known throughout Wales as 'Pantycelyn', and Cwm Rhondda, his most
famous hymn, was originally written
in Welsh by Ann Griffiths:

Guide me O Thou Great Jehovah,
Pilgrim through this barren land;
I am weak but Thou art mighty,
Hold me with Thy powerful hand
Bread of Heaven, Bread of Heaven,
Feed me now and evermore,
Feed me now and evermore.

Henry Brinley Richards (1819-1885) befriended Chopin on a study trip to Paris. The composer of 'God Bless The Prince of Wales' (the music for which is the Australian National Anthem). He was regarded as the finest pianist in Britain.

Sir Henry Walford Davies (1869-1941) was a prolific writer of religious music and an influential educator on music through radio talks.

On 2nd October 1996, the **Reverend William Rhys Nicholas** died, aged 82. Rhys Nicholas was honoured as a superb poet, and also assisted in the publication of Welsh poetry at the Gomerian Press and John Penry Press. He was the latest in a line of distinguished hymn writers. An S4C TV programme in 1995 was devoted to his Welsh-language hymns. His most well-known hymn, *Pantyfedwen*, won the 1967 Pantyfedwen Eisteddfod near Lampeter, which was sponsored by the London Welsh millionaire, David James. In 1968 a competition to write a tune for the hymn was won by the Liverpool Welsh composer, Eddie Evans. By the end of the 1970s, this beautiful hymn-tune had become 'a second national anthem', sung at festivals, weddings, funerals and chapel services

Ar Hyd Y Nos (All Through The Night), *Hiraeth*, *Calon Lân*, *Bugeilio'r Gwenith Gwyn*, The Maid of Cefn Iddfa, *Sospan Fach*, *Llwyn On* (The Ash Grove), *Clychau Aberdyfi* (The Bells of Aberdyfi), *Codiad yr Hedydd* (The Rising of the Lark), *Y Deryn Pur* (The Dove), *Y Fwyalchen* (The Blackbird), *Syr Harri Ddu* (Black Sir Harry). *Dafydd y Garreg Wen* (David of the White Rock), *Nos Galan* (New Year's Eve), *Pantyfedwen*, Men of Harlech, *Cwm Rhondda*, *Myfanwy* and *Cartref* are all Welsh songs that are

known across the country and in every choir's repertoire. Some, like Men of Harlech, are over five hundred years old.

'The Maid of Cefn Iddfa' is a lovely tune, and the mansion of Cefn Iddfa in Llangynwyd is now in ruins. It is dedicated to Ann Thomas (1704-1727), the daughter of the mansion, who was said to be made to marry a local solicitor, Anthony Maddocks. Her true love, Wil Hopcyn, left the district in grief, and wrote the beautiful song *Bugeilio's Gwenith Gwyn* (Shepherding the White Wheat) to show his love for her. He returned when she was mortally ill, she died in his arms, and he is buried next to her in Llangynwyd churchyard.

The ninety-year-old Welsh Folk-Song Society, Cymdeithas Alawon Gwerin Cymru, is based in Aberystwyth and collects and preserves old Welsh songs.

CLASSICAL MUSIC
Carlo Rizzi, Musical Director of the Welsh National Opera, believes with George Bernard Shaw that *'the Welsh are the Italians in the rain'*. He feels like that because *'when the Welsh are making music they give back to a flow of emotions which are rare to find in other places'*.

The Welsh National Opera was born in 1946 as an amateur organisation, became professional in 1967, and now employs more than 250 people as one of the most important operatic ensembles in the world. It has had minimal help from the English government and National Lottery, unlike all the London-based opera companies. The WNO was the holder of the first opera 'Oscar' in the International Music Awards of 1993, for the production of Debussy's 'Pelleas and Melisande'. Plans were drawn up for a new Opera House in Cardiff Bay, but a new Arts Centre will house the WNO as well as other arts media.

The Welsh National Opera premiered Sir Peter Maxwell Davies' new opera *The Doctors of Myddfai* in 1996, based on the tale of generations of a family of Welsh doctors (see entry on Magic).

The Welsh National Symphony Orchestra has an international reputation, and Cardiff annually hosts the fabulous 'Singer of the World' competition, giving up-and-coming opera singers from across the globe their chance for international recognition.

The Welsh Philharmonic Orchestra was formed in 1985, and gives concerts all over Wales. It draws its players from all areas, and they include professional, amateur, peripatetic teachers and student instrumentalists. One of the aims of the orchestra was to develop a bridge from the amateur orchestras to the professional ones.

Dame Adelina Patti, the internationally famous 19th century opera singer was the highest paid entertainer in the world. Her home, Craig-y-Nos Castle is a huge 'sham' castle with its own theatre and a beautiful ornamental park on the River Tawe. It is being renovated by a group led by the soprano, **Dame Gwyneth Jones**. Born in 1936, Dame Gwyneth has sung at Vienna, Bayreuth, La Scala and all the world's other great opera houses.

The baritone **Sir Geraint Evans**, 1922-1992, was an 'institution' at Covent Garden, but also performed at great opera houses all over the world. His career lasted from 1948 to 1984. Stuart Burrows comes from Cilfynydd, Sir Geraint's home town. Among the galaxy of leading international opera singers are Rebecca Evans, Dennis O'Neill, Della Jones, Anne Evans, Jason Howard,

Margaret Price, Anne Williams-King and **Bryn Terfel**. The latter, a bass-baritone, gave an unforgettable appearance singing *Rule Britannia* at 'The Last Night of The Proms' at the Royal Albert Hall. Festooned in Welsh colours and flags, and clutching a huge red dragon, he sang a verse in Welsh, and is destined to be one of the true greats of international music.

Margaret Price, born in 1941, started her career with the Welsh National Opera, and has appeared at Covent Garden, La Scala, and the Paris Opera. Now settled in Munich, she often performs with the Bavarian State Opera.

Grace Williams (1906-77) was born in Barry where she lived for most of her life. After graduating from University College, Cardiff, she spent a period of study with Ralph Vaughan Williams at the Royal College of Music, London, where one of her fellow students was Imogen Holst, daughter of composer Gustav Holst.

Her *Fantasia on Welsh Nursery Tunes* was composed in 1940 and such is its popularity that it has unfortunately overshadowed many of her other fine orchestral works. The Fantasia is beautifully orchestrated and includes eight traditional tunes – *Jim Cro, Deryn y Bwn, Migidi Maglidi, Si Lwli' Mabi, Gee Geffyl Bach, Cysga Di Fy Mhlentyn Tlws, Yr Eneth Ffein Ddu* and *Cadi Ha.*

George Walter Selwyn Lloyd, a Cornishman of Welsh origins, composed three symphonies and two operas before being shell-shocked in the Second World War. Later, he composed another opera and eight symphonies.

Ralph Vaughan Williams (1872-1958), of Welsh stock, was the central figure in the British musical rebirth of the first half of the twentieth century. The *Five Tudor Portraits* and *The Pilgrim's*

Progress are fine works among his many symphonies and operas.

Alan Hoddinott and **William Mathias** have been leading classical composers in modern Europe.

Karl Jenkins, from Penclawdd, is the son of a South Wales chapel choirmaster He wrote *Adiemus – Songs of Sanctuary*, a gold record album that reached the top of the classical music charts in 1997 and sold a million copies worldwide. His sublime and joyous *Adiemus II – Cantata Mundi* also was number one in the classical charts. His album 'Diamond Music' features his concerto 'Grosso Palladio' by the London Philharmonic, and was extremely successful. A classically trained multi-instrumentalist and jazz oboist, he worked with Ronnie Scott and joined the progressive rock band Soft Machine in the 1970s, but now concentrates on composing what he calls *'classical music for secular people.'* Hopefully, Welsh lyrics can be set to Cantata Mundi, and Welsh choirs can take the music into their repertoires.

POPULAR MUSIC

Ivor Davies of Cardiff, **Ivor Novello** (1893-1951), not only wrote popular songs, but was an actor-manager, taking the romatic lead in his musicals such as *Glamorous Night* (1925), *The Dancing Years* (1939), and *Gay's The Word* (1951). He also wrote the operettas *Careless Rapture* and *King's Rhapsody*. He was the leading British silent movie star and a matinee idol through the 1920s. His *Keep the Home Fires Burning* became almost an anthem of the troops during the Second World War. Novello's songs have survived as classics of musical theatre.

Pontyberem's **Dorothy Squires** (1915-98) is probably better-known as a wife of Roger Moore, the film actor, but her 'Times' obituary called her *'one of the great popular singers of the century, a chanteuse-realiste with few equals when it came to conveying intense emotion'.* She starred at the London Palladium, Talk of the Town, Albert hall, Carnegie Hall and at the Moulin Rouge in Hollywood, *'where her greatest fan was Elvis Presley, who repeatedly asked her to sing This is My Mother's Day.'* Her life story would make an interesting film – born in poverty, she was once worth two million pounds and fêted in the USA, but after her bitter parting from Roger Moore died in poverty, much of her earnings lost in divorce litigation. Frank Sinatra called her *'the only British singer with balls'.* His daughter Nancy, after hearing Dorothy Squires sing 'My Way' in Los Angeles, commented *'I think my dad must have been half asleep when he recorded his record'.* Even Edith Piaf thought that Squires' recording of 'If You Love Me' was better than her own.

Thomas Jones Woodward (**Tom Jones**), from Treforest, signed the largest contract in British television in 1968, receiving an estimated nine million pounds for eighty-five shows spread over five years. *It's Not Unusual* and *What's New Pussycat* were probably his greatest hits.

Shirley Bassey, from Cardiff, is another internationally renowned singer, perhaps best known for the James Bond film themes *Goldfinger* and *Diamonds are Forever*. Both Bassey and Jones are 'transatlantic' entertainers of international fame.

Swansea-born **Steve Balsamo**, from a bit-part in the Welsh TV 'soap', *Pobol y Cwm*, was chosen to star in *Jesus Christ Superstar* by Andrew Lloyd-Webber in 1996, and stole the show. **Peter Karrie**, presently starring in the lead role in *Phantom of the Opera*, and a

West End stalwart, is from Bridgend, Glamorgan.

ROCK MUSIC

In the 1960s/70s, Wales produced Man, Mary Hopkins, Amen Corner with Andy Fairweather-Low (*Bend Me, Shape Me, If Paradise Was Half As Nice, Wide-Eyed and Legless*), Rockpile with Dave Edmunds, Racing Car (*They Shoot Horses, Don't They?*) and Badfinger who all did well in the UK/US charts. **Mary Hopkins**'s *Those Were The Days*, especially written by The Beatles for her, was a massive world-wide hit. The famous recording studio at Rockfield, near Monmouth, often pulls rock personalities like Lemmie from Motorhead into nearby hostelries for a jar or two.

Man modelled their act on the American West Coast band, Quicksilver Messenger Service, with twin lead guitars. Their leader, Deke Leonard, wrote an autobiography called *Rhinos, Winos and Lunatics*, also the name of their best LP. A great live band, more appreciated in Europe, they split up in 1976 after 10 years of drunken, drugged, whoring mayhem – their manager commented that it was a miracle that they lasted that long.

The Ivys were re-christened **Badfinger** when they came to the attention of The Beatles and signed to their Apple label. Badfinger were the chosen successors of The Beatles when the 'Fab Four' split up, appearing on all their solo projects and backing the Peter Sellers/Ringo Star film *The Magic Christian*. Badfinger had a smash hit with *If You Want It, Come and Get It*, written for them by Paul McCartney, but were also the writers of the world-wide hit, *Without You*, one of the most moving love songs in history. A number one for Nilsson in 1972 and again for Mariah Carey in 1994, it has been recorded by hundreds of artists, earning massive annual royalties. A film is to be written about the song-writers, Pete Ham and Tommy Evans, who died tragically before the millions started rolling in, penniless and thinking that their careers were over.

In 1975, the two men went into a pub, and Ham drank a great deal of whisky – he telephoned his manager, suggesting that they break up the group and quit the music business. The Americans told them *'they were in too deep'*, and the last words Ham said to Evans were *'I know a way out, I'll see you in the morning'*. Next morning, Pete Ham's pregnant girlfriend found him hanging in the garage. He was just 27.

In 1983, Tommy Evans was desperately trying to get royalties from *Without You*, the world number one of 1972. Still bereaved and depressed following Ham's death, he hanged himself from a tree in his garden – and was found by his six-year-old son.

The surviving members of the band, and their manager, somehow then won an equal right to all past, present and future royalties, leaving the partners of Ham and Evans still almost penniless. At a 1995 awards ceremony in Los Angeles celebrating Mariah Carey's hit, the widowed Marianne Evans was speechless with rage in the audience, as the surviving Badfinger members accepted plaques as 'co-writers' of the song. This moving story is reminiscent of Greek tragedies.

Bonnie Tyler in the 1980s made several international hits including the massive *Total Eclipse of the Heart* and a duet with MeatLoaf. **Shaking Stevens**, of Cardiff, shook off his Sunsets group to become a crossover act that appealed to teenagers and adults with covers of old rock numbers. Mike Peters, with The Alarm, flew the flag of Welsh rock in the 1980s, along with Geraint Jarman. The 1980s New Romantic group, Visage, were the creation of Steve Strange from Wales, and Scritti Politti, aka Green Gartside from Newport hit the album and singles charts in the States and Europe. Later acts were The Darling Buds, and Pooh Sticks.

John Cale, from Garnant, went to the States in the 60s after studying viola, piano and composition in London, and co-founded the Velvet Underground with Lou Reed. He has since written and made some superb albums, including collaborating with Lou Reed on *Songs for Drella*, their tribute to Andy Warhol. Among the dozens of albums he has produced is *Horses* by Patti Smith. His latest album, *Walking on Locusts*, features a collaboration with David Byrne, the ex-Talking Head.

In the 1990s **Waterfront**, from Cardiff, had a US number one record, as did **Donna Lewis**, also from Cardiff, with 'I Love You Always Forever' in September 1996. K-Klass from Wrexham specialised in 'house' music.

However, the Welsh rock scene now is possibly leading the rest of the world, with Cwmbran's Manic Street Preachers, challenged by Super Furry Animals, 60 Foot Dolls, K-Klass, Cwmaman's Stereophonics, Ether, Rachel James, Mogwai, Peter Bruntnell, Catatonia and Gorki's Zygotic Mynci (the latter two bands also record in Welsh) all big players on the UK rock scene. **The Stereophonics** received the 'best newcomer' award at 'The Brits' in 1998 and many top band awards in 1999. Feeder is another promising Welsh band, made up of two Cardiffians and a Japanese bass-player. *The New York Times* described Newport as '*the new Seattle*' for its vibrant music scene, with over 60 bands, including Dub War, Novocaine, The Five Darrens, Rollerco, Suck, Disco, Choketeens and the

wonderful 60 Foot Dolls, the current favourite students' band across the UK. Flyscreen has a contract with MCA, and Dub War fuse trash and dub with attitude. The late Kurt Cobhain, of the Seattle grunge band Nirvana, proposed to Courtney Love of Hole in Newport.

The Manic Street Preachers are perhaps *the* band of the 90s. Their album *Everything Must Go* released a year after the mysterious disappearance of their songwriter/guitarist, Richey James, is a work of poetic magnificence. It was awarded the album of year award by most music magazines in 1996, but their second and third albums, *Gold Against The Soul* and *The Holy Bible*, are also essential for any record collection. Their latest album issued in 1999 is *This is my truth, tell me yours*, a quotation from Aneurin Bevan. The Manics are still following the Welsh culture and political tradition and have also won the BRIT award two years in succession.

The Manics' mentor and manager, Philip Hall, died of cancer in December 1993, and the co-lyricist/guitarist/star of the group, Richey James, vanished in 1995. The group took almost a year before they could perform without him, and now leave the left-hand side of the stage empty for him. They had been friends for years – James Bradfield and songwriter/guitarist Nicky Wire (née Jones) were in the same class from the age of five. Richey James (née Edwards) lived in the same street as Wire. Drummer Sean Moore is Bradfield's cousin and, when he was ten, went to live with Bradfield's family.

Newport's **60 Foot Dolls** are punkish, lager-swilling, and superb live, with an excellent debut LP. Carmarthen's **Gorki's Zygotic Mynci** have been called '*psychedelic bizarros*'. The drummer's father is the Chief Druid of Wales, and the bassist is the son of a sackbut player in a mediaeval orchestra. A very young band with diverse influences, they expect the audience to sing along some choruses in Welsh. With four albums blending pop, folk, punk and psychedelia. An article in *The Independent on Sunday* claimed that in one song they sound like The Fall circa 1978 and The Grateful Dead. Their singer/keyboardist Euros Childs defends against criticism that they do not sing all their songs in English with *'No-one would dare say that if we were African.'* The New York Times rated their album *Bwyd Time* (Food Time) one of the ten best of 1995, calling it *'mystical and whimsical . . . smart and graceful . . . (and) criminally obscure.'*

Cardiff's **Catatonia** has a dreamy, haunted sound, at odds with the persona of their female lead singer, Cerys Mathews, waving cans of Stella Artois at the crowd. Their publicist worked with Julian Cope, old acid-head himself, and says that at last he's *'finally found a group that's even further out there than he is.'* Their first album, *Way Beyond Blue*, was called a *'supreme debut'* by Time Out, and *'this year's best guitar album'* by the NME in 1997. Their alcohol-fuelled lead singer used to be a psychiatric nurse, and her singing has been variously described as *'Bjork skinning up in a nunnery'* and *'Marilyn Monroe on acid'*. The album was mainly produced by The Cranberries producer, Stephen Street, and Mathews describes it as *'big tunes and psychodramas for the end of the century.'* Their guitarist/songwriter Mark Roberts commented in 'Q' magazine that *'Britain used to belong to Wales and we want it back. So we're going to start by taking over the airwaves.'* Catatonia's second album, 1998's *International Velvet*, fea-

tures the massive hit 'Mulder and Scully', and the refrain of 'I am the Mob' is a singalong *'Every day when I wake up, I thank the Lord I'm Welsh.'* The album reached number one in the record charts, and *Road Rage* was another hit single from it. Cerys also shared a hit with Space with *The Ballad of Tom Jones*. Their latest (1999) album is called 'Equally Cursed and Blessed' and went straight to No. 1 in the UK album charts.

Also from Cardiff, **Super Furry Animals** hold the record for the longest song title in the universe, *Llanfairpwllg w y n g y c h g o g e r y c h w y r n d r o - b w c h w l l a n t i s i l i o g o g o g o c h y n g o f o d (inspace)*. From touring with the Welsh cult band Anrhefn and recording with Ankst records, they have moved to Creation Records. They record in Welsh and English – as they say, *'It's no wonder the Welsh language and Welsh culture have no international profile at all. If we were just a Welsh-language band we could stay in Wales and do gigs in cowsheds for the benefit of Welsh television and that would be fine. But because of the type of music we play, we need to go on the road with it. If people hear Welsh being sung and buy Welsh songs, they'll get to know what Wales is really about.'* The Daily Telegraph commented on their 'Radiator' album that *'it's a sight more entertaining than anything stable mates Oasis have yet managed to achieve.'* Gruff Rhys formed the band when he left his native Bethesda and the Welsh language band Ffa Coffi Pawb. He joined up with Bunff and Guto, from the Welsh-language band U-thant, Daf the former drummer from Catatonia, and Daf's younger brother Cian. Caitlin Moran (*The Times*, May 22, 1998) raved about the band's second album, inventing *'an entirely new music'*, and also about their live performances *'the most febrile crowd* reaction I've seen since Radiohead toured with "The Bends"'. . . 'It looks as if Super Furry Animals will be the next and last of the Terminal Indie Underachievers to go Big Top Ten, taking their place alongside Radiohead, the Verve and Catatonia.'

Oasis were discovered in a Manchester pub, by Marcus Russell from Ebbw Vale. Rumour has it that he leaped onto the stage, declaring that he had seen the future of rock and roll. Pre-viously Russell had managed Johnny Marr and the band Electronic, and true to his roots has invested heavily, in ensuring that Ebbw Vale Rugby Club stays financially sound.

Geraint Jarman has pioneered Welsh rock music, and **Dafydd Iwan** Welsh folk music. Iwan's record 'Carlo', a popular name for a dog, coincided with his protests against Prince Charles' investiture as Prince of Wales.

MUTATIONS

The modern words mum and dad seem to come from the Welsh 'mam' and 'tad', where the 'tad' is soft-mutated to 'dad'. This is the major area of difficulty in learning the Welsh language – sometimes intial consonants change, for instance Cardiff is 'Caerdydd' in Welsh, and 'in' is 'yn'. However, 'in Cardiff' becomes 'yng Nghaerdydd'. 'To Cardiff' in Welsh is not 'i Caerdydd' but 'i Gaerdydd'. 'And Cardiff' is 'a Chaerdydd'. Only some initial consonants change, for instance the initial letters c, p and t are subject to soft, nasal and spirate/aspirate mutations, whereas b, d and g are subject to just soft and nasal mutations and the consonants of ll, m and rh only soft mutate.

For anyone learning Welsh, usually locals will correct you, although you can get by without knowing the rules for mutating words. The table below explains better:

Consonant	Word	Soft	Nasal	Spirant
c	Caerdydd Cardiff	Gaerdydd	Nghaerdydd	Chaerdydd
p	pen head	ben	mhen	Phen
t	tad father	dad	nhad	Thad
b	bach small	fach	mach	
d	dyn man	ddyn	nyn	
g	glas blue/green	las	nglas	
ll	llawen merry	lawen		
m	mam mother	fam		
rh	rhyd ford	ryd		

N

NAMES

Because of the relatively few numbers of Welsh Christian names and surnames, e.g. Ioans (Jones, John, Johns), Roberts, Davieses, etc., it became usual for Welshmen to acquire nicknames. In some villages there might be 'Jones the Milk', 'Jones the Butcher', 'Jones the Top Farm', 'Jones the Coal' and so on. The great entrepreneur David Davies was known as 'Davies Top Sawyer', then 'Davies the Railway', and finally 'Davies the Ocean' (see David Davies). A much decorated war veteran was nicknamed 'Dai Alphabet' because of all the initials he was entitled to wear.

Other descriptive names like Fechan, 'the Small', and Goch, 'the red-haired', transmuted over time into Vaughan and Gough or Gooch. The emigré painter, Josef Herman, said that he knew he was accepted by the mining community at Ystradgynlais when he was called Jo Fach, Little Joe. Some leading Welsh families took Norman names, for instance William ap William of Raglan Castle (Black William) was forced to take the name of Herbert by the English crown during The Wars of the Roses. Similarly the Lord Gruffydd ap Gwyn-wynwyn was forced to drop the ancient suffix of the Prince Gwenwynwyn of Powys, by Edward I. Edward not only made him renounce his royal titles, but made him accept the title Baron de la Pole (Pool or Powys), or forfeit all his estates around Powys Castle.

Surnames that usually denote a Welsh ancestry are on the following list. Ap Evan, son of Evan, often became Bevan with the language mutation before vowels (similarly ap Owen became Bowen etc.), and many other surnames are prefixed with p, for example ap Robert became Probert.

Brangwyn
Cadwallader, Cadwaladr
Caradoc, Craddock
Cecil (from the Welsh Seisyllt, in turn from the Roman Sextilius)
Cethin – Gethin (from the Welsh for 'fierce')
Charles
Clwyd (a region of Wales)
Caradoc, Caradog, Cradock (from the Roman Caractacus, Caratacus)
David, Davids, Davis, Davies, Dafydd (perhaps from the Princedom of Dyfed)
Dee – from du, black
Dyfed
Edward, Edwards – supposedly from Iorwerth
Emyr
Evans, Evan – Bevan
Eynon, Einion – Beynon (possibly from Justinian)
Gough, Gooch – from coch, goch, red-haired
Griffith, Griffiths – from Gruffydd
Gwynne, Wynn – from gwyn, wyn 'white' or from the Princedom of Gwynedd
Gwynedd
Harry – Parry, Barry – from Harri
Herbert
Henry – Penri
Hopkin, Hopkins – an old Flemish settler diminutive
Howel, Howells, Hywel – Powell
Hughes, Huw – Pugh, Puw, Pew
Iestyn – from Justinian
James

Jenkin, Jenkins – from Siencyn

Jones, John, Johns – from Latin
Ioannes, which became Ieuan, Ifan,
Evan

Llywelyn, Llywelyn, Lewelyn

Lewis

Lloyd, Loyd from Llwyd 'grey'

Madoc, Maddocks

Map, Mapp – 'son'

Mathew, Matthew, Matthews

Medwyn, Medwin – Bedwin, from
Edwin

Meredith (from Maredudd)

Meurig, Merrick

Morgan, Morgans – from the
princedom of Morgannwg

Morris, Morus – from Meurig, Latin
Mauricius

Nash

Owen, Owens – Bowen

Phillips, Philip

Powys – the princedom

Powell (ap Hywel)

Pugh, Puw (ap Huw)

Rhydderch – Pritchard

Rhys, Rees, Reese, Reece, Rice –
Preece, Price

Richard, Richards – Pritchard

Robert, Roberts – Probert

Rosser – Prosser

Rowlands

Samuel, Samuels

Thomas, Tomos

Traherne, Treharrne

Tudor, Tewdwr – from Celtic
Teutorigos, Teutoris

Vaughan, Fychan, Vernon – from the
diminutive y fechan of bach 'small' =
the small one

Vivian, Vyvyan

Watkins, Watcyn, Gwatkin– from the
diminutive Flemish

Williams – Gwilliam

Yale, Ial – from the region around
Wrexham

Yorath (from Iorwerth)

The telephone directory for the small towns of Gaiman, Trelew and Port Madryn in Patagonia demonstrate the small number of Welsh surnames – there are: 108 Jones, 85 Williams, 42 Pugh, 40 Roberts, 38 Hughes, 31 Thomas, 22 Evans, 14 Owen, 13 Lloyd, 13 Lewis, 11 Price, 8 Griffiths and 5 Davies.

NATIONAL PARKS AND AREAS OF OUTSTANDING NATURAL BEAUTY

Wales has three National Parks, five Areas of Outstanding Natural Beauty, over seven hundred Sites of Special Scientific Interest, dozens of Natural Nature Reserves and several Royal Society for the Protection of Birds sanctuaries. The Forestry Commission owns vast chunks of Wales and fortunately more recent policy has allowed the planting of some deciduous trees that leaven the dark green slabs of conifer cash crops disfiguring our mountains and valleys.

National Parks:

1. Brecon Beacons. This mountain range of 519 square miles (1344 sq. km.) was designated in 1957, and covers parts of four counties, Mid-Glamorgan, Powys, Gwent and Carmarthenshire.

2. Pembrokeshire Coast National Park of 225 square miles (583 sq. km.) was designated in 1952, the only coastal national park in England and Wales.

3. Snowdonia National Park. 838 square miles in Gwynedd (2170 sq. km.), designated in 1951.

Areas of Outstanding National Beauty:

1. Gower Peninsula – the *first* area of land in Britain to be declared an 'AONB' in 1956, the peninsula is around five miles wide and juts out into the sea for fourteen miles. Many sheltered sandy beaches with clean water make it ideal for holidays and it includes the famous Penclawdd cocklebeds, where cockles are still picked by hand for the markets of Swansea and Neath (73 square miles, 189 sq. km.)

2. The Wye Valley – the fifteen miles between Monmouth and Chepstow, passing one of Wordsworth's favourite beauty spots, Tintern Abbey, and the 800 feet (244m) Wyndcliff where one can watch peregrine falcons hunting. Covering 45 square miles (117 sq. km.), there is a further part of it in England.

3. Isle of Anglesey Coastline (Ynys Môn), designated in 1966, 83 square miles (215 sq. km.)

4. The Llŷn Peninsula Coastline, designated in 1966, 60 square miles (155 sq. km.)

5. The Clwydian Ranges, designated in 1985, 60 square miles (155 sq. km.)

Three other outstandingly beautiful areas of Wales belong to the Ministry of Defence – Germans trained their Panzer divisions for decades across great swathes of coastal Pembrokeshire. Mynydd Eppynt in Powys and the Brecon Beacons are also home to military manoeuvring. There are also thirty-one country parks designated across Wales, and forty per cent of the superb Welsh coastline is designated as 'Heritage Coast Area'. Skomer Island is an official Marine Nature Reserve and there are marine conservation areas existing at the Menai Straits and Bardsey Island.

Wales has fifty National Nature Reserves, nineteen local nature reserves, and ten important Nature Reserves run by the RSPB (Royal Society for Protection of Birds). A further eight Special Protection Areas for wild birds are specified under an EC Directive. Wales also has no less than seven wetlands of international importance and almost nine hundred sites of Special Scientific Interest.

NATIONAL TRUST

The *first* piece of land bought by the National Trust is Britain was the viewpoint of Dinas Oleu near Barmouth. There are dozens of properties and places being conserved by the National Trust or Cadw in Wales.

National Trust properties include Penrhyn Castle, Plas Newydd, Powis Castle, Erddig, Conwy Suspension Bridge, Chirk Castle, Erddig, Aberconwy House, Bodnant Garden, Tenby Tudwr Merchant's House, Llanerchaeron, Dinefwr Park, Colby Woodland Garden, Aberdulais Falls, Segontium Roman Fort, Plas yn Rhiw, Tŷ Mawr, Ty'n y Coed Uchaf, Aberdulais Falls and Dolaucothi Gold Mines.

NATIONALISM

'The present Nationalist Movement is largely the creation of ex-servicemen who saw, during the War, the incongruity of fighting for the freedom of nations abroad, while their own was still in bondage'. (Gwynfor Evans, 1945).

The Plaid Cymru nationalist party is covered in the Politics section. One of the reasons that there are nationalists in Wales is the denial of its history. In 1953, the Principal Garter King of Arms, George Bellew of the College of Heraldry, stated categorically that Wales could never have a national flag as *'it had never been a kingdom'*. This view was upheld by the Assistant Secretary of State, Sir Austin Strutt. Wales was a kingdom hundreds of years before the English had to search Europe for German princes and princesses of areas the size of the Isle of Wight to become their rulers. The present German 'dynasty' has less right to a 'royal' flag representing Britain than virtually anyone walking the streets of Newcastle or Liverpool. This is a major reason for the 'rewriting of history' in Britain (see entry) by Hanoverian and Victorian scholars.

Welsh kings and princes were directly descended from Cunedda, around AD400. This was why the Normans, Plantagenets and the House of Lancaster were so keen to exterminate the bloodline, killing off family prisoners and assassinating the last Prince of Gwynedd, Owain Llaw Goch (Owain Lawgoch, see Assassination) in France in 1378. Wales is a nation, and will still be so when England splits into regions.

O

OFFA'S DYKE

About AD450, the Celtic King Vortigern was in the middle of internal strife in Britain and asked the Saxons to come to his aid. They came and assisted him but stayed, pushing Vortigern into what is now Wales. A fluctuating border between Celtic tribes and Saxons advancing from the West was solidified in the 6th century by two great battles. In 577 the three British-Celtic kings, Conmail, Condidan and Farinmail were beaten at the Battle of Dyrham, near Bristol, forming a wedge between the South-West Britons and the rest of the British tribes. The south-west tribes were slowly pushed back westward and became the Cornish, with a similar language to those of Brittany and Wales.

Forty years later, Aethelfrith of Northumbria won the battle of Bangor-is-Coed (Bangor on Dee) near Chester, beating Brochfael the Fanged (whose arms were three severed Saxon heads. Ednyfed Fychan, the ancestor of Henry VII, took over this emblem). Aethelfrith massacred the monks who had been supporting the Britons, and this fateful battle marked the final separating of the Welsh from their fellows (Cymry) in the Lake District and Cumbria. The border with Wales, between Celtic nation and Saxon-controlled Britons, had been formed, and is still virtually the same.

From Prestatyn on the North Coast to Chepstow on the South Coast, the hundred and sixty-eight mile Offa's Dyke Path attracts walkers from all over Europe. Offa, the eighth century Saxon King of Mercia, built this to serve as a border and the present bank and ditch still serves as much of the present border. As well as a political barrier, it may have been a customs barrier for trade and cattle, because there are some notable places where it is missing. Near Knighton (Tref y Clawdd, or Town of the Dyke), the height of the bank to the bottom of the ditch is even now around sixteen feet to twenty feet (5-6m). The width of the ditch is sixty feet (18m), the ditch being on the Welsh side of the raised dyke. The Offa's Dyke Footpath is one of Britain's most beautiful. John Davies has called the dyke *'perhaps the most striking man-made boundary in the whole of Western Europe'*. In effect, it solidified the border between Wales and the Saxons and Mercians, with the notable exception of Herefordshire, much of which stayed 'Welsh' for another eight hundred years.

This national border, much of which the Dyke marks, is one of the oldest in Europe, older than that between Spain and Portugal, or France and Germany. In the past, a Welshman caught east of Offa's Dyke had an ear cut off. East of Offa's Dyke lies the earlier Wat's Dyke, a double ditch and embankment running from Basingwerk Abbey near Holywell to Welshpool, via Buckley, Hope, Llay, Wrexham, Ruabon and Oswestry. Less well-preserved than Offa's Dyke, it preceded it and was probably built by King Ethelbald of Mercia. Old legends say that the areas between Wat's and Offa's dykes were a sort of 'No-Man's-Land', where Saxons and Britons met to trade.

OGHAM

This was the ancient alphabet of the Celts, in use from c.AD300 to the seventh century. On ancient stones, the number and position of straight and slanted lines carved into the edges give us characters in Ogham script, common in Ireland and Wales. As some of the Welsh stones were also inscribed in Latin, we now know the Ogham alphabet and can translate many of these standing stones.

Blocks of wood were also carved, and Irish sagas tell us of huge libraries of Ogham texts recorded on bark. The system was named after the Celtic god of eloquence, Ogma and the Celts regarded ability with words greater than physical prowess.

OLD KINGDOMS AND COUNTIES

The Kingdom of Gwynedd, that area roughly now the Snowdonia National Park and the Island of Anglesey, with its capital at Aberffraw, was the key to Welsh independence. Time and time again the frontiers were pushed back to this inhospitable and mountainous corner of Wales. Without the prolonged resistance of Gwynedd, Wales would hardly exist as a separate entity from England.

To the East of Gwynedd lay the Kingdom of Powys and South-West were the small kingdoms of Ceredigion (Cardigan), Dyfed (Pembroke) and Ystrad Tywi. These latter three were occasionally unified as Deheubarth. In the Mid-South were Brycheiniog (Brecon) and Buallt (Builth) and below them Morgannwg (Glamorgan) and Gwent (Monmouthshire).

Parts of Herefordshire, Worcestershire and Shrophire, the border counties, were Welsh-speaking until a couple of hundred years ago. Monmouthshire used to pass between England and Wales as an administrative county and part of Flintshire was detached from Wales and surrounded by English administrative areas. However, the traditional Thirteen Counties of Wales were reorganised in 1966 to form eight new administrative units. In the north-east, Flint and Denbigh became Clwyd. In the south-east, Monmouthshire was renamed Gwent. Glamorgan in the south was split into three new counties, East, Mid and South. Radnor and Brecon in mid-Wales formed Powys. Pembroke, Cardigan and Carmarthen in the south-west and west now formed Dyfed. The north-west counties of Merionydd, Caernarfon and Anglesey have reverted to being called Gwynedd. And then in turn in 1996 the Glamorgans and Gwent were reorganised into Monmouthshire, Newport, Torfaen, Blaenau Gwent, Caerphilly, Cardiff, Merthyr Tydfil, Rhondda Cynon Taff, Vale of Glamorgan, Bridgend, Neath Port Talbot and Swansea. Dyfed reverted to Carmarthenshire, Pembrokeshire and Ceredigion (Cardigan). Powys remained, Clwyd became Wrexham, Flintshire and Denbighshire. Gwynedd was divided into three, Conwy, Ynys Môn (Anglesey) and a smaller Gwynedd.

OUTWARD BOUND

The International Outward Bound Movement was founded in Aberdyfi in 1941.

OWAIN GLYNDŴR
– see *Glyndŵr*

OWAIN GWYNEDD – OWAIN AP GRUFFYDD AP CYNAN (1109-1170)

The History of Gruffydd ap Cynan was written in the thirteenth century, a hundred and fifty years after his death. Born around 1055, his family was exiled at the Irish court and he married the daughter of the King of Dublin. He invaded Wales in 1075, beating Trahaern of Gwynedd. Trahaern won a second battle, and Gruffydd turned to piracy for six years. In 1081 with a fellow-prince, Rhys ap Tewdwr, he set out from St Davids and killed Trahaern at the battle of Mynydd Carn. Rhys took control of Deheubarth, but Gruffydd returned to piracy and ended up being imprisoned in chains by the Normans.

After his rescue, and Rhys' death at the Battle of Brycheiniog against the Normans in 1093, Gruffydd at last took control of Gwynedd and Deheubarth. King William II, William Rufus, invaded but was repulsed. The Marcher Lords attacked with revolting cruelty, but returned to their border fortresses. In 1099, King Henry I attacked Wales. Gruffydd, by diplomacy, evaded battle and kept quiet until his peaceful death in 1137 at the age of eighty-two. He was ruler of most of Wales and Bangor Cathedral holds a tomb believed to be his – the earliest tomb of a Welsh prince.

During the two hundred years of battles with the Normans and Plantagenets, three political entities in Wales remained fairly stable and relatively independent, the princedoms of Powys, Deheubarth and Gwynedd. Gruffydd's son, Owain Gwynedd ex-tended his possessions over Offa's Dyke into England, and down into the other two princedoms. This ensured the predominance of the Princes of Gwynedd, Rhodri Mawr's descendants, in the continuing Welsh fight for independence. Owain ap Gruffydd thus became known as Owain Gwynedd. Owain's grandson was Llywelyn ap Iorwerth, Llywelyn the Great, whose own grandson was Llywelyn ap Gruffydd, Llywelyn Olaf (Llywelyn the Last).

Owain's reign saw the strongest Norman attacks on Wales. His whole reign was focused upon protecting Wales from the Marcher Lords. He was also known as Owain Fawr, 'Owain the Great', and repulsed an invasion by Henry II so easily that no other Plantagenet king attempted to subjugate Wales until his death. Gwalchmai, his *pencerdd* (chief household bard) wrote in *The Triumphs of Owain*:

> *'Owain's praise demands my song*
> *Owain swift and Owain strong;*
> *Fairest flower of Rhodri's stem,*
> *Gwynedd's shield, and Britain's gem*
> *Lord of every regal art*
> *Liberal hand and open heart*
> *Dauntless on his native sands*
> *The dragon-son of Mona* stands'.*

(*Mona is the English translation of Môn (Anglesey), the holy island of Wales, where the princes of Gwynedd had their chief court at Aberffraw.)

From his accession to the crown of Gwynedd in 1137, Owain Gwynedd was faced with major problems from his brother Cadawaladr and Owain's sons Hywel and Cynan defeated him and forced him to flee to Ireland. In 1145, Owain lost his favourite son Rhun and fell into a long period of grieving. However, Hywel Hir and Cynan took the mighty Norman fortress of Mold (Wyddgrug) and razed it to the ground, restoring his spirits. In 1149 Madoc ap Maredudd, Prince of Powys, joined the Norman Earl of Chester to gain lands off Owain. Their army was slaughtered in a battle in the woods of Consyllt.

In 1156 Owain's brother Cadwaladr, and Madoc ap Maredudd now stirred the English king to invade Wales, to exterminate this over-powerful neighbour. Henry II's first campaign against Owain ended in a truce in 1157. Owain, with his sons Dafydd and Cynan, had waited for Henry's army in the woods at Coed Eulo (Cennadlog) near Basingwerk, on the Dee estuary. They almost took Henry prisoner and the Earl of Essex threw down the Royal Standard and escaped through the woods. Knights from Henry's fleet ravaged Anglesey, where one of the King's sons was killed, while Henry waited for reinforcements at Rhuddlan. With the 1157 truce, Owain gave King Henry hostages, promising not to attack England, and allowed the King to keep the land around Rhuddlan.

In 1160, with the death of Madoc ap Maredudd, Owain attacked Powys and extended his influence in the east. In 1166, the Council of Woodstock tried to make the Welsh princes vassals, and there was an uprising led by Owain and his nephew Rhys ap Gruffydd (The Lord Rhys) in South Wales. A monk of St David's wrote, '*All the Welsh of Gwynedd, Deheubarth and Powys with one accord cast off the Norman yoke.*'

Henry then tried again to subjugate Wales, but failed and Owain's son, Dafydd, captured the important King's castles of Basingwerk and Rhuddlan in 1166 and 1167. Henry recaptured them,

and set up to invade from a base in Shrewsbury. With his brother Cadwaladr and The Lord Rhys, Owain called his forces to Corwen. Henry moved through the damp Berwyn Mountains, cutting a road through the heavy forests to keep away Welsh archers and raiding parties. Even today the road is called *Ffordd y Saeson* ('The English Road'). Welsh guerrilla attacks and bad weather defeated the Normans, and they retreated back to the shelter of Shrewsbury (Pengwern). One violent attack by the Welsh guerrilla forces took place at a site now called *Adwy'r Beddau* (The Pass of the Graves).

King Henry, in his rage, killed all his prisoners. He also had four important hostages – Rhys and Cadwaladr, two sons of Owain Gwynedd, and Cynwrig and Maredudd, two sons of The Lord Rhys of Deheubarth (see Rhys ap Gruffydd). He blinded them – '*and this the King did with his own hand*' according to The Chronicles. Few Welsh people know of this terrible event – it is in hardly any British history books. One wonders what would have been written, if the Welsh had ever done this to English princes.

In 1168, diplomatic relations were established between Owain Gwynedd and King Louis VII of France to King Henry's impotent fury. When he died in 1170, after thirty-three years as Prince of Gwynedd, Owain was hailed as '*the king and sovereign and prince and defender and pacifier of all the Welsh after many dangers by sea and land, after innumerable spoils and victories in war . . . after collecting together into Gwynedd, his own country, those who had been before scattered into various countries by the Normans, after building in his time many churches and consecrating them to God*'.

His chronicler states also that his

kingdom *'shone with lime-washed churches like the firmament with stars'*. Owain had encouraged monasticism, especially in Gwynedd, but he died excommunicated because he refused to divorce his wife who was his cousin. Archbishop Baldwin of Canterbury, when he visited Bangor Cathedral in 1188, spitefully ordered Owain's bones to be moved from the Cathedral to the churchyard.

Madog (Madoc, see entry), the son of Owain Gwynedd, was credited as being the Welshman who discovered America. Madog's sister, Gwenllian, was killed after battling the Normans at Cydweli and may have been the author of the 'Mabinogion' (see entry on Gwenllian). The Lord Rhys was Owain's nephew (see entry on Rhys ap Gruffydd). Rhys was the son of Gwenllian who was executed by the Normans when he was just four years old. Rhys ap Gruffydd, Prince of Deheubarth, now took the mantle of chief defender of Wales against the invading Normans.

OWAIN LAW GOCH
– see Assassinations

OWEN, ROBERT (1771-1858)

In 1771, Trenewydd (Newtown) in mid-Wales produced a man who changed society across the world with his thoughts and actions. Karl Marx and Freidrich Engels both paid generous tribute to him in the development of their theories. When Robert Owen took over the cotton mills in New Lanark in Scotland, in 1800, he improved housing and sanitation, provided medical supervision, set up a co-operative shop and established the first infant school in Great Britain. Owen also founded an Institute for the Formation of Character and a model welfare state for New Lanark.

His example was largely responsible for bringing about The Factory Acts of 1819, but disappointed at the slow rate of reform in England, he emigrated to America in 1821 to set up another model community. From 1817 Owen had proposed that 'villages of cooperation', self-supporting communities run on socialist lines, should be founded, to ultimately replace private ownership. He took these ideas on co-operative living to America and set up the community of New Harmony, Indiana, between 1824 and 1828 before he handed the project over to his sons and returned to Britain. The USA community failed without his inspiring idealism, but he carried on encouraging the fledgling trade union movement and co-operative societies. In 1833 he formed the Grand National Consolidated Trades Union.

From 1834, Owen led the opposition against the deportation of The Tolpuddle Martyrs, a group of Dorset farm labourers, who had stopped working in a cry for higher living wages. Because of his criticisms of the organised religion of the day, where positions were granted as favours, he lost any support from those in power and whose families benefited from the system.

He wrote about the barbaric nature of unrestrained capitalism in *Revolution in Mind and Practice*. He wanted political reform, a utopian socialist system with a transformation of the social order, in which individuals should co-operate and not compete.

He was a fore-runner of the co-operative movement, a great inspirer of the trades union movement, and probably the modern world's first socialist. Those that followed his teachings, who called themselves Owenites, gradually changed their name to Socialists, the first recorded use of the term. Owen is a Welshman of international stature, who is hardly acclaimed in his own land, but his socialism is a thread that runs through Welsh history from the Laws of Hywel Dda in the tenth century, to the election of the first Labour MP in Britain in 1910, to the whole-hearted support for the Miners' Strike in 1984, to the present state of left-wing support in Wales (see Politics).

As the pioneer of co-operation between workers and consumers, his understanding of the 'value chain' and wealth creation has not been equalled until Michael Porter in recent years and, although mistakenly identified as a Scotsman in *The Witch Doctors*, The 1997 Global Business Book Award, he is deemed by the authors to be *'the pioneer of personnel management'*.

In April 1840, an editorial in *The Cambrian* referred to Robert Owen in an article. It reads:

> 'The discontent of the lower and working classes has assumed a new form which threatens to become far more mischievous than mere political agitation, however fiercely carried on. We allude to the institution and spread of Socialism. Under pretence of improving the condition of the poor, Socialism is endeavouring, permanently, to poison their happiness, by depraving their morals, and depriving them of all those consolations flowing from the principles of religion. It is of little use to show that Mr. Owen is a lunatic.'

His son, Robert Dale Owen, was prominent in the abolitionist movement in the USA, writing *The Policy of Emancipation* and *The Wrong Slavery*. He became a Congressman and Ambassador to India, but, like his father, returned to Newtown and died in 1858. 'Hiraeth' is a strong emotion. A memorial museum is now in the house where his father was born.

FOOTNOTE:
Another museum in Newtown is in the High Street, with mementoes about W. H. Smith, the leading British newsagent chain that started in 1792. Newtown also saw the birth of the mail-order idea, started by Sir Pryce Pryce-Jones in 1861 to sell Welsh linens. One of his more famous customers was Queen Victoria. His business base, the Royal Welsh Warehouse is still being used.

P

PEACE UNION, THE

This was founded through the hard work of Joseph Tregelles Price, a humanitarian Quaker who tried desperately to save the doomed Dic Penderyn (see Riots). Its first secretary was Evan Rees of Montgomeryshire, author of *Sketches of Horrors of War*. He was followed as secretary by Henry Richard, and the secretaries for the first hundred years were all Welsh. The pacifist Henry Richard of Tregaron (1812-1888), was known as *Apostol Heddwch* ('The Apostle of Peace') in Wales. The Peace Union was the forerunner of the League of Nations, which in turn changed into The United Nations.

A Congregational minister in London from 1835 to 1850, he became Secretary of the Peace Society in 1848. A nonconformist radical and a friend of Richard Cobden, he travelled widely in Europe, holding peace conferences and encouraging the use of arbitration in international disputes.

Richard was elected MP for Merthyr Tydfil at the age of fifty-six, and thoroughly repudiated 'The Blue Books' which maligned Welsh education. His first act in The House of Commons was to condemn those landlords who evicted their Welsh tenants for voting Liberal. As an MP, he was passionately interested in Welsh education, land reform, disestablishment of the English church in Wales, and the protection of the Welsh language. His interests led to his nickname as 'The Member for Wales'.

PHILOSOPHERS

Richard Price (1723-1791) of Tynton, Glamorgan, has been mentioned previously (see America). A unitarian minister and moral philosopher, he argued against David Hume, believing that *'morality is a branch of necessary truth'*. In 1776 he published *Observations on the Nature of Civil Liberty*. He also provoked Burke's anger with his support for the French Revolution (*A Discourse on the Love of Our Country* 1789), in which he sermonised *'Tremble, all ye oppressors of the world . . . you cannot now keep the world in darkness'*. Price also supported the American Revolution with several books. He was honoured in both these countries. This *'Friend of the Universe, the Great Apostle of Liberty'* was asked by the newly established American Congress, through his friend Benjamin Franklin, to accept American citizenship and to set up a financial system in the new republic (see Marx).

He also influenced William Pitt the Younger with his writings on The National Debt, and helped to set up the first scientific system for life insurance and pensions with his *Observations on Reversionary Payments* in 1771. He had been admitted to The Royal Society in 1765 for his work on probability. This statistician, preacher and philosopher had a political influence upon radicals in both the Old and New Worlds. John Davies calls Price *'the most original thinker ever born in Wales'*. He was officially mourned in Paris, when he died in 1791.

David Williams, who founded the Royal Literary Fund, was born near Caerphilly in 1738. A friend of many eminent thinkers, in 1777 he gave refuge to Benjamin Franklin when he stayed in Wales. Williams advanced Price's philosophy that parliamentarians are trustees of the people, in his *Letters on Political Liberty* in 1782. His opinions were regarded so highly that he was asked to become a French citizen by French revolutionaries and to take a seat in their Convention of 1792. He refused, although he accepted an invitation to criticise and amend the draft of the First Constitution of the French Republic

Bertrand Russell (1872-1970), born in Trelleck near Monmouth wrote numerous books ranging from the influential *Principia Mathematica* and *Problems of Philosophy*. He spent much of his life at his family home of Plas Penrhyn in North Wales. He was a notable supporter of the Campaign for Nuclear Disarmament and was awarded the Nobel Prize for Literature in 1950.

Henry Habberley Price (1899-1985) from Neath, was Professor of Logic at Oxford, whose major works included *Perception* in 1932, *Thinking and Experience* (1953), *Belief* (1969) and *Essays in the Philosophy of Religion* (1972).

PIRATES

Llewelyn Penrose's *Journal* was one of the earliest stories of buried treasure, upon which Edgar Allen Poe based his *Gold Bug*. We have seen that Wales produced the most famous buccaneer in history, Sir Henry Morgan. It also produced a notable series of pirates, including the greatest and most curious them all, **Black Bart**, **Bartholemew**

Roberts, whom Newsweek called the *'last and most lethal pirate'*, also known as *'The Black Pirate'*. Daniel Defoe called his aspect *'black'*, as he had black hair and a dark complexion and he was simply the most formidable pirate in history.

To put piracy into context, the English Navy was a bitterly cruel organisation, and deserters were common. It had to 'press-gang' most of its unfortunate seamen from British ports. Conditions were not as bad in the merchant navy, but there was still a constant flow of dissatisfied seamen men willing to sail under the black (or red) flag of piracy. Bartholomew Roberts wrote of the motives for becoming a pirate: *'In an honest service there is thin rations, low wages, and hard labour; in this, pleanty, satiety, pleasure and ease, liberty and power; and who would not balance creditor on this side, when all the hazard that is run for it, at worst, is only a sour look or two at choking (dying)? No, a merry life and a short one shall be my motto.'*

Black Bart (*Barti Ddu*) captured an amazing four hundred ships between 1719 and 1722, bringing commerce in North America, the West Indies, West Africa and the whole Atlantic almost to a standstill. Born in 1682 at Little Newcastle near Haverfordwest, Bartholomew Roberts went to sea as boy and became a skilled navigator. We first hear of him as the thirty-seven year old third mate on the Princess galley, picking up slaves from the Gold Coast. He was captured by two pirate ships, captained by another Welshman, Hywel Davis, and given the choice of joining them, which he did, despairing of lack of any promotion because of his class. Black Bart's favourite oath was *'Damnation to him that ever lived to wear a halter!'* He was known as 'pistol-

proof', as he was expert in ship-hand-
ling, crew control, and the tactics of
naval warfare.

Within six weeks, Hywel Davis was
dead in an ambush by the Portuguese,
and Roberts was voted the new captain. Accepting, he said *'If I must be a
pirate, it is better to be a commander than
a common man'*. He swiftly avenged
Davis's death, attacking a Portuguese
fleet (although outnumbered forty-two
merchant ships to his own ship). Roberts
escaped with the richest merchantman
in the fleet – £50,000 in the currency of
the day – the most profitable raid in
West Indian pirate history.

He allowed no boys or women on
his ships, was a teetotal tea-drinker,
and the ship's band played hymns for
Sunday services. No drinking or gambling was allowed on board on Sundays. The band also played Black Bart
into battle – he dressed in red damasks
and velvet from head to toe, with a
three-cornered red hat with a huge
scarlet plume, armed with cutlasses
and pistols. His demeanour and scarlet
dress were such that French traders
called him *Le Joli Rouge* – the origin of
the 'Jolly Roger'. It is also said that
Black Bart's flag was the origin of the
skull and crossbones – a skeleton with
an hourglass.

Suffering mutinies, internal fights,
and terrible deprivations at times, he
was feared by all sea-going vessels. Being
annoyed at the persistent attempts of
the governors of Barbados and Martinique to imprison and execute him, he
designed a personal flag and plate for
his cabin door, with ABH (a Barbad-
ian's head) and AMH (a Martinican's
head) illustrated on them. He later
captured, and hanged, the Governor of
Martinique in October 1720 from his
yardarm.

Roberts's crew was drunk when he
was finally ambushed by a special con-
voy of Royal Navy frigates. It seems
that Roberts deliberately sought death.
He was tired of trying to control a
drunken, womanising rabble. Black
Bart could have escaped, but inexplic-
ably ordered his ship to turn to face his
pursuers, although the majority of his
crew were incapable of standing, let
alone fighting the Royal Navy. Captain
Ogle was knighted for his singular
service in killing *'the great pirate Roberts'*,
the only naval man honoured for service against the pirates. Black Bart was
not yet forty years old. Ogle himself
made a fortune, from illicitly purloin-
ing the plundered gold dust he found
in Roberts's cabin.

Of the two hundred and fifty-four
pirates captured, fifteen died en-route
to the Gold Coast, and four more in
the slave hole there during the trial.
Some musicians and 'forced men' were
acquitted. 'The House of Lords', the
hardest and longest-serving members
of the crew, had followed Hywel Davis,
and regarded themselves as the 'aristocracy' of the pirate profession, giving
each other honorary 'lordships'. They
were not contrite at their trial. Seventeen of Roberts's crew were committed
to prison in London, of whom thirteen
died in transit. Of the fifty-two members of Roberts's crew hanged on the
Gold Coast, a third were from Wales,
and a third from the West country. (After
an act of betrayal, Roberts would allow
no Irish to serve with him). The oldest
to be executed was forty-five, and the
youngest just nineteen.

The bodies of the eighteen worst
offenders, the members of the famous
'House of Lords', were dipped in tar,
bound with metal strips and hung in
chains from gibbets on three prominent

hills overlooking the sea-lanes. The shock of the death of this most famous, brave and dreaded pirate helped end the so-called "golden age" of piracy.

The man responsible for Black Bart's adventures, Monmouthshire's **Hywel Davis**, also is famous in pirate annals. He was serving as a mate on the 'Cadogan' in 1718, when it was captured by Captain Edward England, who invited him to become a pirate. Davis refused, whereupon England gave him the 'Cadogan' and sailed away. Carrying on to its destination, Barbados, the authorities were suspicious of Davis's story and clapped him in irons. After three months with no evidence, they released him, but no-one trusted him any longer, and he could not get employment. The frustrated Davis stole a ship, the 'Buck', in late 1718 and made a short speech to the volunteers with him, '*the substance of which was a Declaration of War against the Whole World.*' He was noted for his mercy, affability and good nature, unlike most other pirates.

The pirates sailed from the Caribbean to the Guinea Coast, plundering and acquiring a new and better ship, 'King James'. After attacking the island of Sao Tiago, Davis set sail for Gambia, sailing into the harbour with English ensigns flying and most of his crew hidden below decks. He went ashore to see the Governor at the Royal African Company fort, pretending to be a merchantman fleeing from the French. He noted the defences, and being entertained by the Governor at dinner that night drew his pistols and gave a signal for his men to over-run the fort. Having looted Gambia, there was then an equally successful attack on Sierra Leone, with Davis now commanding three pirate ships.

In the Gulf of Guinea, sailing alone again, the pirates took on a heavier-armed Dutch vessel and a terrible fight lasted thirty-two hours, with Davis eventually taking over the Dutch ship. He renamed her the 'Royal Rover' as his own ship was sinking. With the 'Royal Rover', he took another Dutch vessel with £15,000 in sterling on board, a fortune in those days.

One of Davis's cleverest exploits was the capture of two French ships in 1719. He forced the prisoners from the first ship to masquerade as pirates and hoisted a dirty tarpaulin as a black pirate flag. Bluffed into believing that the captured French ship was another pirate boat, the second ship surrendered. At the Portuguese island of Principe off Gabon, he repeated his 'friendly merchantman' trick, but an officer of a plundered French ship managed to get word to the Governor. Just before the evening's meeting, Davis was fatally shot in the stomach in an ambush, and Bartholomew Roberts, a Welshman just captured, was chosen captain in his place.

Apart from Bartholomew Roberts and Hywel Davis, Wales had some other major contributions to make to pirate history. **Captain John Bowen** (fl.1701) operated between the Red Sea and Bengal, with headquarters in Madagascar. He retired to Mauritius with a vast fortune. His movement into piracy began with his capture by French pirates. A Captain James also operated in these South Seas.

The Welsh Captain **Charles Bellamy** was a socialist, orator and pirate who ravaged shipping off the coasts of Carolina, New England and Newfoundland. Wrecked off Eastham, Massachusetts, he was tried and hanged at Boston in 1726. One of the best pieces of his invective is recorded against a merchant master who refused to join him in piracy:

> *'Damn you! You are a squeaking puppy, and so are all those who will submit to be governed by laws which rich men have made for their own security. For the cowardly whelps have not the courage otherwise to defend what they get by their knavery. But damn* **ye**, *altogether ! Damn* **them** *for a pack of crafty rascals, and* **you**, *who serve them, for a parcel of hen-hearted numbskulls ! They vilify us, the scoundrels do, when there is only this difference:* **they** *rob the poor under the cover of law, forsooth, and* **we** *plunder the rich under cover of our own courage; had ye not better make one of us, than sneak after the arses of those villains for employment?'*

The most fabulous treasure trove in the world is reputed to be in Cocos Island, where hundreds of expeditions have searched for Edward Davis's gold since the eighteenth century.

Daniel Defoe, under the pseudonym Captain Charles Johnson, recounted the story of **Captain John Evans**. An unemployed sloop master, he stole a pirogue (canoe) in Jamaica, then took over a sloop which he called the 'Scourer'. He then attacked and plundered a Spanish sloop, before taking the 'Dove' from New England off to Puerto Rica. In 1723, the 'Lucretia and Catherine' was taken, which replaced the 'Scourer' and they took another merchantman before resting to careen (clean) the ship in the Grand Caymans. However, an argument with the boatswain ended in a challenge to a duel on shore, the normal way of ending such proceedings in pirate etiquette. The boatswain refused to take part, so

Captain Evans hit him with his cane for being a coward, turned to return to the ship, and was shot in the back by the cowardly boatswain. The crew captured and summarily shot the boatswain and discussed what to do next. As they could not agree on a captain, thirty pirates stayed on the Cayman Islands with around nine thousand pounds in loot, leaving the mate and a boy to sail the 'Lucretia and Catherine' into Jamaica's Port Royal.

Captain Lewis has a chapter to himself in the 1837 publication *The Pirate's Own Book*. Starting from Jamaica, he operated off the Carolinas, Virginia and Newfoundland and then Guinea, taking English, French, Dutch and Portuguese ships. Eventually killed by French pirates, he leaves a strange epitaph:

> *'He was the mildest manner's man, That ever scuttled ship or cut a throat; With such true breeding of a*
> *   gentleman,*
> *You could never discern his real*
> *   thought.*
> *Pity he loved an adventurous life's*
> *   variety,*
> *He was so great a loss to good society.'*

Captain John Phillips operated the Revenge off the coast of America, and, like Bart Roberts's, his ship's articles survive, amongst which it is noted that the punishment for *'meddling with a prudent woman'* was death.

Other famous Welsh pirates included Captain David Williams and Captain John Bowen, who operated around Madagascar and the Red Sea, and Captains Harris, Owen, Vaughan, Powel and Hughs.

A notably villainous pirate who operated in the Bristol Channel was John Callice in Elizabethan times. Even earlier there was the Breton, Colyn Dolphyn. In 1449 he had captured Henry, son of the Lord Stradling of St Donat's Castle. After his father paid a large ransom, Henry was released, but four years later he managed to lure Dolphyn onto the rocks, by a false light in a new watchtower he had built. He handed him over to the local people. The terrorised people of Llanilltud Fawr (Llantwit Major) buried him up to his neck in nearby Tresilian Bay, and calmly watched as the incoming tide washed over the infamous villain. Dolphyn's effigy was burnt for many years at Llanilltud Fawr.

PLAID CYMRU

Michael D. Jones, who founded the Patagonian Welsh colony, returned to Wales and set up the Bala-Bangor Theological College and campaigned for Welsh causes. He is now regarded by many as the father of modern Welsh nationalism.

During the National Eisteddfod in Pwllheli in 1925, representatives from *Y Mudiad Cymreig* ('The Welsh Movement') and *Byddin Ymreolwyr Cymru* ('The Army of the Welsh Home Rulers') met to join and form *Plaid Cymru* ('The Welsh National Party'). Saunders Lewis (see Literature) was a founder and later president. In 1936, with two friends, he set fire to a hangar at the RAF bombing range of Penberth, at Penrhos on the Llŷn Peninsula. Little damage was caused and the three turned themselves into police the next day.

The Welsh jury in Carmarthen acquitted the three – Saunders Lewis had said in court: *'What I was teaching the*

young people of Wales in the halls of the university was not a dead literature, something chiefly of interest to antiquarians, but a living literature of the Welsh people. This literature is therefore able to make demands of me as a man as well as a teacher.' The English authorities could not accept the verdict of a Welsh jury, and had the three retried in London, giving them nine months in prison.

The Welsh former Prime Minister, David Lloyd-George, railed against the injustice of it all – *'They yield when faced by Hitler and Mussolini, but they attack the smallest country in the kingdom which they misgovern. This is a cowardly way of showing their strength through violence . . . This is the first government that has tried to put Wales on trial at the Old Bailey . . . I should like to be there, and I should like to be 40 years younger.'* Saunders Lewis was asked if he wanted to see a bloody revolution, and answered *'So long as it is Welsh blood and not English blood.'* He died in 1985, a poet-philosopher-nationalist-pacifist, still without much honour in his own land, who did more than anyone since Bishop William Morgan to keep the Welsh language alive.

Saunders Lewis was shamefully blacklisted by the University of Wales for his nationalism and it was not until 1951 that was he accepted back into academe, at Cardiff University, and this bias still goes on.

In 1979, the Welsh people voted against a National Assembly. A 1996 poll gave 2:1 opposing the Assembly. In 1997 the referendum for a Welsh Assembly was passed by the tiniest minority, mainly because Welsh Nationalists threw everything into supporting the proposal – they see it as a half-way house to full devolution and independence for Wales. Scotland also voted for limited independence, but they will have their own Parliament, with far greater powers than the Welsh Assembly.

Originally Plaid was too identified with the under-populated Welsh-speaking North and West of Wales and not with the eighty per cent of the nation that lives in South and South-East Wales. As a result, the organisation has become fully bilingual, and has renamed itself 'Plaid Cymru – The Party of Wales'. The party now knows that it must take Cardiff, Swansea and Newport if it wants to be serious about Welsh nationalism. Its fundamental concerns of the Welsh language, Welsh identity and Christianity in Wales gave it too narrow an appeal in the past. It is certainly the only party that Labour fears in the country.

POETRY

Poetry is at the heart of all Welsh culture (see Literature). Wales has the oldest recorded poetry in any living Western language, from the *cynfeirdd*, first poets, *Aneirin* and *Taliesin* in The Dark Ages. The saga of *Llywarch Hen*, a ninth century tragedy, tells of the King mourning the death of all his twenty-four sons in battle. Many of the oldest poems still exist, having been passed down verbally through the centuries before being written in the eleventh and twelfth centuries (see Bards, Literature). It was said that the old Celtic bards, or poets, had to train for twelve years to become a full bard, learning eighty long story-poems in the first six years. In the next three years they had to learn another ninety-five, and in the final three years another one-hundred and seventy-five heroic odes, each taking over an hour to retell. The oldest surviving poems use many mnemonics

(aids to memory), stemming from this tradition of having to intimately know over three-hundred and fifty hours of poetry.

In 1282, **Gruffudd ab yr Ynad Coch** wrote his moving elegy to Llewelyn the Last (see Literature, Llywelyn ap Gruffydd).

Dafydd ap Gwilym (c1320-c1370) is the most celebrated Welsh poet, who is said to be buried under the old yew tree in the churchyard adjoining the ruins of Strata Florida Abbey. Indeed, he is one of the greatest of all European mediaeval writers. Many of the Welsh princes are also believed to be buried with him at Strata Florida, the Anglicised version of *Ystrad Fflur*, 'The Way of the Flowers'. He innovated in his use of language and metrical techniques. The seven-syllabled rhyming couplet form known as *cywydd* became his true 'metier'. His reputed birthplace at Llanbadarn Fawr is marked by a celebratory plaque.

Ted Hughes and Seamus Heaney named their verse compendium for young people 'The Rattle Bag' after Dafydd ap Gwilym's poem. Many of the features of his poetry cannot be translated into English, but *'Morfudd fel yr Haul'* (Morfudd like the Sun, translated by Rachel Bromwich, *Dafydd ap Gwilym Poems*, 1982) begins with the lines:

> *Gorllwyn ydd wyf ddyn geirllaes,*
> *I woo a softly spoken girl,*
>
> *Gorlliw eiry man marian maes;*
> *Pale as fine snow on the field edge;*
>
> *Gwyl Duw y mae golau dyn,*
> *God sees that she is radiant*
>
> *Goleuach nog ael ewyn.*
> *And brighter than the crest of foam,*

Goleudon lafarfron liw,
White as the glistening garrulous
wave's edge,

Goleuder haul, gwyl ydyw.
With the sun's splendour; gracious
is she.

Breconshire's **Henry Vaughan**, 'The Silurian' (1622-1695) practised as a country doctor in the Usk Valley, and is buried at Llansantffraid. His twin brother Thomas was a noted 'alchemist', who *'disseminated a purer conception of God and Man'* (see Literature). However, Henry is the more famous as one of the 'metaphysical' poets, combining insight into nature with deep religious conviction:

'I saw Eternity the other night,
Like a great ring of pure and endless
light,
All calm, as it was bright;
And round beneath it, Time in hours,
days, years,
Driv'n by the spheres
Like a vast shadow mov'd; in which the
world
And all her train were hurl'd.'

His vision of the innocent mysticism of childhood was later taken up by Wordsworth.

John Donne (1571-1631) was of Welsh origin – a metaphysical poet of great popularity in the 20th century. 'The Bait' begins:

'Come live with me, and be my love,
And we will some new pleasures prove
Of golden sands, and crystal brooks,
With silken lines, and silver hooks.'

Intriguingly, Professor Glanmor Williams noted the familiarity to the lines

from 'The Passionate Shepherd to his Love' by Christopher Marlowe (1564-1593):

'Come live with me, and be my love,
And we will all the pleasures prove,
The valleys, groves, hills and fields,
Woods or steepy mountain yields.'

William Shakespeare (1564-1616) also wrote in his 'Sonnets to Sundry Notes of Music':

'Live with me and be my love,
And we will all the pleasures prove.
That hills and valleys, dales and fields,
And all the craggy mountain yields.'

It seems that the original was by Marlowe, because Sir Walter Raleigh (c.1552-1618) wrote in his 'Answer to Marlowe':

'If all the world and love were young,
And truth in every shepherd's tongue,
These pretty pleasures might me move
To live with thee, and be thy love.'

The Herberts are a famous family in the history of Wales, being Earls of Montgomery and Pembroke, and were patrons of Shakespeare. William Herbert was the first Welshman known to have addressed the House of Commons, and was an educational pioneer who wished to establish a Welsh college in the ruins of Tintern Abbey. Shakespeare's sonnets appear to be addressed to William Herbert (W.H.), as he was a great supporter of the arts in Elizabethan London. His kinsman Richard Herbert, buried in Montgomery Church, had two famous sons, the poet/cleric George Herbert, and the philosopher and diplomat Lord Herbert of Cherbury, who lived in Montgomery Castle.

George Herbert was born in Montgomery in 1593, and died in 1633 before he reached 40. A devotional poet, his work is described by D. J. Enright as follows:

'. . . *the poems that make up The Temple are flawless and irresistible, and – for the tone of voice is immediately recognisable as his and his alone – unique. They are among the very finest we have in English; in them we hear a man pleading with God or arguing with him, or disputing with himself, but always talking to other men'.*

Some of his aphorisms are also well-known, such as *'he that lives in hope dances without music'* and *'who aimeth at the sky shoots higher much than that he means a tree'.*

Some of Herbert's finest poems are better known as hymns, for example:

'*Let all the world in ev'ry corner sing My God and King'*

and

'*The God of love my shepherd is, And he that doth me feed, While He is mine, and I am His, What can I want or need.'*

His brother Edward, Lord Cherbury, was hailed as 'The Father of Deism' and also published poetry – perhaps his most evocative line is :

'*Now that the April of your youth adorns The garden of your face'.*

John Dyer (1699-1757) wrote 'Grongar Hill', and Wordworth addressed a sonnet to this:

'*Bard of the Fleece, whose skilful genius made The work a living landscape fair and bright.'*

Dyer had given up law to become an intinerant painter, and 'Grongar Hill' was inspired by the Towy valley. He published *The Ruins of Rome* in 1750, and became ordained in 1751, publishing his longest work, *The Fleece* in 1757.

William Williams of Pantycelin is revered by some as Wales' finest poet of all time (see Music). Besides superb prose, he wrote over nine hundred hymns. Ann Griffiths (1776-1805) is also included in the music section.

Sir Lewis Morris (1833-1907) from Carmarthen, wrote verse and drama, largely drawing on incidents in Welsh history and mythology, as in *The Epic of Hades*. He campaigned tirelessly for a national university in Wales.

Gerard Manley Hopkins (1844-1889), of *Glory be to God for Dappled Things* fame, tried to replicate *'cynghanedd'* in the rhymes and rhythms of his poetry. Hopkins wanted his poetry burnt on his death, but it survived. The poems appear to have given a great impetus to the feelings and style of Dylan Thomas' work, a half-century later. A deeply religious man, he studied theology at St Beuno's in North Wales, where he also learned Welsh. *The Wreck of the Deutschland* and *Henry Purcell* are among the best works of this major poet. His poem about the kestrel, *The Windhover*, begins:

'*I caught this morning morning's minion, kingdom of daylight's dauphin, dapple-dawn-drawn Falcon',* and his *Pied Beauty* says:

>   *'Glory be to God for dappled things . . .*
>   *'All things counter, original, spare,*
>   *strange;*
>   *Whatever is fickle, freckled (who*
>   *knows how?)*
>   *With swift, slow; sweet, sour;*
>   *adazzle, dim;*
>   *He fathers-forth whose beauty is past*
>   *change:*
>
>   *Praise him.'*

The most famous bard of this century was *Hedd Wynn* ('White Peace'), the shepherd-poet **Ellis Evans** from Trawsfynydd, who was killed at Flanders in the First World War. He enlisted with the Royal Welsh Fusiliers at the age of thirty, early in 1917, and the poison gas took his life on 31st July in the same year, just before he would have received the chief Bardic prize at the National Eisteddfod in Birkenhead.

In September of that year, the winning poet was called to take the Bardic Chair for his strict metre poem *Yr Arwr* ('The Hero'). Hedd Wynn could not reply to the summons, and the Chair was draped in black on the stage. The assembled Welsh wept openly, and the event is still referred to as 'The Black Eisteddfod'. The moving Welsh-language film commemorating the story was nominated for an Oscar in 1995. His birthplace is next to Trawsfynydd Lake, which provided the cooling waters for the now closed Nuclear Power Station, set in one of the most beautiful spots in Europe.

Edward Thomas, born in 1878, was a superb poet and was one of the few Welshmen in history to disdain the English – his book *Wales*, published in 1905, has been in print ever since. His tragic death in the First World War in 1917 robbed Europe of a major poet. A line of his that always is remembered from *Early One Morning*, is *'The past is the only dead thing that smells sweet.'* F. R. Leavis called him *'an original poet of rare quality.'*

An Anglo-Welsh poet tragically extinguished in the same war was *Wilfred Owen*, from Plas Wilmot near Oswestry on the Welsh border, (1893-1918):

>   *'Red lips are not so red*
>   *As the stained stones kissed by the*
>   *English dead'.*

Concussed at the Somme, he later was awarded the MC, and was killed just a week before the Armistice. Only five of his poems had been published while he was alive but Siegfried Sassoon who had met him in War Hospital collected the rest for publication in 1920. Owen's bleakly realistic poems were chosen by Benjamin Britten for his 'War Requiem'.

In 1937, **David Jones** (1895-1974) wrote *In Parenthesis* (*seinnyesit e gledyf ym penn mameu*). TS Eliot wrote that he was 'deeply moved' by the typescript and that it was *'a work of genius'* in his introduction to it. Part poem, part book, it mingles Jones's cathartic experiences in the First World War with Arthurian legend, Welsh mythology and the Roman occupation of Britain. Eliot places Jones in the same literary representation as himself, Ezra Pound and James Joyce. Jones, a writer, painter, calligrapher and illustrator, was obsessed with the way technocracy had taken us away from faith and sacrament. The intensity of inspiration from his historical roots is probably only rivalled by Arthur Machen and W. B. Yeats.

Also according to the great poet W. H. Auden, David Jones's *The Anathemata* was *'very probably the finest* long poem written in English this century'. This considered meditation on the history and mythology of Celtic-Christian Britain was intelligent, ambitious and influenced TS Eliot's own work. Jones was also a fine painter and calligrapher (see Artists), influenced strongly by Eric Gill. Jones's *Epoch and Artist* is dedicated to Saunders Lewis, the Welsh Nationalist writer. All his writings show his alienation against the world of machines, existentialism, modernism and the analytical philosophy that eradicates metaphysics and the signposts of history.

Rhymney-bred **Idris Davies**, a miner as a fourteen year-old, became a London teacher and extra-mural lecturer. He was the poet of the valleys and died of stomach cancer, aged only forty-eight, in 1953. His *Gwalia Deserta* was published in 1938 with his poems recommended by TS Eliot: '*They are the best poetic document I know about a particular epoch in a particular place, and I think that they really have a claim to permanence.*'

Gwalia Deserta shows a socially and politically committed poet, full of the imagery of mining-valley life in the terrible days of the 1930s. Much of his work describes the impact of the Industrial Revolution, and its terrible decline, upon his beloved countryside and people. A Celtic Christian Socialist, he epitomised Welsh bardic tradition with a respect for fellow mankind, rather than for wealth based upon property:

'Any subject which has not man at its core is anathema to me. The meanest tramp on the road is ten times more interesting than the loveliest garden in the world. And instead of getting nearer

to nature in the countryside I find myself craving for more intense society'.

Quotations from Idris Davies are scattered around this book. He is the most approachable of all our poets, and verse XV, The Bells of Rhymney, of his *Gwalia Deserta* was set to music by Pete Seeger and also recorded by The Byrds amongst many others.

W. H. Davies (1871-1940), the 'tramp poet' from Newport, Gwent, wrote in *Leisure*:

'What is this life if, full of care,
We have no need to stand and stare?'

and in *The Kingfisher*,

'It was the rainbow gave thee birth
And left thee all her lovely hues.'

A descendant of the French criminal-poet, Francois Villon, he lost a leg in 1899, in a railroad accident while wandering across the Klondyke, and ended up living in doss-houses and selling shoe-laces on the streets of London. The poems of *The Soul Destroyer* in 1905 recount his experiences with hobos like Frisco Fatty and red-Nosed Scotty and with prostitutes like Kitty and Molly. George Bernard Shaw wrote the introduction to his *Autobiography of a Super-Tramp*, which opened the doors of admirers like Vita Sackville-West, Ottoline Morrell and Edith Sitwell to the peg-legged tramp. Davies later married and settled in Gloucester, in a house he named Glendower (the Anglicised version of Glyndŵr). Spurning convention to the last, his pet was a toad called Jim, which he fed saucers of milk.

Waldo Williams (1904-1971) is as close to a saint as Wales has produced this century. 'The Poet of Mynach-logddu' (up on the Preseli Hills), was imprisoned more than once for his pacifism. In the 1950s he refused to pay his income tax while conscription to the armed forces still existed, so bailiffs took away his furniture. He gave up his teaching job, because income tax was deducted from his pay, an element of which went on military expenditure. (It should be remembered that when all the Welsh councils declared themselves nuclear-free zones in the 1980s, Wales was the first region in Europe to ban nuclear weapons from crossing its lands – pacifism has always been a strong element in Welsh culture.) He despaired of the loss of the Welsh language in the Preseli area, and stood as a Plaid Cymru candidate.

Dylan Thomas is the Welsh poet in essence, throwing words around like confetti, unlike the more restrained (and Christian) R. S. Thomas. His radio play *Under Milk Wood*, was later filmed in Lower Fishguard with Elizabeth Taylor and Richard Burton. The boathouse near Laugharne Castle, where he wrote much of his work, is open to the public. Buried at Laugharne in a simple grave, many visitors go to Browns Hotel where he used to become famously drunk. He died, allegedly of alcoholic poisoning, on a reading tour of the United States, possibly burnt out as a poet. Evidence, discovered in 1997, points to the failure in not treating Thomas for a diabetic coma as the possible cause of his death.

Probably strongly influenced by Gerard Manley Hopkins, his writings are emotive and a link to Wales for anyone who leaves the country to find work. The free-form thought processes, refined by dozens of rewrites, have given us poetry that will last forever.

Dylan throws thoughts, ideas and words into a magical blender. His *Do Not Go Gentle Into That Good Night* was recently voted the second most popular poem written in English – he asked his dying father to '*rage, rage against the dying of the light*', as '*old age should burn and rave at close of day.*' In his short life (1914-1953) before he succumbed in the States, he kick-started Welsh poetry into word-plays never seen before in the English language. One could pick just about any passage from Dylan's prose and poetry and be thrilled with its spine-tingling *joie de vivre*:

> '*Years and years and years ago, when I was a boy, when there were wolves in Wales, and birds the colour of red-flanneled petticoats whisked past the harp-shaped hills . . . when we rode the daft and happy hills bareback, it snowed and snowed.*' (*A Child's Christmas in Wales*).

> '*It is spring, moonless night in the small town, starless and bible-black, the cobblestreets silent and the hunched, courters'-and-rabbits' wood limping invisible down to the sloeblack, slow, black, crowblack, fishing-boat bobbing sea.*' (*Under Milk Wood*).

> '*It was my thirtieth year to heaven, Woke to my hearing from harbour and neighbour wood And the mussel pooled and the heron Priested shore.*' (*Poem in October*).

> '*Though they go mad they shall be sane Though they sink through the sea they shall rise again; Though lovers be lost love shall not; And death shall have no dominion.*'

> (*And death shall have no dominion*).

Ceri Richards, in his wonderful suite of lithographs dedicated to Dylan Thomas, uses *Prologue* as his inspiration.

Alun Lewis of Aberdare (1915-1944) died of gunshot wounds in Burma, during the Second World War – his poems *In Hospital: Poona I, In Hospital: Poona II, Song (on seeing dead bodies floating off the Cape), Sacco Writes to His Son,* and *The Sentry* were all read by Dylan Thomas on BBC Radio. Like Edward Thomas, the war took him away too early, at the age of just 29 years. His poems have a recurring theme of isolation and death and he was indebted to Edward Thomas to whom he dedicated one of his best poems.

Vernon Phillips Watkins (1906-1967), called by some a 'neo-romantic' poet, was another Welshman rated very highly by his great friend Dylan Thomas. *The Collier* is a simple and moving poem about the effect of the pit on a young man with aspirations.

John Ormond Thomas (1923-1990), a superb and neglected poet, switched effortlessly between literature, academe and TV production. He made around 70 films, many on poets and painters like Graham Sutherland, Kyffin Williams and Vernon Watkins. John was awarded the Cholomondeley Award for English poetry in 1975.

His *Selected Poems* were short-listed for the Whitbread Prize on 1989. *Cathedral Builders* touched a chord with all Welshmen, where the workers stand well back from the glittering fat bishop at the consecration, and one stares up at the spire and mutters sotto voce '*I bloody did that*'. Possibly his crowning achievement was *Definition of a Waterfall*, a short poem which took several years to complete:

'*Not stitched to air or water but to both*
A veil hangs broken in concealing
   truth . . .'

R. S. Thomas, a poet-priest, was nominated for the 1996 Nobel Prize for Literature. Born in Cardiff in 1913, he studied classics at Bangor University. 'RS' became an Anglican priest in 1936, retiring in 1978. Now aged 84, he lives in the Llŷn Peninsula and is possibly the finest poet writing in English today, with no sign of any weakness in his powers to transfix the reader with visions of bleakness and beauty. He represents the uncompromising conscience of a Wales, under ceaseless alien attack, and tries to work out our difficult relationship with God.

His poem *Reservoirs* sums up his disgust with abandoned communities ('*smashed faces of farms*'), with the alien conifers of the Forestry Commission ('*gardens gone under the scum of forests*'), with tourist '*strangers*' to whom these reservoirs have '*the watercolour's appeal to the mass*'. He has become, over time, a committed Welsh Nationalist. R. S. Thomas displays a scorn for those complicitous in the loss of language, and the turning of Wales into some quaint theme parks for the richer, more sophisticated English:

'*Where can I go, then, from the smell*
Of decay, from the putrefying of a dead
Nation? I have walked the shore
For an hour and seen the English
Scavenging among the remains
Of our culture, covering the sand
Like the tide and, with the roughness
Of the tide, elbowing our language
Into the grave that we have dug for it.'

Ted Hughes wrote that R. S. Thomas's poetry '*pierces the heart*', and Thomas's indignation at the way history has treated the Welsh demonstrates this:

'. . . *an impotent people,*
Sick with inbreeding,
Worrying the carcass of an old song.'
(from *Welsh Landscape*, 1955)

Dannie Abse (b.1923), the Cardiff doctor and poet, has published at least six volumes of poetry, a novel and a volume of an autobiography.

POLITICS

Mention has been made of Jefferson's contribution to American democratic thought and his writing of the Declaration of Independence and the Constitution (see America).

A Welsh minister, **David Williams** of Eglwysilian, published *Letter of Political Liberty* in 1782, a schedule for revolution and reform. Its French translator was imprisoned in the Bastille, but after the Revolution, Williams was invited to Paris to assist in the writing of the new Constitution, and made an honorary citizen of France.

Observations on the Nature of Civil Liberty, by the radical writer **Dr Richard Price** of Llangeinor (1723-1791), influenced the French Jacobins, and when Price died the French Assembly went into mourning (see entries on America and Philosophers).

The Liberal Party surged into power in Wales with its opposition to landlords and anti-establishment policies, and by the turn of the 20th century was virtually in total control. The Liberal **David Lloyd George** had grown up in Llanstumudwy, near Cricieth. He introduced Old Age Pensions (1908) and National Health Insurance (1911) when Chancellor of the Exchequer from 1908-1915. Previously as Minister for the Board of Trade (1905-1908) he was responsible for the passing of three important acts involving merchant shipping, the production census and patents. The rejection of his budget by The House of Lords in 1909-1910 led to Parliamentary reform and a lessening of the nobility's power. A radical Welsh nationalist and a pacifist, he compared the Boers, in their fight against the Empire, to the Welsh. He only moved from pacifism with the invasion of Belgium by Germany in 1914.

After being Minister of Munitions, then Minister of War in 1915-1916, he became coalition Prime Minister from 1916 until his General Election defeat in 1922. By his forceful policy he was, as Adolf Hitler later said, '*the man who won the war*'. One of the 'Big Three' at the peace negotiations, he was shown to be a brilliant diplomat. His defeat in 1922 was mainly due to his ceding of 'The Irish Free State' – the modern day Eire was given its independence by him against strong opposition by the Conservatives in his government. Lloyd George is also notable in world history for approving the Balfour Declaration, promising the Jews a national state in Palestine. So Wales has had a world statesman who has changed the face of the twentieth century.

Clement Davies, who controlled Montgomery for years (even now this is one of the only two Liberal seats remaining in Wales), was leader of the Liberal Party in the House of Commons from 1945 to 1956, refusing ministerial office under Conservative governments in order to keep the Liberal Party separate. He conducted a brilliant parliamentary defence against Labour and Conservative colonial secretaries in support of Seretse Khama which led to Khama becoming Prime Minister of Bechuanaland and President, when it was renamed Botswana.

Merthyr, a town subjected to grinding oppression by the ironmasters, was the first town in Britain to elect a Socialist MP, **Keir Hardie** in 1900. With the coming of the Socialist/Labour Party, at last the people had a chance to protest against the right wing of the moneyed status quo. However, with Labour moving into the ground vacated by the Left Wing of the Conservative Party, it may be that Plaid Cymru poses the greatest threat to traditional Labour domination of the Welsh political scene. Certainly local Labour politicians see Plaid as the problem of the future.

Gwynfor Evans won Plaid Cymru's first seat, in Carmarthen, in 1966, and it now controls the old heartlands of the Princes of Gwynedd, with four MP's. Plaid is working steadily away at the local level to build up its base in the more highly populated areas of Wales.

The National Health Service, the jewel that was pioneered in Britain and copied in civilised countries all over the world, was largely based upon the example of a Welsh valley community scheme. Tuberculosis and pneumoconiosis were rife in nineteenth century Wales, but in Tredegar was established the Workmen's Medical Aid Society (with its own doctors), in the 1890s. Workers paid three old pence in the pound, equivalent to just over one per cent of their income, for dentistry services, spectacles and midwives. Its doctors included A. J. Cronin, who wrote about the scheme and its effects in *The Citadel*. In 1923, **Aneurin ('Nye') Bevan** was elected to the Hospital Committee, allied to the Medical Aid Society, and as Minister of Health just over three decades later, he launched the National Health Service.

A leader in the Welsh Miners' strike in The Great Strike of 1926, Bevan had become a Labour MP in 1931, and in World War II was frequently a *'one-man opposition'* to Winston Churchill. One of the most attractive aspects of Nye's personality was that he never tried to disguise his roots. Nye Bevan was unequivocal in his attachment to the working classes: *'No amount of cajolery, and no attempts at ethical and social seduction, can eradicate from my heart a deep burning hatred for the Tory Party . . . So far as I am concerned they are lower than vermin.'* Aneurin Bevan is commemorated in a statue at the West end of Cardiff's Queen Street.

Bevan resigned from the post-war Attlee Government over charges being introduced for teeth and spectacles. However, the real reason was the foreign and defence policy of that labour government. The scale of the arms budget, forced upon Britain by the U.S. government during the Korean War, was unsustainable. Even his implacable enemy Winston Churchill later acknowledged that Bevan was right.

The dominance of Labour on the Welsh political scene is shown in the voting at the last two General Elections.

Order of Voting	*1st*	*2nd*	*3rd*	*4th*
1992				
Labour	27	4	6	4
Conservative	6	28	–	4
Plaid	4	2	5	27
Liberal	1	4	23	10
Total Seats	38			

Order of Voting 1997	1st	2nd	3rd	4th
Labour	34	4	2	–
Plaid	4	5	3	28
Liberal	2	8	21	9
Conservative	–	23	14	3
Total Seats	40			

The swing from Liberal to Labour in Wales in the last century is demonstrated below, to show the solidity of the left-wing vote in Wales. The Liberals used to be the more left-wing party until Wales elected the first Labour MP, Keir Hardie.

Welsh MPs	Lab	Tory	Lib	Plaid	Other
1900	1	6	26		1
1906	1	–	28		4
1910 Jan	5	2	27		
1910 Dec	5	3	26		
1918	10	3	2		20
1922	18	6	2		3
1923	19	4	11		1
1924	16	9	10		
1929	25	1	9		
1931	15	6	8		6
1935	18	6	2		9
1945	27	3	4		1
1951	27	5	3		1
1955	27	5	3		1
1959	27	6	2		1
1964	28	6	2		
1966	32	3	1		
1970	27	7	1		1
1974 Feb	24	8	2	2	
1974 Oct	23	8	2	3	
1979	21	11	1	2	1 (The Speaker)
1983	20	14	2	2	
1987	24	8	3	3	
1992	27	6	1	4	
1997	34	–	2	4	

In the last 25 years, Conservative support in Wales in voting patterns has stayed between 25% and 32% – by the 1994 European Parliamentary elections it slumped to 14.6% of the vote, less than Plaid Cymru. In the 1995 elections to Wales's twenty-two new unitary councils, the Tories gained only 3% of the seats. All of Wales' five Members of the European Parliament are Labour.

In 1888, Keir Hardie (a Christian pacifist socialist who bitterly opposed the First World War) made a pledge on Home Rule and Devolution was 'pledge number 3' in Labour's General Election Manifesto in 1918. In 1924, Labour introduced its first devolution bill, but it was talked out. In 1929, the pledge on devolution had dropped to sixty-third position out of sixty-three in its General Election Manifesto, as the party realised that Wales and Scotland were easy votes for them. When Labour achieved power in 1945, it dropped its commitment to constitutional reform. Labour's proposals for a toothless Welsh Assembly in 1997 paralleled its 1978 Wales Bill, with the 1979 Referendum.

Before the 1997 election, the 'golden scenario' for Ron Davies, the Welsh Labour MP, was a totally Tory-free Welsh zone, as all Tory seats were in marginal Anglicised areas. The most marginal (a 19 seat majority), Vale of Glamorgan, had an English MP, Walter Sweeney. Ex-Tory MP Matthew Parris commented in *The Times* that '*Mr Sweeney is in the Tory Party, because as yet Parliament does not have a Neanderthal Party*'.

The largest Tory majority in Wales was six thousand and fifty in Clwyd North-West, held by Rod Richards, who resigned his Welsh Office post in 1996 after publicity of an adulterous affair. He memorably once called Welsh Labour councillors '*short, fat, slimy and fundamentally corrupt*' and had to make a belated apology. Both Sweeney and Richards and their four other Conservative colleagues lost their Welsh seats as MPs. The 1997 election blew away the remaining vestiges of the Conservative Party in Wales. Like Scotland, it now has no Tory MPs.

PRINCE OF WALES

Ystrad Fflur, Strata Florida Abbey, sees the annual celebration of 19th October 1238 which marked the voluntary unification of Wales where all the princes met there to swear allegiance to Llewelyn the Great and his son. In 1237, Llywelyn's wife Joan had died, and he had suffered a stroke, so he presented his son and heir Dafydd to all the other princes of Wales. Llywelyn had been recognized as overlord by King Henry III, and he wished to secure the succession before he retired as a monk to Aberconwy Abbey, where he died just two years later. Charles, the current Prince of Wales, refused an invitation to attend the celebration, because of prior commitments.

The last native Prince of Wales, Llywelyn ap Gruffydd, was killed in 1282. Edward I proclaimed his own son to be Prince of Wales in 1301. By the Statute of Rhuddlan in 1284, King Edward had declared all Welshmen subjects of the English Crown. The myth that Edward II was presented to the Welsh in 1284 as a baby in Caernarfon dates from 1584. This first Anglo-French Prince of Wales was invested at Lincoln when he was 17 years old. If his older brother Alphonso had survived, we would have seen a Prince Alphonso of Wales. Since this first investiture, all but one of the Princes of Wales have been French, English, German, and a mixture of all types of European nationalities except Welsh.

The one exception was Prince Arthur, the Welsh-speaking son of Henry VII, Harri Tudur, who died early, with his brother Henry VIII becoming King of England. Lady Diana Spencer, Princess of Wales, when berated by the English press for buying German cars, told Andrew Neil, editor of The Sunday Times, *'I think it's very unfair. After all, I married a German.'*

If one looks at the 'lineage' of minor German families that make up this present 'Prince' of Wales, one can see his Welsh connections. His mother was a Saxe-Coburg-Gotha (the family renamed itself Windsor when Britain was fighting the First World War against the Germans, for obvious reasons). Prince Charles's father was supposedly a Battenburg (Phillip's uncle, Lord Mountbatten, similarly changed his name from something less Germanic, and wanted Prince Charles to take the surname Mountbatten-Windsor). However, 'Duke' of Edinburgh Phillip Mountbatten's real surname is Schleswig-Holstein-Sonderburg-Glucksburg. As far as history is concerned, Charles Windsor, 'Prince of Wales', is really Charles Saxe-Coburg-Gotha-Schleswig-Holstein-Sonderburg-Glucksburg, 'Prince of anywhere-but-Wales'.

PRINCES AND KINGS OF GWYNEDD

The history of Gwynedd is the history of Welsh independence and language – its rocky crags, Anglesey with the royal court at Aberffraw and the Llŷn Peninsula are the real heart of Wales. As much as we know of the royal lineage is shown below, with those with separate headings italicised:

Ruler	From	To
Cunedda	c400	450
Einion Wyn		
Cadwallon Llawhir ab Einion		
Maelgwn Hir ap Cadwallon		549
Rhun ap Maelgwn		
Beli ap Rhun		
Iago ap Beli		616
Cadfan ab Iago		c625
Cadwallon ap Cadfan		635
Idris ap Gueinoth	635	637
Cadafael ap Cynfedw		655
Cadwaladr ap Cadafael	655	664
Cadwaladr Fendigaed ap Cadwallon		682
Idwal ap Cadwaladr ap Cadwallon		
Rhodri Molynwog ab Idwal		754
Caradog ap Meirion		798
Cynan Dindaethwy ap Rhodri		
Molwynog	798	816
Hywel Farf-fehinog ap caradog	798	825
Merfyn Frych ab Etthil ferch Cynan	825	844
Rhodri Fawr ap Merfyn Fach	844	878
Anarwd ap Rhodri	878	916
Idwal Foel ab Anarwd	916	942
Hywel Dda ap Cadell ap Rhodri	942	950
Iago ab Idwal Foel	950	979
Hywel ab Ieuaf ab Idwal Foel	979	985
Cadwallon ab Ieuaf ab Idwal Foel	985	986
Maredudd ab Owain ap Hywel Dda	986	999
Cynan ap Hywel ab Ieuaf	999	1004
Llywelyn ap Seisyll		1023
Iago ab Idwal ap Meurig ab Idwal Foel	1023	1039
Gruffydd ap Llewelyn ap Seisyll	1039	1063
Bleddyn ap Cynfyn	1063	1075
Trahaearn ap Caradog	1075	1081

Gruffydd ap Cynan ab Iago	1081	1137
Owain Gwynedd ap Gruffydd ap Cynan	1137	1170
Iorwerth Drwyndwn ab Owain, Cynan ab Owain, Dafydd ab Owain (Dafydd I), Maelgwyn ab Owain – sharing	1170	1195
Llywelyn Fawr ab Iorwerth (Llywelyn I)	1195	1240
Dafydd ap Llywelyn (Dafydd II)	1240	1246
Owain ap Gruffydd, Llywelyn ap Gruffydd – sharing	1246	1255
Llywelyn ap Gruffydd (Llywelyn II – Llywelyn the Last)	1255	1282
Dafydd ap Gruffydd (Dafydd III)	1282	1283

The last descendant of the House of Gwynedd, owing to the English attempts to kill off the family, was the grandson of Llywelyn ap Gruffydd's brother, Owain ap Rhodri. Owain Llaw Goch, (Owain Lawgoch) as he was known, was regarded as a 'mab dar-ogan' ('son of prophecy', or 'promised deliverer') by the Welsh, and styled himself as Prince of Wales. This Welsh hero spent much of his life outside Wales, fighting across Europe, until he was assassinated in 1378 on the orders of the English crown (see Assassination).

R

RAIL

A plaque in Raglan Church commemorates the first practical steam engine, built by the Marquis of Worcester at Raglan Castle in 1663.

The first recorded steam locomotive that ran, drew wagons with men at Penydarren, Mid Glamorgan, on 22nd February 1804. It was built by Richard Trevithick and predated George Stephenson's Locomotion by twenty-one years. The engine pulled ten tons of iron and seventy passengers from Merthyr Tydfil to Quaker's Yard at around five miles per hour.

The world's oldest passenger railway opened in 1807 in Mumbles, Swansea, and operated until 1960 after being bought by a competitor, South Wales Transport, a local bus company. Built by engineer Benjamin French, it ran along the front of Swansea Bay, from Swansea to Oystermouth. The railway made Mumbles famous in Victorian times. The first train was pulled by horses, then steam trains, then electric power. Plans are now under way, however, to run electric trams along part of the old Mumbles Railway route.

According to The Guinness Book of Records, John Drayton of Newport, Gwent, gave British Rail 31,400 suggestions for improvement between 1924 and 1987, of which one in seven were adopted. 100 were accepted by London Transport.

Britain's longest electric-powered Cliff Railway, at Aberystwyth, takes the visitor to the world's largest Camera Obscura, overlooking 1000 square miles of sea and landscapes, including twenty-six mountain peaks.

The summit of the Great Orme, Llandudno, can be reached by Britain's longest cable car (5320 feet) or by a funicular railway built in 1877. From the top one can watch guillemots, kittiwakes and razorbills on the cliff ledges.

Wales and West Regional Railways operates The Heart of Wales, one of the finest scenic rides in Britain, linking Shrewsbury with Swansea. Of equal quality is the Cambrian Coast Railway northwards along Cardigan Bay from Aberystwyth.

THE GREAT LITTLE TRAINS
OF WALES
Wales is famous for its narrow gauge steam railways, many built for transporting slate to the sea ports:

Talyllyn Railway – runs from Tywyn to Abergynolwyn in Snowdonia. Passengers can alight at Dolgoch to see the Dolgoch Falls. This railway has operated continuously since its opening in 1865. This former quarry train runs seven miles on 27 inch gauge around the foothills of Cader Idris. It is the oldest narrow gauge railway in the world, and formerly carried slate to Tywyn. When it came to the end of its working life in 1951, a group of enthusiasts, including the author of the *Thomas the Tank Engine* stories, bought the railway and kept it going. It carried three quarters of a million passengers in 1995.

Ffestiniog Railway – the oldest railway, climbs thirteen miles through wonderful scenery from Porthmadog to the slate town of Blaenau Ffestiniog. On 23.5 inch gauge, it links two British Rail lines, and passes in a long tunnel through a mountain of slate. From 1832 the trains ran down to the coastal port by gravity, before being hauled back up to the slate quarries by horses. In October 1863, the Princess and Mountaineer locomotives entered service and were followed by The Prince and Palmerston. Also in 1863, the Board of Trade gave permission for passenger trains to run along the railway, the first on a narrow gauge in Britain.

In 1870, some of the leading railway engineers of the time and the Imperial Russian Commission saw the first demonstration of the Fairlie double-engine Little Wonder, the forerunner of a new generation of Ffestiniog locomotives. The decline of the slate industry and World War Two lead to the line closing in 1946, but the line was restored from 1954, and the railway carried over 300,000 passengers in 1996.

The Welsh Highland Railway has been restored for a short section from Porthmadog on 24 inch track, and will stage exclusive *Ivor the Engine* days. The Millennium Commission has given a £4.3 million grant to help restore the service through the heart of Snowdonia, between Porthmadog and Caernarfon. The route will eventually be twenty-five miles of some of the most stunning scenery in Europe.

Snowdon Mountain Railway – from Llanberis to the summit of Snowdon, this is the only rack and pinion railway in Wales, on 27.5 inch gauge. Completed in 1896, the one in five climb takes the seventy year old engine and carriages about an hour. Its first engine came off its track, so the existing locomotives are known as Numbers 2, 3, 4 and 5.

Llanberis Lake Railway – a short 24 inch gauge section along Llyn Padarn has been restored, of what used to be

the slate line to Port Dinorwig on the Menai Straits.

Bala Lake Railway – from Bala to Llanuwchllyn, following the lakeside for four miles on 24 inch gauge, on what used to be the Bala-Corwen line.

Fairbourne and Barmouth Steam Railway – along sand dunes to the mouth of the Mawddach with a connecting ferry to Barmouth, this has the narrowest of narrow gauges, just over 12 inches (31cm). It was built as a horse-drawn tramway to carry building materials for the construction of Fairbourne, and steam was introduced in 1916. It is the last narrow-gauge boat train in Europe.

Brecon Mountain Railway – from Merthyr Tydfil up the Beacons, almost four miles of 24 inch track on the bed of the former Brecon and Merthyr Railway.

The Welshpool to Llanfaircaereinion Light Railway Line runs twelve miles, and was built in 1903 to enable local people to get their produce to Welshpool market. It descends nine miles to the River Banwy on 30 inch gauge.

Great Western Railway from Llangollen along the Dee Valley, on standard 56.5 inch gauge, this runs through the gorge of the Dee, and is being extended along the old Barmouth-Ruabon line.

The Vale of Rheidol Railway has been taking passengers from Aberystwyth to the beauty spot of Devil's Bridge since the early 1900s. This is a superb twelve mile run on 13.5 inch gauge.

The Teifi Valley Railway runs a short distance near Newcastle Emlyn.

The Pontypool and Blaenafon Steam Railway runs three quarters of a mile between two restored platforms, and the one hundred and ten year-old Crane Street Station at Pontypool is being transferred there, brick by brick.

The Vale of Glamorgan Line runs a short distance from Cardiff Bay, and hopefully will link up in future years across the old Vale line through Rhoose and Gileston.

RELIGION AND RELIGIOUS LEADERS

Mention has been made elsewhere (see entries on Cathedrals, Religion, Llan) of the fact that Wales was a Christian country before England was converted by Irish missionaries and St Augustine. Augustine prophesied doom for the Welsh in *The Anglo-Saxon Chronicle* when he said that *'if the Welsh will not be at peace with us, they shall perish at the hands of the Saxons'*.

The nascent Roman-English church hated its Celtic Christian predecessor, and called upon all the powers of Rome to subdue it by any means. The Roman missionary to England, Saint Augustine had also previously condemned these monks at the Synod of Chester for their refusal to bow to Rome. He wanted the Welsh to obey him as Archbishop of Canterbury and help him evangelise the English and drop some of the Church's customs. At his first meeting with the Welsh bishops, probably in Wiltshire in 602-603, he stated that *'The Brythons said they could not give up their customs without getting their people's consent.'* The bishops had tended to a Christian people for a hundred years after the Romans left, while the rest of Europe was heathen – as they saw it, they were the true keepers of Christianity, not this arrogant foreign priest.

Seven British bishops of the Celtic Church went to the second meeting with Augustine, c.604, with a large party of monks from the nearby monastery of Bangor-is-Coed. Bede told the tale of the bishops consulting a hermit before they met Augustine, as to whether they should follow this newcomer's ideas and authority. The hermit told them that they should follow Augustine *'if he is a man of God'*. The bishops asked how they would know, and the hermit quoted the Gospel according to Saint Matthew: *'Shoulder my yoke and learn from me, for I am gentle and humble in heart'*. If Augustine was gentle and humble, they should follow him as their Archbishop. If he was proud and severe, Christianity was not in him. They asked the hermit how to judge this, and he told the Celtic bishops to arrive late for the meeting. *'If he gets to his feet when you come to him, listen humbly to him, for he is the servant of God; but if he scorns you by remaining seated and not rising when you arrive, you being accompanied by a greater number than he is, then you must treat him with contempt.'*

Augustine did not rise, the Welsh did not follow him or listen to any of his recommendations for changing the date of Easter from the traditional one, for changing their method of tonsure, etc. As Gwynfor Evans stated in *Land of My Fathers*, spiritual pride was seen as the worst sin by the socialist Celtic Church and this arrogant Roman interloper threatened them with war. The Celtic Church remained intact until being largely broken up by the Normans eight hundred years later, and finally killed off by the Act of Union in 1536.

The Venerable Bede stated that the

Welsh had no desire to Christianise the pagan English and added in 731 that '*It is to this day the fashion among the Britons (Welsh) to reckon the faith and religion of Englishmen as naught and to hold no more converse with them than with the heathen*' (*Historia Ecclesiastica Gentis Anglorum*).

He went on to claim that '*The Britons for the most part have a natural hatred for the English and uphold their own bad customs against the true Easter of the Catholic Church; however they are opposed by the power of God and man alike.*' When he recorded the great Saxon victory by Aethelfrith at Chester in 613, he noted the English massacre of Welsh monks at Bangor-is-Coed for their sinful support of the Welsh King of Powys, Selyf. He recounted with some glee that 1200 of the 2100 monks were slaughtered by the pagan Aethelfrith. The Venerable Bede refers to what Welsh bards called 'The Massacre of the Saints', calling the Welsh '*treacherous men*', and their army '*an atrocious militia*'. This early rewrite of history shows Bede's massive prejudice against men defending their own country against foreign attack. He quotes the words of Aethelfrith when he urged his victorious soldiers to rampage through the great monastery, murdering the monks who were kneeling in prayer: '*If they call upon God against us they are fighting us as surely as those who bear arms*'.

Bede's abhorence of the Celtic Church was probably inflamed by his hatred of Pelagius and the famous Pelagian doctrine. Pelagius (c360-c420) was a British monk whose name was a Greek translation of the Celtic Morgan ('sea-born'). His European friends called him Brito, as he hailed from the Celtic Church of the Britons. Settling in Rome

about 400, he wrote *On the Trinity, On Testimonies* and *On the Pauline Epistles*. His doctrines were examined and he was accused of heresy before the synod of Jerusalem in 415. His heresy was that he did not believe in Original Sin or predestination, but in free will and in man's innate capacity to do good. This impeachment failed, so the Catholic authorities tried again at the synod of Carthage in 416. Pope Zosimus banished him from Rome in 418, but Pelagianism has often returned to plague the church authorities, particularly with Arminius and Jansen in the seventeenth century.

Pelagius was the first real critic of the Greek Orthodoxy of these times, and his contemporary St Augustine of Hippo was forced into formulating a repudiation of Pelagius. Bishop Honoratus of Arles tried to reconcile Pelagius and Augustine. With another Briton, Celestius, also later excommunicated, Pelagius believed '*si necessitas est, peccatum non est; si voluntatis, vitiari potest – if there be need, there is no sin; but if the will is there, then sinning is possible*'. Pelagius was condemned by the Venerable Bede, for his '*noxious and abominable teaching*'.

Hywel Harris (1714-1773) founded Welsh Calvinistic Methodism, and formed a Protestant monastery which he called his 'family' in Trefeca in 1752. **Hugh Price Hughes** (1847-1902) was a Welsh Wesleyan minister, born in Carmarthen. He founded 'The Methodist Times' and combined Methodism with socialism. He was a friend of Griffith Jones, who by his death had been responsible for educating 160,000 Welsh children. He was also a friend of William Williams of Pantycelyn, one of the greatest figures in Welsh literary history. Unfortunately, Harris's Calvinism was based on three important principles: God was supreme, only the pre-ordained would go to heaven, and man was utterly depraved. The Methodism which swept Wales almost killed off its culture, especially folk-dance, as all forms of enjoyment and closeness to the opposite sex were deemed sinful.

THE REWRITING OF HISTORY

The fact that nations rewrite their histories to suit nationalist principles is well-documented, and mentioned in the introduction to this book. To the sins of omission of early British/Welsh contributions to British history, we can trace a deliberate path of manipulation, distortion, suppression and destruction by Normans through to Hanoverians and Victorians, in a desperate attempt to gain legitimacy for conquering a nation. This sad strategy has been normal for all victorious countries – the Chinese in Tibet, the Australian settlers and Aborigines, the Indonesians and East Timor, the Spanish in South America and so on.

Many Welsh standing stones have been broken up, taken away or covered over. Old treasure hoards, showing remarkable Celtic artistry, have been lost or melted down. Very little early writing remains, compared to Eire. Much of what we know about the early saints, predating by hundreds of years the Roman Church of England, comes from the Breton *Vitae* (Lives of Saints).

As the Normans took over the great monasteries at Llancarfan and Llanilltud

Fawr (Llantwit Major), their treasures were taken to English abbeys, but their ancient libraries to The Tower of London. When Welsh princes were imprisoned in the Tower, they took their libraries with them, where they stayed. All of this information from the Dark Ages was destroyed by fire, by a monk called Ysgolan in 1300. Early non-Roman religion was suspect, tarred with the brush of Pelagianism (see Religion). These ancient Welsh books also conflicted with the view that Britain was heathen, before Rome and Augustine came to save its citizens. Of course, Viking raids such as those on St David's, Llancarfan and Llanilltud had damaged libraries, but much was recollected through the oral traditions and mnemonics that enabled the bards and monks to remember history. The next great threat was the Reformation and the Dissolution of the Monasteries. These events, along with the burning of the great libraries at Raglan and St Donat's castles, have destroyed many Welsh sources. The one man who did more to put everything back together, Edward Williams of Flemingston (Iolo Morganwg), has been savaged by academics, many with no Welsh language capabilities.

Richard II (1367-1400) attempted to ban writing in Wales, and his deposer Henry Bolingbroke (Henry IV) had an Act of Parliament passed prohibiting the importation of all writing materials and equipment into Wales. Richard III saw the danger of the invention of the printing press, and prohibited its use in Wales. Even though a Welsh King, Henry VII, defeated Richard in 1485, it was not until 1694 that an Act of Parliament allowed printing presses to be set up in Wales.

The Stuart and Hanoverian kings and queens related themselves back to Scottish origins, and had little interest in Welsh traditions and history, and even less in the language. When German George Hanover somehow became King of England in 1714, history changed in its teaching and emphasis. The *Bruts*, or Chronicles (see Literature, Brut y Tywysogion) and the twelfth century *History of the Kings of Britain* were no longer used as source materials. The Stuarts were still trying to regain the throne, backed by two Scottish rebellions in 1715 and 1789.

This new German dynasty had to be established in its rightful place to stop nationalist feelings flaring up in England. The 1789 French revolution reinforced this view, and the *Bruts* disappeared into the backwaters of knowledge. The marriage of Queen Victoria of Hanover to Prince Albert of Saxe-Coburg and Gotha sparked a 'Saxon' revival, with a cult growing up around King Alfred who led the Anglo-Saxons against the Vikings in the ninth century. (Incidentally, Alfred asked for Welsh scholars to set up what later became Oxford University, and insisted that the Welshman Asser, Bishop of St David's, moved to England to work with him as his advisor). The Victorians then suffixed Alfred 'the Great' and used his court's version of early British history *The Anglo-Saxon Chronicles*, rather than earlier or concurrent Welsh sources, for the early history of Britain. For instance, although Welsh sources identify King Arthur with Arthmael ap Meurig ap Tewdrig in south Wales, he is not mentioned in The Anglo-Saxon Chronicles, so real history was ignored.

After 'The Treachery of the Blue Books', Welsh teachers were replaced with English ones, and the disgusting 'Welsh Knot' instituted in schools for children caught speaking Welsh. In 1866, Bishop William Stubbs wrote *The Constitutional History of England*, revolutionising the teaching of British history from the 'noble' and civilising influence of the Romans to 1485. His Germanophile book was written to be the official curriculum for all schools – the history of Romans, Anglo-Saxons and Normans – not the history of the British people.

Bishop Stubbs further wrote, in his *Select Charters from the beginning to 1307* (Oxford 9th edition, published in 1931), the following piece of pre-Hitlerian dogma:

> 'The English nation is of distinctly Teutonic or German origin. The Angles, Jutes and Saxons . . . entered upon a land . . . whose inhabitants were enervated and demoralised by long dependence, wasted by successive pestilences, worn-out by the attacks of half-savage neighbours and by their own suicidal wars . . . This new race was the prime stock of our forefathers, sharing the primaeval German pride of purity of extraction . . . and strictly careful of the distinction between themselves and the tolerated remnant of their predecessors . . . It is unnecessary to suppose that any general intermixture either of Roman or British blood has affected this national identity . . . from the Briton and the Roman of the fifth century we have received nothing . . . The first traces, then, of our national history must be sought not in Britain but in Germany.'

The above demonstrates the worthlessness of the British, i.e. Celtic people. They count for nothing in history, and their 'Age of Saints', fighting off the pagan Saxons was merely 'enervating'. Welsh history of 'The Age of the Saints' and King Arthur was wiped from the record and replaced by the so-called 'Dark Ages', not worthy of mention.

The single major problem in researching the documents remaining that give us an insight into early Christianity, Caratacus, Arthur and the role of southeast Wales in leading the British defence against successive waves of barbarians, is that the sources are in too many places – London, Cardiff, Oxford, America, Aberystwyth and elsewhere. One of the great tragedies was the theft of Llandaf Cathedral's *Chartulary*, the illuminated manuscript that was the source of the old Llandaf Charters. It was stolen in the late seventeenth century and renamed the *Book of St Chad*, and is displayed at Lichfield Cathedral. It is a precious Welsh relic, annotated in the margins with notes about Welsh saints. The Llandaf Charters, a superb recounting of Welsh kings and saints, was collated from many sources by Galfrid in 1108, the principal one being the chartulary. Galfrid's original work is possibly now in the Vatican Library. St Chad was an English bishop of Lichfield who died in 672. In Ireland, we can see the fabulous *Book of Kells* in Trinity College Library, in a wonderful exhibition area. The Welsh equivalent was stolen by the Church of England, which will not return it.

The three major British treasures of the sixth century are The Book of Kells, The Lindisfarne Gospels and the Llandaf Charters. It is time that the Charters were returned to Wales as a great tourist attraction and reminder of our past. There is constant pressure for The Lindisfarne Gospels to go home to the north-east of England from London. Why is there no such pressure for the stolen Llandaf opus?

RHODRI MAWR – RHODRI AP MERFYN FRYCH AP GWRIAD – RHODRI THE GREAT (820-878)

Possibly because of the lasting Roman influence in Wales, and their much later adoption of Christianity, the Saxons and neighbouring Mercians were regarded as uncultured and aggressive pagans by the Welsh, but the border held against them, albeit with some fluidity. There were also constant Pictish attacks on the coastal areas of Wales. However, the next severe threat to Wales was that of the Norsemen, whose first recorded attack was in 850. Merfyn Frych spent his reign fighting against the Danes and Mercians, and fell at Cetyll against Burchred of Mercia in 844.

Rhodri Mawr unified most of Wales to move it towards statehood, thanks in part to the need to fight this Viking threat. A descendant of Llywarch Hen, the warrior-bard, he had succeeded his father in 844, and it is notable that Wales achieved national unity under him, whereas England had to wait for statehood until the coronation of Edgar at Bath in 973. Rhodri was the only Welsh King to be called 'The Great', and earned thanks from Charlemagne for his victories against the Viking threat, killing the Viking leader Horm, off Anglesey in 856. (Orme's Head at Llandudno may be named after Horm). In fact, Alfred and Charlemagne were the only other rulers to be bestowed with the title of 'Great' in this century. Nora Chadwick called Rhodri *'the greatest of all the kings of Wales'*.

Until his death in battle in 878, he held Wales together, even making an alliance with King Alfred of Wessex against the Norsemen. He had assumed the throne of Gwynedd upon his father's death, taken control of Powys upon the death of his uncle Cyngen (on a pilgrimage to Rome) in 872, and ruled Seisyllwg from 872 when he married the sister of its last king. Now leader of nearly all Wales, his inherent hatred of Mercians led him to ally himself with the Danes against a Mercian invasion in 878, and he died in battle against them, protecting Powys from invasion. His son Gwriad fell at his side.

His dominions were divided, with Anarawd becoming King of Gwynedd, Cadell King of Deheubarth, and Merfyn King of Powys. Three years later at the Battle of Conway, the Welsh victory under Anarawd was known as *Dial Rhodri* ('Rhodri's Revenge') – 'God's vengeance for the slaughter of Rhodri'.

The practice of partible inheritance, gavelkind, meant that each of Rhodri's six sons had a part of Wales to control. Unusually for Welsh sons, they seemed to work well together, with the result that Rhodri's grandson, Hwyel Dda eventually came to rule Wales.

The Viking raids carried on until 918, and the rule of Hywel Dda, and restarted on his death in 952, especially focusing upon Welsh monasteries. St David's Cathedral was sacked by them for the sixth time, as late as 1091.

RHYS AP GRUFFYDD – ARGLWYDD RHYS – THE LORD RHYS (1132-1197)

In 1136, Gwenllian led her army against the Normans at Cydweli. One son was killed, another imprisoned, and towards the end of the fighting, she was captured and executed. The battlefield is still called Maes Gwenllian, a mile from the castle, and a stone marks the place of her death. She left a four year-old son, to be known as 'The Lord Rhys', the grandson of Rhys Tewdwr who was slain by the Normans at Brycheiniog in 1093. His father was Gruffydd ap Rhys, who was named 'Gruffydd the Wanderer' from his days in hiding in the great forest of Ystrad Tawi. He died in the same year as Gwenllian, so their remaining children were brought up by Owain Gwynedd. Rhys was born in 1132, and grew up in the shadow of his uncle Owain Gwynedd, but from Owain's death in 1170 until his own death in 1197 was the pre-eminent Welsh leader, based in the castle he built at Dryslwyn and his principal residence at Cardigan.

After Gruffydd's death in 1137, his four sons worked together to consolidate the princedom of Deheubarth. However, Anarawd was assassinated by raiders from North Wales in 1143, Cadell was severely wounded by Normans from Tenby after reconquering Ceredigion, and Maredudd died in 1155, leaving Rhys in charge. Rhys burnt Cydweli Castle in 1159, to avenge his mother's execution, and thirty years later rebuilt it. However, from this time, there was heavy pressure from King Henry II until 1165. Cantref Bychan and Ceredigion were restored to their Norman lords, but Rhys successfully attacked Llandovery in 1162.

Gwenllian had operated out of the forests of Caio, retaking Welsh land until her death at Cydweli. Her efforts and death had served to build bonds between rival Welsh princes, rather like Jeanne d'Arc in France. In 1167, the Princes of Gwynedd, Powys and Deheubarth had united, putting aside their normal quarrels. Their army, led by The Lord Rhys and Owain Gwynedd, annihilated an invasion force in the Berwyn Hills. The aggressors were made up of armies from England, Scotland, Flanders, Anjou, Gascony and Normandy, supported by a Danish fleet and financed by London merchants. King Henry blinded two of Rhys' hostage children in revenge, along with two of Owain Gwynedd's sons.

This victory brought home to the Welsh a need for a united front, and Rhys took over leadership upon Owain Gwynedd's death. Like Hywel Dda with the Saxons, he realised the necessity of friendship and accommodation with the Normans to preserve Welsh independence, and diplomatically befriended Henry II. He allowed Henry through Wales on his way to Ireland in 1171, and Henry in turn officially recognised Rhys as ruler of Deheubarth. Ceredigion and other territories were restored to the house of Deheubarth. On Henry's return, he appointed Rhys Justiciar of South Wales, in return for Rhys' support. This gave Rhys effective overlordship of most of South Wales including Glamorgan and Gwent.

Rhys held the first Eisteddfod that can be authenticated in Cardigan in 1176 (where his father is also said to have held this great event), and twelve years later entertained Giraldus Cambrensis and Archbishop Baldwin of Canterbury. Also know as Rhys *Mwyn Fawr* ('The Greatly Courteous'), he established the Abbey of Ystrad Fflur (Strata Florida) in Ceredigion (Cardiganshire) in 1186.

After Henry II's death, Rhys gained more of Wales back from the Norman Marcher Lords, campaigning constantly. In 1196 the Normans of the East encroached on his territories, under Roger Mortimer and Hugh de Say. He put them to flight, capturing Painscastle and burning Maes Hyfaidd.

He died aged around sixty-five in 1197, hailed as the chieftain who did more than any to preserve South Wales from the Normans. He was also renowned as a patron of bards and monks, and was commemorated as '*the head, and the shield, and the strength of the south, and of all Cymru; and the hope and defence of all the tribes of the Britons'*.

His tomb is in St David's Cathedral, along with that of Giraldus Cambrensis. Rhys ap Gruffydd's effigy is the recumbent figure of a knight in the north presbytery. Strangely enough, just like Owain Gwynedd, he died in a state of excommunication, mainly because of a quarrel with Bishop Peter. However, the Celtic Church still buried him, like Owain Gwynedd, in a cathedral despite the wishes of Canterbury.

Upon Rhys' death, the ruling power in Wales passed to the royal line of Powys, in the shape of Madog ap Maredudd, who is described in *The Dream of Rhonabwy* in the Mabinogion. From Madog, power passed to Owain Cyfeiliog, his nephew, and a poet who consolidated Powys. Owain Cyfeiliog was also excommunicated by Canterbury, but was buried in at Ystrad Marchell, the Cistercian Abbey he had founded. The violent Gwenwynwyn of Powys succeeded (he features in Walter Scott's novel *The Betrothed*), but he was decisively defeated. Leadership of Wales passed from Deheubarth and Powys back to the House of Gwynedd – to Llywelyn the Great.

RIOTS

A melange of people, from all over Britain, had flocked for work to Merthyr, Wrexham, Swansea, Neath, Monmouthshire and the Rhondda Valleys in the Industrial Revolution. Faced with appalling working conditions, having to buy all their provisions at company-owned high-priced 'truck shops', and living at poverty levels in shanty towns, there was political upheaval – the awakenings of real and persistent social discontent. In 1793, hundreds of copper workers and miners marched to Swansea protesting about the high price of grain, cheese and butter, but were dispersed. Three Merthyr men were executed for rioting in 1801. After the 1815 Corn Laws which pushed bread to artificially high prices for the benefit of landed interests, the situation became worse. In the 1820s fifty men from the Neath Abbey steelworks were sacked for trying to form a union, and *The Cambrian*, Wales' leading newspaper called their leaders *'gin-swilling degenerates'*. The Calvinistic Methodists called union activity *'devilish'*, but by 1831 a Merthyr miner told the magistrate that *'My Lord, the union is so important to me that I would live on sixpence a week rather than give it up.'*

Serious violence broke out at Merthyr Tydfil in 1831. Troops were called in, and after two pitched battles, order was restored. In the brutal suppression, over twenty were killed, more than in the 'Peterloo Massacre' of Manchester Weavers in 1819, but Welsh deaths did not receive anything like the same publicity or notoriety in history.

THE MERTHYR RISING

The Great Depression of 1829 led to massive unemployment and wage cuts, making the working classes even more indebted to their masters. William Crawshay had lowered wages at his Merthyr iron foundries, there was a crisis among tradesmen and shopkeepers, and the Debtor's Court was busy confiscating workers' property to pay off debts. Thomas Llywelyn, a miner, demanded compensation and led a demonstration that released prisoners and marched on Aberdare. At the same time in nearby Hirwaun, when the Debtors' Court had seized the truck of Lewis Lewis, miners, iron workers and tradesmen joined the political radicals – they had had enough.

In this year of 1831, in The Merthyr Rising, hungry iron and coal workers took over the town for five days, and paraded under a sheet daubed symbolically with the blood of a lamb and a calf. On its staff was impaled a loaf of bread, showing the needs of the marchers. This was probably the first time that the 'red flag' of revolution was raised in Britain. (It may the first time anywhere in the world). A ten thousand-strong crowd battled with soldiers at the Castle Inn in August 1831, and up to two dozen men, women and children died in the fighting. Unemployment and reduced wages had fomented the unrest, and the workers burnt Court records and their employers' property. The tyrannical ironmasters Crawshay and Guest were locked up in the Castle Inn, defended by Scottish soldiers, who opened fire on the mob. The Argyll and Sutherland Highlanders were reinforced by the Glamorgan Yeomanry, and the supporting Swansea Yeomanry were forced back to Neath. Major Richards called out the equivalent of the Home Guard, the Llantrisant Cavalry, to rescue the regular soldiers, who sustained no losses.

Lewis Lewis, the truck owner whose loss sparked off the initial revolt, was sentenced to death, commuted to exile for life. A 23-year-old collier, Dic Penderyn (Richard Lewis) was accused of riotous assault and a 'felonious' attack upon Private Don Black of the 93rd Highland Regiment. Dic Penderyn was hanged at Cardiff, his last words being *'Arglwydd, dyma gamwedd'* ('Oh God, what an injustice'), as an example *pour les autres.* Other defendants were transported to Australia. Forty years later, an immigrant from Merthyr, Ieuan Evans, confessed on his deathbed in the USA that it was he that wounded the soldier. The carter who took Penderyn's body back to Aberafan asked to be, and is, buried next to Dic Penderyn in the churchyard of St Mary's.

The Merthyr Rising was described by John Davies as *'the most ferocious and bloody event in the history of industrialised Britain.'* Gwyn Williams pointed out that *'these defeats inflicted on regular and militia troops by armed rioters have no parallel in recent British history.'* Publicity was suppressed – after all the starving Welsh working class did not matter in the grand scheme of things. In June 1831 a Mrs Arbuthnot noted in her diary: *'There has been a great riot in Wales and the soldiers have killed twenty-four people. When two or three were killed at Manchester, it was called the Peterloo Massacre and the newspapers for weeks wrote it up as the most outrageous and wicked proceeding ever heard of. But that was in Tory times; now this Welsh riot is scarcely mentioned.'* Gwyn Williams commented that *'bodies were being buried secretly all over north Glamorgan . . . widows did not dare claim poor relief.'*

SCOTCH CATTLE

Around the same time in Monmouthshire, arose the mysterious 'Scotch Cattle' raiders dressed in animal skins and women's clothes, with blackened faces. The leader of each group, Tarw (Bull) wore horns on his head, and they would attack unpopular managers, unfair employers, strike-breakers and profiteers, and smash windows and furniture, around midnight. For fifteen years in the 1820s and 30s this secret society of separate 'herds' organised strikes, frightened blacklegs and employers but 'Scotch Law' held, whereby no-one was ever betrayed to the authorities.

Dr D. J. V. James, in *Rebecca's Children,* describes a typical visit to blacklegs, strike-breakers, or non-supporters of strikes . . . *'The leaders of the party were disguised by masks, handkerchiefs, and cattle skins; the remained had blackened faces, and wore women's clothes, 'their best clothes', or simple reversed jackets. They announced their arrival by blowing a horn, rattling chains, and making 'low' noises. At the home of their victim the Cattle smashed the windows with stones or pickaxes and broke down the door. Once inside, it was a relatively easy matter to destroy the furniture and earthenware, and to set fire to clothes and curtaining. The inhabitant might be ill-treated or given a further warning; then the Cattle disappeared as quickly as they had arrived, leaving their glistening red mark on the open door.'* The movement petered out in 1835, when a miner, Edward Morgan, was hanged in Monmouth for his part in a disturbance.

CHARTISM

This new working-class militancy was a strong breeding ground for the doomed Chartist Movement. Chartism was a campaign for basic human rights in the 19th century. The 1838 People's Charter called for universal male franchise, payment of MP's, equal electoral districts, secret elections and the abolition of property qualifications to vote. Llanidloes was a hotbed of Chartist activity, and the mayor asked for three policemen to be sent from London, *'a course which combined the maximum of irritation with the minimum of security'* according to a local commentator. Mayor Thomas Marsh had already appointed three hundred local special constables, fearing a threat to the established order. In 1839, Marsh provoked a riot, and the three policemen were briefly held imprisoned in the Trewythen Arms, for which three ringleaders were transported for fifteen years. The mob had controlled Llanidloes for a few days before troops from Brecon had restored order.

Most activity supporting Chartism, trying to stop wealthy landowners buying votes from the enfranchised few, took place in the industrialised parts of South Wales. Newport's Chartist Uprising ended when troops killed twenty-four Chartists. The seven thousand marchers, mainly miners, came down Stow Hill to be met by a hail of bullets by soldiers hiding in The Westgate Hotel. Queen Victoria knighted the mayor, who gave the order to shoot the marchers, whose eight ringleaders were sentenced to be hung, drawn and quartered. This was in 1839. The political show-trial was called by Michael Foot *'the biggest class-war clash of the century'*. Public protest led to the sentence being commuted to transportation for life without a last meeting with their families. The historian, Macaulay, called the ringleaders *'great criminals . . . who would, if their attempt had not been stopped at the outset, have caused such a destruction of life and property as had not been known in England for ages.'*

Just like the Merthyr Rising, there was negligible publicity in England. As Coupland says: *'Nothing happened in England to match the march of some five thousand Welshmen down from the coal valleys through the darkness and drenching rain of a winter night to Newport . . . nobody remarked that the trouble was suppressed by English soldiers who were paid to do it and shot down twenty Welshmen and wounded several others in the doing.'*

One million, four hundred thousand people signed a petition asking for the pardon of the ringleaders, but most died as convicts in Australia. John Frost, a former Mayor of Newport and JP, was pardoned when he was seventy-one and returned to be honoured in Newport, being carted through the town in a flower-bedecked carriage. It was drawn by his former Chartist comrades. The main square in Newport is now named after him, and you can still see bullet holes in the Westgate Hotel. The Corn Laws were repealed in 1846, making bread cheaper, and 1867s Great Reform Bill doubled the electorate, adding another one million voters. At last some working people could vote – Chartism had helped change British history.

The Anglicisation of Newport and its environs since this time has been rapid. John Frost had addressed the Chartists in Welsh, and Gwent, even on its Herefordshire borders, was a Welsh-speaking county. A few years earlier, Iolo Morganwg had stated that Gwent had the highest proportion of monoglot Welsh speakers of all the counties in Wales. (It is now probably the most Anglicised county).

In 1847, the Government's official 'Report on the State of Education in Wales' at least apportioned some blame for the rise of Chartism: *'I regard the degraded condition (of the people of Monmouthshire) as entirely the fault of their employers, who give them far less tendance and care that they bestow on their cattle, and who with few exceptions, use and regard them as so much brute force instrumental to wealth, but as no wise involving claims upon humanity'* . . . *'Brynmawr contains 5000 people, nearly all of whom are the lowest class . . . Not the slightest step has been taken to improve the mental or moral conditions of this violent and vicious community'*. At this time, the ironmasters and colliery owners like Crawshaw Bailey were living in heavily defended castles and mansions, guarded from the hatred of their employees.

THE REBECCA RIOTS

In rural West Wales, rioting took place against the hated toll gates and work-houses, simultaneously supporting the Chartist protests. This last peasant revolt in Britain began at the hamlet of Efailwen, with the destruction of the tollgate and burning of the tollhouse, in May 1839. Improvements to roads were necessary, and roads had been put in charge of 'road trusts'. These made their profits from large numbers of toll gates, set up along the roads. Local farmers were crippled by the charges, and could not afford to take their produce or herds to market. Local uprisings occurred, with groups of men dressed in skirts with blackened faces, demolishing turnpikes and toll gates. The leader was thought to be Thomas Rees, known as Twm Carnabwth, and their targets also included some of the hated workhouses in South West Wales. (Many tollhouses can still be seen, often hexagonal in shape, and converted to private houses).

These 'Daughters of Rebecca' were such a force that the government moved quickly to reduce and make uniform the tolls. Genesis XXIV, 60 states: *'And they blessed Rebekah and said to her, "Thou are our sister, be thou the mother of thousands of millions, and let thy seed possess the gates of those which hate them".'* The leader of each band of night raiders was called Rebecca, and his followers 'daughters'. These mounted raiders were sick of heavy taxes, tithes to an alien church, high rents to English absentee landlords, the acceleration of enclosure of common land where they could once graze their animals, the English placemen who served as priests, landlords and judges, the price of bread and so on. Anglican clergymen were sent letters addressed to 'Ministers of the National Whore.'

A statement in *The Welshman* in 1843 expressed the feelings of the demonstrators: *'The people, the masses, to a man throughout the counties of Carmarthen, Cardigan and Pembroke are with me. O yes, they are all my children . . . Surely, say I, these are members of my family, these are the oppressed sons and daughters of Rebecca.'*

The toll gates had finally tipped the balance from passive acceptance to action in 1839. Finding the official authorities helpless against the code of silence that protected them, the Maids of Rebecca extended their activities to encompass social justice. They made fathers pay for illegitimate children, or even marry the women involved. Unjust sentences were righted, men were made to go back to their wives, a family bible seized for non-payment of tithes was returned. Only when some ringleaders were transported to Australia for life (Shoni Sgubor Fawr, Dai'r Cantwr and Jac Tŷ-isha) did the dissent slowly fade away, but an 1844 Act of Parliament did reform the iniquitous toll road system.

Dai'r Cantwr (David the Singer) was born David Davies at Treguff near Llancarfan. A farm labourer and local preacher, he also taught people to sing and led the church choir. Tried at the Carmarthenshire Sessions with thirty-nine others, he was found guilty of destroying the gates at Spudder's Bridge. He was chained by each leg to another prisoner, moved to London and then went on a horrific seventeen week journey to Tasmania. While in prison, he composed several songs, one of which was sold in village fairs all over Wales *Cân Hiraeth y Bardd am ei Wlad* ('The Poet's Longing for his Country'). Also in prison he wrote, *'The fame which might have been mine, I have forfeited, and no more will I see Llancarfan the haunts of my youth.'* He never returned to Wales.

Gelli-Goch, near Machynlleth, is the birthplace of Hugh Williams (1796-1874). In Carmarthenshire, Williams was supposed to have been the mastermind behind Rebecca and her children. Openly sympathetic, as a solicitor he defended any protesters brought to court, without taking any fees. He compiled an anthology of radical verse, addressed Working Men's Association and Chartist meetings and was watched by the police.

THE TONYPANDY RIOT

In 1910 there was another rising for which Winston Churchill is still hated by many of those with a knowledge of Welsh history, for sending in troops with fixed bayonets to restore order. Upon 8th November, more than sixty shops were attacked by miners and one collier, Samuel Rays was killed by police. Colonel Lindsay, Chief Constable of Glamorgan, had asked the Home Secretary, to send troops to restore order. First, Churchill had sent mounted police and London policemen, and then troops. The friendship between army officers and pit owners was noted in these days of repression. *The Times* recorded that there was in the Rhondda: *'the same oppressive atmosphere that one experienced in the streets of Odessa and Sebastopol during the unrest in Russia in the winter of 1904. It is extraordinary to find it here in the British Isles.'*

This period of 'The Great Unrest' amongst an impoverished and overworked people also saw major disturbances in the Cynon Valley, a riot among seamen in Cardiff docks in 1911, and the Llanelli Riot. When a crowd harassed the occupying soldiers, two young Llanelli men were shot and killed. It was just two days since the start of the National Railway Strike of 1911, which ended on the night of the killings. The 2.30 train from Cardiff to Milford haven had been stopped, and the 1st battalion of the Worcester Regiment had been called in to disperse the rioters. The troops were ordered to fire at the people, and Private Harold Spiers, a Welshman, refused to do so upon unarmed civilians. John Francis was hit in the throat, Ben Hanbury in the hand. John John and Leonard Wurzel were killed. This occurred while no-one was threatening the troops. It was the last time that workers in Britain were shot and killed by the army in an industrial dispute. Following this, ninety-six trucks were destroyed, shops were damaged and four people killed in an explosion. On the same day and following, there was disorder in Tredegar, Bargoed and across the coalfield. Thousands lined the streets of Llanelli for the funerals.

Spiers had been arrested for refusing to fire into the crowd, but escaped from his guards, and was re-arrested two weeks later in New Radnor. He was charged and tried for desertion, but a couple of days later there was a report in *The South Wales Daily News*, stating: '*We are officially requested to deny the statement made by Private Spiers on his arrest*' . . . '*Spiers was never ordered to fire by the Officer in Charge. It is extremely doubtful whether he was amongst the troops on the Railway at all, and he was not under arrest at the time he deserted*'.

This farrago of lies was concocted by Winston Churchill, the Home Secretary, who did not wish to make Spiers into an imprisoned working class hero (according to recently released Public Records Office papers). Churchill was already hated throughout South Wales for sending the troops into Tonypandy in 1910, and was an ambitious politician. In a Parliamentary reply in December 1911, a War Office official firmly denied that any soldier in Llanelli had refused to fire, but stated that Spiers had been imprisoned for two weeks for going absent without leave. Also in December, Spiers bought himself out of the army, but enlisted again and fought throughout the First World War.

All these attempts for a people to control part of its own destiny are virtually forgotten. However, the feeling of inequity has always persisted in Wales. The last people to hold out in the Great Strike of 1926 were the Welsh miners. The last pits to return in the last coal strike of 1984 were Welsh (see Coal).

RIVERS

The longest river in Britain, the Severn (Hafren) begins in Pumlimon's foothills on the West coast, cuts across to Shrewsbury (Pengwern), and follows the Welsh borders to exit into the Bristol channel, a journey of 220 miles (354 km). The Wye (Gwy) follows a similar route from Pumlimon for 130 miles. The Dee (Dyfrdwy) runs 111 miles from Llyn Tegid (Lake Bala) to the Wirral in Lancashire. The River Mynwy (Monmow) is 35 miles long and forms part of the Anglo-Welsh boundary.

Cardiff is unusual for a Capital City in that it sees the exit of three rivers, the Taff or Taf (41 miles), Rhymni (36 miles) and Elai (Ely, 26 miles). Other major Welsh rivers are the Wysg (Usk 85 miles), Teifi (73 miles), Tywi (68 miles), Clwyd (40 miles), Dyfi (Dovey 37 miles), Ithon (37 miles), Alyn (36 miles), Conwy (36 miles), Taf (35 miles) and Cothi (34 miles). Wales is a fisherman's paradise, especially for salmon and sewin (sea-trout), and the following rivers are all over 25 miles in length – Elwy, Tawe, Ebbw, Nedd (Neath), Llwchwr (Loughor), Rheidol and Irfon.

There are estimated to be fifteen thousand miles of rivers in Wales. They are of international ecological importance, fed by Wales's estimated one metre rainfall per year. The Elan Valleys were dammed to supply Birmingham in the English midlands. England, with a dryer climate and twenty-five times the population, needs more water, especially in its Thames region. The problem is that Wales could have rivers like the River Kennett, which in Swindon, Wiltshire, has been drained dry by Thames Water. Since the 1970s England has been looking again at Wales for water. There is a plan to use Carreg Goch to supply Birmingham, to build up the level by Severn-Trent Water, and destroy landscape of European importance. A sequence of valleys like Trywerin have been flooded to supply English industry.

ROBBERS

Tregaron-born **Twm Sion Cati** (c.1530-1609), the 'Welsh Robin Hood', used to hide in a cave on Dinas Hill, near Llyn Brianne, from the Sheriff of Carmarthen. Dinas Hill is now a Royal Society for the Protection of Birds Sanctuary, near the beautiful Rhandirmwyn and Llyn Brianne. An educated but illegitimate squire's son, he was a highwayman for a few years, supposedly only robbing the rich. Twm's mother was named Catherin, so he was nick-named 'Cati' after her, but his full name was Sion ap Dafydd ap Madog ap Hywel Moetheu of Porth-y-Ffin. In 1559 Twm was officially pardoned for his crimes. There are many stories and legends about his trickery in his 'bandit years' before he became 'respectable'. He retired near Cilycwm, as Thomas Jones, a respected Justice of the Peace, landlord, poet and historian, noted for his knowledge of genealogy and heraldry. It is interesting that Robin Hood is the subject of a Disney film and a thriving tourist industry, but never existed, whereas Twm Sion Cati is unknown. The Dinas RSBP bird sanctuary with Twm's cave has goosanders, golden ringed dragonflies, dippers, common sandpipers, pied flycatchers, polecats, peregrine falcons, purple hairstreak butterflies and redstarts, around where the River Tywi joins the River Doethie. Often red kites can also be seen – it is a marvellous part of Wales.

In the 16th century a band called **Gwylliaid Cochion Mawddwy** ('the Red-haired Robbers of Mallwyd') terrorised Mid-Wales, before many were caught and executed by Baron Lewis Owen. Around eighty were rounded up and condemned at a place where the house Collfryn ('Hill of Loss') stands. They were hanged in 1554 two miles from Mallwyd on Rhos Goch ('Red', or 'Bloody Moor') and a mound, 'Boncyn-y-Gwylliad', is supposedly where they were buried en masse. A few weeks later, the baron was ambushed and murdered by surviving members at *Llidiart-y-Barwn* ('the Baron's Gate') near Mallwyd. As well as Llidiart-y-Barwn, the nearby Brigands' Inn is named after these red-headed rogues. Local place names recalling the event abound, such as Mwynt y Gwylliad (where there is an old cemetery), Pont y Lladron ('Bridge of Thieves'), Sarn y Gwylliad (a ford), Ffynnon y Gwylliad (a well) and Ceunant y Gwylliad (a ravine). People with red hair in Merioneth and Montgomery are still sometimes called 'red bandits'.

ROME

In 55BC, Julius Caesar invaded Britain, and wrote in his 'Gallic Wars' that '*All the Britons paint themselves with woad, which gives their skin a bluish colour and makes them look dreadful in battle.'*

Caractacus (Caradoc), son of Cunobelinus (Cymbeline) fought against the Roman invasion of Britain from AD43-50, but was betrayed by Cartimandua, Queen of the Brigantes of the North of England. He was exhibited in triumph by the Emperor Claudius in Rome, and died about AD54. Tacitus refers to the legions being awestruck at their first sight of the druids, being *'ranged in order, with their hands uplifted, invoking the gods and pouring forth horrible imprecations'*.

Roman influences in Wales run from the language (see Language) to places beginning with Caer (see Caer) to the effects on surnames (Sextilius > Seisyllt > Cecil) and Christian Names (Justinus, Justinian to Iestyn). Magnus Maximus, the commander at Caernarfon, was accompanied by a Welsh bodyguard when he invaded the Continent in AD381 to claim the Imperial Throne. He left the government of Wales in the hands of Romanised Welshmen, thereby Wales was the first Roman territory to attain peaceful self-government. He was killed at Aquileia in 388, and is known in Welsh history as Macsen Wledig, a hero of the Welsh, from whom later princes claimed descendence. One of the most famous Welsh medieval stories, *The Dream of Macsen Wledig*, refers to Segontium, the Roman fort of Caernarfon.

Within a hundred years, around 510, the Emperor Honorius had no troops to spare for British garrisons, and the Welsh nation came into existence. With the final withdrawal of Rome, Britain found itself divided into three areas; Gaelic/Goidelic Scotland, Germanic England and Brythonic Wales, Strathclyde and Cornwall.

RUGBY

Rugby Union has always been regarded as Wales's national game. Wales's current coach the New Zealander, Graham Henry, was quoted as saying: *'Rugby is not part of Welsh culture; it is Welsh culture'*.

It is believed that rugby was first played at St David's College in Lampeter in 1850, after a Reverend Williams introduced the game he had played at Cambridge University.

The first club to be formed was Neath in 1871 and the first rugby organisation was established in 1874. This was the South Wales Football Union and became the Welsh Rugby Union (WRU) in 1881. That body selected a Welsh team to play England in the same year.

In the late 1870s large crowds would attend matches in the South Wales Challenge Cup, but due to local rivalry with violent outbreaks both on and off the field the tournament was abandoned in the late 1880s.

At a similar time there were disputes between the Home Nation Unions over alleged Welsh professionalism and international matches were cancelled. However, after the differences were resolved Wales recommenced its international programme and the period between 1900-11 brought Wales its first 'Golden Era'. During the recession of the 1920s and 30s the game waned but after the Second World War there was a major revival with games such as the 1951 Cardiff vs. Newport attracting a crowd of nearly 50,000, a Welsh club record.

Wales's recent and second most 'golden age' was during the 1970s. Then it seemed that Wales were playing magical rugby. Indeed, possibly the try of the century, that scored by the Barbarians against New Zealand, featured six Welsh internationals in a passing movement that covered the field.

The dream half-back pairing of Barry John and Gareth Edwards was ended when 'King' John retired prematurely from the game. Edwards went on to make a record 53 consecutive appearances from 1967 to 1978, when he retired. J. P. R. Williams, who brought an attacking dimension to full-back play, holds the Welsh record of 55 appearances. He never lost in eleven appearances against England, scoring five of his six international tries against his old foe. Probably his greatest game was when Wales were 13-0 down to England at half-time, with the great Gareth Edwards off injured. J.P.R. scored one of Wales's four second-half tries (then worth only 3 points each), which with a conversion and drop goal gave a 17-13 victory, and one of the most stirring come-backs of modern times.

A poll of 200 players, coaches, managers and writers across the globe, to find the greatest rugby player of all time, was published by *Rugby World* in October 1996. The highest Englishman, at 12th, is Fran Cotton. Top was Gareth Edwards, followed by Serge Blanco, and three other members of 'the golden team', Gerald Davies, Barry John and J. P. R. Williams, were all in the top 10. Edwards won three Grand Slams, 5 successive Triple Crowns, captained Wales 13 times and scored 20 tries. He went on three British Lions tours, including the successes of New Zealand in 1971 and South Africa in 1974. His try mentioned previously, in the 1973 Barbarians defeat of New Zealand, was manufactured almost entirely by Welsh players, and is arguably the most memorable try in recorded history.

Over the past two decades, Welsh rugby has been in decline and in 1998 the team suffered two humiliating results against England and France, where Wales lost by a record margin to each.

It is interesting to note that there are 117 Welsh internationals currently playing club rugby at top levels in England and Wales. Cardiff alone have 17 current and recent internationals. In the 1970s, Wales used about 30 players in a decade, all of them intelligent, passionate and none of them playing for the £10,000 a match appearance money. For twenty years there has been an overweight, overpaid bureaucracy supervising Welsh rugby not knowing how much the national game means to the Welsh man or woman in the street. A new coach, Graham Henry from New Zealand, has been appointed and he appears to have rekindled the pride in wearing a Welsh shirt that bypassed the chosen players of the last twenty years, reversing 1998's defeats against both France and England in 1999 and reaching the quarter-finals of the 1999 Rugby World Cup for the first time since 1987.

In the past, Wales often lost its best rugby union players to rugby league, for instance Maurice Richards (who memorably scored 4 tries against England), David Watkins and the legendary Billy Boston. Cardiff's Billy Boston was the second highest try scorer in the history of rugby league, who played 564 times for Wigan, and 31 times for Great Britain. Joining Wigan from Cardiff, he was chosen for the Great Britain team to tour Australia in 1954 after just five league matches. He scored 36 tries on the tour. Lewis Jones scored the most rugby league points in a season, for Leeds, in 1956/57, with 36 tries and 194 goals, totalling 496. David Watkins scored the most goals, 221, for Salford in 1972/73. Cardiff's Jim Buller Sullivan of Wigan kicked the most goals, 2867, in a glittering career that spanned from 1921-1946. He also made the most appearances for one club, Wigan – 774 of a record first-class appearances. The giant of the game also played for Wales at baseball, a game the Welsh played before the Americans discovered it, and still popular in Cardiff. The longest continuous career was of an Augustus John (Gus) Risman, from Barry, who played his first game for Salford in 1929 and his last game for Batley in 1954. His son, Bev, went on to play for England at rugby union before turning to league. Widnes paid a world record fee for Jonathan Davies, the Welsh outside-half, to turn to rugby league. He later returned to play rugby union for Cardiff and Wales, after representing Great Britain at rugby league.

Probably the most remarkable rugby player in the history of league and union has been David Watkins, now Chairman of Newport Rugby Club. He is the only player to have captained Britain in both Rugby Union (the British Lions) and in Rugby League. He is also the only man to have captained Wales in Union and League. He was also captain of Newport rugby union club for 4 years, and of Salford rugby league club for 7 years.

Arguably the most famous rugby club side in the world is Cardiff. They have beaten New Zealand, Australia, South Africa and Maori first XV's as touring teams treat Cardiff as an international fixture – the club to beat. Similarly both Newport, Swansea and Llanelli have defeated major touring sides in their illustrious histories.

Wales, the host nation of the fourth Rugby World Cup (1999), now has the new Millennium Stadium on the site of the former National Stadium, in Cardiff. The W.R.U. have built the most modern sports arena in Europe and only one of two stadia outside the USA with a retracting roof.

RUSSIA

In the 17th century, **Henry Lloyd** of Gwynedd fought for the Austrians, then the Prussians and finally the Russians. As a general in their army, he commanded armies against Sweden and the Turks, and wrote a seminal military textbook used in military academies across Europe.

The first steel mills were built in the Russia of the Tsars by **John Hughes** of Merthyr, who founded the town of Hughesovka. The Russians called it Yuzovska, renamed Stalino under the dictator, and since re-renamed Donetsk.

S

SAINTS

The first known Welsh saints, **St Julius** and **St Arvan**, were martyred at Caerleon in 305, and three Celtic bishops attended the Synod of Arles in 314 and the Council of Ariminium in 359. Celtic bishops were probably at the Council of Nicea in 325, and bishops from Britain were also signatories at Tours in 461, Vannes in 465, Orleans in 511 and Paris in 555. The Welsh Triads say that Caractacus and his father Bran, after seven years' captivity in Rome, brought the religion to Wales, and there is a tradition that St Paul preached in Celtic Britain. St Clement's Epistle to the Corinthians, written around AD95, states that Paul had gone to 'the very limit of the West.' It seems that Christianity reached Wales in the first century, possibly reinforced by waves of Christian Gauls escaping the Aurelian persecution of 177.

The teaching of Pelagius became popular in Britain, and St Germanus (St Garmon) travelled from Auxerre in 429 and in 447 to preach against the doctrine. In this second visit he led the Celtic Britons against the invading Picts and Scots, defeating them with the battle cry of 'Alleluia'. Tradition has the battle placed at Maes Garmon near Mold in Flintshire.

Monasticism in Wales dates from around 420, with the first notable saints being **Dyfrig (Dubricius)** and **Illtyd**. A second generation, who followed them around the middle of the century, were mainly taught by them, for instance Samson, Dewi, Gildas, Teilo, Catwg/Cadog, Cybi and Padarn. Many of these also set up their own holy settlements, for instance Llandeilo, Llangybi and Llanbadarn (see Llan).

St Dyfrig died on the Isle of Saints, Bardsey Island, and his remains were moved to Llandaf Cathedral in 1120 by Bishop Urban. He seems to have been bishop of Llandaf, and was succeeded there by St Illtud. St Illtyd was a Breton disciple of St Garmon, who became head of the most famous monastery in Britain, Llanilltud Fawr (Llantwit Major), after studying at Llancarfan. His pupils included St Samson of Dol (regarded as the patron saint of Brittany), St Cybi, Gildas the historian, and Maelgwn Gwynedd. Dewi Sant was probably educated here, also. St Illtud died around 505, and is said to be the model for Sir Galahad in Arthurian romance. The Life of St Samson calls him *'of all the Britons the most learned in the scriptures.'* St Samson moved on to Caldey Island, and visited Ireland and Cornwall before going to Brittany.

Possibly born in the late fifth century, but more probably in the early sixth, **Dewi Sant**, **Saint David** spent his life reforming the church in Wales, and fighting druidic remnants of belief. He was born on the shore of St Bride's Bay, and the chapel dedicated to his mother St Non is said to mark the place, and possibly dates from this period. Not far away is St David's Cathedral, on the spot where Dewi founded a monastery. Like Illtud, he was an ascetic with a strong sense of discipline, and a vegetarian. He was known as *Dewi Ddyfrwr*, 'David the Waterdrinker'. Over fifty churches are still dedicated to this patron saint of Wales. A casket said to contain his bones, plus those of St Justinian and St Caradoc, was discovered more than a century ago in St David's Cathedral, and the bones are being carbon-dated at Keble College, Oxford.

St David held a meeting in the church at Llanddewi Brefi to denounce the Pelagian Heresy. In this Synod of Brefi, legend says that the ground rose so that he could be heard by the crowds, and the old church stands on a prominent mound. He seems to have died around 589, and was reputed to have been a centenarian. He was canonized during the reign of Pope Calixtus II, around 1120. In 1398 the Archbishop of Canterbury decreed that the Festival of St David be held on March 1st, and the Welsh continued to keep this special saint's day all through the period of the Commonwealth, when saints' days were forbidden. March 1st is Wales's national day, when Welshmen all over the world wear the symbols of leeks and daffodils.

Saint Patrick (Padrig), Ireland's patron saint, was thought to have been born in Pembrokeshire in 389, and was carried off by Irish raiders in 406, becoming Bishop of Armagh in AD432, consecrated by St Garmon at Auxerre. Recent evidence seems to point to his birth in Banwen, near Swansea. In St Patrick's 'Confessio' he states he was born at Banaven Taberiar, a smallholding near a Roman fort, which could be Tafarn-y-Banwen, a farm near an old Roman stronghold. This is also on the strategically important Sarn Helen, once the major Roman road through Wales. Local custom says that Patrick came from Banwen, and there are placenames such as *Hafod Gwyddelig* ('Irish Summerhouse') and a *Nant Gwyddelig* ('Irish Stream'). George Brinley Evans also points to the nearby Hirfynydd Stone, the extremely rare early Christian carving of a man in prayer, surrounded by Irish symbolic patterns. (Note that 'Gwyddelig', the Welsh for 'Irish', is similar to 'Goidelic'. The Welsh were the Brythonic Celts, and the Irish were the Goidelic Celts – see Language).

St Teilo, said to have been a cousin of Dewi Sant, was born at Penally, near Tenby, and was a pupil of Dyfrig. He left his monastery at Llandeilo Fawr to escape the Yellow Plague in 547, and after seven years in Brittany returned to Llandaf, possibly succeeding Illtud. In 577, with his monks he accompanied Iddon ap Ynys in a decisive battle against the Saxons on the banks of the River Wye. St Teilo's skull was kept by the Melchior family near Llandeilo, who up to the 1930s were offering pilgrims drinks of water from it, to cure their ills.

St Cadog, or **Catwg**, was born about 497, the son of Gwynlliw, a prince of Dyfed and Gwladus. Educated in Caerwent, he founded the famous monastery at Llancarfan in 535, where there are still traces of the settlement. He visited Brittany and Strathclyde, and was killed in England, his body being buried back at Llancarfan. St Deiniol, who founded the monastery at Bangor, the precursor of the cathedral, was taught by St Cadog.

The most important saints in Brittany are the seven Founding Saints – St Malo, St Brieuc (Briog), St Samson of Dol, St Patern (Padarn, or Paternus), St Tugdual (Tudwal), St Pol Aurelian and St Corentin. Of these only St Corentin was not Welsh. (He was Cornish-Welsh). Most were taught at Llancarfan and Llanilltud Fawr monasteries.

Mention should be made of the family of Brychan Brycheiniog, a contemporary of Cunedda and Vortigern in The Dark Ages. From his kingdom of Breconshire, many of his children became saints commemorated across Wales. His male offspring who became saints include Cynog, Clydog and Berwyn. Other sons included Arthen, Gwen, Gerwyn, Pasgen. Cynin Cof fab Tudwal Befr (Cynin, son of Bishop Tudwal) was a grandson of Brychan and a character in the Mabinogion story of Culhwch and Olwen.

Some of Brychan's many daughters commemorated as saints are Arianwen, Tudful (martyred at Merthyr Tudful), Tybïe (Llandybie), Dwynwen (Llanddwynwen), Hawystl, Mwynen, Cain (Llangain and Llangeinor), Eleri, Ceingar the mother of Saint Cynidr (Llangynidr), and Meleri the grandmother of Dewi Sant. Other daughters included Bechan or Bethan, Ceindrych, Ceinwen, Goleuddydd, Gwen (Gwenllian or Gwenhwyfar, who may have married King Arthur), Gwawr (the mother of the poet-soldier Llywarch Hen), Tangwystl (Ynystanglws, near Swansea). Brychan's daughter, Saint Gwladys, married Saint Gwynlliw, King of Gwent (after whom St Woolos Cathedral in Newport is named), and their son was Saint Catwg, who established the famous monastery at Llancarfan and churches throughout South Wales, Cornwall and Brittany.

In 1970, **Richard Gwyn** of Llanidloes, a Catholic schoolteacher was canonised. Four hundred years earlier, he had refused to take the Oath of Supremacy, and to attend church in the reign of Elizabeth I. He was tortured and spent four years in jail. Upon being heavily fined, and asked how he would pay, he smiled and said, '*I have something towards it – sixpence*'. The response to this jest was fairly humourless – he was sentenced to be '*drawn on a hurdle to the place of execution where he shall hang half-dead, and so be cut down alive, his members cast into the fire, his belly ripped open unto the breast, his head cut off, his bowels, liver, lungs, heart thrown likewise into the fire*'. Gwyn responded '*What is all this? Is it any more than one death?*' and he met his grisly end in 1584.

The first Welsh Puritan martyr was the Presbyterian **John Penry** from Breconshire, executed in 1593. Educated at Cambridge and Oxford, his second book was secretly printed in 1588, the year of the Armada. He appealed to Parliament in it for Welsh-speaking preachers in '*my poor countrie of Wales*'. He described the Welsh bishops of the established Church of England as '*excrements of Romish vomits*', and pleaded for the sovereignty of the individual conscience (see Religion).

David Lewis, rector of Cwm near the Skirrid Mountain, ministered secretly to Catholics in Wales for thirty years, and was known as *Tad y Tlodion*, 'Father of the Poor'. He was arrested with seven other priests by the fanatical Protestant, John Arnold MP. After painful interrogation, he was prosecuted for papacy by Arnold, who was closely related to the judge. In 1679 at Usk, Lewis was found guilty, hanged, cut down barely alive, disembowelled, dismembered and beheaded. He was canonised by Pope Paul VI three centuries later.

Many churches dedicated to Welsh saints were renamed by Normans in the 11th and 12th centuries, as St John, St Mary, etc., but many survive, and it is interesting how many have Romano-British names.

FEAST DAYS OF THE EARLY SAINTS

Date	Saint	also known as	Flourished
Jan 1	Medwyn	Medwin	C7th
Jan 13	Elian	Eilian	C6th
Jan 15	Lleudadd		C6th
Jan 23	Ellyw	Elli	C6th
Jan 25	Dwynwen (Wales' Valentine)		c.460
Jan 29	Gildas	Badonicus	c.500-c.570
Jan 31	Aidan	Madog, Maidoc, Aidus	C6th
Jan 31	Melangell		Died c.590
Feb 1	Ffraid	Brigid	c.450-c.525
Feb 3 (Feb 1)	Abbot Seiriol		C6th
Feb 9	Bishop Teilo		died 580
Feb 13	Dyfnog		C7th
Mar 1	Bishop Dewi	David, Patron Saint of Wales	c.520-588
Mar 3	Abbot Gwynno		
Mar 5 (Mar 2)	Non	Dewi's mother	C5th-C6th
Mar 17	Patrick	Patron Saint of Ireland	
Mar 27	King Gwynlliw	Woolos	died c.500
Apr 5	Derfel		C6th
Apr 7	Abbot Brynach		C5th-C6th
Apr 15	Bishop Padarn	Paternus	C5th-C6th
Apr 20 or 21	Abbot Beuno		died 642
Apr 27	Cynidir	Enoder	C6th
May 1	Briog	Brieuc (Britanny), Briavael	C5th
May 5	Bishop Asaff	Asaph	C5th-C6th
May 16	Carannog		C5th
May 21	Collen		C7th
May 28	Abbess Melangell		
June 4	Pedrog		C6th
June 16	Curig		fl550
June 20	Arfan	Aaron	exec. c.305
June 20	Julius		exec. c.305
June 20	Govan		C6th
July 2	Bishop Euddogwy	Oudoceus	died c.615
July 3	Abbot Peblig	Publicius	C5th
July 17	Cynllo		Fl.550

Date	Saint	also known as	Flourished
July 28	Bishop Samson		c.490-c.565
Aug 23 and Dec 5	Stinan	Justinian	C6th
Aug 23	Tudful	Tydfil	Died c.480
Sep 7	Abbot Dunawd	Donat	C6th
Sep 11	Bishop Deiniol		C6th
Sep 21	Mabon		C6th
Sep 25 and Jan 24	Catwg	Cadoc, Cadog, form of Cadfael	c.497-c.577
Oct 8	Cain		C5th-C6th
Oct 9	Abbot Cynog		
Nov 1	Aelhaern	Elhaearn	C7th
Nov 1	Cadfan		C5th-C6th
Nov 3	Clydog	Ruler of Ewyas, (Herefordshire), Welsh until 1536	Fl.500, martyred
Nov 3	Abbess Gwenfrewi	Winifrede	C7th
Nov 5 (6, 7, 8)	Abbot Cybi		C6th
Nov 6	Abbot Illtud		C5th-C6th
Nov 12	Abbot Tysilio		C7th
Nov 14	Bishop Dyfrig	Dubricius, Dyfan	Fl.475
Nov 15	Bishop Malo		died c.640
Nov 22	Bishop Paulinus		died c.505
Nov 27 (and 7)	Cyngar		C6th
Dec 8	Bishop Cynidr		C6th
Dec 12 (and Feb 23)	Ffinian		C6th
Dec 26 (Dec 30)	Bishop Tathan	Tatheus	C5th

SCIENTISTS

Llyn y Fan Fach (see Lakes), in the mountains near Llanddeusaint, is known as the place where Myddfai of Blaen Sawdde farm met the 'lady of the lake'. After Myddfai offered her three kinds of bread, the beautiful woman promised to marry him on the condition that he would never hit her three times without a cause. Her father gave the couple livestock, and they lived at Esgair Llaethdy farm and had three sons. However, Myddfai tapped her thoughtlessly on three occasions; when she did not want to attend a baptism, when she cried at a wedding and when she laughed at a funeral. She disappeared with all the animals, but reappeared to her sons on several occasions, at *Llidiart y Meddgon* (Physicians' Gate) and *Pant y Meddygon* (Physicians' Hollow). She taught them how to heal with herbs and plants, and her eldest son, *Rhiwallon*, became physician to Rhys Grug, Lord of Dinefwr. Rhiwallon's three sons were Rhys Grug's doctors when he died in 1234, and they founded a long line of physicians culminating in John Williams, Queen Victoria's eminent doctor. The places still exist, where the ancestors of this longest line of medical men in recorded history learned their profession. John Williams edited the thirteenth century manuscript of the earliest folk remedies *The Physicians of Myddfai* and it was translated into English by John Pughe in 1861.

Dr. John Dee (see Magic) was born to a Welsh court official in 1527, becoming one of the foundation fellows of Trinity College Cambridge in 1546. He moved to Louvain (Leuven) University in modern-day Belgium because English humanism was not scientific enough, and made contact with some of the finest minds in mathematics and geography, such as Mercator, Ortelius and Gemma Phrysius. *'An astounding polymath . . . the lectures of this twenty-three-year-old at Paris were a sensation; he was to be courted by princes all over Europe. He returned to England with navigational devices like the balestila or cross-staff, was taken up by the Queen, the retinue of the Earl of Leicester and the Sidneys, and at the heart of the Elizabethan Renaissance.'* (*Welsh Wizard and British Empire* by Professor Gwyn Alf Williams). A brilliant mathematician like Robert Recorde of Pembrokeshire before him, he published an augmentation of Recorde's *Grounde of Arts*, a mathematical textbook which ran to twenty-six editions by 1662 and wrote his own seminal Preface to the English edition of *Euclid*, which has been called a *'landmark in mathematical thought.'*

'With his remarkable library at Mortlake, (Dee) became the thinker behind most of the ventures of the English in their search for the North-East and North-West Passages to Cathay, pouring out treatises, maps, instructions, in his characteristic blend of technology, science, imperialism, speculation, fantasy and the occult' (*Welsh Wizard and British Empire*, ibid.). He was imprisoned by Queen Mary for trying to 'enchant' her, and a London mob sacked his fabulous library in 1583 as the den of a black magician. He is said to have been the model for both Shakespeare's white Prospero and Marlowe's black Faust.

Dee seems to have invented the term 'British Empire', as 'philosopher' to Queen Elizabeth, as he worked to justify her title to an Atlantic empire based upon Madoc's discovery of America.

Back in the 16th century, the aforementioned **Robert Recorde** of Tenby (c1510-1558) was a leading mathematician, the writer of the first English language texts on algebra and arithmetic, and incidentally invented the equals (=) sign, to *'avoid the tedious repetition of equals to'*. His arithmetic book went into fifty editions and was notable in being innovative in two respects. It was written as a dialogue between a master and pupil to keep it interesting and it used the device of pointing fingers, precursing Windows icons! Recorde studied at Oxford, qualified as a Doctor of Medicine in Cambridge, was a doctor in London and in charge of mines in Ireland, but died in prison because of a lawsuit taken out by the Duke of Pembroke.

Edward Lhuyd (Lluyd) 1660-1709, from Glanfred, near Llandre (Llanfihangel Genau'r-glyn) was the first noted taxonomist of zoology, transformed Oxford's Ashmolean Museum, and also revised the 1695 edition of Camden's *Encyclopaedia Britannica* (see Language).

And nearly three hundred years ago, **William Jones** was the first mathematician to use *pi*, the ratio of a circle's circumference to its diameter, in a publication (see Mathematics).

Wales is more renowned for its literary output, but has contributed to the scientific field in many areas. **Wendell Meredith Stanley**, an American biochemist of Welsh descent, won the Nobel Prize for Chemistry in 1946, for isolating, crystallising and demonstrating that the Tobacco Mosaic Virus was infectious.

Catherine Alice Evans (1881-1975), of Neath, Pennsylvania (a strongly Welsh settlement) was a noted microbiologist. Her research into bacterial contamination of milk led to the recognition of the dangers of unpasteurised milk. Until her research publication in 1918, brucellosis in humans and cattle was thought of as two different diseases.

Another American-Welshman, **Thomas Hunt Morgan**, won the 1933 Nobel Prize for Medicine for his pioneering work in genetics, using the fruit fly, Drosophila. He helped establish that genes were located on the chromosomes, discovered sex chromosomes, and invented the techniques of genetic mapping.

Cecil Frank Powell was awarded the Nobel Prize for Physics in 1950 for his discovery of the pion (pi meson) in cosmic radiation. He worked extensively on the photography of nuclear processes.

Oliver Evans (1755-1859) was born in Newport, Delaware. He was an engineer who developed high pressure steam engines and machines powered by them. Joining a flour mill owned by his two brothers, he built machines using water power to drive conveyors and escalators. By his work, one operator could control all the mill's processes, making Evans a pioneer of production-line techniques. Moving on to Philadelphia, he built over fifty stationary steam engines, and invented a steam dredger that could move on both land and water.

Richard Roberts (1789-1864) was a mechanical engineer and inventor, born in Carreghofa. Self-taught, he improved Maudsley's screw-cutting lathe and built one of the first metal-planing machines. He developed Crompton's spinning mule and set up in business making self-acting spinning mules and railway locomotives, starting with the 'Experiment' for the Liverpool and Manchester railway in 1833.

The American-Welshman **Gilbert Newton Lewis** (1875-1946) *'probably did more to advance chemical theory this century than any other chemist'* (Chambers Biographical Dictionary) with his pioneering work in transferring ideas from physics into chemistry. Born in Massachusetts, this theoretical chemist set out the electronic theory of valency.

William Morris Davis (1850-1934) was an American physical geographer from the Welsh heartland of Philadephia, who developed the concept of the regular cycle of erosion.

Sir Thomas Lewis (1881-1945), the cardiologist and clinical scientist, was the first man to master the electrocardiogram and fought hard for funding for research into clinical science.

There is a society of Welsh scientists, *Y Gymdeithas Wyddonol Genedlaethol*, based in Aberystwyth. Wales's contribution to science has been greatly undervalued, a situation which was redressed by Professor Phil Williams of the University of Wales, Aberystwyth, in his article, *Land of Poets and Scientists* (*Planet* magazine).

His information is remarkable for the disproportionate contribution that Welshmen make to science today, yet we still honour our poets, sportsmen and singers more. He remarks that at one meeting of the Space Physics Research Grants committee, six of the seventeen scientists were Welshmen, and another, Hughes, was the grandson of Welsh teacher. In the same year, at an international conference on the ionosphere in Belgium, nearly every speaker was Welsh, although they were working in three different countries. Incidentally, *The Computus Fragment* is part of a manuscript on the stars written in Welsh by a monk at Llanbadarn around 940. Also Lewis Morris Rutherfurd, 1816-1892, who studied at Williams College Massachusetts, was the leading spectroscopist and astronomical photographer of his day.

As well as space physics, the atmospheric physics field is full of Welsh scientists, with the head of the Meteorological Office nearly always being Welsh. And *'the fundamental period of atmospheric oscillation is known internationally as the Brunt period after a scientist from Llanidloes'*.

In the 1850s, a young scientist, **Alfred Russell Wallace** from Usk, working in the Pacific, sent a paper on the tendency of varieties of species to depart from the original type. He sent it to Charles Darwin. Darwin looked at it, and presented it as a joint paper while Wallace was abroad, thereby making his name with the greatest single discovery in the Life Sciences. Wallace is now almost forgotten, while Darwin and *The Origin of the Species* are known the world over. 'The Wallace Line' between the islands of Bali and Lombok, and between Borneo and The Celebes, showed the first biogeographers the division between flora and fauna in similar climates. Wallace had spent four years in the Amazon basin, and another eight years collecting specimens in the Malay Archipelago, those hundreds of islands that make up

modern Indonesia. The *'greatest field biologist of the nineteenth century'* (*The Song of the Dodo*, David Quammen, 1996) . . . *'is famous for being obscured'* . . . *'for a variety of reasons, some good and some shabby, Darwin received most of the recognition.'*

Wallace had a feeling for equality that Darwin lacked. Darwin was independently wealthy, whereas Wallace was apprenticed to a builder at 14, and became a trainee land surveyor in rural Wales. In the 1840s he was employed redrawing property boundaries as common land was enclosed and the rich squirearchy divided up the land. He later called this *'a legalised robbery of the poor'*. From 1848 to 1852 Wallace explored South America, but his ship sank on the voyage home, and all his precious specimens were lost (except for those he sent home earlier). He was in the Malay Archipelago from 1854 to 1862, collecting 125,000 specimens, and in 1869-1870 in Borneo. In Adrian Desmond's and James Moore's biography, *Darwin*, 1997, we see Wallace as a *'self-taught socialist'* who *'saw humanity as part of a progressive world governed by natural law'* and who *'had learned to see morality as a cultural product'*. Wallace adapted Malthusian logic on the overpopulation of mankind to the animal kingdom. Thus Wallace's more rounded theory of selection and evolution was that the environment extinguished the unfit, rather than Darwin's 'competition between species'. He also regarded natives such as the Dyaks in Borneo with admiration for their adaptation to their environment. On the other hand, Darwin was disgusted by the natives of Tierra del Fuego.

'And Wallace was to post the question dismissed by Darwin – what was the purpose of natural selection? Evolutionary forces worked towards a just society, this

was the point – *"to realise the ideal of perfect man."* Darwin accepted nothing so utopian.' In *The Song of the Dodo* we see Darwin's 'Watergate' (pp. 110-114) where some of his lies are documented, crucial letters went *'missing'* and *'somebody cleaned up the file'* to give the great man credit for Wallace's work. Unfortunately, this lack of recognition forms a theme running through Welsh scientific discovery. The story of this attractive and humane man, Wallace, not part of the upper-class establishment, who contributed vastly to science, needs to be widely told. Wallace's books included *A Narrative of Travels on the Amazon and Rio Negro* (1853), *On the Law Which Has Regulated the Introduction of New Species* (1855), *The Malay Archipelago* (1869) and *Contributions to the Theory of Natural Selection* (1870). He also pioneered zoogeography with his 1876 'Geographical Distribution of Animals'. Wallace was before his time – he campaigned strongly for women's suffrage, receiving sneers from the academic community for this, and also proposed the nationalisation of land and socialism.

Another example of an unknown Welsh contribution to science is that of **David Hughes**, who invented the teleprinter (from 1855, this telegraph-typewriter was widely used). In 1878 he invented the microphone and the induction balance. In 1879, he held an experiment in Great Portland Street. At one end of the street he had a spark transmitter to generate electro-magnetic waves, and at the other a *'coherer'*, a piece of equipment to receive the waves. He had proposed the theory to Clark Maxwell, and the President and Secretary of the Royal Society witnessed the success of the experiment. A Welshman had proposed and demonstrated the first radio transmitter and receiver in the world, and thereby proved the existence of electro-magnetic radiation. The English committee was not impressed, however, and attributed the effects to Faraday induction rather than electro-magnetic radiation. A polymath, from 1850-53 Hughes had been a Professor of Music at Bardston College, Kentucky, and he left a fortune to London hospitals. (Readers might note that Bardstown was where the Evan Williams family set up American bourbon whisky production, and the area has strong Welsh links.) Ten years later, a German scientist named Hertz managed to transmit such radiation just from one side of his room to the other, not exactly the length of a London street, and was honoured with the unit of radio frequency, the Hertz, being named after him.

Sir William Robert Grove, born in Swansea in 1811, after studying law, invented the Grove Voltaic Battery in 1839. Appointed a FRS, he became Professor of the London Institution, writing *Correlation of Physical Forces*. Returning to legal work, this remarkably rounded character became a High Court judge, dying in 1896.

Around the same time, **Sir John Dillwyn-Llewelyn** (1810-1882) of Penllergare was a considerable scientist, also becoming a FRS. In 1841 he invented an 'electro-galvanic apparatus' to propel his boat around his private lake, and worked with Professor Wheatstone to develop the telegraph. They also proved that electric currents passed through sea-water in experiments at Mumbles. He collaborated with Claudets on Daguerrotypes, and helped **Henry Fox Talbot**, the inventor of the modern process of photography. Fox Talbot himself was brought up in Penrice Castle in Gower. Dillwyn-Llewelyn was also an outstanding botanist.

Hugh Owen Thomas (1833-1891) pioneered orthopaedic surgery across the world, and his 'Thomas Splints' are still used for hip and knee illnesses. He was descended from a long line of famous 'bone-setters' from Anglesey, supposedly descended from a survivor from a shipwreck of the Spanish Armada in 1588. Other sources say that it was a shipwreck in 1745 at the Skerries or West Mouse Island when a young Spaniard struggled to the shore-line. Dyfrig Roberts, a descendant, believes that twins speaking a 'strange tongue' struggled ashore during the Jacobite rebellion, and that they could have been Scottish, Manx or Spanish. One of them was skilful in dealing with bone injuries, and set himself up in Liverpool as a sort of 'quack doctor'. However, all five of his sons qualified as real doctors. The one survivor called himself Evan Thomas, and specialised in settling dislocated bones, passing his skills on to his children. There is a memorial in Llanfair PG to him. Four generations later the 'Thomas Splint' cut fatalities from broken femurs from 80% to 20%, and the splint is now mainly used for children with femur fractures.

Dr. James Cowles Prichard, a Border Welshman from Herefordshire, argued for a single human species in his 1813 *Researches into the Physical History of Mankind*. Later, in 1831, he was the first to establish Celtic as an Indo-European language with close affinity to Sanskrit, Greek, Latin and the Teutonic languages ('The Eastern Origin of the Celtic Nations'). He also wrote on Egyptian mythology and on the natural history of mankind.

Percy Carlyle Gilchrist and his cousin **Sidney Gilchrist Thomas** are mentioned more extensively in the entry on 'Min-erals – Iron and Steel'. When Bessemer revolutionised steel-making with his 'process' of using a converter to make bulk steel in 1856, he did not know that it could not be used for iron ores that included phosphorous. He had used pig-iron from Blaenavon, which was phosphorous-free. Phosphorous made steel very brittle, and was present in over 90% of European iron ores, and around 98% of American ore. In 1877/1888 the cousins found out how to remove the phosphorous, and Thomas died just seven years later, probably as a result of his experiments, at the age of thirty-five. Gilchrist died in 1935, having sold the patents to Andrew Carnegie who then opened up American steel production. An obelisk in Blaenavon commemorates the cousins for the *'invention (which) pioneered the basic Bessemer or Thomas process'*. In 1890, Britain was the world's greatest steel producer, but by 1902 this great invention had allowed Carnegie and Krupp of Essen to propel the USA and Germany into the first two places in steel production. Everyone has heard of the Scot Andrew Carnegie and his philanthropy, but no-one knows the Welshmen. At least Carnegie had the grace to admit that the 'Carnegie Process' was not his – *'These two men, Thomas and Gilchrist of Blaenavon, did more for Britain's greatness than all the kings and queens put together. Moses struck rock and brought forth water. They struck the useless phosphoric ore and transformed it into steel, a far greater miracle.'*

Sir Tanatt William Edgeworth David KBE (1858-1934) was a distinguished geologist and KBE who won the DSO in World War One. He also was one of the party of three which reached the South Pole in Shackleton's 1909 expedition.

In 1937, **Evan Williams** of Llany-bydder made one of the most important discoveries in physics, detecting a new fundamental particle, the meson. To ensure academic and scientific integrity, he waited for the detection of another particle before publishing. In the meantime, the American, Anderson, detected the particle, did not wait for the expected confirmation, published a paper within a month and received the Nobel Prize.

Professor Miller from Llanymddyfri was the founder of atomic crystallography, and as a young man appointed to the life Chair of Mineralogy at Cambridge. Succeeded by another young Welshman, they held the chair for an astonishing 94 years between them.

Sir William Henry Preece (1869-1913) from Caernarfon was instructed by Michael Faraday and became a pioneer of wireless telegraphy and telephony. Inspired by David Hughes, he improved railway signalling and introduced the first telephones to Great Britain as engineer-in-chief of the Post Office.

Edward John Bevan studied chemistry at Manchester and in 1892, with Charles Cross, patented the viscose process of rayon manufacture. Using cellulose, either yarn (rayon, or artificial silk) or film (cellophane) could be manufactured giving the world a quantum leap in materials technology.

Ernest Jones (1879-1958) was a life-long friend of Sigmund Freud's, and introduced psychoanalysis to the USA and Britain. Dr Jones learned German in order to more fully understand Freud's theories, and was instrumental in the furthering of Freud's work on neurosis.

The late **Dyfrig Jones** first gave, in the science lecture at the Abergwaun Eisteddfod, 'Voyager' data from Jupiter and Saturn, that vindicated his theory of planetary radiation. He waited until he could give the results to his countrymen in his own language. Honoured in America and amongst the worldwide space community, he was again hardly known in Wales.

One man who might turn out to be *'the most influential Welshman of all time'* is Cardiff's *Brian Josephson*, who specialises in Low Temperature Physics and designed the 'Josephson Junction', which probably will become the basic component of hyper-powerful computers. A Nobel Prize winner, his is, all to sadly, an unfamiliar name in Wales.

Professor Myron Evans is probably the most prolific and original physicist of the second half of this century in the world at present. His Evans/Vigeur Field Theory is a revolutionary Photon Emission Quantum Theory accepted by adjudication worldwide. This theory was formulated by mind-bending mathematics in conjunction with Professeur Vigeur of the Marie Curie Universite in France, a member of the *Legion d'Honneur* who is regarded as a national hero in France.

Vero Wynne-Edwards was, according to his obituary (*The Independent*, 11th January 1997) *'one of the 20th century's greatest scientific naturalists and original thinkers on population regulation in animals'*. His 1962 publication *Animal Dispersion in Relation to Social Behaviour* sold an astonishing 350,000 copies world-wide. His thinking was that animals are not always trying to increase their numbers, as Darwinism indicated, but that they are programmed to regulate them by various mechanisms such as territorial behaviour and social displays.

Perhaps the only Welsh scientist familiar to the public is the distinguished forensic pathologist **Professor Bernard Knight** of Cardiff, who retired in September 1996 after 48 years and over 25,000 post-mortem examinations. His knowledge was used during the Fred and Rosemary West trial. This unassuming man started at the age of seventeen as a laboratory technician, trained to become a doctor, and studied to become a barrister while working as a doctor. This multi-talented man also writes novels.

Dr. David Dalby is a Welsh academic who has travelled for thirty-five years looking for endangered languages, and had established the world's largest register of extant languages and dialects. He has identified ten thousand living languages. Preserving a multilingual world is his obsession, '*Monolingualism is as bad as illiteracy . . . there is something very sinister about a group of upper-class English people who dominated the world in the days of Empire and then imposed their own language on subdued peoples . . . The last line of my national anthem, Land of My Fathers, is "May the old language live forever"; could there be any better motto for those of us who care about the wealth of living language in this world?*'

Professor Phil Williams's theory is that there are so many Welshmen in science, including John Meurig Thomas, President of the Royal Institution, because '*science was a field, unique in Britain, where ability was the only qualification for success. To get on in the Civil Service, the City, the Army, the Church, it was a prerequisite to wear the right tie and speak with the right accent. But in science – and only in science – the talented student from Wales could get right to the very top. And once a few Welshmen had made their mark, they served as role models for the next generation.*'

Mention must be given to **Elaine Morgan**, whose *Descent of Woman* was published in 1972, adding to the feminist debate by querying the role of women during evolution. A respected novelist and playwriter, she resented the Desmond Morris hypothesis in *The Naked Ape* that women had developed breasts purely to attract men. She went on to develop her theories in *The Aquatic Ape, The Scars of Evolution, The Descent of the Child* and *The Aquatic Ape Hypothesis*. She believes, unlike most biologists and paleoanthropologists, that mankind spent between one and two million years of its evolutionary life in water. Fat only occurs in two types of mammal, hibernating or aquatic. Unlike the apes, human infants are born fat and become fatter, as they had no need to live in trees. We have skin adapted for water, rather than layers of fur, human babies can swim from birth, and there appears to be no-one who can disprove this remarkable woman's theories.

SETTLEMENTS

The antiquarian Camden, noted *Anglia Transwallania* – 'England Beyond Wales'. That part of Pembrokeshire south of the Preseli Hills was known as the 'Englishry', with a line of fortifications protecting it from the 'Welshry' in north Pembrokeshire. The place names north and south of this line are Welsh and English respectively, divided by the invisible line known as the 'Landsker'. Similarly, Flemings were settled in the south of the Gower (*Gŵyr*) peninsula, and there is also an Englishry-Welshry border there. From 1111, many Flemings were settled in Pembrokeshire by Henry I, to work the fish, wool and wine trades. Tenby became a Flemish stronghold, and many places like St Florence, near Manorbier, and Flemingston display old cottages with the distinctive massive Flemish chimneys.

Llangwm, another Flemish settlement near Haverfordwest, used to have a distinctive distrust of strangers, and was actively hostile. Jealous of their fishing rights in the Cleddau creeks, the villagers collected bass, mullet, herring and salmon from distinctive black-tarred boats, descendants of the smaller two thousand year-old coracles. The women used to row and walk miles to Milford and Pembroke markets with the fish and shellfish catches.

There were Viking settlements in Pembroke, with Norse place-names – Milford, Haverfordwest, Herbrandston and Hubberston. The names of many Welsh islands have a Scandinavian origin, ending in holm (islet) or ey (island), e.g. Anglesey (Island of the Angles), Bardsey, Caldy, Skokholm, Grassholm, Flat Holm, etc.

SEVERN BORE

A 'bore' is a surge of tidal water up an estuary or river, caused by the funnelling of the rising tide into a narrowing mouth. The River Severn is the longest river in Britain, and meets some of the highest tides in the world where it opens out into the Bristol Channel. An extremely high tide, especially in Spring, can be assisted by wind and build up where it is resisted by the river current against it. It will eventually break through the current, and the broken wave will surge for miles up the Severn, even uprooting trees on the banks. Every year people try to surf up

the River Severn, on this 'Severn Bore', which can reach up to six feet high.

SEVEN WONDERS OF WALES

*'Pistyll Rhaeadr and Wrexham Steeple,
Snowdon's Mountain, without its people,
Overton yew trees, St Winifrede's Wells,
Llangollen Bridge and Gresford's Bells.'*

The 'Seven Wonders' are as follows:

1. *Pistyll Rhaeadr* (see Waterfalls) plunging two hundred and forty feet (73m) near Llanrhaeadr ym Mochnant.
2. *Wrexham Steeple* on the Church of St Giles, a superbly decorated one hundred and thirty-six foot (41m) tower, completed in 1520. Endowed by Margaret Beaufort, Henry VII's mother, the Perpendicular tower has twenty nine sculptures. The superb 1720 wrought-iron gates are by the Davies brothers of Bersham. Elihu Yale, the founder of Yale University is buried in the churchyard, and Parliamentary forces melted the organ pipes in The Civil War, to make bullets.
3. *Snowdon* (see Mountains), or *Y Wyddfa Fawr*, is the highest mountain in the British Isles after Ben Nevis in Scotland. Many paths and trails run up its 3560 feet.
4. *The Yew Trees* in the churchyard at St Mary's, Overton. Overton was once an important borough with its own castle.
5. *St Winifrede's Well* (see Wells) at Holywell was visited by several English kings. From the 13th century until the Reformation, it was in the care of the Cistercian monks of nearby Basingwerk Abbey, which gained a healthy income from pilgrims.

6. *Llangollen's Trefor Bridge,* named after John Trefor, Bishop of St Asaph, dates from 1345, was rebuilt in the 16th century and later widened for modern traffic.

7. *The bells at Gresford Parish Church,* Clwyd, which also has superb mediaeval stained glass and a fourteen-hundred year-old yew in its churchyard.

SPORTS

(Rugby has a separate entry)

The ancient Welsh game, *cnapan,* was played by up to fifteen-hundred naked Welshmen at a time, until the 17th century. It survived until the 19th century, with up to six-hundred participants from rival villages, some on horseback, trying to hit or carry the ball to its destination, usually around 2 miles away. A bowl of heavy wood was fought over cross-country between villages, as one mob tried to force it into the opposing village. Some claim it to be the spiritual ancestor of rugby (see Rugby).

Other old games that lasted until the last century were *bando,* like hockey, and *chwarae pêl,* a handball game similar in concept to 'fives'. Chwarae pel was traditionally played against the walls of churches until in the eighteenth century courts started to be built – there were three in Llantrisant alone. Bando was played between an indeterminate number of players, with deadly inter-village rivalry, and The Margam Bando Boys are featured in a famous song. The most famous teams were Kenfig, Pyle, Margam and Llantwit Major.

ATHLETICS
Lynn Davies (Lynn the Leap) set the still unbeaten UK record for the long jump of twenty-seven feet (8.23m) in Switzerland in 1968, and had won the gold medal in the Olympic Games at Tokyo in 1964.

Every New Year's Eve, there is a 6km Race in Mountain Ash, with international athletes, to commemorate the 18th century shepherd Guto Nyth Brân, who died after running twelve miles in 53 minutes. Born in 1700, his death at the age of thirty-seven was attributed to being slapped on the back after winning the race. It was said that he could beat horses in races, keep up with hounds, and out-run a hare. A broken heart features on his gravestone in the churchyard of St Gwynno at Llanwynno.

Steve Jones won the London Marathon in a record 2 hours 8 minutes and 16 seconds in 1985, and won the New York Marathon three years later. He is still the UK record holder. In 1948 Tom Richards of Pontnewydd, *'an ardent beer-drinker who habitually ran in Woolworth's Red Flash daps'* (i.e. plimsolls, quote from *The Western Mail,* 7th August 1998), was just beaten for the gold medal in the Olympic Games marathon. He thought he was lying in fourth position until he entered Wembley Stadium, and just saw two runners in front of him, so accelerated and caught one of them to achieve what he thought was the bronze. A mix-up at a drinks station had cost him over ten seconds, and he finished in far better shape than the Argentinian winner. His initial euphoria at finishing second when he thought he was lying fourth, turned to anger in later years when he realised he could have won the race. He had a few pints that night to celebrate, and started work at 6.30 the next morning as a hospital nurse.

Wales's most well-known runner is

Colin Jackson, who set the World record for the 110m hurdles in Stuttgart in 1993, and has won the World Championship. He also set the world indoor record for 60m hurdles in Stuttgart in 1994. A new star in the making is Christian Malcolm, who easily won the World Junior 100m in a championship record time in 1998. Other currently successful athletes are **Iwan Thomas** (World Champion 400 metres) and **Jamie Baulch**.

BOXING
Boxing was a traditional route out of the Welsh valleys. 'Peerless' **Jim Driscoll** became featherweight champion of the world in 1909. He died in 1924, his funeral procession watched by one hundred thousand Welshmen, the largest funeral ever in Wales. His exploits inspired Percy Jones from the Rhondda to win a world title.

Freddie Welsh (F. H. Thomas) was world welterweight and lightweight champion in from 1914-1917. He had crossed the Atlantic, after leaving a Pentre foundry at the age of seventeen, to seek his fortune in America. **Jimmy Wilde**, known as The Tylorstown Terror, or The Mighty Atom, was flyweight champion from 1916 until 1923. He lost only four fights out of four hundred and sixty four. **Howard Winstone** was world featherweight champion in 1968, and **Colin Jones** drew the world welterweight championship in 1968. In one of the great fights in history, **Tommy Farr** almost beat Joe Louis in his prime at Madison Square Garden in 1938.

In December 1997, **Barry Jones** won the WBO super-featherweight championship to join **Robbie Regan** and **Joe Calzaghe** as current world champions. **Steve Robinson** held the WBO featherweight championship in the 1990s also.

CRICKET
Glamorgan has won the Cricket County Championship on three occasions, 1948, 1969 and 1997, and the Sunday league in 1993. In 1997, 14 players received Championship medals, eleven of whom had come through the Wales Schools system, and two of whom had played for Glamorgan Colts. Their only overseas player was Waqar Younis, the Pakistani bowler. In recent years Majid Khan of Pakistan and Viv Richards of the West Indies have also chosen to play for the county. Glamorgan's batsman Steve James topped the batting averages in 1996-97, and was chosen as the Cricketer of the Year by his fellow-professionals, the cricket writers, and Wisden – a hat-trick of the game's three top awards. However, he was not chosen for the MCC touring team for the West Indies by its English selectors. In 1998, James was eventually chosen for just one match against the South African tourists. His average over the three seasons had been 76, from 4274 first-class run, better than any of the 30 batsmen chosen before him to play for the MCC.

One of Britain's best spin bowlers, **Robert Croft** of Glamorgan was picked to tour the West Indies in 1998 and Australia in 1999.

Probably the finest cricketer from Wales was Cardiff's **Maurice Turnbull**, who was capped by the MCC, and also played for Wales at rugby, after winning a double Cambridge 'Blue' in both games. He was tragically killed in the Second World War.

Wales has produced two captains of England, **Cyril Walters** in 1934 against Australia and **Tony Lewis** in 1969 for the M.C.C. tour to the Far East and in 1972 against India.

St Fagans has won the Village Championship Trophy three times, Marchwiel twice and Gowerton once, the only times these trophies have been taken out of England.

FOOTBALL

In football, the oldest international in the world was **William Henry (Billy) Meredith** from Chirk, who played right wing for Manchester City, Manchester United, and Wales. At twelve years old he was working in Black Park Colliery. The conditions marked him for life, and he decided to become a professional footballer, signing for Ardwick (Manchester City) for a £5 fee. He made his debut while still working down the pit. He scored twice on his home debut and quickly became the favourite player of the supporters. One Friday after working he took the 2am train on Saturday morning to Newcastle, arriving at 11am, played a match and was back home at 10.30pm to go to work the next day.

This moustachioed lynchpin of the City team took them to promotion and in the next year became their captain. His trademark was that he chewed a toothpick while playing. As captain, he took Manchester City to the Cup Final, scored the winner, and took the FA Cup back to Manchester for the first time. He had started to become a 'star' and all on a maximum wage of £4 a week. He was bought by the newly promoted Manchester United, and has a place of honour in their football museum. As Bobby Charlton stated, Billy Meredith was their 'earliest star'. Football at this time was a 'hard man's game', but Meredith missed hardly any matches as United won the League in 1908. In his position of authority in the game, he chaired the first meeting of the Professional Footballers' Association – Manchester United were suspended, but the new players' union survived,

and Meredith was the last player to return to play after the strike for better conditions.

He was Manchester United's key player when they won the FA Cup in 1909, and he became soccer's first media personality, with personal appearances and product endorsements – he was football's first 'superstar' in any country in the world. Meredith returned to Manchester City for the final three years of a glittering career.

He played against England aged almost forty-six, in 1920, and his international career spanned a record twenty-six years. He was in the team for Wales's first victory against England, and was selected seventy-one consecutive times for his country from the age of twenty-one, but only played forty-six times because Manchester City often stopped him playing. Meredith played for thirty years in the English First Division and hardly missed a game until he was well into his fifties. Obsessed with training and fitness, he scored nearly five-hundred goals from his position of outside-right and was still a sporting celebrity in his seventies. However, he died in 1958 aged eighty-three, and is buried in an unmarked grave in Manchester. The great Stanley Matthews was compared with him, but Meredith could also score goals – he said Matthews *'would never have made the grade in my day'*.

When **Cardiff City** won the FA Cup against Arsenal in 1927 (courtesy of a Welsh goalkeeper in the Arsenal team making a dreadful mistake) it was the only time the FA Cup left England. In 1925, Cardiff had lost the final 1-0 to Sheffield United. However, by 1932 they were bottom of the 3rd Division, and have never since been a major football force. However, there is massive potential for a first-class football team in Cardiff. In 1968 they reached the semi-finals of the European Cup-Winners' Cup, losing to SV Hamburg.

The most expensive football player in history was **Bryn Jones** of Arsenal, who cost £14,000 in 1939. Unfortunately the war years coincided with his playing career. The youngest Welsh cap was **Ryan Giggs** of Manchester United, aged seventeen. Wales in fact has had a remarkable number of world-class forwards, including Giggs, Wyn 'The Leap' Davies (Manchester United, Manchester City, Newcastle), Trevor Ford (Aston Villa and PSV Eindhoven), Ivor Allchurch (Swansea, Newcastle and Cardiff), John Charles (Leeds, Juventus and Roma), Gerry Hitchens (Arsenal, Cardiff and Torino), John Toshack (Liverpool and Sporting Lisbon), Mark Hughes (Barcelona and Manchester United), Ian Rush (Juventus and Liverpool) and Dean Saunders (Aston Villa, Liverpool, Nottingham Forest and Galatsaray). In October 1986, Juventus set the British transfer record when they paid £3.2 million for **Ian Rush**, hoping for a repeat of the service that John Charles gave them. In 1984, he had won the European Golden Boot Award on scoring 32 goals in the 1983/84 season. Another Liverpool player was voted one of the best 22 players in the 1998 World Cup. **Michael Owen** was born in Hawarden, Flint, and could have played for Wales, but unlike Ryan Giggs, chose the greater glamour of the English national team. This eighteen year-old is valued at £30,000,000 transfer value and insured for £60,000,000, £10,000,000 more than the Brazilian Ronaldo.

Trevor Ford, a two-footed centre-forward, scored a hat-trick for Swansea in the 1950s against Aston Villa,

who bought him. He scored 59 goals in just three seasons before moving on to Sunderland for a record £30,000 transfer fee, PSV Eindhoven and Cardiff. Called 'the first modern centre-forward', he scored 177 goals in 259 games for Swansea. Another Swansea player, the 'golden boy' of Welsh football, **Ivor Allchurch** played his first game for them in 1949 and achieved 69 Welsh caps. Another two-footed player, he was the most respected footballer of his generation, known as 'the Prince', and 'the prince of inside-forwards'. He made 450 league appearances for Swansea.

John Charles was the first British £50,000 transfer when he left Leeds in 1957 for a distinguished career with Juventus from 1957, where he was nick-named 'the gentle giant', and still remembered with affection. A statue of him stands outside the ground, and he also played for Roma. The problem is that every Welsh soccer-playing schoolboy wants to be a goal-scorer, to be in the limelight, ever since John Charles scored 42 goals for Leeds in the 1953-54 season. He was not fit for the Wales team that narrowly lost in the World Cup quarter-finals in 1958, 1-0 to Brazil. He had been savagely and constantly kicked in the preceding game, because of his influence on the Welsh team. It is fair to say that if he had been able to play, and get on the end of the constant stream of crosses served up by Cliff Jones, Wales could have won and been known world-wide. Such is the power of football. Brazil went on to win this World Cup in Sweden, starring the young Pele. John Charles' brother Mel was a noted international who also played against Brazil, and was a long-time Arsenal player.

Two more famous Welsh forwards starred in the Tottenham Hotspur league and cup double side of 1961, operating on the wings, **Cliff Jones** and **Terry Medwin**. Cliff Jones' father Ivor also played for Wales, as had his uncle Bryn, the most expensive footballer up to the war years. Cliff Jones played 59 times for Wales, and played for Spurs for ten years, scoring 176 goals. He had cost the club a British record fee for a winger of £35,000. The only international player of note that has not been a forward is the former Everton goalkeeper, **Neville Southall**, with over 80 Welsh caps, an intriguing character who refused to celebrate victories with his clubmates, preferring to return home to his wife and children.

John Toshack is another interesting character. Having won every honour in the game with a great Liverpool team, he became manager of Swansea, and took them from the Fourth Division to the First Division in three years, briefly even being top of the Football League. The legendary Liverpool manager, Bill Shankly, called Toshack 'manager of the century' for this feat in taking a small Welsh town above the likes of Manchester United, Tottenham Hotspur and Liverpool. A fluent Spanish-speaker, he then took Real Sociedad from being a perennial struggler to being one of the top clubs in Spain. After four years, he was invited to become the coach of Real Madrid in 1988, and won the League with them. After another spell at Real Sociedad, and 47 days as manager of Wales, he moved to be coach of Deportivo La Coruna, challenging Barcelona and Real Madrid for the title again. He was then recalled as the Real Madrid coach.

GOLF
Dai Rees was the captain of the European team to beat the USA for the first time in The Ryder Cup in 1957, and

Ian Woosnam was recently the world's leading golfer in the order of merit, after he won the American Masters' Tournament in 1991, and the World Match-Play Championship in 1987 and 1990. He also won the European Open in 1988. Wales also won the World Cup in 1987 (Woosnam and Llewelyn) and 1991 (Woosnam and Price).

ICE-HOCKEY
Cardiff Devils are one of Britain's leading ice-hockey teams, being virtually invincible in the mid-to-late 1990s.

SHOW-JUMPING
In the Helsinki Olympics, **Sir Harry Llewellyn** on Foxhunter, won Britain's only Gold Medal in the Games, winning the Show Jumping Team event. **Richard Meade** won an individual gold in Munich in 1972, and team golds in Mexico and Munich. **David Broome** was World Show Jumping champion three times between 1961 and 1969.

SNOOKER
Ray Reardon was world champion six times between 1970 and 1978, and **Terry Griffiths** won the title in 1979. The current leader in the world rankings is **Mark Williams**.

TENNIS
In 1873, a court was established at Nantclwyd Hall, Llanelidan, and the game of Lawn Tennis first played anywhere in the world, invented by Major Walter Wingfield. He invented and patented nets for this new outdoor game he called 'sphairistike'. The old game of tennis had only been previously played indoors.

TABLE TENNIS
The relatively unknown **Roy Evans**, OBE, died in 1998 at the age of eighty-

eight. He and his wife played table tennis for Wales, but it was as the head of the International Table Tennis Federation that he was asked to fly to China. He inaugurated the first sporting links with Red China since the second world war, facilitating Richard Nixon's 'ping-pong diplomacy' and the re-entry of China in world affairs.

STATELY HOMES

The best that are open to the public are:

The 17th century **Tredegar House**, Newport, stands in a country park and was the home of the powerful Morgan family. Sir William Morgan entertained King Charles I here. Captain Henry Morgan, the privateer, was a nearby cousin. Godfrey Morgan, Viscount Tredegar, survived the charge of the Light Brigade in 1854. His horse, Sir Briggs, is buried near the house. Here in the 1920s and 30s, Viscount Evan Morgan dabbled in black magic and kept a menagerie of exotic animals. There are events throughout the year. The last Morgan of Tredegar died in Monaco, having spent the family fortunes and sold the house.

Bodelwyddan Castle in Clwyd is an outpost of the National Portrait Gallery, with opulent Victorian interiors.

Powys Castle has evolved from a border castle to a stately home with a golden state bedchamber dating from 1688, and has strong connections with Clive of India. The superb formal gardens were created between 1688 and 1722 by the .Welsh architect William Winde, and are the only formal gardens in Britain of this date which survive in their original form. In the reign of Edward I, the Gwenwynwyn family, to keep the castle had to renounce all claims to Welsh princedom of Powys, and took up the name De La Pole.

Erddig Hall, near Wrexham, has been called *'the most evocative upstairs-downstairs house in Britain'*.

Chirk Castle was built by Edward I, and has been the home of the Myddleton family since the 16th century – the huge iron gates are a true Welsh masterpiece, made by local brothers Robert and John Davies of Bersham between 1718 and 1724.

Penrhyn Castle was rebuilt with money from the slate mines, in neo-Norman style, with slate everywhere, even a huge slate bed where Queen Victoria slept.

Plas Newydd is a splendid 18th century mansion built by the Marquess of Anglesey, one of Wellington's commanders at Waterloo. On horseback, when a cannon ball took off his leg during the battle, he turned to Wellington and exclaimed *'Begod, there goes me leg!'*, to which the phlegmatic Duke replied *'Begod, so it do!'*, and carried on supervising the battle. His artificial leg, made of wood, leather and springs, was the world's first articulated leg, and is on display in the hall's Cavalry Museum.

At Ystrad Fflur, Strata Florida Abbey, the White Cistercian monks kept a healing cup made of wood from Christ's Cross. Later it transmuted into The Holy Grail, used at the Last Supper and sought in legend by Arthur and his knights. It passed to nearby **Nanteos Mansion**, where the Powell family became its custodians.

T

TALIESIN

Regarded as the greatest of the Welsh bards, it seems he lived in the sixth century and was the son of Henwg the Bard, St Henwg from Caerleon. St Henwg is said to have travelled to Rome to ask Constantine to send missionaries to Britain. Taliesin was educated at the bardic school of Cattwg (Cadoc) of Llanfeithyn near Llancarfan, and died at Bangor Teifi. A cairn near Aberystwyth may mark Taliesin's burial place.

Legends about Taliesin ('Radiant Brow') run through Welsh history and mythology, in association with Arthur, Maelgwn and Brân the Blessed. Sometimes confused with Merlin, the tale of his magical birth was appended to the 'Mabinogion' by Lady Guest.

TECHNIQUEST

This Science Discovery Centre, in Cardiff Bay, has one hundred and seventy hands-on exhibits, looking over *'Europe's most exciting waterfront development'*. It is the largest activity-based science centre in the UK, with seven hundred thousand visitors a year, and has recently moved to new £7.5 million premises.

THEME PARKS

The first theme park in Wales was **Oakwood**, on a site near Canaston Bridge in Pembrokeshire. It attracts almost half a million visitors a year, and has the largest wooden roller coaster in Europe, Megaphobia. It was voted 'best wooden roller coaster in the world' in 1997, and gives passengers a 2.75 G force on one eighty foot drop. The hundred and forty foot Skycoaster is the largest in Britain, giving the brave an opportunity to free fall bungee-style from the equivalent of fourteen stories at speeds up to 65mph.

Still at the planning stages is *Legend Park* at Magor near Newport. It will incorporate Pencoed Castle into its infrastructure. The project will have a massive transparent covering, the largest in Europe, enabling the site to be open throughout the year. Originally scheduled to open in 2001, the site will cover 800 acres and will give serious competition to Disneyland Paris and Alton Towers.

Rhyl's **Sun Centre** cost almost £5,000,000 in 1985, and has 6,400 square metres enclosed by glass and a tinted PVC roof. The structure houses Europe's only indoor surfing pool, a monorail unique in the world and a 200 feet (60m) waterslide. Open from Easter to September, the heated pools are surrounded by suntan beds, restaurants, a cabaret and tropical plants.

THIRTEEN TREASURES

Myrddin (Merlin), procured these 'Thirteen Precious Curiosities of Britain' and sailed away with them in his glass boat, never to be seen again. In legend, he is buried with them on the Island of Enlli (Bardsey Island), off the remote tip of the Llŷn Peninsula.

1. *Mwys Gwyddno* – 'the Hamper of Gwyddno Garanhir', which will turn meat for one person into meat for a hundred. Gwyddno was 'Dewrarth Wledig', king of the lost lands of Cantre'r Gwaelod, which lies under the waters of Cardigan Bay.

2. *Cadair, neu car Morgan Mynafawr*, 'the Chair or Car of Morgan Mynafawr', which will carry a person wherever he or she wishes to go.

3. *Cyllel Llawfrodedd*, 'the Knife of the Hand of Havoc', a druid sacrificial knife.

4. *Modrwy Eluned*, 'the Ring of Eluned', which made the wearer invisible. Sometimes the Halter of Eluned is added to the thirteen treasures, to make one's mount invisible, and also a stone belonging to Eluned has been included in the past.

5. *Tawlbwrdd* (Throwboard), a type of chess or backgammon board with men of silver on a surface of gold, who could play by themselves. It was also referred to as the 'Gwyddbwyll board of Gwendolau'. Gwyddbwyll was an ancient Celtic board game (in Irish, 'Fidchell'), meaning 'wood sense'. The board was the world in miniature, and ritualistic combat games were played, possibly to resolve disputes and arguments without resorting to bloodshed. The Welsh Myrddin poems say that Gwendolau was Merlin's lord, who died at the Battle of Arfderydd against his cousins Peredur (Sir Perceval of Arthurian legend) and Gwrgi. A replica of this game predating the ninth century, and described in The Laws of Hywel Dda, is now on sale, and two players compete to capture or defend the King.

6. *Llen Arthur*, 'the Veil of Arthur', which made the wearer invisible – this is a later addition to the list.

7. *Dyrnwyn*, 'the Sword of Rhydderch Hael', which would burst into flames from the cross to the point if anyone except Rhydderch drew it. Rhydderch appears to have been a Celtic King of Strathclyde, who fought against Myrddin's side in the Battle of Arfderydd. This battle, Arthuret, was fought in 575 for a 'lark's nest', possibly the important harbour at Caerlaverock near Dumfries, which translates as Fort Lark. At this battle, possibly because of the loss of Gwendolau, Myrddin is said to have lost his reason after fighting and gaining a golden torc in the battle. Gwendolau's 'faithful company' fought on for six weeks after his death. Dyrnwyn may be the precursor of Excalibur.

8. *Dysgyl a Gren Rhydderch*, 'the Platter of Rhydderch', upon which any meat desired would appear. Sometimes a plate with the same properties that belonged to Rhygenydd is included in the treasures.

9. *Corn Brangaled*, 'the Horn of Brangaled', which could provide any drink a man desired. The Celts were great men for their drink.

10. *Pais Padarn*, 'the Cloak of Padarn Redcoat', which made the wearer invisible.

11. *Pair Drynog*, 'the Cauldron of Drynog', in which nothing but the meat of a brave man would boil.

12. *Mantell*, 'the Robe' that would always keep the wearer warm, which possibly had belonged to Tegau Eufron. The wife of Caradoc Freichfras, her other treasures of a cup and a carving knife are also both sometimes included in the list. This Caradoc 'Strongarm' possibly founded the Kingdom of Gwent in the 5th Century, and was the original ancestor of a dynasty of Welsh kings.

13. *Hogalen Tudno*, 'the Whetstone of

St Tudno', which could only sharpen the weapon of a brave man. Tudno hailed from the lost kingdom of Cantre'r Gwaelod, and his father, Seithenyn, was named as the sluice-keeper who became so drunk that he forgot his duties and allowed the sea to take over the kingdom.

Other Welsh treasures are mentioned in 'The Book of Taliesin'. Manawyddan and Pryderi (characters in The Mabinogion) are joint rulers of Annwn (Hades), warders of a 'magic cauldron' of inspiration which the gods of light attempt to capture, and which became famous later as 'The Holy Grail'.

After the death of Pwyll, Prince of Dyfed, with his court at Narberth, his widow Rhiannon married Manawyddan, and 'The Three Birds of Rhiannon' were another treasure which could sing the dead to life, and the living into the sleep of death. Their rarity is shown in one of the ancient Triads:

> *'There are three things which are not*
> *   often heard:*
> *The Song of the birds of Rhiannon,*
> *A song of wisdom from the mouth of a*
> *   Saxon, and*
> *An invitation to a feast from a miser.'*

TOURISM

Catherine Zeta Jones was used to advertise Wales in 1996, in a £2.5m campaign with the Saatchi and Saatchi catch-line, *'Wales – a different holiday every day'*. It was hoped that there would be an increase on the 735,000 overseas visitors who spent an estimated £198m in 1995. Tourism was in total worth £1.9 billion to the Welsh economy in 1996 (overall spending by day visitors and holiday makers). This was 13% better than 1995, despite the Sea Empress oil spill disaster.

Tourism now accounts for more than 7% of Wales Gross Domestic Product, compared to 5% of GDP for the UK in general. Unfortunately this is mainly tourism from the rest of the UK. Only 3.3% of overseas visitors to the UK come to Wales, and the majority of them on their way through to Ireland. Welsh spending accounts for only 1.9% (£190 million) of their spending in Great Britain. Wales is not known throughout the world.

There were around 11,000,000 visitors to Wales in 1996 and 1997. Many tourist operators are deeply critical of the Wales Tourist Board's promotional campaigns. Wales spends £5,000,000 per annum on promotion, compared to Ireland's £60,000,000, with just twice the Welsh population. A condemnation of this board is that the number of jobs created by tourism, about 95,000, are exactly the same as twenty years ago.

There is growing pressure for St David's Day, 1st March, to be declared a national holiday. As the economy is the lowest GDP per head in the UK already, many Welsh people believe that it could be beneficial, especially linked with a tourism push. Other countries and towns have festival days.

TREACHERY

The defining moment that rings through Welsh poetry from the earliest times was the *'Treachery of the Long Knives'*, where the flower of Celtic nobility was slaughtered at a feast by the Saxon invaders. The next thousand years showed the Welsh distrust of Saxon, Norman and Plantagenet motives towards their people and lands. It is said that on May Day, the Britons came to Stonehenge or Old Sarum in Wiltshire to meet the

Saxon leader Hengist from Kent, to ratify the existing peace, to grant land to the Saxons, and to restore Vortigern to power in AD472. According to the Chronicles, the British were unarmed at a great feast, and the Saxons had concealed knives or daggers ('seaxas'). When Hengist shouted *'Nemet oure seaxas'*, they slew the seated Britons. This 'Plot of the Long Knives' (*Twyll y Cyllyll Hirion*) is referred to as the second of the 'three treacherous meetings of Britain' . . . *'The second was that of the Mount of Caer Caradawg, where the treason of the long knives took place, through the treachery of Gwrtheyrn (Vortigern); that is to say, through his counsel, in league with the Saxons, the nobility of the Cymry were nearly all slain there'.* The period of mourning for this terrible event for hundreds of years after was at the annual kindling of the Omen Fires (*Coelcerthi*) on the last night of October, All Saints Eve. The bard Cuhelyn ap Caw wrote about the event as early as the sixth century, as did the obscure Ymarwar Lludd Mawr *' I know when the battle was caused over the wine feast'.* Golyddan's seventh century *Destiny of Britain* scorns the feeble Vortigern and his dealings with the invading Saxons, before and after the massacre:

'For the chieftain of the Saxons and
their darling
Distant was the journey's end unto
Gwrtheyrn Gwynedd (Vortigern),
The joint course of the Germans into
migration.
No man attaineth what the earth will
not undo.
They know not who migrate into every
estuary.
When they bargained for Thanet
through lack of discretion

With Horsa and Hengist, who were in
their career,
Their prosperity was derived from us,
to our dishonour,
After the secret, pregnant with results,
of the servile man at the confluence.
Imagine the drunkenness of the great
potation of mead,
Imagine the terrible deaths of many,
Imagine the dreadful lamentations of
the women.
It is the feeble sovereign who stirs up
the grief.'

According to the *Brut Tysilio*, in these times *'a shriek was heard over every hearth in Britain on the night of every May Day, and so struck every man and beast to the heart, that the men lost their strength, the women miscarried, the youth of either sex became senseless, and the beasts and trees unproductive'*. The event was allegorised when Llefelys told his brother Lludd ap Beli that *'the shrieks arise from a contest between the dragon of Britain, and the dragon of a foreign nation which on the night of May-Day endeavours to conquer her, and the shriek you hear is given by your dragon in her rage and distress'*. He then told Lludd to bury the dragons deep in the earth, so no calamity should befall Britain. These underground dragons resurface in the legends of Merlin and the red dragon of Wales.

The truth of the matter may never be known, but most Welshmen believe that Llywelyn Olaf (see Llywelyn the Last), 'our last prince', was killed through a Norman trap, just outside Builth Wells. The history of the Norman Kings and Marcher Lords is peppered with tales of treachery, torture, lies and savagery, and the following few pages highlight some of the more well-known treacherous deeds.

The Norman Hugh the Fat, Earl of Chester, asked Meirion Goch to bring Gruffydd ap Cynan, Prince of Gwynedd, to arrange peace in 1082. He then clapped Gruffydd in chains, until Gruffydd managed to escape, twelve long years later (see Gruffydd ap Cynan).

The last native King of Glamorgan, Iestyn ap Gwrgant, lived at Llanilltud Fawr. He was in conflict with Rhys ap Tewdwr, who was encroaching on his lands from the west, so in 1091 he asked Robert Fitzhamon to bring Norman mercenaries from England to help retain his lands. The battle won, the Normans returned to England and Iestyn sent his warriors back to their fields. However, the Normans turned their boats around on that same night and seized the castles along the coast of the fertile Vale of Glamorgan. Iestyn fled to Bristol, and Fitzhamon wrote to William Rufus saying that his conquest of South Wales had been successful. The new Lord of Glamorgan took Boverton, Llanilltud Fawr, Cowbridge, Dinas Powys and Cardiff, and shared the rest of Glamorgan among his Norman retainers.

The Normans did anything to get hold of Welsh lands. In 1104 Gerald treacherously slew Hywel ap Goronwy to take Ystrad Tywi and Gower (Gŵyr). Hugh Mortimer blinded Rhys ap Hywel in 1148, to take over his territories around Bridgnorth. Blinding was a common Norman practice – King Henry II personally took out the eyes of his child hostages, the two sons each of Owain Gwynedd and The Lord Rhys.

In 1175, William de Braose, the Norman Lord of Brecon and Abergavenny, held vast tracts of land which he had conquered in south-east Wales. Seisyllt ap Dynwal, Lord of Upper Gwent, held the manor of Penpergwm and Castle Arnold for de Braose as his feudal overlord. The Norman invited Seisyllt and another seventy local Welsh lords to Abergavenny castle for a feast and to hear a royal declaration. Hidden outside the banqueting hall were soldiers under the command of Ranulph Poer, Sheriff of Hereford. Seated during the feast, the Welsh nobles were massacred by Norman troops. Only Iorwerth ab Owen (see Heroes) escaped, snatching a sword and fighting his way out of the castle. The antiquary Camden noted that Abergavenny *'has been oftner stain'd with the infamy of treachery than any other castle in Wales'*.

William de Braose then raced to Castle Arnold, seized Sisyllt's wife Gwladys, and murdered Seisyllt's only son, Cadwaladr, before her eyes. Norman law stated that conquest of Welsh territories by any means whatsoever was fair. Iorwerth led his men to Abergavenny, forcing De Braose to flee to his stronghold in Brecon Castle. In 1182, Seisyllt's kinfolk managed to scale the high walls of Abergavenny and took the castle, but unfortunately de Braose was absent. Seisyllt ap Eudaf had told the Constable of the castle that he would attack the castle at a certain angle, in the evening. The Normans waited all night for the attack, and were all asleep at dawn, whereupon the Welsh threw up their scaling ladders in the area that Seisyllt had said, taken the castle and burnt it to the ground.

Ranulph Poer and de Braose marched to Dingestow (Llandingat) near Monmouth to begin building another castle. The Welsh attacked and Poer was killed, and de Braose only just escaped with his life. This battle is known from the descriptions of the capacity of the bowmen of Gwent. Arrows could penetrate a depth of four fingers of oak. One arrow passed through a Norman's armour plate on his thigh, through his leg, through more armour and his saddle, killing his horse. Another Norman was pinned through armour plating around his hip to his saddle. He wheeled his horse, trying to escape, and a further arrow pinned him to the saddle through the other hip.

Like his king, the Norman Marcher Lord de Braose was notable for blinding and torturing any Welshman he could lay his hands on. In 1197 he pulled Trahaiarn Fychan through the streets of Brecon behind a horse, until he was flayed alive. Maud de Valerie, his huge wife, also enjoyed seeing prisoners tortured. With the death of The Lord Rhys, de Braose pushed even more into Welsh territories. However, he fell out of King John's favour, and escaped to France in 1204, leaving his wife and eldest son behind. John took them to Corfe Castle and locked them up with just a piece of raw bacon and a sheaf of wheat – this was this Angevin king's favourite form of execution.

After eleven days they were found dead. King John even murdered his nephew Arthur, the son of Geoffrey of Boulogne. De Braose was known to the Welsh as 'the Ogre', and all the great lords brutalised the Welsh – the Laceys, Carews, Corbets, Cliffords, Mortimers, Despensers, Baskervilles and Turbervilles were all vicious, murdering brutes. It was said of Robert of Rhuddlan that he spent fifteen years doing nothing but trying to take Welsh lands and kill its rightful owners – '*Some he slaughtered mercilessly on the spot like cattle, others he kept for years in fetters, or forced into harsh and unlawful slavery.*' The

Normans and Angevins left a legacy in Wales of cheating, torturing, raping and stealing.

Before Llywelyn the Great's death in 1240, King Henry officially recognised Dafydd ap Llywelyn as de facto ruler of Wales. However, in 1245 Henry III reneged on his promises and again invaded Wales, but was defeated by Dafydd in the only significant battle at Deganwy, and retreated back to England. Upon the tragically early death of Dafydd ap Llywelyn Fawr in 1246, a new power struggle took place to control Wales, only to be resolved by Llywelyn the Last. Mystery surrounds Dafydd II's death. It may be that he was poisoned on Henry's orders.

In 1282, the final war between Llywelyn Olaf and King Edward, the King called for a truce and began negotiations for peace. However, Luke de Tany, the commander of his army that had landed in Môn (Anglesey), built a bridge of boats at Moel y Don, trying to end the war quickly. On 6th November he crossed to the Arfon side of the Menai Straits, but Llywelyn demolished his army, and left Dafydd to hold Gwynedd while he went on his fateful journey to Builth.

The circumstances of Llywelyn the Last's death are mysterious. There is still no understanding of how Llywelyn came to be so far detached from his main forces in his Gwynedd stronghold. King Edward had offered him exile and an English earldom in return for unconditional surrender. Archbishop Pecham of Canterbury had been negotiating between Llywelyn and Edward on the terms of an end to the war, and the documentation still exists. In 1282 Llywelyn had a small army on one side of the Irfon Bridge, and two English armies were approaching from the other side. One version of events is that a few miles from his army, Llywelyn and a small bodyguard of eighteen men were waiting for someone at Irfon Bridge. Archers suddenly appeared, some of his men were killed, and Llywelyn rode away, but not to rejoin his army. Some time after, it appears that he had stopped again, and was speared by Stephen (or Adam) de Frankton, a Norman. Perhaps Llywelyn had thought that the arrival of the archers was a mistake, and was still waiting for his contact to arrive.

According to Pecham's later letters, a document was found on Llywelyn inviting him to go to the Irfon Bridge, sent by the Marcher Lords. This document disappeared, and also a copy sent by the Archbishop to the Chancellor. It looks like Llywelyn was killed by Norman treachery – the treachery on the bridge is a recurrent theme in Welsh literature, and for centuries the inhabitants of Builth were known as traitors in Wales. (*Bradwyr Buallt*, 'Builth Traitors' became a common term of abuse). Also according to Archbishop Pecham, de Frankton's spear did not kill him, and Llywelyn lived on for hours, asking repeatedly for a priest, while his army was being slaughtered a couple of miles away. He was refused one, while his captors waited for the Marcher Lord Edward Mortimer to come to the scene. The French/Latin recording of the times, 'The Waverley Chronicle', states that Mortimer executed Llywelyn on the spot. Probably he also took possession of the letter in Llywelyn's pocket at this same time. It may have been that de Frankton was given a large farmstead at Frampton, just north of Llanilltud Fawr, in the 'safe'

Vale of Glamorgan, in return for keeping quiet about the affair

The Norman Marcher Lords were in a strange position. Their great power was tolerated by successive Norman and Angevin Kings of England as a necessary buffer against the unconquered Welsh princes. They knew that if Wales was conquered completely, their lands would be the next to be crushed by the power of the throne. Therefore there had been some intermarriage between Norman and Welsh noble families, hedging their bets as it were. Another version of this fateful day is found in English sources. Llywelyn I had married King John's daughter, and Llywelyn II was married to Elinor de Montfort. An English chronicler of the day states that Llywelyn was led to believe that Edmund Mortimer of Wigmore wanted to come over to the Welsh side. The Mortimers were his cousins, descended from his father's sister Gwladys, daughter of Llywelyn I. The chronicler says that Mortimer did this to please King Edward. Llywelyn could not trust Edward because of his ongoing treachery, but he would trust a Mortimer. He had even spared the life of Edmund Mortimer's father in the past.

The other baron involved seems to have been John Giffard, whose lands lay next to the Mortimers, and who had just been appointed Constable of Builth Castle. He had married Maud Longsword (Longespee) a cousin of Llywelyn. However, Llywelyn knew that he had fought for de Montfort against the English crown, and then deserted de Montfort in his hour of need. Llywelyn knew that Giffard (as Giffard's surviving documents show), would be willing to change sides to improve his situation. Llywelyn believed that Builth Castle would be surrendered to him. The story goes that Llywelyn crossed the ford on the River Irfon with just one squire, Goronwy Fychan (son of his minister Ednyfed Fychan). He left his picked bodyguard of eighteen men to guard the ford, upon being summoned 'by a gentlewoman' to meet local chiefs at Aberedw. She was not there, and he hid in a cave (still called Llywelyn's Cave), while Mortimer's troops swarmed across the area. He returned in a blizzard to meet his bodyguard, but the river had risen too high to cross, so they had to move on to the bridge at Builth Castle to cross and rejoin his army across the River Wye.

Mortimer's men chased the small band, and they destroyed the bridge behind them. Llywelyn asked the garrison at Builth to surrender, but they refused. Mortimer's chasing soldiers crossed the Wye at Erwood (Y Rhyd), eight miles down the valley. Llywelyn pushed on to the bridge of Orewyn, over the Irfon, near Llanynys Church, and told his men yet again to guard the bridge. The prince went to sleep in the nearby farmhouse at Llanfair, when the troops of Mortimer, and Giffard's men reached the bridge. Elias ap Philip Walwyn, one of Giffard's captains, knew of a nearby ford, and eventually the eighteen men were cut to pieces fighting on both sides. Goronwy Fychan had run back to warn Llywelyn and was run through with a lance. Llywelyn was unarmed in his rush to escape, and was trying to get back to his main army, but was overtaken. On foot, he was slowed down by a great spread of broom, ironically a symbol of Plantagenet Kings, when he was speared by de Frankton.

John de Warenne (1231-1304) was the half-brother of Henry II. With Roger Mortimer, another Marcher Lord, he was entrusted with the care of the two sons of Griffith ap Madog. Griffith had the Lordship of Bromfield, and other territories surrounded by Norman lords, and so he was forced to fight with them against Llywelyn the Last. Mortimer and de Warenne murdered their young charges by drowning, with Lord de Warenne taking their estates of Bromfield and Yale, and Roger Mortimer taking the Lordship of Chirk. Roger Mortimer was entrusted with the government of North Wales as the Justice of Wales, by Edward I, in recognition of his hard attitude against the Welsh, and he used the post to accumulate as much Welsh territory as possible.

The Marcher Earl Warenne murdered the two eldest sons of Gruffudd ap Madog when he died, in order to take the lordship of the eldest. This was Gyndyfrdwy, a seventeen mile long valley of the river Dee, taking in Llangollen, Llandysilio, Llansantffraid and Corwen. However, for some reason he granted this land in 1282 back to Gruffudd Fychan, the third brother. Eventually, Gruffudd's great grandson took over the Lordship, Owain Glyndŵr.

In 1318, the last true Lord of Glamorgan, Llywelyn Bren, was ritually tortured to death on the orders of Hugh Despenser, the Norman lord as he said that it was on King Edward II's orders. This was a treacherous lie, and Despenser was executed in Cardiff Castle (see Heroes, and Ghosts).

In 1378, an entry was made in the English King's Rolls of the Exchequer, noting the payment to John Lamb for assassinating the last heir to the House of Gwynedd. That charismatic hero

Owain Llawgoch (see entry on Assassination) was not even safe in France from Edward III's reach.

In 1399, Lord Grey had tried to capture Gruffydd ap Dafydd by offering him a pardon. Gruffydd gave himself up at Oswestry, but was lucky to escape with his life. Lord Grey then asked Glyndŵr to discuss Welsh grievances at Glyndŵr's great manor of Sycharth in 1400. Glyndŵr did not trust the Norman Marcher Lord, who was desperate for more Welsh lands. He therefore asked that Grey brought only a small band of men with him. Grey hid a large body of cavalry in the woods near Sycharth in order to capture Glyndŵr, but Owain Glyndŵr was fortunately warned by his bard Iolo Goch, and managed to escape. This event started the Glyndŵr uprising that lasted for over fifteen years. During the ensuing war, Owain Glyndŵr asked Henry Percy (Hotspur), son of the Earl of Northumberland, to try to arrange a peace with Henry IV in 1401. The King was inclined to agree, but Lord Reginald Grey of Rhuthin hated Glyndŵr, and Lord Somerset wanted more Welsh estates, so they agreed to use peace talks as a device to capture Glyndŵr. Fortunately, Hotspur, an honourable Northerner, refused to be take part, warned Glyndŵr, and later became his ally (see Glyndŵr).

Gruffydd Vaughan, of Garth in Montgomery, distinguished himself fighting for Henry V, and was knighted on the field of Agincourt for his bravery. He captured the renowned warrior Sir John Oldcastle, the enemy of the Lord of Powys, Harry Grey, and delivered him to Grey at Montgomery Castle. A poem by Dafydd Llwyd describes how

Grey lured Gruffydd, under a lure of safe conduct, into the castle. There he was murdered, for Grey wanted his neighbouring lands.

TRIADS

Trioedd Ynys Prydein, the Triads of the Isles of Britain, stem from the 'Age of Saints' in the fifth and sixth centuries onwards. They were mnemonics, aids to memory, for the bards to recollect long stories. There are many different versions of the hundreds that have passed down to us. Some are contained in the *Peniarth Manuscript*, some in the *Llyfr Coch Hergest* (The Red Book of Hergest), some in The Black Book of Carmarthen and also in the *Llyfr Gwyn Rhydderch* (The White Book of Rhydderch). The White Book was collated in the early 1300s.

Some are recounted below:

The three principal cities of Ynys Prydain, the Isle of Britain: Caer Llion upon Wysg in Cymru (Caerleon upon Usk in Cambria); Caer Llundain in Loegr (London in Loegria); Caer Evrawg in Deifr and Brynaich (York in Deira and Bernicia).

The three tribal thrones of the Island of Britain: Arthur as Chief Prince in Mynyw, and Dewi as Chief Bishop, and Maelgwn Gwynedd as Chief Elder; Arthur as Chief Prince in Celliwig, and Bishop Bytwini as Chief Bishop, and Caradwg Strong-Arm as Chief Elder; Arthur as Chief Prince in Pen Rhionydd in the North, and Gerthmwl Wledig as Chief Elder, and Cyndeyrn Garthwys as Chief Bishop.

The three oppressions that came to this island, and not one of them went back: One of them was the people of the Coraniaid who came here in the time of Caswallawn son of Belli, and not one of them went back, and they came from Arabia (*Twrch Trwyth*, Vandals, who killed one of Arthur's sons). The second oppression: the *Gwyddyl Ffichti* (Goidelic Picts). And not one of them went back. The third oppression:

the Saxons, with Horsa and Hengist as their leaders.

Arthur's three great queens: Gwenhwyfar daughter of (Cywryd) Gwent; Gwenhwyfar daughter of Gwythyr son of Greidiawl; and Gwenhwyfar daughter of Gogfran the Giant.

U

URDD GOBAITH CYMRU – LEAGUE OF THE YOUTH OF WALES

The Urdd was founded in 1922, with two hundred boys who responded to an invitation to camp at Llanuwchllyn, and now comprises three hundred youth clubs, fifty two thousand members and runs an Urdd National Eisteddfod. Gwynfor Evans has pointed out the essential difference between Welsh 'nationalism' and other, more sinister forms of national pride:

'When the Urdd was growing strongly in the 30s there was a powerful youth movement in Germany. The aims and ethos of the Hitler Youth were as different from the Welsh movement as Nazism was from Welsh nationalism, as the three-fold pledge of the Urdd indicates: "I will be faithful to Wales and worthy of her, to my fellow human being whoever he may be and to Christ and his love".'

The nationalism of the Welsh movement was Christian and international. Handbooks were published for use in Christian services; an Urdd Sunday was held; and in the month of May each year a Message of Goodwill was broadcast to the countries of the world.

W

WARS

It appears that Wales is alone of all the older nations in the world in its non-aggressive behaviour and its non-declaration of invasive wars. However, the last war was declared upon Germany on behalf of England, Scotland, Wales and Monmouthshire. The peace treaty omitted Monmouthshire, so this county is still technically at war with Germany. This anomalous position arose because of Monmouth's position as a kind of 'buffer-state', a no-man's land between England and Wales, and its administrative control used to rotate between the two countries.

Nora Chadwick wrote about the Welsh attitude towards power and aggression:

'. . . the gradual approximation to a Wales united under a single family. It is I think the most remarkable feature of early Welsh history that the union of most of these kingdoms should have come about gradually with no record of conquest and no bloodshed. Those historians who speak of the Welsh as a warlike people see Wales only through the eyes of the Norman conquerors, when the whole country became an armed fortress on the defensive. The early history is very different – a history of peaceful development, of gradual unification by policy, and by a series of royal marriages.'

In 1982, Wales became the first nuclear-free country in Europe when all eight of its county councils agreed never to allow nuclear weapons on their soil.

WATERFALLS

At Aberdulais Falls, **Rhaeadr Aberdulais**, in the Vale of Neath, there is Europe's largest electricity-generating waterwheel. This is a National Trust site that includes reminders of the area's industrial heritage.

Blaenrhondda Waterfalls, north of Treherbert are home to grey wagtails, dippers and sparrowhawks.

Pistyll Rhaeadr in the Berwyn Mountains is the highest waterfall in England and Wales, near Llanrhaedr Ym Mochnant, plunging 240 feet (73m) in two stages, one of 150 feet, over a sheer cliff, and passing under a 'fairy bridge' on its way down. One of the 'seven wonders of Wales', George Borrow in 1854 called it in *Wild Wales*, *'. . . an immense skein of silk agitated and disturbed by tempestuous blasts, or by the long tail of a grey courser at furious speed. Through the profusion of long silvery threads or hairs, or what looked such, I could see here and there the black sides of the crag down which the Rhaeadr precipitated itself with something between a boom and a roar.'*

The *second* highest waterfall is *Pistyll-y-Llyn*, which falls 230 feet (70m).

Ceunant Mawr, on the outskirts of Llanberis is 60 feet high, and superb in winter. Its smaller sister, Ceunant Fach, can be seen from the Snowdon rack and pinion railway.

Near Llanbrynmair, **Ffrwd Fawr** drops 150 feet from a sandstone rock amphitheatre to the valley floor of the Twymyn River.

Swallow Falls, between Betws-y-Coed and Capel Curig, are three falls pouring down a deep ravine, which has been a tourist attraction since Victorian times.

The famous **Horseshoe Falls** near Llangollen were man-made in 1801 to divert water from the River Dee to the Llangollen Canal.

At **Dyserth** in Clwyd there is a 60 foot waterfall, and many falls in the Vale of Ffestiniog, Gwynedd, including Cynfal Falls.

Cenarth Falls is possibly the best place in Wales to watch salmon leaping, up the River Teifi.

Dolgoch Falls is a series of falls in a deep wooded glen near Tywyn.

The famous Torrent Walk near Dolgellau, follows the banks of the **Clywedog** as it cascades though a deep valley, wooded with hornbeam and small-leafed lime trees. Notable for ferns, wood fescue, Tunbridge filmy-fern and beech fern can be seen here

Nearby **Coed Garth Gell** is a stream gorge with a ruined mine overlooking the spectacular Mawddach estuary. Pied flycatchers, wood warblers and grey wagtails are in the oak and birch woodlands.

The waterfall at the head of the valley at **Abergwyngregyn** (near Penmaenmawr) sees the Rhaeadr-fawr river plunge 120 feet over the cliffs.

To the West of Conwy, the largest of the Aber Falls, **Rhaeadr Mawr** is 160 feet high, and there are many cascades and cataracts in the surrounding oakwoods.

Where the rivers Conwy and Machno meet, near Penmachno, there is a series of falls, up to 50 feet high through a wooded gorge, ending up in the **Fairy Glen**, a noted beauty spot.

Devil's Bridge near Aberystwyth is possibly the best-known beauty spot in Wales, consisting of three bridges, all stacked one above the other, spanning a narrow 300 foot (91m) gorge. The top

bridge is the modern road bridge, built in 1901. Underneath it is the stone bridge built in 1753. The lowest bridge is **Pont-y-gŵr-Drwg** ('The Bridge of the Evil Man'), built by Cistercian monks in the 12th century. From the viewing platform under this bridge, one can see 'The Devil's Punch Bowl', where the swirling River Mynach has made strange shapes in the rocks, before cascading over a series of superb falls. Just later, the river joins the River Rheidol, which itself has just encountered the Gyfarllwyd Falls.

Coed y Brenin forest ('King's Wood'), near Ganllwyd used to be an estate of the Princes of Gwynedd. In the 35 square miles of wood, there is a superb visitor centre, gold-mining remains, polecats, buzzards, an arboretum and the beautiful waterfalls of **Pistyll Cain** (150 foot drop) and **Rhaeadr Mawddach** (60 feet in three steps). Nearby is **Rhaeadr Ddu**, the Black Waterfall where the river Gamlan falls over 50 feet through black rocks in an old oak wood.

The limestone rock around Ystradfellte is a paradise for cavers, and at Porth Yr Ogof a huge cave swallows up the River Mellte (see Caves). A quarter mile downstream the Mellte reappears, leading to the spectacular waterfalls, **Sgwd Clun-Gwyn** ('White Meadow Fall'), the impressive **Sgwd Isaf Clun-Gwyn** ('Lower White Meadow Fall') and **Sgwd y Pannwr** ('Fuller's Fall'). The most famous fall is **Sgwd yr Eira** ('Fall of Snow'), where one can walk behind the fall of water and not get wet.

Clydach Gorge has no less than seventeen waterfalls, and Cwm Clydach is a nature reserve with Britain's oldest beech wood, surviving fourteen thousand years on the side of the gorge. Plans to upgrade the A465 'Heads of the Valleys' road will mean the disruption of some of the falls, and the possible elimination of the rare Lesser Horseshoe Bat.

WDA

Wales has a history of creating businesses – the largest shipping corporation in the world, Lloyd's of London, Lloyds Bank, and the stores of Dickins and Jones, Owen Owen, D. H. Evans, Iceland, Laura Ashley, Lewis's of Liverpool and John Lewis/Waitrose, the last being a very successful partnership of employees. Robert Owen was the founder of the Co-operative Movement. However, since the last war, Wales has only seen the decline of its economic base.

The Welsh Development Agency, a quango, is responsible for regenerating the Welsh economy. The WDA has been successful in attracting foreign firms to Wales (see Inward Investment). Although many companies have relocated in Wales, indigenous industry has not been assisted. This is just one of the major flaws in EU law and economic policy, that countries can assist other countries' firms to set up with tax breaks, free factories and rent, greenfield sites and the like.

Under the new Labour Government, the 'Economic Powerhouse for Wales' has been set up, combining the WDA, the Development Board for Rural Wales and the Land Authority for Wales.

WELLS

The most famous spa town in Wales is **Llandrindod Wells**, an almost perfectly preserved (but fading) Victorian gem of a place. It was created almost from scratch in the 1850s, and still has the ambience of a century ago. A famous Victorian Festival, where all the locals dress up in Victorian costume, is held for one week every August. Up to eighty thousand visitors a year used to use the wells. Advertisements of the day claimed that '*saline, sulphur, magnesian and chalybeate waters are very efficacious in the treatment of gout, rheumatism, anaemia, neurasthenia, dyspepsia, diabetes and liver affections*'. A chalybeate spring spouts out of a public drinking fountain in Rock Park Gardens. In the Pump House Tea Rooms at the Rock Park Spa, one could choose from draught saline, sulphur or magnesium water. Happily, they are being restored and are soon to reopen.

The people of **Builth Wells** have had a nickname until this century of *bradwyr Buallt*, 'Builth traitors', because of the story that they would not let Llewelyn Olaf (see Llywelyn the Last), into their gates just before he was killed. Llanfair-ym-Muallt, the Welsh name for Builth, means 'The Church in the Cow Pasture'. Its sulphur waters were known as far back as 1740. Saline water was first discovered there in 1830, and by the late nineteenth century, the spa had a Central Pavilion for gentlemen and ladies to come and 'take the waters'. The wells were most popular around 1890, when the chalybeate and saline springs were used by those suffering from heart, kidney and gout disorders. The Royal Welsh Agricultural Show, held over four days every year on a special site, is one of Europe's finest shows of its kind.

Llangamarch Wells is a third notable Welsh spa town. Llangamarch, on the River Irfon, attracted David Lloyd George and foreign heads of government to its barium wells. Barium chloride allegedly helped cure heart disease, gout and rheumatism. The spring is in the grounds of the Lake Hotel, formerly known as the Pump House Hotel. Nearby Cefn-Brith was the home of John Penri (Penry), who was put to death aged thirty-four in 1593 for his pamphlets denouncing absenteeism and immorality in the clergy. He left his four children all he possessed, a Bible each (see Saints).

Llanwrtyd Wells claims to be the smallest town in Britain. Its well was documented in the fourteenth century as *Ffynnon Drewllwyd* or *Droellwyd* ('Smelly Spring'), as its overpowering smell is due to its having the highest sulphur content in Britain. The spring was rediscovered in 1732 when the local vicar saw a frog come out of it, and realised that it must be safe to drink. The Reverend Theophilus Evans then announced his cure of the 'grievous scurvy', and encouraged people to come and partake the waters, because the presence of healthy frogs meant that the water was pure. However, not until the Victoria Wells were exploited by piping the water in 1897 (thereby removing the frogs), did the range of magnesium, saline and chalybeate treatments become popular.

At **Trefriw**, in Gwynedd, Romans tunnelled into the mountain to find mineral-rich waters bubbling up from a fissure in the rocks. The original Roman cave, and the eighteenth century stone bath house with slate bath can be visited, and the Victorians laid on steamboats from Conwy to take patients to the spa's pump room. The Victorian boom died away, but you can still buy the water in liquid or dried form. The Church of St Mary was founded by Llywelyn the Great, and

Trefriw Woollen Mill still demonstrates the traditional methods of making Welsh woollens (see Crafts).

HOLY WELLS

St Non's Well, not far from the chapel of St Justinian, a sixth century hermit, celebrates the mother of St David. David was in legend born on the slopes of St Non's Bay, and a ruined chapel marks the spot. St David's Cathedral is in a nearby sheltered hollow.

St Winifrede's Well in Trefynnon (Holywell), Clwyd, has a shrine which has been a place of pilgrimage and healing since the seventh century, and is known as 'The Lourdes of Wales'. Kings and queens have prayed and given offerings at the well, where a young virgin was decapitated when she spurned the advances of a prince. Her uncle, St Beuno, was present at the killing, and restored her head to her body, a white scar around her neck being witness to her living martyrdom. In the fifteenth century the well was covered by superb Renaissance fanvaulting on elaborate pillars, paid for by Henry VII's mother, Margaret Beaufort. Richard I (The Lionheart) and Henry V were patrons of the well, which became one of the greatest shrines in Christendom. St Winifred has two commemorative days in the Calendar of the Saints, 22nd June for her martyrdom and 3rd November for her second death. Her remains were moved to Shrewsbury Monastery in 1138. This practice, like the removal of Dyfrig's remains from Bardsey island to Llandaff Cathedral, was a particularly Norman practice. They wished to give their churches a holier aura and greater status.

People even attended the well during the Reformation, when pilgrimages were punishable by death, and the Catholic King James II came here to pray for a son and heir in 1686, the last royal pilgrimage in the British Isles. Since 1873 it has been cared for by resident Jesuits. On the nearest Sunday to 22nd July, pilgrims still come to see a relic, part of St Winifrede's thumb bone, and enter the well three times to cure their ailments. This is perhaps a throwback to the Celtic rite of triple immersion, three being the holiest number for the Celts. (St Myllin, in the sixth century, was the first person in Britain to baptise by immersion in water.) The spring was used by the Romans, who used the waters to cure gout and rheumatism. The spring, although smaller than in earlier times, is the most copious in Great Britain, pouring from 2000 to 3000 gallons per minute.

Ffynnon Asa, in the Halkyn Mountains at Newmarket, is Wales' second largest spring. Newmarket is alleged to have had race meetings long before its Cambridge namesake. The nearby Gop is the largest limestone cairn in Wales, eighty feet long and supposedly the grave of Queen Boadicea (Buddug).

St Dwynwen, daughter of the Welsh chieftain Brychan, led a pure life after an unrequited love affair, at **Llanddwyn Island** near Newborough Warren, Anglesey. There are the remains of an abbey and some huge stone crosses commemorating the fifth century saint, and the well on the island was famous for telling whether lovers would stay faithful. The handkerchief of the faithful lover will float on the surface, while that of the faithless lover will be attacked by a sacred eel. Fresh wheaten bread must be cast in the well to wake the eel, before the handkerchief is spread on the surface of the water. The well is

sometimes covered by high tides. St Dwynwen now features on the Welsh equivalent of Valentine Cards.

The following description is by William Williams, Llandygai, in 1807:

'The place was much resorted to formerly and continued in repute to our days. There was a spring of clear Water, now choked up by the sands, at which an old woman from Newborough always attended and prognosticated the lover's success from the movement of some small eels which waved out of the sides of the well, on spreading a suitor's handkerchief on the surface of the water. I remember an old woman saying that when she was a girl, she consulted the woman of this well about her destiny with respect to her husband. On spreading her handkerchief, out popped an eel from the North side of the well: then the woman told her that her husband would be a stranger from the south part of Caernarvonshire. Sometime after it happened that three brothers came from that part and settled in the neighbourhood where the young woman was: one of whom made his addresses to her, and in a little time married her. This is the substance of the story as far as I remember it. This couple were my mother and father.'

The well of **Mair Saint**, Holy Mary, at Penrhys between the two Rhondda valleys, was broken up in the Reformation, and is in a poor condition today, but once was almost as famous as St Winifrede's.

St Cybi's Well, Ffynon Gybi, used to draw people to its healing waters at Llangybi, as in the eighteenth century a spa developed around it. Its two elaborate well-chambers were beneficial for 'scrofulous cases'.

Ffynnon Fair (Mary's Well) is at the foot of Grisiau Mair (Mary's Steps) where pilgrims used to take their last drink before undertaking the dangerous crossing from Porth Meudwy (Hermit's Port) to the holy island of Ynys Enlli (Bardsey).

Penmon Priory has an ancient holy well, in Anglesey, and the nearby sixteenth century dovecote could hold a thousand birds.

There are many holy wells associated with saints in Wales. Nearly all were smashed up in the 1536 reformation, but restored could assist Welsh tourism. *The Holy Wells of Wales*, by Francis Jones, a 1954 book, has just been reprinted, and lists 437 holy wells, plus 125 wells with topographical names, 104 wells associated with lay names, 93 with adjectival names, 61 wells named after birds and animals, 32 with occupational names, and 25 named after trees. There are hundreds more 'lost' wells in Wales.

OTHER WELLS

Barri Island features a strange 'Roman Well', and the spring of Patrisio in the Black Mountains was used by Father Isio, a Celtic hermit who was murdered by Saxons.

Taff's Well, just north of Cardiff, is only a few yards from the River Taff, and was used for over two-hundred years to cure muscular rheumatism. The pale green water is almost identical chemically to that of Bath, and is a constant 67 degrees Fahrenheit.

There were many 'cursing wells' in Wales, the most noted being the well of Eilian, near Llaneilian-yn-Rhos in Clwyd. To cast a curse, the guardian of the well wrote it on paper and threw it in. The church authorities blocked off this particular well in 1929. Sarah Hughes

was said to make £300 a year from the well, years before it passed into the hands of the notorious John Evans, 'Jac Ffynnon Eilian', who had the well water piped into his garden. In 1831 he was imprisoned for illegally obtaining money, and died in 1854. The saying *fel Ffynnon Eilian* ('like Eilian's Well') was used for many years after to mean great troubles.

At Llandrillo-yn-Rhos near Colwyn Bay, a cursing well was still being used in the first part of this century, when a gipsy who had threatened a Welshman by 'putting him in the well' was tried at the local assizes. Up until 1918, the ancient fish-weir here paid a tithe of salmon to the church.

At Llanfyllin near Welshpool, St Myllin established a church and holy well. He was the first person in Britain to baptise by immersion, in the 6th century, and the citizens of the town used the well for centuries to cure their ills.

Llanbadarn Fynydd well in Powys was used to cure sick animals, used in living memory by farmers bringing dogs, cows and sheep.

King Tewdrig controlled much of south-east Wales, and fought with Constantine the Blessed against the invading Saxons. He is said to have founded the college of Cor Worgan, or Cor Eurgain later to become famous as Llanilltud Fawr. (Cor Tudus is marked on old maps of the town). After Constantine's death, he allied with Vortigern to keep the peace, and passed on his kingdom to his son Meurig. Tewdrig retired to Tintern, where he was attacked by Saxons. A stone bridge in the nearby Angidy valley is called *Pont y Saeson*, 'Bridge of the Saxons', and this may be where the fight took place. The enemy were driven off, but not before Tewdrig was mortally wounded. His son Meurig arrived and took his father on a cart to a well in Mathern. A plaque there reads *'By tradition at this spring King Tewdrig's wounds were washed after the battle near Tintern about 470AD against the pagan Saxons. He died a short way off and by his wishes a church was built over his grave'*.

Mathern is the corruption of *Merthyr Teyrn*, 'the site of martyrdom of the sovereign'. In 822, Nennius described the well as one of 'the marvels of Britain', and also referred to the Well of Meurig. Meurig became known as Uther Pendragon ('Wonderful Head Dragon', leader of the Celtic army), and was the father of Arthmael, the King Arthur of legend.

In Llanddona, Gwynedd, is the famous Ffynnon Oer (Cold Well). It lies near the shore, and was said to have issued forth when three witches landed and commanded it to appear. Bela Fawr, Sian Bwt and Lisi Blac lived by begging, married smugglers and chanted their curses near the 'cold well'. One curse has been translated as:

> *'Let him wander for many centuries;*
> *At each step a stile;*
> *On each stile a fall;*
> *In each fall a breaking of bone;*
> *Neither the largest or smallest*
> *But the neck bone every time.'*

Wells were sacred to the early Celts, and they used the hot springs of Bath before the Romans came to Britain. Aqua Sulis, or Bath, is named after the Celtic Goddess Sulis.

'Brecon Spring Water' is available in most of the major UK supermarket chains, and 'Tŷ Nant' spring water, from a well in Bethania, near Lampeter, is well-known for its distinctive blue bottle. Around fifty million bottles of Tŷ Nant were sold around the world in 1996, 75% going to export.

WELSH COSTUME

The traditional Welsh costume seems to be a survivor from Stuart times, which lasted so long in remoter parts, that eighteenth century English travellers took it to be the national costume. The last sighting of a lady wearing the tall hat seems to have been in 1871 at Llancattwg by Kilvert, and it was still common in Cardiganshire in the 1860s but dying out in North Wales. The tall, originally beaver, hat had a narrower brim and taller crown in West Wales than in Monmouthshire. The white lace cap worn under the hat has four rows of goffered frills over the ears, but does not show on the forehead.

The dress consists of *ffedog, pais a betgwn* ('apron, petticoat and gown'). The gown is looped up and pinned behinds, or has a tight bodice with a basque. There should be many petticoats, with the top one being usually striped or checked. The aprons are plain white, striped or checked. A shawl (*fichu*) is worn over the shoulders, and crossed in front and secured at the waist, or tucked into the bodice. Buckled shoes were worn for best, but clogs for everyday wear. Some of the old costumes have been passed down through generations, and some can be seen at The Museum of Welsh Life, Saint Fagans.

WELSH NOT

In 1799, a traveller to Flintshire noted that in the schools, *'If, in the colloquial intercourse of the scholars, one of them is to be detected in speaking a Welsh word, he is immediately degraded with the "Welsh lump", a large piece of lead fastened to a string, and suspended round the neck of the offender. The mark of ignominy has had the desired effect: all the children of Flintshire speak English very well.'*

The 'Welsh Not' was a system of punishment in the 19th century to ban the use of the Welsh language in schools. The Education Act of 1870 led to an English-orientated system of schools, and even in rural primary schools where the population were monoglot-Welsh speakers the speaking of Welsh was cruelly punished.

Earlier in 1845 the National Society proclaimed the inadequacy of education in Wales and this led to an inquiry culminating in a report of some 1,183 pages known as the Blue Books, published in 1847. Due to the commissioners general ignorance of things Welsh there was general outcry to the report's unsympathetic stance towards the language, people and culture of Wales, it became known as 'The Treachery of the Blue Books'. But even in this report it was recorded:

> *'My attention was attracted to a piece of wood, suspended by a string round a boy's neck, and on the wood were the words "Welsh stick". This, I was told, was a stigma for speaking Welsh.'*

One person over whom this unjust system had a deep and lasting influence was Sir Owen M. Edwards (1858-1920) who later became Chief Inspector of Schools for Wales. He wrote in *Cylch Atgof* (1906), on having been taken by his mother to his new school in Llanuwchllyn near Bala:

> *'The school's door was opened; I heard a strange din, and I could see the*

children packed tight on many benches. There were two open spaces on the floor of the school, and I could see two people on their feet, one in each open space. I understood later that they were the assistant master and mistress. The schoolmistress took me to one of them, but I only recall the words "a new boy" from what she said. I could read Welsh quite well by then, and I was put in a class of children who were beginning to read English. The reading book was one of the SPCK's, and I still loathe those letters, on account of the cruelty I suffered while trying to read from that book. The teacher was a pleasant fellow, and he was kind to me, but after the reading-lessons he went back to his other pupils. The word soon went round that someone new, and ridiculous at that, had come to the school. Several of the cruel children had their eye on me – I knew about them all, loud-mouthed children from Y Llan most of them were, and they never amounted to much. The teacher had whispered to me not to speak a word of Welsh; but these naughty boys did all they could to make me raise my voice, and in the end they succeeded. I lost my temper and began to speak my mind to the treacherous busybody who had contrived to torment me. As I began to speak my rich Welsh everyone laughed, and a cord was put around my neck, with a heavy wooden block attached to it. I had no idea what it was, I had seen a similar block on a dog's neck to stop it running after sheep. Perhaps it was to prevent me from running home that the block was hung round my neck? At last it was mid-day, the time to be released. The school-mistress came in with a cane in her hand. She asked a question, and every servile child pointed a finger at me. Something like a smile

came across her face when she saw the
block around my neck. She recited some
long rhyme at me, not a word of which
I could understand, she showed me the
cane, but she did not touch me. She
pulled off the block and I understood
that it was for speaking Welsh that it
had been hung around my neck.

That block was around my neck hundreds of times after that. This is how it
was done, – when a child was heard
uttering a word of Welsh, the teacher
was to be told, then the block put around
the child's neck; and it was to stay there
until he heard someone else speaking
Welsh, when it was passed on to the
next poor child. At school's end the one
who was wearing it would be caned on
his hand. Each day the block, as if by
its own weight, from all parts of the
school, would come to end up around
my neck. Today I take comfort from the
fact that I never tried to seek respite
from the block by passing it on to another.
I knew nothing about the principle of
the thing, but my nature rebelled
against the damnable way of destroying
the foundation of a child's character. To
teach a child to spy on a smaller one
who was speaking his native language,
in order to pass the punishment to
him? No, the block never came off my
neck and I suffered the cane daily as
school drew to its close.'

(translated by Meic Stephens)

This sad pattern of enforcement, taking the laguage out of the children, was
repeated all over Wales for decades as
Victorian England tried to standardise
its nearest piece of Empire.

However, in 1909 Sir O. M. Edwards
said: *'Every H.M.I. will see that Welsh is
put in its right place in the curriculum of
every school.'* This was the command of
the Chief Inspector.

WELSH PLACE NAMES

Knowing the following will help your
enjoyment in touring Wales – for example Rhyd y Groes ('ford of the
cross'), Aberdulais ('mouth of the black
water'), Nantgarw ('stream' or 'valley
of the deer'), Nantymoel (stream of the
bare mountain), Rhandirmwyn ('district
of minerals') – most place names are
easily translated:

aber – mouth of river, estuary
afon – brook or river
allt – height or steep slope
ap – son of
bach (fach, bychan, fechan) – small or
　little
ban – bare hill, peak
banc – mound, bank or hillock
bedd – grave or sepulchre
bedwen – birch
berth – hedge
bettws – secluded place or chapel
blaen – source of stream, head of
　valley
braich – arm
bro – region
bran – crow (brain – crows)
bron – hillside, slope
bryn – hill
buarth – farmyard, enclosure
bwlch – mountain pass
bwthyn – cottage
cader (cadair, gadr) – stronghold, chair
　or seat
cae – field or enclosure
caer – stronghold, fort, camp
canol – centre
cant – hundred
capel – chapel
carn – cairn, rock
carreg – (cerrig) rock or stone(s)
cartref – home
carw – deer, stag
castell – castle

cefn – ridge or back
cil – cell
clogwyn – precipice
clun – meadow
clwyd – gate, perch
coch (goch) – red
coed (goed) – wood, trees
cors – bog
craig (crug) – rock, crag, stone-pile
crib, cribyn – comb, crest, ridge
croes (groes) – cross
cwm – valley
cwrt – court
cymer – junction, confluence
cyntaf – first
dan – under, below
De – South
derw – oak
din, dinas – fortified hill, fortress (pre-
    Roman), town
dôl – meadow, valley, field
dros – over
drum (trum) – backbone
drws – door, passage
du (ddu) – black
dulas -black water
dŵr – water
Dwyrain – East
dyffryn – river valley
eglwys – church
elwy – gliding water
esgair – cliff, long ridge
fan (ban) – high, height
fford – road, way, gate
fforest – forest
ffridd – forest
ffynnon – well, source
gallt – steep
gardd – garden
garth – hill
garw (arw) – rough
gelli – grove
glan (lan) – shore, river bank
glas (las) – blue, green
glo – coal
Gogledd – North

Gorllewin – West
glyn – glen, deep valley
gwern – bog, swamp
gwyn (wyn, gwen, wen) – white, fair
gwy (wy) – water
gwyrdd – green
gyrn – peak, pike
hafod – summer retreat
heli – salt
heol – road
hen – old
hir – long
isaf – lower
llan – holy place, church, clearing
lle – place
lledr – bare
llwyn – bush, grove
llyn (lyn) – lake, pool, tarn
llys – palace, court
maen (faen) – boulder, stone
maes (faes) – meadow, field
mawr (fawr) – big, great
melin (felin) – mill
melyn – yellow
merthyr – burial place of saint, martyr
moel (foel) – a rounded, or bare
    mountain
môr – sea
morfa – sea marsh
mynydd (fynydd) – mountain, hill
nant – valley, stream
neuadd – hall
newydd – new, new dwelling
nos – night
ogof – cave
pandy – mill
pant – hollow, vale
parc – park
pen – head, top of
pentre – village
pistyll – waterfall, water spout
plas – hall, mansion
pont (bont) – bridge
porth – door, port, mouth, entrance
pwll – pool
rhaeadr – waterfall

rhandir – division or district

rhiw – incline, sometimes a pathway
  across a hill

rhos – moor, wet meadow

rhudd – red, crimson

rhyd – ford

sarn – causeway

scwd – waterfall

stryd – street

sych (sech) – dry

taf – dark

tal – front, end

tomen, domen- mound

tan – under

traeth – estuary, strand, beach

tref (tre) – town, dwelling

twll – hole, chasm

ton – grassland

traeth – beach, shore

tref/tre – hamlet, town

troed – foot

twˆr – tower

tŷ – house

uchaf – highest, upper

uwch – higher

un – one, a

waun – moor, uncultivated land

wern – swamp, wood

wrth – near, by

y (yr) – the

ynys – island

yspytty – hospital

ystrad – vale, street

North – Gogledd

South – De

East – Dwyrain

West – Gorllewin

WHISKY

In the America section, we have seen
that American whisky owes its roots to
Welsh settlers (see America). Welsh
whisky was made from around AD365.

There was a monastery distillery on
Bardsey Island, first produced by a
monk Rhaullt Hir , but manufacture
gradually died out in Wales because of
the growth of non-conformist religion
(whereby enjoyment was deemed sinful), and by increasing taxation. Irish
and Scottish distillers were far enough
away from London to disguise or hide
their production figures, so whisky
today is now associated with those
countries. Whisky was started off by
fermenting barley, as in today's bourbon
whisky, because of the prevalence of
barley in the Welsh economy. In fact,
whisky was distilled beer without hops.

Bardsey Island, Ynys Enlli, was
formerly known as Ynys Afallach, the
Isle of Apples, so Apple Brandy – Cal-
vados – could have been made there. It
is still made unofficially on farms all
over Britanny.

Whisky was first used as a medicine,
and the distilling process found its
way to Ireland with the interlinking
with Irish monks, and thence it crossed
to the Scottish Western islands. Most
Welsh production was in Pembrokeshire
and Cardiganshire, often by farmers
using their excess barley.

The largest whisky distillery in Wales,
R. J. Lloyd Price's in Bala, closed down
in 1906, but at one time was so important that it had a railway line leading to it. Edward VII was presented
with an enormous commemorative
bottle of the whisky on a visit to Bala.
The disused works was used to house
German prisoners-of-war, and then to
imprison Irish rebels after the Easter
Rising of 1916. From June in that year
until his release in December, internee
number 1320 spent his time learning
Welsh and devising guerrilla tactics.
His name? Michael Collins.

Whisky manufacture was resurrected

by a Brecon company, whose owner, Dafydd Gittins, saw an old bottle of Bala whiskey in a bar at Ruthin Castle.

WINE AND MEAD

In mediaeval times, monasteries produced wine, and before that the native Welsh princes had their own vineyards. In more recent times the Marquess of Bute had large vineyards near Castell Coch. Some of the following vineyards are open to the public, for example Llanerch Vineyards near Hensol, which makes white and rose wine and elderflower cordials. Andrac of Llanvaches, Gwent makes quality sparkling wines. Cwm Deri of Narberth produces white and red country wines and mead, and Tŷ Brethyn near Llangollen makes traditional meads and fruit wines. Other vineyards are Glyndŵr at Cowbridge, Brecon Court at Usk, Tintern Parva at Tintern and Sugar Loaf at Abergavenny.

The ancient Greeks elevated mead to a 'food of the gods', and Norsemen celebrated weddings for a whole lunar month – hence the word 'honeymoon'. However, the Welsh monasteries found that the honey flavours of the drink were too strong, and diluted the honey with fruit juices. (Honey was used to ferment drinks in these times because there was no sugar available). The Laws of Hywel Dda gave permission for court stewards to have a daily ration of mead, and laid down rules for its production. Tŷ Brethyn Meadery, at Maesmor Hall near Corwen, makes traditional meads, including a pink one with redcurrants for use at weddings.

Mead is an ancient drink made from barley and honey, still popular in our sister-nation, Brittany, where it is known as *houchen*, and in the West Country. Could this be the derivation of the US slang for alcohol, hooch ? Elizabeth I had the finest *metheglyn* (mead), sent annually to her from Anglesey. Mead was so strong and popular that the Church tried to persuade people to turn to ale, which had replaced it as the popular drink by the 18th century. By the middle of the nineteenth century, mead was very much a minority drink in Wales, but is always used as the toast drink, at recreations of medieval banquets in stately homes and castles.

Meads such as metheglyn, hyppocras, pyment and cyser, combining honey with spices and fruit, were sold at the Royal Welsh Show. Metheglyn is spiced with cloves, ginger, rosemary, hyssop and thyme. Under the Tudor Dynasty, mead became the most popular alcoholic drink in England. However, from the 17th century, sugar was imported from the West Indies, replacing honey as a sweetener, and mead declined in the face of competition from ale, gin and rum.

The following quotation was found in *Yr Haul*, the magazine of the Church in Wales, in July 1932:

'Getting drunk on mead meant a dreadful drunkenness, damaging to the body, people getting so drunk that they could not sober up for many days. In addition to this, its effect on the body's equilibrium was very different from the effect of getting drunk on beer. A man who gets drunk drinking beer leans forward, and such a drunkard moves forward, but mead would make one lean backwards, and a drunkard drunk on mead would be impelled 'backwards' despite all efforts to move forwards'.

WOMEN'S RIGHTS

In 1865, the Welsh colony in Patagonia was the first society anywhere in the world to give women the vote.

Celtic women, such as Buddug (Boadicea) of the Iceni, and Cartimandua of the Brigantes, held real power. Queen Teuta fought the Greeks and Romans between AD71 and AD83. Women landowners in Ireland were expected to fight as warriors until Saint Adamnan forced a change of the laws in the sixth century. Women in Celtic Gaul were butchers, chemists, doctors and sellers of wine. This equality passed down and was enshrined in the Laws of Hywel Dda, who codified the old Welsh laws. In medieval times, Welsh women had amazing rights compared to all their European contemporaries. The union of marriage was a contract rather than a sacrament, whereby the woman received property which remained hers completely and in perpetuity, the exact opposite of the dowry system practised elsewhere. She had equal rights in a divorce case, and if married for seven years, could leave her husband with half of his property. The widow had the same right on a husband's death, and she could make a will leaving property. In England, women had no right to hold property apart from her husband until an act of 1882 (see Hywel Dda).

There is the old joke that the Welsh are so scared of their wives that they chose one for the national flag – a dragon. The natural respect accorded to women in Wales, and the willingness of husbands to assist in household duties (that in other countries are the 'prerogative' of women) is a refreshing part of Welsh nature. In Celtic law, a man was fined for calling a woman ugly, making up a nickname, making fun of a weakness or telling a lie about a female.

Gwenllian's heroism is mentioned previously (see Gwenllian) – she was the mother of The Lord Rhys, the sister of Owain Gwynedd, the mother of Nest, and possibly the author of the 'Four Branches' of the Mabinogi, the main tales of the Mabinogion. She died aged thirty-eight, executed after battle with the Normans.

Last century, Ernest Reuan wrote:

> 'It was through the Mabinogion that the Welsh influenced the Continent; it transformed, in the twelfth century, the poetic art of Europe and realised this miracle, that the creation of a small nation which had been forgotten had become a feast of imagination for mankind over all the earth . . . Above all else, by creating woman's character the Welsh romances caused one of the greatest revolutions known to literary historians. It was like an electric spark; in a few years the taste of Europe was transformed.'

He carried on to say that this was the first flowering of chivalry that helped raised the status of women in Europe.

Z

ZULU WARS

The Victoria Cross is the highest British award for gallantry in wartime. The greatest number of VCs won in a single action were by the Welsh at Rorke's Drift over two days in 1879. This was shortly after an English army had suffered their worst defeat in its history, being massacred at Isandhlwana. Nearly seventeen hundred soldiers of the 1st/24th Foot Regiments were annihilated, but a detachment of the 2nd/24th held out days later against the victorious Zulu Impi.

Just eighty-two men manned the small mission hospital and supply depot, facing four thousand Zulu warriors. Only twenty-seven men died at Rorke's Drift, fighting throughout their flaming encampment.

The South Wales Borderers received a Full Battle Honour, and eleven Victoria Crosses were earned in the engagement. When the Zulus retreated, they sang to a brave, outnumbered foe, as encaptured in the 1961 film *Zulu*, starring Stanley Baker and Michael Caine. Sir Stanley Baker produced the film, which had recovered its costs more than eight-fold by the time of Baker's death in 1978.

BIBLIOGRAPHY

The following books are referred to in the text and to the authors I owe my gratitude. There will be other very useful books upon Wales that I have not used in this compilation. Future editions will add to this reference book list as I add to my library.

In future editions, I hope very much to add information from individuals. There is so much local information about our past, that eventually dies with us, and which we need to collate and publish about Wales. The memory of just one old lady, who saved lost and forgotten folk-dances, should be an inspiration to all of us.

Allen, J. Romilly, *Celtic Crosses of Wales* (1978).
Ambrose, S. E., *Undaunted Courage* (USA, 1996).
Aneirin, *Y Gododdin* (translated by Kenneth Jackson, 1990).

Barber, Chris & Pykitt, David, *Journey to Avalon* (1993, pb).
Barker, R. J., *Christ in the Valley of Unemployment*.
Beazley, Elizabeth & Brett, Lionel, *North Wales* (1991).
Black Book of Carmarthen (translated by Jeff Davies, 1999).
Blamires, David, *David Jones: Artist and Writer* (1978 pb).
Borrow, George, *Wild Wales* (1862).
Breeze, Andrew, *Welsh Mediaeval Literature* (1991).
Brooks, J. A., *Hosts and Legends of Wales* (1987 pb).
Brown, Dee Alexander, *Morgan's Raiders* (1995).

Caesar, Julius, *Britannicus* (translated by Handford, S. A., 1951).
Cahili, Thomas, *How the Irish saved Civilsation* (1995 pb).
Carradice, Phil, *The Last Invasion: The story of the French Landing in Wales* (1992).
Chatwin, Bruce, *In Patagonia* (1977).

Connolly, Peter, *Greece and Rome at War* (1981).
Conran, Tony, *Welsh Verse* (1987).

Dafydd ap Gwilym, *Poems* (translated by Rachel Bromwich, 1982).
Davies, Glyn, *A History of Money* (1994).
Davies, Idris, *Collected Poems* (1993).
Davies, John, *A History of Wales* (1993).
Davies, Norman, *Europe – A History* (1997).
Davies, R. R., *The Revolt of Owain Glyndŵr* (1997 pb).
Delaney, Frank, *Legends of the Celts* (1989 pb).
The Celts (1993 pb).
Desmond, Adrian & Moors, John, *Darwin* (1997).
Dixon-Kennedy, Mike, *Celtic Myth and Legend* (1993 pb).

Eluere, Christiane, *The Celts: First Masters of Europe* (1996 pb).
Evans, Admiral Edward R. C. R., *South with Scott* (undated).
Evans, Robert & John, Brian, *The Pembrokeshire Landscape* (1973 pb).
Evans, Gwynfor, *Land of my Fathers: 2000 Years of Welsh History* (1992).

Ffowc-Elis, Islwyn & Jones, Gwyn, *Twenty-five Welsh Short Stories* (1971 pb).
Fraser, Maxwell, *Wales Volume I; The Background* (1952).
Wales Volume II: The Country (1952).

Gerald of Wales, *The Journey Through Wales* (translated by Lewis Thorpe, 1978 pb).
Gilbert, Adrian; Wilson, Alan, & Blackett, Baram, *The Holy Kingdom: The Quest for the Real King Arthur* (1998).
Greenslade, David, *Welsh Fever – Welsh Activities in the US and Canada Today* (1986).
Gruffydd, W. J., *Folklore and Myth in the Mabinogion* (1950 pb).
Gwyndaf, Robin, *Chwedlau Gwerin Cymru/Welsh Folk Tales* (1995 pb).

Heywood, Thomas, *The Life of Merlin* (1812).
Hodgkin, R. H., *A History of Anglo-Saxons*.
Holmes, Michael, *King Arthur: A Military History* (1996).

James, D. J. V., *Rebecca's Children*.

Jarman, A. O. H. & Hughes, Gwilym Rees, *A Guide to Welsh Literature*, Vol. 1 (1976).

Jones, Francis, *The Holy Wells of Wales* (1954).

Jones, J. Graham, *A Pocket Guide to the History of Wales* (1990 pb).

Knightly, Charles, *A Mirror of Mediaeval Wales: Gerald of Wales and his Journey of 1188* (1998).

Laing, Lloyd & Jennifer, *The Origins of Britain* (1987 pb).

Lewis, Eiluned & Peter, *The Land of Wales* (1949).

Lloyd, D. M. & E. M. (Editors), *A Book of Wales* (1953).

Lloyd. J. E., *Owen Glendower* (1931).

Lofmarch, Carl, *A History of the Red Dragon* (1995).

Macalpine, Joan, *The Shadow of the Tower* (1971 pb).

McElroy, Joseph, *Jefferson Davis* (USA 1995).

May, John, *Reference Wales* (1994 pb).
A Chronicle of Welsh Events (1994 pb).

Meehan, Aidan, *Celtic Design: Knotwork, the Secret Method of the Scribes* (1991 pb).

Morgan, Gerald, *The Dragon's Tongue – The Fortunes of the Welsh Language* (1996 pb).

Morton, H. V., *In Search of Wales* (1935).

Morris, Jan, *The Matter of Wales* (1984 pb).

Olson, Don, *Prince Madoc: Founder of Clark County Indiana* (USA, 1999).

Ordnance Survey, *Guide to Castles in Britain* (1087).

Owen, Trefor M., *A Pocket Guide to the Customs and Traditions.*
Welsh Folk Customs (1959).

Palmer, William T., *Odd Corners in North Wales* (1948).

Parry-Jones, David (Editor), *Taff's Acre – A History and Celebration of Cardiff Arms Park* (1984).

Pennant, Thomas, *A Tour in Wales* (1778).

Petrie, Pamela, *Travels in an Old Tongue – Touring the World Speaking Welsh* (1997).

Pliny, *Natural History* (translated by William Stearns Davis, 1912).

Pugh. T. B. (Editor), *Glamorgan County History, Volume III – The Middle Ages* (1971).

Raine, Kathleen, *David Jones and the Actually Loved and Known.*

Redknapp, Mark, *The Christian Celts: Treasures of late Celtic Wales* (1991 pb).

Reese, David, *The Son of Prophecy: Henry Tudor's Road to Bosworth* (1985 pb).

Rees, Gustave, *Music in the Middle Ages* (USA, 1940).

Richards, Alun, *A Touch of Glory – 100 Years of Welsh Rugby* (1980).
The New Penguin Book of Welsh Short Stories. (Editor), (1995 pb).

Sager, Peter, *Pallas Guide: Wales* (1991 pb).

Sale, Richard, *Owain Glyndŵr's Way* (1996).

Senior, Michael, *Portrait of South Wales* (1974).

Skidmore, Ian, *Owain Glyndŵr. Prince of Wales* (1978).

Stephens, Meic (Editor), *A Book of Wales – An Anthology* (1987).

Stephenson, David, *The Last Prince of Wales* (1983).

Tacitus, *Annals.*

Thomas, Clem & Thomas, J. B. G., *Rugby in Wales* (1970).

Thomas, Dylan, *Collected Poems* (1952).

Thomas, R. S., *Selected Poems 1946-1968* (1973).

Tuchman, Barbara W., *A Distant Mirror: The Calamitous Fourteenth Century* (1978 pb).

Underwood, Peter, *Ghosts of Wales* (1978).

Valentine, Mark, *Arthur Machen* (1995 pb).

Williams, Alice E., *A Welsh Folk Dancing Handbook* (1990).

Williams, David L., *John Frost: A Study in Chartism* (USA, 1969).

Williams, Gwyn, *Presenting Welsh Poetry* (1959).

Williams. Gwyn A., *Madoc: The Making of a Myth* (1979).
When was Wales (1985).
Welsh Wizard and British Empire: Dr John Dee and a Welsh Identity (1980 pamphlet).

Williams, Huw, *Welsh Clog/Step Dancing* (unknown).

Williamson, James A., *The Tudor Age* (1964).

Williams, Herbert, *Davies the Ocean: Railway King and Coal Tycoon* (1990).

Zaczek, Iain, *Chronicles of the Celts* (1996).